'ABDU'L-BAHÁ

The Centre of the Covenant
of Bahá'u'lláh

'ABDU'L-BAHÁ

'ABDU'L-BAHÁ

*The Centre of the Covenant
of
Bahá'u'lláh*

by

H. M. BALYUZI

GEORGE RONALD
OXFORD

First published by
George Ronald
46 High Street, Kidlington, Oxford, OX5 2DN

First paper edition 1972
Second Edition, with minor corrections 1987
Reprinted 2002

ISBN 0 85398 043 8

TO

THE EVER PRESENT SPIRIT

OF

THE GUARDIAN OF THE CAUSE

OF GOD

WHOSE

BELOVED GRANDFATHER'S STORY

THIS BOOK ATTEMPTS TO TELL

Contents

Part III

EUROPE AND THE CLOSING YEARS

APPENDICES

Illustrations

The author wishes to thank the Audio-Visual Department, Bahá'í World Centre, Haifa, Israel, for kindly making available seven of these illustrations.

Foreword

The first chapter of this book was written as long ago as 1939. The book owes its inception to a gracious remark by Shoghi Effendi, the Guardian of the Bahá'í Faith. When my booklet on the life of Bahá'u'lláh was issued by the Publishing Trust of the Bahá'ís of the British Isles in June 1938, and copies were sent to him, he expressed his hope in a letter to the National Spiritual Assembly that companion volumes would be written on the life of the Báb and the life of 'Abdu'l-Bahá. I set about organizing an outline for a book on the life of 'Abdu'l-Bahá, which, because of the abundance of available material, would necessarily be of vaster proportions than the slim booklet on the life of Bahá'u'lláh. That booklet was reprinted in *The Bahá'í World*, Vol. VIII (1938–40). In future years with added material it grew into a small book and came from the press in the Centenary year of the Declaration of Bahá'u'lláh.

The onset of the Second World War halted my work on the life of 'Abdu'l-Bahá. And it was not resumed until more than a score of years had passed. Then I had to recast my outline of the book, because more material had come into my possession and to my knowledge. I had also come to feel strongly, for a variety of reasons, that Professor Edward Granville Browne's connections with the Faith of the Báb and Bahá'u'lláh had to be explored and explained. It took a considerable time to put the material on Edward Browne into a coherent shape. But when I had done so it became apparent that a diversion of that magnitude was inappropriate in a book on the life of 'Abdu'l-Bahá. It was suggested to me (with which suggestion I readily concurred) that the chapter on Edward Browne should be extracted and made into a monograph, to be published separately. Having decided on that course I realized that more research was required before an adequate monograph could be produced.

That research, although time-consuming, was highly re-warding. *Edward Granville Browne and the Bahá'í Faith* was published in 1970, having been thrice rewritten and recast.

I then went back to continue the story of 'Abdu'l-Bahá. My principal source was now Shoghi Effendi's *God Passes By* which was published in 1944, five years after I had prepared my first outline. Other books mainly consulted were Ḥájí Mírzá Ḥaydar-'Alí's *Bihjatu'ṣ Ṣudúr, Memories of Nine Years In 'Akká* by Dr Yúnis Khán-i-Afrúkhtih, *Badáyi'u'l-Áthár* by Mírzá Maḥmúd-i-Zarqání (Diaries of 'Abdu'l-Bahá's occi-dental tour), *Khátirát-i-Ḥabíb* (Memoirs of Ḥabíb) by Dr H. Mu'ayyad, *The Chosen Highway* by Lady Blomfield, and *Abdul Baha's First Days in America* by Juliet Thompson. *Abdul-Baha In London, Paris Talks* and *The Promulgation of Universal Peace* provided the texts of the Talks delivered by 'Abdu'l-Bahá in the West. Certain discrepancies had to be reconciled, and particular difficulties with the dates of 'Abdu'l-Bahá's talks and engagements in the West had to be resolved. These dates as given in Zarqání's Diaries and *The Promulgation of Universal Peace* did not tally on many occasions, and sometimes differed considerably. I decided to accept the version provided by the latter work, since the compiler was himself a Westerner and more qualified to use the Western calendar correctly. Dates relating to 'Abdu'l-Bahá's second visit to Europe had likewise to be adjusted, whenever Zarqání's version differed from accounts pro-vided by Western sources. A number of minor alterations have been made in the translations of 'Abdu'l-Bahá's Talks, wherever the available Persian or Arabic text suggested a better rendering.

A word on the photographs of 'Abdu'l-Bahá. The first photographs that we have of Him were taken in Adrianople. Then there were none until He reached London in 1911 and press photographers attempted to photograph Him. 'Abdu'l-Bahá said, as reported by Lady Blomfield, 'If the

photographs must be, it would be better to have good ones.'
Therefore a number of studio portraits were taken in
London, and again in Paris a month later. In the United
States 'Abdu'l-Bahá was photographed frequently. On His
return to the Holy Land, and in the closing years of His
life, when pilgrims came again with their cameras, He was,
once more, frequently photographed. No studio photograph
was ever taken in the Holy Land.

As the year 1970 sped by and the opening months of 1971
were upon me, setbacks made it obvious that it would be a
desperate race against time to complete the book to be
available for the fiftieth Anniversary of the Passing of
'Abdu'l-Bahá. Unstinted help given to me by Marion and
David Hofman facilitated my task considerably, for which I
am eternally grateful.

I am much indebted to the Bahá'í Publishing Trusts of
Great Britain and the United States for their kindness in
allowing very lengthy quotations from their publications;
and to Mrs Doris Holley and Dr Edris Rice-Wray for per-
mitting the reproduction of long extracts from the writings
of the Hand of the Cause, Horace Holley, and from *Portals
to Freedom*, respectively, as well as to the National Spiritual
Assembly of the Bahá'ís of Canada for excerpts from
'Abdu'l-Bahá in Canada.

My sincere thanks also go to Miss Angela Anderson, Mrs
Beatrice Ashton, Mr and Mrs David Lewis, and Mr Rustom
Sabit for their meticulous care in reading the proofs. Several
of the photographs have been reproduced beautifully by Mr
Horst W. Kolodziej, for which, too, I am very thankful.

Finally, without the encouragement, patience and suggestions of my wife this book would not have reached its
readers thus soon.

H. M. BALYUZI

London
 May 1971

Quotations are reproduced in their original form, even though differing from the spelling and transliteration of Persian words adopted in this book. The author has deemed it appropriate, however, because of the extent of his quotation from *The Promulgation of Universal Peace*, to edit these extracts in respect to transliteration of Persian names, capitalization, the use of English spellings, and occasional punctuation. He has also omitted the honorific 'His Holiness' (Ḥaḍrat' in the original Arabic and Persian) preceding the names of the Manifestations of God, which was not used by the Guardian of the Faith in his translations, and for which there is no acceptable equivalent in English.

Persian texts not published in English have been translated by Mr Balyuzi.

He is, and should for all time be regarded, first and foremost, as the Centre and Pivot of Bahá'u'lláh's peerless and all-enfolding Covenant, His most exalted handiwork, the stainless Mirror of His light, the perfect Exemplar of His teachings, the unerring Interpreter of His Word, the embodiment of every Bahá'í ideal, the incarnation of every Bahá'í virtue, the Most Mighty Branch sprung from the Ancient Root, the Limb of the Law of God, the Being '*round Whom all names revolve*', the Mainspring of the Oneness of Humanity, the Ensign of the Most Great Peace, the Moon of the Central Orb of this most holy Dispensation—styles and titles that are implicit and find their truest, their highest and fairest expression in the magic name 'Abdu'l-Bahá.

SHOGHI EFFENDI

PART I

YOUTH, IMPRISONMENT AND FREEDOM

CHAPTER I

THE MASTER

Here is a life, abundant, spacious, immeasurable. It cannot be adequately described. It cannot be encompassed. It lies beyond the range of assessment, because every event in the life of the Son of Bahá'u'lláh carries a major accent. He was eight years old when He was taken to the dungeon of Ṭihrán and saw His beloved Father bent under the weight of chains. From that tender age to His seventy-seventh year when, His work done, He left His mortal frame, 'Abdu'l-Bahá lived a life of total self-abnegation, of unbroken, unqualified service to God and to man. In this field He did not spare Himself toil or pain. Bahá'u'lláh had given Him these designations: 'the Greatest Branch', 'the Mystery of God', 'the Master'. But once the mantle of authority came to rest on His shoulders, He chose to be known as 'Abdu'l-Bahá—the Servant of Bahá.

'Abdu'l-Bahá sorrowed with the sorrowful and the stricken and the afflicted, in deep compassion. He rejoiced with the truly joyous. Thousands thronged to His door to seek relief. Some of them sought worldly goods. But many more desired the relief which only the goods of the spirit can bestow. To them all, 'Abdu'l-Bahá gave freely and abundantly. No one found His door shut. No one was turned away. No one left His presence empty-handed. He did not merely wait for the oppressed and the bewildered and the fallen to come to Him. He went out to find them and to serve them. The learned and the wise also came to Him and drank deeply at the fount of His knowledge. Rulers and potentates, statesmen and generals, the mighty and the great came as well, and found in 'Abdu'l-Bahá a counsellor whose motives were generous and disinterested.

It would be erroneous to imagine that by this description we have given a complete portrait of 'Abdu'l-Bahá and have encompassed Him. What we have said of Him can be said of saints and seers of all ages. No description can measure up to the theme of a life which transcended every barrier to its total fulfilment. Once an observer remarked that 'Abdu'l-Bahá walked 'the mystic way with practical feet'. Dr T. K. Cheyne, the celebrated Biblical scholar and higher critic, spoke of Him as: 'The Ambassador to Humanity'.

Edward Granville Browne, the eminent orientalist of Pembroke College, Cambridge, visited 'Akká in April 1890, and met 'Abdu'l-Bahá. Later he wrote:

Seldom have I seen one whose appearance impressed me more. A tall strongly-built man holding himself straight as an arrow, with white turban and raiment, long black locks reaching almost to the shoulder, broad powerful forehead indicating a strong intellect combined with an unswerving will, eyes keen as a hawk's, and strongly-marked but pleasing features—such was my first impression of 'Abbás Efendí, 'the master' (Áká)* as he *par excellence* is called by the Bábís. Subsequent conversation with him served only to heighten the respect with which his appearance had from the first inspired me. One more eloquent of speech, more ready of argument, more apt of illustration, more intimately acquainted with the sacred books of the Jews, the Christians, and the Muhammadans, could, I should think, scarcely be found even amongst the eloquent, ready, and subtle race to which he belongs. These qualities, combined with a bearing at once majestic and genial, made me cease to wonder at the influence and esteem which he enjoyed even beyond

* Áqá.

the circle of his father's followers. About the greatness of this man and his power no one who had seen him could entertain a doubt.[1]

Thornton Chase, the first Bahá'í of the American continent, wrote in the early years of the century:

The fame of him has gone round the world. Many, from this country, led by various motives, have visited him, and we have seen and heard them after their return. Without exception they have agreed in declaring that they have seen the most powerful being upon the earth. They tell how, going before him with varied expectations, curiosities or hopes, and finding themselves in his presence, they were overwhelmed with awe, shame, fear, love, abasement or exaltation, emotions differing according to the conditions of each. They tell how they fell at his feet and longed to kiss even the dust on which he trod . . .

Strong men, with tears streaming down their cheeks and voices broken with emotion, have told us of the unspeakable love, gentleness, majesty and power radiating from that simple man of slender build and medium height . . .

We are told how the little children love him; how he takes them in his arms and bears them on their way to school and enters into their hearts with his sweet sympathies; how the poor and afflicted hover around his steps and feed upon his words, while he blesses them with both material and spiritual gifts; how the friends brave all things, endure all things and bear all trials to gain the briefest visit to him; how his enemies bow and bend like willows before the gentle forgiveness of his look; how no soul can enter and leave his presence without being changed—for better, or for worse.[2]

Horace Holley,[3] another distinguished Bahá'í of the United States—who was appointed a Hand of the Cause of

God by the Guardian of the Faith—met 'Abdu'l-Bahá on the shores of Lake Leman in August 1911. This is his testimony:

He displayed a beauty of stature, an inevitable harmony of attitude and dress I had never seen nor thought of in men. Without having ever visualized the Master, I knew that this was he. My whole body underwent a shock. My heart leaped, my knees weakened, a thrill of acute, receptive feeling flowed from head to foot. I seemed to have turned into some most sensitive sense-organ, as if eyes and ears were not enough for this sublime impression. In every part of me I stood aware of Abdul Baha's presence. From sheer happiness I wanted to cry—it seemed the most suitable form of self-expression at my command. While my own personality was flowing away, even whilst I exhibited a state of complete humility, a new being, not my own, assumed its place. A glory, as it were, from the summits of human nature poured into me, and I was conscious of a most intense impulse to admire. In Abdul Baha I felt the awful presence of Baha'-o'llah, and, as my thoughts returned to activity, I realized that I had thus drawn as near as man now may to pure spirit and pure being . . .

During our two days' visit, we were given unusual opportunity of questioning the Master, but I soon realized that such was not the highest or most productive plane on which I could meet him . . . I yielded to a feeling of reverence which contained more than the solution of intellectual or moral problems. To look upon so wonderful a human being, to respond utterly to the charm of his presence—this brought me continual happiness. I had no fear that its effects would pass away and leave me unchanged . . . Patriarchal, majestic, strong, yet infinitely kind, he appeared like some just king that very moment descended from his throne to mingle with a devoted people . . .[4]

Howard Colby Ives was a Unitarian minister in Jersey City at the time of 'Abdu'l-Bahá's visit to the United States. On the day of 'Abdu'l-Bahá's arrival in New York (April 11th 1912), Howard Ives went to see the venerable Teacher about Whom he had heard a great deal from his Bahá'í friends:

A glimpse was all I succeeded in getting. The press of eager friends and curious ones was so great that it was difficult even to get inside the doors. I have only the memory of an impressive silence most unusual at such functions . . . At last I managed to press forward where I could peep over a shoulder and so got my first glimpse of 'Abdu'l-Bahá. He was seated. A cream colored fez upon His head from under which white hair flowed almost to His shoulders. His robe, what little I could see of it, was oriental, almost white. But these were incidentals to which I could pay little attention. The impressive thing, and what I have never forgotten, was an indefinable aspect of majesty combined with an exquisite courtesy . . . Such gentleness, such love emanated from Him as I had never seen. I was not emotionally disturbed. Remember that at that time I had no conviction, almost, I might say, little or no interest in what I came later to understand by the term His 'Station' . . . What was it that these people around me had which gave to their eyes such illumination, to their hearts such gladness? What connotation did the word 'wonderful' have to them that so often it was upon their lips? I did not know, but I wanted to know as I think I had never known the want of anything before.[5]

Months later Howard Ives gave his allegiance to 'Abdu'l-Bahá:

Here I saw a man who, outwardly, like myself, lived in the world of confusion, yet, inwardly, beyond the possibility of doubt, lived and worked in that higher and real world. All His concepts, all His motives, all His actions, derived their springs from that 'World of Light'. And, which is to me a most inspiring and encouraging fact, He took it for granted that you and I, the ordinary run-of-the-mill humanity, could enter into and live and move in that world if we would.[6]

Arminius Vambéry, the renowned Hungarian orientalist, met 'Abdu'l-Bahá in Budapest in 1913. A few months later, shortly before his death, he wrote Him this letter:

I forward this humble petition to the sanctified and holy presence of 'Abdu'l-Bahá 'Abbás, who is the center of knowledge, famous throughout the world, and loved by all mankind. O thou noble friend who art conferring guidance upon humanity—May my life be a ransom to thee . . .

I have seen the father of your Excellency from afar. I have realized the self-sacrifice and noble courage of his son, and I am lost in admiration.

For the principles and aims of your Excellency, I express the utmost respect and devotion, and if God, the Most High, confers long life, I will be able to serve you under all conditions. I pray and supplicate this from the depths of my heart.[7]

Lord Lamington, one-time Governor of the Bombay Presidency, wrote thus of 'Abdu'l-Bahá:

There was never a more striking instance of one who desired that mankind should live in peace and goodwill and have love for others by the recognition of their inherent divine qualities.

At Haifa, in 1919, I well remember seeing a white figure seated by the roadside; when he arose and walked the vision of a truly and holy saintly man impressed itself on me. I think it was on this occasion that he took his signet ring from off his finger and gave it to me.[8]

IN THE DAYS OF HIS FATHER

'Abdu'l-Bahá, the eldest Son of Bahá'u'lláh, was born in Ṭihrán on May 23rd 1844,[9] the midnight of the same evening that the Báb revealed His Mission in Shíráz. He was named 'Abbás after His grandfather, but, as already mentioned, took the name of 'Abdu'l-Bahá after the ascension of Bahá'u'lláh. He was only eight years old when—in the wake of a desperate and futile attempt on the life of Náṣiri'd-Dín Sháh, by two half-crazed men—Bahá'u'lláh was imprisoned, and the Bábís were ferociously persecuted. Bahá'u'lláh's house was pillaged, His lands and goods were confiscated, and His family reduced from opulence to penury. One day, while in Europe, 'Abdu'l-Bahá recalled the sufferings of those bleak times:

Detachment does not imply lack of means; it is marked by the freedom of the heart. In Ṭihrán, we possessed everything at a nightfall, and on the morrow we were shorn of it all, to the extent that we had no food to eat. I was hungry, but there was no bread to be had. My mother poured some flour into the palm of my hand, and I ate that instead of bread. Yet, we were contented.

And again:

At that time of dire calamities and attacks mounted by the enemies I was a child of nine.* They threw so many

* In the reckoning of the lunar year.

stones into our house that the courtyard was crammed with them . . . Mother took us for safety to another quarter, and rented a house in a back alley where she kept us indoors and looked after us. But one day our means of subsistence were barely adequate, and mother told me to go to my aunt's house, and ask her to find us a few qiráns . . .* I went and my aunt did what she could for us. She tied a five-qirán piece in a handkerchief and gave it to me. On my way home someone recognized me and shouted: 'Here is a Bábí'; whereupon the children in the street chased me. I found refuge in the entrance to a house . . . There I stayed until nightfall, and when I came out, I was once again pursued by the children who kept yelling at me and pelted me with stones . . . When I reached home I was exhausted. Mother wanted to know what had happened to me. I could not utter a word and collapsed.[10]

Bahá'u'lláh's imprisonment lasted four months in a dark, verminous dungeon. He was in the company of cut-throats and highwaymen. With Him also were many Bábís who loved and revered Him, and were happy to be near Him and to share His sufferings. The agonies of the Bábís were intense, and when death came to them they walked with radiant faces into its embrace, though it was attended by tortures beyond belief. And as they went out of their cell to die they knelt in front of Bahá'u'lláh and kissed the hem of His garment, grateful for this last reward of their total dedication.

Bahá'u'lláh Himself once related the story of those days to Mullá Muḥammad-i-Zarandí, entitled Nabíl-i-A'ẓam, the historian and chronicler of His Faith:

All those who were struck down by the storm that raged during that memorable year in Ṭihrán were Our fellow-

* Iranian silver coin of the period.

prisoners in the Síyáh-Chál, where We were confined. We
were all huddled together in one cell, our feet in stocks,
and around our necks fastened the most galling of chains.
The air we breathed was laden with the foulest impurities,
while the floor on which we sat was covered with filth
and infested with vermin. No ray of light was allowed to
penetrate that pestilential dungeon or to warm its icy-
coldness. We were placed in two rows, each facing the
other. We had taught them to repeat certain verses which,
every night, they chanted with extreme fervour. 'God is
sufficient unto me; He verily is the All-sufficing!' one
row would intone, while the other would reply: 'In Him
let the trusting trust.' The chorus of these gladsome voices
would continue to peal out until the early hours of the
morning. Their reverberation would fill the dungeon,
and, piercing its massive walls, would reach the ears of
Náṣiri'd-Dín Sháh, whose palace was not far distant from
the place where we were imprisoned. 'What means this
sound?' he was reported to have exclaimed. 'It is the
anthem the Bábís are intoning in their prison,' they
replied. The Sháh made no further remarks, nor did he
attempt to restrain the enthusiasm his prisoners, despite
the horrors of their confinement, continued to display.[11]

One day 'Abdu'l-Bahá, anxious to see His Father, was
taken to the dungeon. This is His account of that awesome
visit:

They sent me with a black servant to His blessed presence
in the prison. The warders indicated the cell, and the
servant carried me in on his shoulders. I saw a dark, steep
place. We entered a small, narrow doorway, and went
down two steps, but beyond those one could see nothing.
In the middle of the stairway, all of a sudden we heard
His blessed voice: 'Do not bring him in here', and so they
took me back. We sat outside, waiting for the prisoners
to be led out. Suddenly they brought the Blessed

Perfection* out of the dungeon. He was chained to several others. What a chain! It was very heavy. The prisoners could only move it along with great difficulty. Sad and heart-rending it was.[12]

At last came release, but also banishment. Bahá'u'lláh and His family were expelled from their native land. Despoiled and destitute they travelled in the heart of winter over the snow-bound peaks of western Írán. Ill-equipped for such an arduous journey, their sufferings were great. Some seventy years later, Bahá'íyyih Khánum,† the daughter of Bahá'u'lláh, entitled the Greatest Holy Leaf, was relating her experiences of those far-off days to an English lady who was devoted to the Cause of her Father. Noticing tears in the eyes of her companion, she said: 'This time is very sad, Laydee, I shall make you grieve if I tell of it.' And Lady Blomfield said: 'Oh, I want to be with you in my heart through all your sadness, dearest Khánum.' Bahá'íyyih Khánum's reply was: 'Well, well! If I did not live in my thoughts all through the events of the sad days of our lives, I should have naught else in my life, for it has been all sorrow; but sorrow is really joy, when suffered in the path of God!'[13]

'Abdu'l-Bahá at that early age was a victim of consumption. Sixty years later, when speaking of the illness which was keeping Him in the French capital for a period longer than expected, He brought to mind those years of His childhood:

> I have been travelling for two years and a half. Nowhere was I ill except here. Because of that I had to stay a long time. Were it not for this illness I would not have stayed in Paris more than a month. There is a reason for this . . . It has been so from the early years of my life. The wisdom of whatever has happened to me has become apparent

* One of the designations of Bahá'u'lláh.
† Bahíyyih Khánum.

later. While I was a child in Ṭihrán, seven years of age, I contracted tuberculosis. There was no hope of recovery. Afterwards the wisdom of and the reason for this became evident. Were it not for that illness I would have been in Mázindarán.* But because of it I remained in Ṭihrán and was there when the Blessed Perfection was imprisoned. Thus I travelled to 'Iráq in His company. And when the time came, although physicians had despaired of my recovery, I was suddenly cured. It happened in spite of the fact that all had said a cure was impossible.[14]

The exiles reached Baghdád in April 1853. The hardships of imprisonment and a difficult journey in midwinter had left their marks on the health of Bahá'u'lláh. The members of His family were ill with exhaustion. Their foes were jubilant. They rejoiced over the apparent eclipse of a fortune that had once dazzled the sight of a nation.

Bahá'u'lláh knew His mission and destiny. In the twilight of the dungeon of Ṭihrán He had seen the brilliance of the Sun dawning in His own Person. There He had received the intimation that He was the Redeemer Whose advent the Báb had heralded and all the Scriptures of mankind foretold. But the time for His declaration had not arrived. We are told that 'Abdu'l-Bahá was conscious of the station of His beloved Father. His attitude towards Bahá'u'lláh was not merely that of a son to his father. It expressed a higher devotion, a worthier obedience. The Báb states that the first one to believe in a Manifestation of God is the essence of the achievement of the preceding dispensation; and so, 'Abdu'l-Bahá, the first to believe with His whole being in the Mission of His Father, was the most eminent representative of the virtues called forth by the Báb. And He was also to be 'the embodiment of every Bahá'í ideal, the incarnation of every Bahá'í virtue . . . '

* The province bordering on the Caspian Sea where Bahá'u'lláh's ancestral home was.

Exactly a year after His arrival at Baghdád, Bahá'u'lláh decided to seek the seclusion of the mountain and the wilderness. His health restored, He had arisen to fulfil the pledge made in the dungeon of Ṭihrán, to revitalize the broken community of the Báb. But bitter adversaries attacked from within, and their action threatened disruption and chaos.

Bahá'u'lláh left Baghdád (on April 10th 1854), His destination disclosed to no one, to make it plain that His aim was not the assertion of leadership.

'Abdu'l-Bahá grieved over this cruel separation, but though a child of no more than ten years of age, His mien and bearing were assured and serene. His youthful shoulders had to bear responsibilities which mature men prefer to forgo. He read avidly what He could find of the Writings of the Báb. No school had ever moulded His mind, the unfoldment of which had been the loving care of Bahá'u'lláh. Some years later, still in His teens, He wrote a lucid, illuminating commentary on the well-known tradition ascribed to the Prophet Muḥammad: 'I was a Hidden Treasure and loved to be known, therefore I created beings to know.' He undertook this task at the request of 'Alí Shawkat Páshá, a nobleman, highly-cultured and deeply-read. 'Abdu'l-Bahá's commentary not only reveals profound knowledge, striking mastery of language, and rare qualities of mind, but above all it shows the most profound understanding.

'Abdu'l-Bahá oftentimes walked among the learned who were wise with the wisdom of age and competent with experience, and conversed with them on their themes and topics. They respected the speech of the young boy, because it was mature and enlightening, and because the speaker was modest and charming. Once a redoubtable enemy of Bahá'u'lláh remarked that had He no other proof to substantiate His exceptional powers, it were sufficient that He had reared such a son as 'Abbás Effendi.

The news was brought to Baghdád of a sage who had

appeared in the mountains of the north, a remarkable person possessed of unique qualities. 'Abdu'l-Bahá recognized in this news tidings of His Father. His uncle, Mírzá Músá, Bahá'u'lláh's faithful brother, thought likewise. Shaykh Sulṭán, an outstanding Arab Bábí of Karbilá, accompanied by Jawád the woodcutter, also a Bábí of Arab origin, set out to seek Bahá'u'lláh and entreat Him to return. Bahá'u'lláh's long absence had shown beyond doubt that the community of the Báb stood in dire need of Him. He went back in March 1856 amidst joy and jubilation.

Bahá'u'lláh gave the Bábís vision and hope and character which they had lost. But as yet only the chosen mind of 'Abdu'l-Bahá had received the full impact of the station of His Father. It was during this period that Bahá'u'lláh bestowed upon His Son the designation 'Sirru'lláh'—the Mystery of God. Those who sought the presence of Bahá'u'lláh found in His eldest Son traits and qualities which evoked high praise and marvelling admiration.

Enemies were active again. Because the fame of Bahá'u'lláh was spreading far and wide, they gathered their forces for a further onslaught. Their voices became strident, and Náṣiri'd-Dín Sháh was alarmed. Responding to the pleadings of the Iranian Ambassador, the Ottoman Government decided to call Bahá'u'lláh to Constantinople. Prior to His departure, Bahá'u'lláh moved to the garden of Najíb Páshá on the outskirts of Baghdád. Later the Bahá'ís came to know it as the Garden of Riḍván. There Bahá'u'lláh revealed His Station and His Mission. The Day of Days had come – 'the Day whereon naught can be seen except the splendours of the Light that shineth from the face of Thy Lord, the Gracious, the Most Bountiful.'

In a letter which 'Abdu'l-Bahá wrote during the twelve-days' sojourn in the Garden of Riḍván, He traced the course—three years long—of plots, negotiations, and pressures that had been brought to bear on the Ottoman Government. A request to deliver Bahá'u'lláh and His dependants to the Persian officials was firmly rejected. Other governments were next asked to use their powers of persuasion. In the end the Sublime Porte* agreed to move Bahá'u'lláh away from the vicinity of Persia. 'Abdu'l-Bahá further related:

The third day after Ramadán[15] when, in observance of the festival, my uncle and I called on the Páshá,† he expressed his eagerness to meet Him [Bahá'u'lláh]. The Páshá, however, wanted the meeting to be at his own house. He [Bahá'u'lláh] replied that He did not wish to go to the Governorate, but if the Páshá desired to meet Him, the meeting could take place in the mosque. He went to the mosque, as did the Páshá, but on entering it the Páshá turned back and went away. Later he sent his own vizier to Bahá'u'lláh's presence, with letters from the Ṣadr-i-A'ẓam (prime minister), and also this message: 'I came to the mosque, but was ashamed to broach such matters at the first encounter.' The vizier gave an account of all that had transpired. Then he said: 'What the Páshá asked to know was this—whether you preferred not to leave. Should it be so, if you will write and inform the Ṣadr-i-A'ẓam, we shall forward your letter to him. But if you should desire to leave, that would be your own choice.' He [Bahá'u'lláh] replied: 'If the Government displays proper respect, I will choose, for certain reasons, to reside awhile in those regions.' Then the Páshá sent Him this message: 'I shall carry out your wishes and do what you say.'

The Governor-General, 'Abdu'l-Bahá further wrote, had called in person at the garden of Najíb Páshá, to pay his

* Báb-i-'Álí—a designation of the seat of power in Constantinople.
† Námíq Páshá, the Válí (governor-general) of 'Iráq.

respects to Bahá'u'lláh and to show his esteem and affection. And the discomfiture of the foe is apparent in these, the concluding lines of that historic letter:

Such hath been the interposition of God that the joy evinced by them hath been turned to chagrin and sorrow, so much so that the Persian Consul-General in Baghdád regrets exceedingly the plans and plots which the schemers had devised. Námíq Páshá himself on the day he called on Him [Bahá'u'lláh] stated: 'Formerly they insisted upon your departure. Now, however, they are even more insistent that you should remain.' They plotted and God plotted, and God is the best of plotters.*

On May 3rd 1863, the exiles set out on their long journey to the capital of the Ottoman Empire. Unlike the lonely exodus of ten years before, this time they were accompanied by a number of devoted people for whom the reality of heaven was the presence of Bahá'u'lláh. It was a triumphal march. Everywhere Bahá'u'lláh was received with reverence by the officers of the state. 'Abdu'l-Bahá was then a youth of nineteen, handsome, gracious, agile, zealous to serve, firm with the wilful, generous to all. He strove hard to make the toil of a long journey less arduous for others. At night He was among the first to reach the halting-place, to see to the comfort of the travellers. Wherever provisions were scarce, He spent the night in search of food. And at dawn He rose early to set the caravan on another day's march. Then the whole day long He rode by the side of His Father, in constant attendance upon Him. It took them one hundred and ten days to reach the port of Sámsún on the Black Sea, where they embarked for Constantinople, and arrived at the metropolis of the Ottoman Empire on August 16th 1863.

* See Qur'án iii. 47.

What could await Bahá'u'lláh and His family in Constantinople? He arrived serene and unperturbed, sought no favour, solicited no benefaction. He neither called on the officials and the grandees of the capital, nor did He return their visits. He calmly waited for the decision of the Ottoman ruler. Early in December, Sultán 'Abdu'l-'Azíz ordered the banishment of Bahá'u'lláh and His family to Adrianople. Náṣiri'd-Dín Sháh's ambassador, Ḥájí Mírzá Ḥusayn Khán, the Mushíru'd-Dawlih, played a conspicuous part in effecting Bahá'u'lláh's exile to the fringes of the Turkish Empire. The man who brought the Sultán's edict to Bahá'u'lláh was received by 'Abdu'l-Bahá and His uncle, Mírzá Músá.[16] Then it was that Bahá'u'lláh made the first public proclamation of His Mission to circles beyond the community of the Báb. It was contained in a Tablet (the text of which is not extant) revealed in answer to the imperial edict, and delivered three days later to the same man who had brought that edict. That Tablet, admonitory and severe, was addressed to the person of the Sultán. Referring to it its Author said:

Whatever action the ministers of the Sultán took against Us, after having become acquainted with its contents, cannot be regarded as unjustifiable. The acts they committed before its perusal, however, can have no justification.[17]

Bahá'u'lláh's third exile was reminiscent of His first. Once again it was the heart of winter. Once again the road led out of the capital city of an Islamic realm, the seat of a corrupt tyranny. Once again the exiles were ill-equipped for the rigours of a winter journey.

'They expelled Us,' wrote Bahá'u'lláh, addressing Sultán 'Abdu'l-'Azíz, 'from thy city with an abasement with which no abasement on earth can compare . . . Neither My family, nor those who accompanied Me, had the necessary raiment to protect them from the cold in that freezing weather . . . The eyes of Our enemies wept over Us, and beyond them those of every discerning person.'[18]

'Abdu'l-Bahá was now beginning to shield His Father from the intrusions of an unbelieving world, as well as from the malice of the envious and the faithless. But Bahá'u'lláh's sorrows had not yet reached their culmination. The last act of treachery, by no less a person than His own half-brother, was yet to come. Likewise a fourth exile and incarceration in a penal colony.

It was a harsh journey to Adrianople. Severe storms raged, and there were forced marches before the exiles reached their destination on December 12th. This town in Roumelia, on the periphery of the Ottoman Empire, was to be Bahá'u'lláh's home for well-nigh five years. Here He would proclaim His Advent to the sovereigns of the world, and the 'Supreme Pen' would move to warn and admonish them. Here also Mírzá Yaḥyá, entitled Ṣubḥ-i-Azal (the Morning of Eternity), a half-brother of Bahá'u'lláh and the 'nominee of the Báb', would openly defy the authority of Bahá'u'lláh and cause that 'great dividing' which ultimately spelled his own ruin.

As a direct result of the intrigues of Mírzá Yaḥyá and his accomplices, and their representations to the Sublime Porte, Bahá'u'lláh was condemned to His fourth and last exile. Sixteen years earlier, in the torrid month of August, He had been subjected to indignities and thrown into the dungeon of Ṭihrán. Now, another August witnessed His final exile.

The firmán (edict) of Sulṭán 'Abdu'l-'Azíz named 'Akká in Syria as the place of Bahá'u'lláh's incarceration, and Famagusta in Cyprus the locality to which Mírzá Yaḥyá was to be banished. The Ottoman ruler did not spare the man who was the prime instigator of mischief. But no one knew what was to happen to the Bahá'ís who had chosen to be near their Lord in Adrianople.

Without warning, one morning in that sweltering summer month, soldiers surrounded the house of 'Izzat Áqá, where Bahá'u'lláh resided. His followers were rounded up, wherever they were in the city, and were told that they had to leave. One of them, Áqá Riḍáy-i-Qannád,[19] a man staunch and steadfast to the end, has recorded: 'Most of our possessions were auctioned at half their value.' There was great consternation in the city. Consuls of European Powers came to offer their assistance to Bahá'u'lláh, but their aid was courteously and emphatically declined. Bahá'u'lláh Himself makes mention of those tribulations in the *Súriy-i-Ra'ís*, a Tablet addressed to 'Álí Páshá, the Grand Vizier of the Ottoman Empire:

The loved ones of God and His kindred were left on the first night without food . . . The people surrounded the house, and Muslims and Christians wept over Us . . . We perceived that the weeping of the people of the Son (Christians) exceeded the weeping of others—a sign for such as ponder.[20]

It was in that same Tablet, revealed during the journey from Adrianople to Gallipoli, that He foretold the nemesis about to overtake the proud Sulṭán and his realms:

The day is approaching when the Land of Mystery (Adrianople), and what is beside it shall be changed, and shall pass out of the hands of the king, and commotions shall appear, and the voice of lamentation shall be raised, and the evidences of mischief shall be revealed on all sides, and confusion shall spread by reason of that which hath befallen these captives at the hands of the hosts of oppression. The course of things shall be altered, and conditions shall wax so grievous, that the very sands on the desolate hills will moan, and the trees on the mountain will weep, and blood will flow out of all things. Then wilt thou behold the people in sore distress.

Later, in a second Tablet from 'Akká, He wrote to the Grand Vizier:

> Soon will He seize you in His wrathful anger, and sedition will be stirred up in your midst, and your dominions will be disrupted. Then will ye bewail and lament, and will find none to help or succor you.[21]

And at Gallipoli, Bahá'u'lláh told Ḥasan Effendi—an official detailed to supervise the transference of the exiles to that town—while he was taking his leave: 'Tell the king that this territory will pass out of his hands, and his affairs will be thrown into confusion.'[22]

Bahá'u'lláh's departure from Adrianople, decreed by the Ottoman ruler—the Caliph of Islám, the recognized successor to the Arabian Prophet—brought to a close a turbulent, disastrous, and yet immeasurably glorious period of His forty-years'-long Ministry, a period that had witnessed the public proclamation of His Faith—His majestic call to the sovereigns of the world and the generality of mankind—as well as the perfidy of Mírzá Yaḥyá whom He had reared with loving care from early childhood.

It was during those five years in Roumelia that 'Abdu'l-Bahá, the Most Great Branch, already styled by His Father 'the Mystery of God', attained the full stature of His unmatched and resplendent manhood. He was nineteen when Bahá'u'lláh and His family were ordered from Constantinople, the seat of the Caliphate, to the remote border of the Turkish dominions within the fringes of the European continent. Now, twenty-four years of age, He was greatly revered and highly esteemed not only in the company of His Father's followers but in circles beyond. Khurshíd Páshá, the Governor of Adrianople, was one of those who saw in 'Abdu'l-Bahá a very remarkable person, and whose regard and admiration for Him were noteworthy. Indeed so attached had <u>Kh</u>ur<u>sh</u>íd Pá<u>sh</u>á become to Bahá'u'lláh and His Son that, when the Sulṭán's firmán reached him, he declined to inform Bahá'u'lláh of its content in person, and delegated that repugnant task to a subordinate. Another prominent Ottoman official, 'Azíz Pá<u>sh</u>á, when raised to the rank of Válí (governor-general), journeyed to 'Akká twice to pay his respects to Bahá'u'lláh, and to hold converse with 'Abdu'l-Bahá.

It was in Adrianople that Bahá'u'lláh revealed a Tablet the significance of which cannot be over-estimated. That Tablet was the *Súriy-i-<u>Gh</u>uṣn* (Súrih of the Branch) addressed to Mírzá 'Alí-Riḍáy-i-Mustawfí, a Bahá'í of <u>Kh</u>urásán— that province in eastern Persia famed in the Bábí Dispensation and to which some momentous prophecies of Bahá'u'lláh specifically apply. Mírzá 'Alí-Riḍá was a high-ranking official in the service of the government, and his brother, Mírzá Muḥammad-Riḍá, the Mu'taminu's-Salṭanih, also a follower of Bahá'u'lláh, was the Vizier of <u>Kh</u>urásán. In the *Súriy-i-<u>Gh</u>uṣn*, Bahá'u'lláh thus extols His eldest Son:

There hath branched from the Sadratu'l-Muntahá this sacred and glorious Being, this Branch of Holiness; well is it with him that hath sought His shelter and abideth beneath His shadow. Verily the Limb of the Law of God hath sprung forth from this Root which God hath firmly implanted in the Ground of His Will, and Whose Branch hath been so uplifted as to encompass the whole of creation. Magnified be He, therefore, for this sublime, this blessed, this mighty, this exalted Handiwork! . . . A Word hath, as a token of Our grace, gone forth from the Most Great Tablet—a Word which God hath adorned with the ornament of His own Self, and made it sovereign over the earth and all that is therein, and a sign of His greatness and power among its people . . . Render thanks unto God, O people, for His appearance; for verily He is the most great Favour unto you, the most perfect bounty upon you; and through Him every mouldering bone is quickened. Whoso turneth towards Him hath turned towards God, and whoso turneth away from Him hath turned away from My Beauty, hath repudiated My Proof, and transgressed against Me. He is the Trust of God amongst you, His charge within you, His manifestation unto you and His appearance among His favoured servants . . . We have sent Him down in the form of a human temple. Blest and sanctified be God Who createth whatsoever He willeth through His inviolable, His infallible decree. They who deprive themselves of the shadow of the Branch, are lost in the wilderness of error, are consumed by the heat of worldly desires, and are of those who will assuredly perish.[23]

Unequivocal is Bahá'u'lláh's statement of the exalted station of His beloved Son, revealed in these stirring words. Stern and fervent is Bahá'u'lláh's command that His Son must be the focus of a Bahá'í's devotion. Unsparing is His condemnation of those who turn away from the Most Great Branch.

On August 21st 1868, an Austrian–Lloyd boat left Gallipoli bound for Alexandria. On it were Bahá'u'lláh, His family and His people, about seventy in number; also Mírzá Yahyá, his family, and his two confirmed adherents: Siyyid Muhammad-i-Isfahání and Áqá-Ján Big. At first the Ottoman authorities were strongly inclined to separate the followers of Bahá'u'lláh from Him. But wiser counsels had prevailed, and at the behest of Bahá'u'lláh, staunchly upheld and pressed by 'Umar Effendi—an Ottoman major in whose custody the exiles were placed—it had at last been decided not to effect this cruel separation.

However, it was ordered by the authorities in Constantinople, whose word constituted the law of the Empire, that four of the Bahá'ís should be sent to Cyprus with Mírzá Yahyá. It was also decreed that a number of the supporters

of Mírzá Yaḥyá should be included among the companions
of Bahá'u'lláh. These included the two already mentioned
who openly adhered to Mírzá Yaḥyá—Siyyid Muḥammad-
i-Iṣfahání, his corrupter and evil genius, the 'Antichrist of
the Bahá'í Revelation'; and Áqá-Ján Big-i-Khamsa'í, an
artilleryman who had served with the Turkish forces. Both
men had been plotting hard and exerting every influence
they could in Constantinople, to make the Ottoman authorities take action against Bahá'u'lláh. The act of placing them
among the followers of Bahá'u'lláh brought dire results in
later years.[24]

In Alexandria, where the Austrian–Lloyd ship put in,
there languished in prison the man who was destined to
become the chronicler of the Faith, Mullá Muḥammad-i-
Zarandí, surnamed Nabíl.[25] After touching at Port Said and
Jaffa, the ship reached Haifa, where the exiles disembarked.
The journey thence to 'Akká, across the bay, in small sailing-
boats in the height of summer, was galling. It was the last
day of August 1868 when Bahá'u'lláh came ashore at the
landing-stage beneath the grim walls of 'Akká.

At the jetty in the shadow of the forbidding citadel that
was to receive the Manifestation of God, stood a group of
misguided inhabitants of that prison-city. They were there
to catch a glimpse of the One referred to as 'the God of the
Persians'. Drawn from the ranks of the blind, unreasoning
mob which inhabits every age and era, they came to the
seashore to mock and jeer. A sense of righteous hatred
filled their souls, an aberration to which men in many times
and circumstances have been prone.

> . . . upon Our arrival at this Spot [wrote Bahá'u'lláh]
> We chose to designate it as the 'Most Great Prison'.
> Though previously subjected in another land (Ṭihrán)
> to chains and fetters, We yet refused to call it by that
> name. Say: Ponder thereon, O ye endued with under-
> standing![26]

This was the prison of desperadoes to which Bahá'u'lláh and His people were consigned. 'Akká had achieved fame more than once in its long history. It had refused to bow to mighty conquerors. Prophets of Israel as well as the Prophet of Arabia had alluded to it in terms that exalted it above other towns and cities of glittering splendour. Hosea had said that 'Akká was 'a door of hope'. Ezekiel had referred to it as 'the gate that looketh toward the east' to which 'the glory of the God of Israel came from the way of the east'. It was Ptolemais in the days when Jesus walked the Mediterranean shore. And Muḥammad had said: 'Blessed the man that hath visited 'Akká, and blessed he that hath visited the visitor of 'Akká . . . A month in 'Akká is better than a thousand years elsewhere.'[27]

But on this awesome and momentous day of August 1868 —awesome and momentous because it witnessed the literal fulfilment of great prophecies reaching back well-nigh three thousand years—'Akká was a forlorn dwelling for man, and its miseries were manifold. Its air was foul, its water was foul, its thoroughfares were foul. Its people were captives of ignorance; benighted, bigoted sycophants. Notable exceptions made the condition of these people even more glaring. The glories of 'Akká had departed. Now the Glory of God came to it.

'The first night,' wrote Bahá'u'lláh in the second Tablet addressed to the Grand Vizier of Turkey, 'all were deprived of either food or drink . . . They even begged for water, and were refused.'[28]

Very soon the pestilential air of 'Akká and the insanitary state of its barracks began to take their toll. All but two of the exiles fell sick. Malaria and dysentery and typhoid swept over them. Three died. 'Abdu'l-Bahá tended the sick, shielded His Father, faced the scorn and the fury of the inhabitants of 'Akká, held His ground with callous gaolers and brutal guards and hostile officials. He never wavered.

His vigil never relaxed. Years later, as related by Hájí Mírzá Ḥaydar-'Alí in his autobiography, Bahá'u'lláh recalled the endeavour and the achievement of His Son:

In Baghdád We Ourselves would go and take a seat in the coffee-house to meet the people—friends and acquaintances, strangers and inquirers alike. We brought those who were remote near to the Faith, and led many a soul into the fold of the Cause. Thus We served the Cause of God, gave victory to His Word and exalted His Name. The Most Great Branch undertook the same task and served in the same way, to a much greater degree, in Adrianople, and then to a far greater extent and with greater efficacy, in 'Akká. The same hardships and afflictions which were Ours in the early days befell Him. In Baghdád We were not prisoners, and the Cause of God had not obtained even a fraction of the fame which it has gained today. At that time the number of its opponents and adversaries and ill-wishers was far less than today. In the Land of Mystery [Adrianople] We used to meet with some and let them come into Our presence. But in the Most Great Prison We do not meet the people who are not within the fold of the Cause. We have closed the doors of social intercourse. It is the Master Who has taken every trouble upon Himself. For Our sake, in order that We may have ease and comfort, He faces the world and its peoples. For Us He has become a mighty stronghold, a mighty armour. At first He rented the Mansion of Mazra'ih. We were there for a while. Then he secured for Us this Mansion of Bahjí. He has arisen with all His power to serve the Faith, and confirmation crowns His effort. This work so occupies His days and nights that He is perforce kept away from Bahjí for weeks. We consort with the Friends and reveal His [God's] Word. He, the Master, is the target and bears all hardships.

The same writer has recorded this utterance of Bahá'u'lláh, which not only mirrors His regard for His Son, but throws great light on the problem of teaching:

A pleasing, kindly disposition and a display of tolerance towards the people are requisites of teaching the Cause. Whatever a person says, hollow and product of vain imaginings and a parrot-like repetition of somebody else's views though it be, one ought to let it pass. One should not engage in disputation leading to and ending with obstinate refusal and hostility, because the other person would consider himself worsted and defeated. Consequently further veils intervene between him and the Cause, and he becomes more negligent of it. One ought to say: right, admitted, but look at the matter in this other way, and judge for yourself whether it is true or false; of course it should be said with courtesy, with kindliness, with consideration. Then the other person will listen, will not seek to answer back and to marshal proofs in repudiation. He will agree, because he comes to realize that the purpose has not been to engage in verbal battle and to gain mastery over him. He sees that the purpose has been to impart the word of truth, to show humanity, to bring forth heavenly qualities. His eyes and his ears are opened, his heart responds, his true nature unfolds, and by the grace of God, he becomes a new creation . . . The Most Great Branch gives a willing ear to any manner of senseless talk, to such an extent that the other person says to himself: He is trying to learn from me. Then, gradually, by such means as the other person cannot perceive, He gives him insight and understanding.[29]

Conditions of life in the cheerless barracks of 'Akká taxed the strength of its inmates to the utmost. The guards were cruel and avaricious and offensive. The townsmen from whom, after a lapse of time, the prisoners were allowed to make some of their necessary purchases, under strict surveillance, were unrelenting in their hatred and contempt. But over and above all afflictions and privations the behaviour of Siyyid Muḥammad-i-Iṣfahání and his associate daily added to their wounds. Their taunts and maligning, their constant spying and ceaseless tortuous denunciations before the authorities made the rigours of incarceration harder to bear. Their odious deeds continued unabated, even after the release of the exiles from the barracks.

Sorrows abounded. But the most poignant was the death of 'Abdu'l-Bahá's brother, Mírzá Mihdí, entitled G͟huṣn-i-Aṭhar—the Purest Branch. He was no more than twenty-two years of age, and served as an amanuensis to his Father. One evening in the gathering dusk, as he paced the roof, occupied with his devotions, he fell through a gap to the level below. The fall, although causing severe internal injuries, did not kill him outright. He begged his Father to accept his life as a ransom for the Bahá'ís who were not allowed to come into the Most Great Prison to meet their Lord. His wish was granted by a Father heavily weighed down by the sorrows of this world. The Purest Branch died on June 23rd 1870, twenty-two hours after receiving his fatal injuries. Within four months, incarceration in the citadel came to an end.

When Bahá'u'lláh was sent to the penal colony of 'Akká His followers had no knowledge of His fate and the place of His exile. They were anxious and distressed. They must have thought that He had quaffed the same cup of martyrdom as His Forerunner, the glorious Báb. The Bahá'ís of Iṣfahán went to the office of the British Indo-European Telegraph and asked for assistance to find what had befallen Him. Before long, Tablets conveying the news of imprisonment in the penal colony reached the Bahá'ís. Those of them who still lived in Bag͟hdád had also been subjected, during this very period, to merciless persecution, and had been herded to Mosul, in chains. Now the burning desire of the Bahá'ís, wherever they were, was to attain the presence of Bahá'u'lláh. But the foe was watchful, distances were formidable, hazards were immense, obstacles well-nigh insurmountable. Some brave men walked over mountains and deserts to 'Akká. The seventeen-year-old Áqá Buzurg of Khurásán was one of them. He found his way into the barracks, and became the bearer of Bahá'u'lláh's Tablet to Náṣiri'd-Dín Sháh. He went on foot and returned on foot to certain martyrdom. Bahá'u'lláh named him Badí'—the unique, the matchless.

A few others succeeded in passing the ranks of guards and arrived at the Most Great Prison. Ḥájí Abu'l-Ḥasan-i-Ardakání, the renowned Ḥájí Amín* of later years, was one of those intrepid men. But to reach the presence of Bahá'u'-lláh, he 'was only able to do so in a public bath, where it had been arranged that he should see Bahá'u'lláh without approaching Him or giving any sign of recognition'. Years later, in 1913, Ḥájí Amín travelled to London to meet 'Abdu'l-Bahá. In the intervening years he had been cast into prison, more than once, for the sake of his Faith. In London, witnessing the triumphal tour of 'Abdu'l-Bahá, he may well have remembered that day in the public bath of 'Akká, when, having journeyed through perils and hardships from his native Persia to the penal colony on the Mediterranean coast, he was denied the bounty of conversing with Bahá'u'lláh. He had known the nadir of the fortunes of the Faith, and was then seeing with his own eyes the ascendancy of 'Abdu'l-Bahá, the homage paid to Him by the people of the West. They asked Ḥájí Amín in London what his feelings were, and he was lost in wonderment.

A few did enter the prison-city and the prison-barracks.

* So known, because Bahá'u'lláh conferred on him the title of Amín-i-Iláhí (Trusted of God). He was, in fact, the first to reach Bahá'u'lláh after his imprisonment in the prison of 'Akká.

But many more, whose tired but unfaltering feet had brought them over high peaks and sandy wastes to the walls of 'Akká, found the gates barred and entry forbidden. They had to stand behind the second of the moats that girded the citadel, and be content with seeing from that distance a dim but majestic Figure, Who stood behind the bars of His cell and raised His hands in their direction. But that one gaze revived their hopes and flooded their hearts with joy.

Among the pilgrims was an old master-builder of Káshán, Ustád Ismá'íl, who had once been the esteemed retainer of a powerful courtier.* But he was forced to forsake his native land. In Baghdád he became a victim of the concerted assaults of the townsmen, and experienced the bitterness of exile to Mosul. Thence, semi-blind, he took the road to 'Akká, to find the gate barred. Behind the second moat he stood to gaze at his Lord. But his impaired eyesight prevented him from seeing that beloved Figure. The members of Bahá'u'lláh's family, who from within the prison-walls beheld Ustád Ismá'íl turn back in grief, wept over his plight. A day did eventually come when he was allowed to enter 'Akká and to attain the presence of Bahá'u'lláh. Meanwhile his home had been made in a remote cave on Mount Carmel. Had not Elijah also lived in a cave on the Mountain of God?

Nearly half a century later, 'Abdu'l-Bahá recounted the moving story of the aged master-builder of Káshán:

He made his home in a cave outside the city, and he obtained a tray in which he displayed a few inexpensive rings, thimbles and pins. With these wares he walked the streets from morn till noon. His earnings varied from twenty to thirty copper pieces a day. His best days

* Farrukh Khán, the Amínu'd-Dawlih of Káshán, who negotiated in Paris the Anglo-Persian Peace Treaty of 1857.

brought him up to forty pieces. Then he would go back
to his cave-home to eat his meagre meals and to praise
and magnify the Name of his Lord. He was always contented and thankful. Thus would he intone: 'Praise be
to God that I have attained to this supreme bounty.
Friends I left behind, and in this cave I found a dwelling.
I became enamoured of the Divine Visage. What blessing
is greater than this?'[30]

Sorrows abounded. But the joy of faith and sacrifice
suffused the face of sorrow.

There would come a day in the distant future, when
'Abdu'l-Bahá would set out in person to take the Message
of His Father to the people of the West. In the United
States, in August 1912, Mrs Parsons, a devoted Bahá'í of
Washington, D.C., invited Him to Dublin, New Hampshire,
where she had an estate. During the summer months, many
people prominent in the life of the capital visited that resort.
Mrs Parsons arranged a luncheon party at her home and
asked some twenty people, all outstanding in various walks
of life, to meet 'Abdu'l-Bahá. Culture, science, art, wealth,
politics, achievement—all were represented. The hostess
was eager that 'Abdu'l-Bahá should tell those leaders of
society about Bahá'u'lláh and the Faith He had proclaimed
to mankind. Probably the guests thought that they were
in for a lecture. But 'Abdu'l-Bahá told them a story which
made them laugh. He Himself laughed heartily, and again
with them when they, encouraged by the lead He had
given, also told amusing stories. 'Abdu'l-Bahá and his guests
were full of mirth throughout that luncheon. It was 'good
to laugh', He told them; 'laughter is a spiritual relaxation'.

At this point He referred to His years in prison. Life was
hard, He said, tribulations were never far away, and yet,
at the end of the day, they would sit together and recall
events that had been fantastic, and laugh over them. Funny

situations could not be abundant, but still they probed and sought them, and laughed. Joy was not, He told them, a by-product of material comfort and affluence. Were it so, dejection would have ruled every hour of their lives in those days, whereas their souls were joyful. Those Americans, distinguished in public life, had received the impact of truth, often absent from their daily experience, and they looked with new eyes at the visitor from the East, eyes that mirrored deep admiration and respect. And the great heart of 'Abdu'l-Bahá enveloped them all. Afterwards He asked His hostess whether she was pleased with Him.

In the year 1870 there were stirrings within the Ottoman dominions and movements of Turkish troops became imperative. The citadel of 'Akká was needed for military purposes, and Bahá'u'lláh and His people were led out of prison. But it was not release from bondage. They had to live within the city walls. In the course of the following months, Bahá'u'lláh and His family were moved from house to house—from the house of Malik to the house of Khawwám, thence to the house of Rábi'ih, and finally to the house of 'Údí Khammár,* where accommodation was so limited and cramped that thirteen people had to live in one small room. Quarters were found for a large contingent of the prisoners in a caravanserai called the Khán-i-'Avámíd. Bahá'u'lláh and His followers found themselves living in the midst of townsmen whose hearts were envenomed, whose minds were warped with prejudice. Dealing with such men called for qualities which only faith could provide.

It was now that the true stature of 'Abdu'l-Bahá was revealed.

There was a Christian merchant in 'Akká who, like many

* This house, together with the one adjoining which was later incorporated with it, is known as the house of 'Abbúd.

of his fellow-citizens, held the Bahá'ís in scant respect. It happened that he came upon a load of charcoal which some of the Bahá'ís had been permitted to buy outside 'Akká. (Inside the town they were denied such purchases.) The merchant, noticing that the fuel was of a fine grade, took it for his own use. For him Bahá'ís were beyond the pale, and so their goods could be impounded. When 'Abdu'l-Bahá heard of the incident, He went to the place where the merchant transacted his business to ask for the return of the charcoal. There were many people about in that office, bent on their trade, and they took no notice of 'Abdu'l-Bahá. He sat and waited. Three hours passed before the merchant turned to Him and said: 'Are you one of the prisoners in this town?' 'Abdu'l-Bahá said that He was, and the merchant then enquired: 'What was the crime for which you were imprisoned?' 'Abdu'l-Bahá replied: 'The same crime for which Christ was indicted.' The merchant was taken aback. He was a Christian, and here was a man speaking of similarity between His action and the action of Christ. 'What could you know of Christ?' was his retort. 'Abdu'l-Bahá calmly proceeded to tell him. The arrogance of the merchant was confronted by the patience of 'Abdu'l-Bahá. When 'Abdu'l-Bahá rose to go, the merchant also rose and walked with Him into the street, betokening his respect for this Man—one of the detested prisoners. From then on, he was a friend, even more, a stout supporter.

In 'Akká also lived a man named Shaykh Maḥmúd. He lustily hated the Bahá'ís. While many of his fellow-townsmen had gradually come to realize how very wrong they had been and were speaking of the prisoners in terms of appreciation and praise, Shaykh Maḥmúd remained adamant in his hatred. One day he was present at a gathering where people were talking of 'Abdu'l-Bahá as a good man, a remarkable man. The Shaykh could bear it no longer and stormed out, saying that he would show up this 'Abbás

Effendi* for what He was. In blazing anger he rushed to the mosque, where he knew 'Abdu'l-Bahá could be found at that hour, and laid violent hands upon Him. The Master looked at the <u>Sh</u>ay<u>kh</u> with that serenity and dignity which only He could command, and reminded him of what the Prophet Muḥammad had said: 'Be generous to the guest, even should he be an infidel.' <u>Sh</u>ay<u>kh</u> Maḥmúd turned away. His wrath had left him. So had his hate. All that he was conscious of was a deep sense of shame and bitter compunction. He fled to his house and barred the door. Some days later he went straight into the presence of 'Abdu'l-Bahá, fell on his knees, and besought forgiveness: 'Which door but thine can I seek; whose bounty can I hope for but thine?' He became a devoted Bahá'í.†

It must not be assumed that the passions of the people of 'Akká were stilled within the space of a few months. In fact it took many a month, each laden with perils, before a change became apparent. During that period a crisis of extreme severity, damaging to the reputation of the Faith, overtook the community. Those who provided the ground for this crisis, and provoked its occurrence, were the adherents of Mírzá Yaḥyá who had been included, by the edict of Sulṭán 'Abdu'l-'Azíz, in the company of the followers of Bahá'u'lláh. From the start they had shown open defiance. They spied, made accusations, incited the populace, spread alarming rumours. 'Abdu'l-Bahá mentions the vigil kept by them to discover the arrival of Bahá'ís at 'Akká:

In the days of the Blessed Perfection, when the regulations of the Most Great Prison were extremely rigorous, none

* 'Abdu'l-Bahá was known as such by the generality of the people in that region.

† This story of <u>Sh</u>ay<u>kh</u> Maḥmúd was related to the present writer, nearly forty years ago, by Ḥájí Mírzá Ḥabíbu'lláh Afnán, a member of the family of the Báb, who as a young man had heard it from <u>Sh</u>ay<u>kh</u> Maḥmúd himself.

of the friends was allowed to leave the citadel, or to enter it. Kaj-Kuláh* and the Siyyid † had their home over the second gate, and by day and night they kept watch. Whenever they saw anyone arriving, they immediately reported to the government that the person newly arrived had brought letters with him and would take letters back. The authorities would then arrest the friend who had come, confiscate his papers, throw him into gaol, and finally expel him. This procedure became the rule and the government followed it for a long time.[31]

The intrigues of these men assumed such proportions that the life of Bahá'u'lláh was placed in jeopardy, and the Bahá'ís were continuously disturbed and agitated. Bahá'u'lláh was constantly urging them not to harbour any thought of retribution. An Arab Bahá'í, who was inclined to violence, was told to return to Beirut.

At this juncture, when mischief was rife and nerves were taut, Bahá'u'lláh revealed a Tablet in Arabic which is known to the Bahá'ís of the East‡ by its opening verse: 'Verily the hearts of the sincere are aflame with the fire of separation.' Among the Writings of Bahá'u'lláh this Tablet has a special place and unique quality. Therein He lays bare the agonies of His soul, laments His plight, grieves over the fickleness, the faithlessness and the waywardness of men, and calls upon God for deliverance. Then He shares with mankind the response that comes to His supplication from Him Whose Supreme Manifestation He was.

Then occurred the horrendous event to which we have referred. Disregarding the reiterated injunctions of Bahá'u'lláh, seven of the exiles decided to rid their community of its tormentors. They spoke to no one of their abominable

* 'Awry-cap'—a nickname given to Áqá-Ján Big.
† Siyyid Muhammad-i-Isfahání.
‡ Arabic and Persian speaking.

plan. One night, when all was quiet in the town, they managed to enter the home of the adherents of Mírzá Yaḥyá and slew them. With Siyyid Muḥammad and Áqá-Ján Big perished a recent recruit to their circle, Mírzá Riḍá-Qulíy-i-Tafríshí. This third victim had time and again broken his word, and all ties between him and the followers of Bahá'u'lláh had finally been severed.

Immediately pandemonium broke loose. The whole city was roused. People felt unsafe. Such were the fears of the populace that 'Abbúd, whose house adjoined the residence of Bahá'u'lláh, added to the thickness of the walls separating the two houses.

Bahá'u'lláh was subjected to fresh humiliations. His house was besieged by troops. In the streets the mob was howling. He was taken to the Governor's quarters and put under arrest. 'Abdu'l-Bahá was seized and conducted to the gaol, where He was chained. Twenty-five of the Bahá'ís were also imprisoned. Even the children did not escape the fury of the people of 'Akká. Coming out of their homes they were abused and stoned. Seventy hours passed before they allowed Bahá'u'lláh and His Son to return to their home. 'My captivity,' He wrote, 'cannot harm Me. That which can harm Me is the conduct of those who love Me, who claim to be related to Me, and yet perpetrate what causeth My heart and My pen to groan.' 'The cup of Bahá'u'lláh's tribulations was now filled to overflowing,' states Shoghi Effendi, His great-grandson, the Guardian of the Bahá'í Faith.[32]

What 'Abdu'l-Bahá had to achieve, in this hour of humiliation, was no less than a miracle. Qualities that He now brought forth amply and visibly demonstrated that He was indeed what His Father had affirmed of Him—the 'Mystery of God'. He was immeasurably, tirelessly patient. He was undeviatingly, unshakably firm. He was magnanimous. He was uncompromising. He was kindness personified. He was stern. He walked in the ways of humility. He spoke in tones unmistakably authoritative. He was meek. He was the archetype of majesty. Divine paradoxes were revealed in His being, His actions, His words.

And a change, at first almost imperceptible, began to appear. The Governor, who was not well-disposed towards Bahá'u'lláh and His people, was replaced by an official of a different calibre. Aḥmad Big Tawfíq, the new Governor, was a man of perception and a just administrator. He it was who begged Bahá'u'lláh to accord him the favour of allowing him—the Governor—to render Him a personal service. Bahá'u'lláh directed him to undertake the repair of the old aqueduct which had once given the inhabitants of 'Akká salubrious water, but had become derelict with the passage of years. Aḥmad Big carried out this task, and the people of 'Akká benefited greatly. A proverb current in that region had it that a bird flying over 'Akká would fall dead, so pestilential was its air. But gradually people began to say that since Bahá'u'lláh had been brought to live among them, conditions had altered. Cholera epidemics repeatedly came close to the walls of 'Akká, but did not touch the town. This same wise and benevolent Governor used to send his son to 'Abdu'l-Bahá for instruction, and in the exercise of justice and sound government turned to 'Abdu'l-Bahá for counsel.

Officials and inhabitants of 'Akká and its environs—the very people charged by a tyrant to keep the exiles in rigorous confinement—were captivated by the supernal charm and the subduing majesty of the Chief Exile and His Son.

Then from Beirut came the Válí, 'Azíz Páshá who had been privileged to know Bahá'u'lláh and 'Abdu'l-Bahá in Adrianople, to pay his respects to Bahá'u'lláh and to profit by the companionship of His Son. Later He repeated this visit. And 'Abdu'l-Bahá, though still formally a prisoner, travelled to Beirut, by the express invitation of one of the most brilliant statesmen of the Ottoman Empire—Midḥat

Páshá, the liberal reformer, who as grand vizier was instrumental in inducing the Sultán to grant a constitution to his
people. Although that régime was short-lived, and 'Abdu'l-
Hamíd restored autocracy and banished the reformer,
Midhat Páshá's reputation endured and he was hailed and
revered as the 'Father of the Constitution'. 'Abdu'l-Bahá's
journey to Beirut must have taken place sometime in 1878,
and on this occasion Bahá'u'lláh revealed a Tablet to commemorate and mark its significance:

> Praise be to Him Who hath honoured the Land of Bá
> (Beirut) through the presence of Him round Whom all
> names revolve. All the atoms of the earth have announced
> unto all created things that from behind the gate of the
> Prison-city there hath appeared and above its horizon
> there hath shone forth the Orb of the beauty of the great,
> the Most Mighty Branch of God—His ancient and im-
> mutable Mystery—proceeding on its way to another
> land.[33]

In Beirut 'Abdu'l-Bahá met, apart from Midhat Páshá,
many of the notables of the Arab world, among them the
celebrated Shaykh Muhammad 'Abduh, future Grand
Muftí of Egypt. This learned and noble Shaykh had been
an associate of Siyyid Jamálu'd-Dín al-Afghání, the stan-
dard-bearer of pan-Islamism and an inveterate opponent of
the Faith of Bahá'u'lláh. Yet so fervent was his admiration
for 'Abdu'l-Bahá that he intended to go to 'Akká in His
company. 'Abdu'l-Bahá dissuaded him because such action
would have harmed him and his standing.

The fame of 'Abdu'l-Bahá (known as 'Abbás Effendi
outside the circles of the Faith) was now widespread. When
He visited Nazareth—the home of Christ—the Muftí of
that town, Shaykh Yúsuf, a man both erudite and powerful,
received Him with high honour. At the bidding of the

Muftí, officials and dignitaries met 'Abdu'l-Bahá a long way out of the town, and escorted Him into Nazareth. Such marks of respect were reserved for governors-general and others of superior rank. Shaykh Yúsuf reciprocated 'Abdu'l-Bahá's visit at a later date, when 'Abdu'l-Bahá accorded him a welcome and reception truly regal.

Aḥmad Big Tawfíq was succeeded as governor by Muṣṭafá Ḍíyá Páshá. Orders from the Sublime Porte had remained unaltered. But the governors of 'Akká could no longer consider Bahá'u'lláh a prisoner consigned to their charge. Muṣṭafa Ḍíyá Páshá made it known that Bahá'u'lláh could, if He so wished, move out of the confines of the town and live in the country. Bahá'u'lláh did not avail Himself of this offer, although in the darkest hours of incarceration within the barracks He had written:

> Fear not. These doors shall be opened. My tent shall be pitched on Mount Carmel, and the utmost joy shall be realized.[34]

But the moment had not arrived.

Nine eventful years ran their course, and still Bahá'u'lláh was immured within the city walls. He, Who found great delight in shaded gardens and green fields and the open vistas of the countryside, had not for all that time set eyes on a rustic scene. 'Abdu'l-Bahá relates what then happened:

> Bahá'u'lláh loved the beauty and verdure of the country. One day He passed the remark: 'I have not gazed on verdure for nine years. The country is the world of the soul, the city is the world of bodies.' When I heard indirectly of this saying I realized that He was longing for the country, and I was sure that whatever I could do towards the carrying out of His wish would be successful. There was in 'Akká at that time a man called Muḥammad

Páshá Ṣafwat, who was very much opposed to us. He had a palace called Mazra'ih,* about four miles north of the city, a lovely place, surrounded by gardens and with a stream of running water. I went and called on this Páshá at his home. I said: 'Páshá, you have left the palace empty, and are living in 'Akká.' He replied: 'I am an invalid and cannot leave the city. If I go there it is lonely and I am cut off from my friends.' I said: 'While you are not living there and the place is empty, let it to us.' He was amazed at the proposal, but soon consented. I got the house at a very low rent, about five pounds per annum, paid him for five years and made a contract. I sent labourers to repair the place and put the garden in order and had a bath built. I also had a carriage prepared for the use of the Blessed Beauty. One day I determined to go and see the place for myself. Notwithstanding the repeated injunctions given in successive firmans that we were on no account to pass the limits of the city walls, I walked out through the city gate. Gendarmes were on guard, but they made no objection, so I proceeded straight to the palace. The next day I again went out, with some friends and officials, unmolested and unopposed, although the guards and sentinels stood on both sides of the city gates. Another day I arranged a banquet, spread a table under the pine trees of Bahjí,† and gathered round it the notables and officials of the town. In the evening we all returned to the town together.

One day I went to the Holy Presence of the Blessed Beauty and said: 'The palace at Mazra'ih is ready for you, and a carriage to drive you there.' . . . He refused to go, saying: 'I am a prisoner.' Later I requested Him again, but got the same answer . . . There was, however, in 'Akká a certain Muḥammadan Shaykh,‡ a well-known

* Known also as the Mansion of 'Abdu'lláh Páshá. Today it is a place of Bahá'í pilgrimage.

† The second residence on the plain of 'Akká to which Bahá'u'lláh moved at a later date.

‡ Shaykh 'Alíy-i-Mírí, the Muftí of 'Akká.

man with considerable influence, who loved Bahá'u'lláh and was greatly favoured by Him. I called this S͟hayk͟h and explained the position to him. I said, 'You are daring. Go tonight to His Holy Presence, fall on your knees before Him, take hold of His hands and do not let go until He promises to leave the city!' He was an Arab ... He went directly to Bahá'u'lláh and sat down close to His knees. He took hold of the hands of the Blessed Beauty and kissed them and asked: 'Why do you not leave the city?' He said: 'I am a prisoner.' The S͟hayk͟h replied: 'God forbid! Who has the power to make you a prisoner? You have kept yourself in prison. It was your own will to be imprisoned, and now I beg you to come out and go to the palace. It is beautiful and verdant. The trees are lovely, and the oranges like balls of fire!' As often as the Blessed Beauty said: 'I am a prisoner, it cannot be,' the S͟hayk͟h took His hands and kissed them. For a whole hour he kept on pleading. At last Bahá'u'lláh said, 'K͟haylí k͟hub (very good)' and the S͟hayk͟h's patience and persistence were rewarded. He came to me with great joy to give the glad news ... I took the carriage the next day and drove with Him to the palace. No one made any objection. I left Him there and returned myself to the city.[35]

It was the Muftí of 'Akká, the religious head of the Muslim community, who went down on his knees and begged Bahá'u'lláh to leave the confines of the city walls. How amazingly the fortunes of God's nascent Faith had changed in the course of nine years.

After a sojourn of two years in the Mansion of Mazra'ih, Bahá'u'lláh took residence in the palace of 'Údí K͟hammár* which was nearer to the city of 'Akká, and from which the forbidding citadel of the ancient town, the gentle blue of the Mediterranean, the silhouette of Mount Carmel across the bay, were all discernible. This last abode of Bahá'u'lláh,

* This was the same man who originally owned the house of Abbúd, the last residence of Bahá'u'lláh in 'Akká.

on the plain of 'Akká, is today known as the Mansion of
Bahjí, and stands adjacent to the building which enshrines
His mortal remains—the most sacred spot on the earth.
During the years of Bahá'u'lláh's incarceration in 'Akká
this mansion had been under construction, and had risen
to be the most magnificent house in the whole neighbourhood. But, in the wake of a sudden epidemic, its owner left
it and fled. Thus it was that 'Abdu'l-Bahá could rent and
later purchase this palace of 'Údí Khammár for His Father.
Bahá'u'lláh designated it the 'lofty mansion' which 'God
hath ordained as the most sublime vision of mankind'.
Its original owner lies buried in a corner of the wall that
surrounds the Mansion.

There was a Christian inhabitant of 'Akká, a fanatical
Protestant, named Jurjus al-Jamál, who owned lands
adjoining the area of the Mansion of Bahjí. With his own
hands he raised an olive plantation which exists to this day.
There were also pine trees on his land, directly facing the
Mansion, under which Bahá'u'lláh walked and sat. When
'Abdu'l-Bahá offered to purchase the land on which the
pine trees stood, Jurjus demanded the fantastic sum of
ten thousand pounds in Turkish gold. He specified in his
will that he should be buried on that very land. Further, he
laid an injunction on his brother not to sell the property,
but to wait, for Bahjí had a brilliant future. His wishes for
burial were carried out. However, his brother did sell the
land, and removed Jurjus's coffin for reburial in Nazareth.

'Abdu'l-Bahá also acquired a garden called Na'mayn,
which was an island in the midst of a stream within a short
distance of 'Akká. It was close to the man-made hill named
after Napoleon Bonaparte, which had been raised to mount
Napoleon's cannons for the bombardment of the city.
'Riḍván', reminiscent of the garden of Najíb Páshá outside
Baghdád where He had first declared His Mission, was the
designation which Bahá'u'lláh bestowed upon the garden of

Na'mayn. Furthermore, He referred to that delightful oasis on the then bare and treeless plain as the 'New Jerusalem' and 'Our Verdant Isle'. To this garden which His followers beautified, Bahá'u'lláh would at times resort. And there were occasions when He stayed in the very modest summer house which had two plain, habitable upper rooms. He vividly portrays in a Tablet a vision of 'the Maid of Heaven' which came to Him by the cool waters of Na'mayn.

Bahá'u'lláh was, at long last and by the efforts of His Son, delivered from the oppression of 'Akká and its people. Now He could devote His time entirely to the nurture of His own followers, to the unveiling of His divine counsel. It was 'Abdu'l-Bahá who lived in 'Akká in the midst of its bleakness, met the officials and the notables and townsmen, protected the Bahá'í community, defended its interests, attended to its welfare, and shielded His Father. To reach the presence of Bahá'u'lláh He always walked the distance between 'Akká and Bahjí. Many years later during His Western visit, while crossing by ship from New York to Liverpool, He paced up and down the deck for a long time; when at last He sat down to rest, He told His attendants: 'I walked 4600 feet, the length of the road between 'Akká and the Shrine of Bahá'u'lláh. I want to practise walking, perchance I might be able to go on foot to the Shrine. In latter times, in the Holy Land, I was too weak to go on foot and was deprived of this bounty.'[36] He was in His sixty-ninth year.

Ṭarázu'lláh Samandarí,* the distinguished Hand of the Cause of God, who at the age of sixteen, during the last six months of Bahá'u'lláh's life, was a pilgrim to His presence, recalled a day that he accompanied 'Abdu'l-Bahá on the walk from 'Akká to Bahjí. It had rained and the ground was wet, but coming round the bend of the road into full sight of the Mansion, 'Abdu'l-Bahá prostrated

* Died 1968 in Haifa.

Himself and laid His forehead on the sodden earth. And innumerable were the occasions that, as 'Abdu'l-Bahá approached Bahjí, Bahá'u'lláh turned to those in His presence and told them: The Master is coming. Haste ye to go out to meet Him and escort Him. To this scores have attested.

Samandarí also recalled another day of his memorable pilgrimage, when Bahá'u'lláh administered to him a gentle, kindly, but highly significant admonition. For several days he had not been called to the presence of Bahá'u'lláh and, encountering a small child of the household, he asked her to be the bearer of a petition for him to Bahá'u'lláh, after ascertaining that He was alone. His petition was for the bounty of admission to His presence. When he attained it, Bahá'u'lláh asked him: Do you not meet the Master every day? Samandarí's answer was affirmative. And Bahá'u'lláh said: Then why do you speak of not having been here in My presence for several days, you who meet the Master every day and receive the honour of His company? He equated meeting 'Abdu'l-Bahá with meeting Himself.

Ḥájí Mírzá Ḥaydar-'Alí, whom we have come to know in these pages, has recorded another testimony by Bahá'u'lláh to the station and the powers of His Son. The Ḥájí had composed a treatise, drawing upon those Islamic traditions which pointed to 'Abdu'l-Bahá. This compilation and commentary he presented to Bahá'u'lláh. Applauding it, Bahá'u'lláh told him that his deductions and conclusions were absolutely right. Furthermore He said:

The force of the utterance of the Most Great Branch and His powers are not as yet fully revealed. In the future it will be seen how He, alone and unaided, shall raise the banner of the Most Great Name in the midmost heart of the world, with power and authority and Divine effulgence. It will be seen how He shall gather together the peoples of the earth under the tent of peace and concord.[37]

On his second pilgrimage to the Holy Land in the life-time of Bahá'u'lláh, the same Hájí Mírzá Haydar-'Alí, with two fellow-pilgrims, travelled by boat from Constantinople with a learned man from 'Akká, one of the notables of the town. This man spoke to the Hájí of 'Abbás Effendi ('Abdu'l-Bahá) in terms of high praise and profound admiration. The Bahá'í pilgrim did not divulge his faith and his destination, as it could have hampered and even prevented his journey, but confined himself to saying that 'Abbás Effendi had many followers in Persia and that he had heard about Him and them. The traveller from 'Akká replied that 'Abbás Effendi was unique and very wonderful. Such was his zeal in extolling the person of 'Abdu'l-Bahá that Hájí Mírzá Haydar-'Alí had to say that, although he was bound for Egypt, he had decided after listening to him to visit 'Akká and meet so remarkable a seer. Later the Hájí learned that his fellow-passenger, who reached 'Akká before him, had recounted the incident to 'Abdu'l-Bahá; 'They will be coming,' he had said.

In Írán during those years persecution, oppression, and martyrdom of Bahá'ís were common occurrences. Year by year the ranks of the martyrs swelled until their numbers approached thirty thousand. But nothing daunted the followers of Bahá'u'lláh. They remained firm and steadfast.

And that which Bahá'u'lláh had promised to His people, from His prison-cell in 'Akká, did assuredly come to pass. His tent was raised on Mount Carmel, more than once. On that holy mountain, in the evening of His life, Bahá'u'lláh gave a particular task to His Son. Standing one day in the shade of some cypress trees, halfway up the mountain, He pointed to the rocks immediately below Him. On that spot, He told 'Abdu'l-Bahá, a mausoleum should rise to enshrine the mutilated remains of His Forerunner, the Báb, which had lain hidden for decades in His native land.

'Abdu'l-Bahá carried out that command as soon as times were propitious, but the task was immense and took many years. It exposed 'Abdu'l-Bahá to great peril and brought Him much sorrow and suffering. But in the end He fulfilled His Father's behest and triumphantly concluded His labours.

CHAPTER 3

THE ASCENSION OF BAHÁ'U'LLÁH

The ascension of Bahá'u'lláh took place in the early hours of May 29th 1892, and the hearts of the Bahá'ís were broken. A cable from 'Abdu'l-Bahá conveyed the news to 'Abdu'l-Hamíd, the Sultán of Turkey: 'The Sun of Bahá has set'.

That same cable informed the Sultán that the earthly temple of Bahá'u'lláh would be laid to rest within the periphery of the Mansion of Bahjí, and 'Abdu'l-Hamíd agreed. At nightfall of the same day—after the dignitaries and leading citizens and vast numbers of ordinary men and women, who were not adherents of His Faith, had paid their last respects to Bahá'u'lláh and gone; and after long hours of commotion —when silence had settled upon the plain of 'Akká, the coffin that contained the sacred remains was taken from the Mansion to a house a few yards away. This house was the home of a son-in-law of Bahá'u'lláh. In it a vault had been prepared beneath the room that had served the Great Afnán* as a chamber for receiving his guests, and in that vault they placed the coffin.

Deep was the sorrow of the people of 'Akká and its neighbourhood. Even more, all Syria and its adjacent territories felt bereaved. Those who had formerly detested the Bahá'ís and scorned them and shunned their company, came to the gates of the Mansion day after day to mourn the passing of Bahá'u'lláh. People who had, in days past, let themselves believe that in the proximity of the Bahá'ís neither their lives, their honour, nor their property were

* Hájí Mírzá Siyyid Hasan, a brother of the wife of the Báb.

safe, were now sadly aware that a great Being had passed out of their midst. Writers and poets, Muslim and Christian alike, from 'Akká and from the renowned cities of the Arab world—Damascus, Beirut, Cairo, Baghdád—composed eulogies that not only extolled Bahá'u'lláh, but also eloquently praised His Son. Among them was Amín Zaydán, the eminent Egyptian man of letters, Christian by faith; and Hájí Muhammad 'Abdu'l-Halq, a Muslim, famed for his piety and learning throughout Syria. And it was to 'Abdu'l-Bahá, and 'Abdu'l-Bahá alone, that they all addressed and offered these expressions of their grief and their esteem.

The wound in the hearts of those who recognized in Bahá'u'lláh the Lord of the Age and the Redeemer of mankind, was graphically and poignantly described by the immortal Nabíl who, unable to live with its pain, drowned himself not long after:

Methinks, the spiritual commotion set up in the world of dust had caused all the worlds of God to tremble . . . My inner and outer tongue are powerless to portray the condition we were in . . . In the midst of the prevailing confusion a multitude of the inhabitants of 'Akká and of the neighboring villages, that had thronged the fields surrounding the Mansion, could be seen weeping, beating upon their heads, and crying aloud their grief.[38]

To Bahá'ís in Persia, in Egypt, Syria, 'Iráq and other Ottoman dominions, in Caucasia and Turkistán and other lands of the East, 'Abdu'l-Bahá sent this, His first message to them:

He is the All-Glorious.

The world's great Light, once resplendent upon all mankind has set, to shine everlastingly from the Abhá Horizon, His Kingdom of fadeless glory, shedding splen-

'ABDU'L-BAHÁ IN ADIRNIH (ADRIANOPLE)

'AKKÁ—THE PRISON CITY

(by courtesy of The Universal House of Justice)

dour upon His loved ones from on high, and breathing into their hearts and souls the breath of eternal life.

O ye beloved of the Lord! Beware, beware lest ye hesitate and waver. Let not fear fall upon you, neither be troubled nor dismayed. Take ye good heed lest this calamitous day slacken the flames of your ardour, and quench your tender hopes. To-day is the day for steadfastness and constancy. Blessed are they that stand firm and immovable as the rock, and brave the storm and stress of this tempestuous hour. They, verily, shall be the recipients of God's grace, shall receive His divine assistance, and shall be truly victorious.

The Sun of Truth, that most great Light, has set upon the horizon of the world to rise with deathless splendour over the Realm of the Limitless. In His *Most Holy Book* He calleth the firm and steadfast of His friends: 'O peoples of the world! Should the radiance of My beauty be veiled, and the temple of My body be hidden, feel not perturbed, nay arise and bestir yourselves, that My Cause may triumph, and My Word be heard by all mankind.'[39]

CHAPTER 4

THE CENTRE OF THE COVENANT

Bahá'u'lláh had raised His peerless Son to be the Centre of His Covenant. In a document which He designated *Kitáb-i-'Ahdí*—The Book of My Covenant—a document the like of which cannot be found in the whole range of the Scriptures of mankind, He made His purpose indubitably clear that 'Abdu'l-Bahá was to be the Head of His Faith, the Expounder of His Word, the Unerring Balance by Whom falsehood was distinguished and separated from truth. This Covenant which Bahá'u'lláh established with His people, and not only with them but with the entire human race, has no parallel in the records of religion.

In the *Epistle to the Son of the Wolf*, the final book revealed by the pen of Bahá'u'lláh, He spoke of His Testament as the 'Crimson Book'. 'The Ark of His Testament'—God's Testament—which we find mentioned in the Revelation of St John, is this Testament of Bahá'u'lláh.

The world had never seen the like of Bahá'u'lláh's Testament. Neither had it seen the like of His Covenant. In the words of 'Abdu'l-Bahá, ' . . . the pivot of the oneness of mankind is nothing else but the power of the Covenant.' Again in His words, ' . . . the "Sure Handle" mentioned from the foundation of the world in the Books, the Tablets and the Scriptures of old is naught else but the Covenant and the Testament.' And again: 'The lamp of the Covenant is the light of the world . . . '[40]

That which can give concrete form to the oneness of mankind, the oneness with which God has endowed His creation, is the teaching and precept of Bahá'u'lláh. Nothing else can make or will make the spiritual unity of mankind a fact indisputably acknowledged and upheld by all the denizens of the earth, the prime principle operative in every sphere of human activity. This and this alone will rescue man from self-immolation. But to do this the teaching of Bahá'u'lláh must not suffer corruption. Otherwise it will assuredly fail. It is the Covenant of Bahá'u'lláh, the invincible power of which has been tested and proved time and again, that has preserved and will preserve the integrity of His teaching. The Covenant and the Covenant alone has stayed the hand of the desecrator.

'Abdu'l-Bahá is the Centre of this Covenant. In Him and Him alone the Covenant found its expression. His alone was the authority to divide the faithful from the faithless.

'In accordance with the explicit text of the *Kitáb-i-Aqdas*,' He Himself has testified, 'Bahá'u'lláh hath made the Centre of the Covenant the Interpreter of His Word—a Covenant so firm and mighty that from the beginning of time until the present day no religious Dispensation hath produced its like.'[41]

A man who was proud and wayward sent 'Abdu'l-Bahá a blank piece of paper to test His powers of reading the hearts and minds of men. 'Abdu'l-Bahá answered him:

O thou who posed a test for 'Abdu'l-Bahá! Is it seemly for a man like thee to test a servant submissive and lowly before God? Nay by God, it is given to the Centre of the Covenant to test the peoples of the world.[42]

Bahá'u'lláh had entrusted His Will and Testament to the care of 'Abdu'l-Bahá. On the ninth day after His ascension its contents became known. Earlier in the day nine of the Bahá'ís, including members of Bahá'u'lláh's family who were chosen by 'Abdu'l-Bahá, gathered to witness the breaking of the seal and to learn the counsel of the Testament. Later, the same day, within the walls of the Shrine of Bahá'u'lláh, Mírzá Majdi'd-Dín—the son of Mírzá Músá, Bahá'u'lláh's faithful brother and valiant supporter throughout forty years, then alas deceased—stood up to read the Will. No doubt could be entertained. It was evident to Whom the Bahá'ís had to turn, and Whom they had to obey, on Whose shoulders the mantle of total authority now rested. No one expressed dissent. Everyone who was there, and heard that 'Abdu'l-Bahá was the successor to Bahá'u'lláh, submitted to what He had ordained. Ṭarázu'lláh Samandarí vividly recalled that felicitous day, and the obedience that was unquestionably rendered to 'Abdu'l-Bahá.

But there was a heart hopelessly stirred by envy. It beat in the frame of the second surviving son of Bahá'u'lláh, Mírzá Muḥammad-'Alí, entitled Ghuṣn-i-Akbar, the Greater Branch, the man whose rank and station the Testament of Bahá'u'lláh had placed next to that of the Centre of the Covenant Himself. This half-brother of 'Abdu'l-Bahá, had already committed an act of astounding perfidy. (To this testifies the letter of repentance, short-lived though that repentance was, of Mírzá Badí'u'lláh, the fourth surviving son of Bahá'u'lláh.) In that document he stated, in no uncertain terms, that two cases which belonged to Bahá'u'lláh and contained His writing materials, seals, and papers were purloined by Mírzá Muḥammad-'Alí, on the very dawn of the day that their Father passed away.

'Abdu'l-Bahá has described how Mírzá Muḥammad-'Alí, by deception, obtained possession of those cases, which had been close to Bahá'u'lláh's bed. When, in that oppressive dawn of May 29th, they were proceeding to wash the body of Bahá'u'lláh and prepare it for interment, he suggested to 'Abdu'l-Bahá to remove the cases to another room, as water might be splashed over them and damage the papers. 'Abdu'l-Bahá had no room in the Mansion of Bahjí. He and

His family lived in 'Akká. (He resided there to be near the majority of the Bahá'ís, and to be accessible to officialdom.) Therefore Mírzá Muḥammad-'Alí took charge of the two cases.

A few days later, a Bahá'í who had been honoured with a Tablet from Bahá'u'lláh, on which His seal was not affixed, asked 'Abdu'l-Bahá whether he could have that bounty. Bahá'u'lláh's seals were in the cases which Mírzá Muḥammad-'Alí had, to his delight, obtained. 'Abdu'l-Bahá asked His brother to bring them, but the latter denied any knowledge of their whereabouts, or that he had ever received them.

Mírzá Muḥammad-'Alí's most cherished object had been to lay hands on the Will and Testament which he knew his Father had written. But that document had been entrusted to 'Abdu'l-Bahá. Thus his first attempt to subvert the Covenant of Bahá'u'lláh proved abortive. But ambition and jealousy drove him on to deeds more wretched, until he ultimately destroyed himself.

In a Tablet addressed to Mírzá Muḥammad-Báqir Khán, a distinguished Bahá'í of Shíráz, 'Abdu'l-Bahá refers to Mírzá Muḥammad-'Alí's deceit:

> The centre of violation purloined, in its entirety, the Divine trust which specifically appertained to this servant. He took everything and returned nothing. To this day the usurper unjustly remains in possession. Although each single item is more precious for 'Abdu'l-Bahá than the dominion of earth and heaven, till now I have kept silent and have not breathed a word, lest it bring us into disrepute amongst strangers. This was a severe blow to me. I suffered, I sorrowed, I wept, but I spoke not.

Before long Mírzá Muḥammad-'Alí set out in earnest to undermine the authority of 'Abdu'l-Bahá, to cast doubts in the minds of Bahá'ís, to band together the ambitious and the

self-seeking. As Mírzá Yaḥyá had his evil genius,* so did
Mírzá Muḥammad-'Alí. His tempter was Mírzá Majdi'd-
Dín, the same man who had read the Testament of Bahá'u'-
lláh in public. He was inordinately proud and arrogant. The
present writer has a vivid recollection of him haughtily
stalking the streets of Haifa in the late twenties. His story
brings that of Lucifer to mind. Married to Mírzá Muḥam-
mad-'Alí's sister, he intended to use the second son of
Bahá'u'lláh as a tool—only too willing and wieldy—to
nullify the authority of 'Abdu'l-Bahá and obtain power for
his own ends. 'Abdu'l-Bahá told him that he would be given
a long life, would live on racked with miseries, welcoming
death, craving for the release which death brings; but balm
would be denied him, until the day when he should see here
in this world the complete frustration of all that he had
contrived, the total defeat of all his schemes—the vindi-
cation and the triumph of the Covenant of Bahá'u'lláh.

'Abdu'l-Bahá's prophecy was fulfilled. Mírzá Majdi'd-
Dín lived to be more than a hundred years old, stricken
down, incapable of movement, shorn of speech, but with
eyes to see. In a house fast becoming derelict, which stood
next to the Mansion of Bahjí, casting a dark shadow
alongside its effulgent radiance, this broken man lingered on
until 1955. He saw the might of the Covenant triumph over
violation. He saw, where he lay, Shoghi Effendi, the grandson of 'Abdu'l-Bahá, the Guardian of the Faith—named,
raised, and appointed by the Centre of the Covenant of
Bahá'u'lláh—in the plenitude of his powers, create for the
Shrine of Bahá'u'lláh the setting and surroundings that
befitted such a mausoleum. Then he died. But before his
unhappy fate overtook him dire was the mischief that he
wrought.

Within a brief period of time Mírzá Muḥammad-'Alí won
over to himself the entire body of the family of Bahá'u'lláh,

* See p. 24.

save for Bahá'íyyih Khánum, the sister of 'Abdu'l-Bahá, and Mírzá Muḥammad-Qulí, a devout and loyal half-brother of Bahá'u'lláh who had shared His exiles and tribulations and now, in the hour of severe testing, stood firm with his wife and children in adherence to the Covenant. Sons and daughters of Bahá'u'lláh with their wives and husbands chose to be violators. So did the sons and daughters of Mírzá Músá. Christ has said: 'For there must be stumbling but woe unto him who causeth stumbling.'[43]

One might well ask how it was that these men and women of the flesh and blood of Bahá'u'lláh broke faith with Him. How could they act as they did? As this story unfolds, we shall see how appalling their actions were. In the lifetime of Bahá'u'lláh they had shown evidence of their envy. 'Abdu'l-Bahá towered over them. He was a spiritual giant and they were dwarfs. That same stalwart and steadfast Bahá'í of Shíráz, Mírzá Muḥammad-Báqir Khán,[44] to whom 'Abdu'l-Bahá confided the account of the perfidy committed by Mírzá Muḥammad-'Alí, reminded the centre of violation that there was a couplet of Persian verse which said that even should the royal phoenix die out, no one would seek the shelter of an owl. The owl, an inmate of ruins, is known in oriental literature as a bird of ill-omen.

Jealousy is a gnawing disease, as testified by Bahá'u'lláh. It destroys the one who harbours it. Insatiable desire for power is equally destructive.

But the fact remained that Mírzá Muḥammad-'Alí was the son of Bahá'u'lláh, named by Him in the Book of His Testament. He was the Greater Branch. Many Bahá'ís could not entertain the thought that this son of Bahá'u'lláh had the makings of a traitor. They were sorely perplexed.

Apart from these fount-heads of violation, there were others who let ambition challenge loyalty. One such was Mírzá Áqá Ján, the amanuensis of Bahá'u'lláh, who, since the days in Baghdád when he was a youth of sixteen, had diligently served Him as attendant and scribe. He was the first person, years prior to the declaration in the garden of Najíb Páshá, to whom Bahá'u'lláh spoke words which pointed to His station. True it was that Mírzá Áqá Ján displeased Bahá'u'lláh in the last years of His life, but this lapse had been forgiven. Although heartily detested by Mírzá Muḥammad-'Alí and his lieutenants, who did not cease to keep fresh the memory of his grave lapse and Bahá'u'lláh's displeasure, and in spite of the fact that 'Abdu'l-Bahá had shielded him, Mírzá Áqá Ján lent himself to their designs and, strangely enough, became their cat's-paw. Emboldened, for four months he took his abode within the Shrine of Bahá'u'lláh, whence he hurled abuse at the Centre of the Covenant.* Áqá Muḥammad-Javád-i-Qazvíní, another eminent Bahá'í of 'Akká, a member of that small company invested with the signal honour of transcribing the Tablets of Bahá'u'lláh, also threw in his lot with the band of the faithless. And there were others. In the rising tide of confusion, even the faithful and the steadfast were bewildered. So heart-broken was Nabíl by the ascension of Bahá'u'lláh and the unmistakable signs of disloyalty in the midst of His family, that he drowned himself in the sea. It was a problem truly baffling and intractable that the sons and daughters of Bahá'u'lláh, whom He had enjoined His followers in His Testament to revere, should ignore that same Testament and contend with the Most Great Branch Whose supremacy was indubitable and Whose incomparable qualities had always been acknowledged.

The time came when 'Abdu'l-Bahá was almost alone.

* It must be remembered that in those years the Shrine was very different from what it is today. There was a courtyard with rooms opening into it. As previously mentioned, the house which became the Shrine had been the home of the Great Afnán, Ḥájí Mírzá Siyyid Ḥasan, the brother of the wife of the Báb. He was deceased, but the property belonged to his son who was already showing signs of disaffection.

CHAPTER 5

OPEN REBELLION

Sedition was at first covert. There were dubious hints, veiled complaints, loaded allusions. Then half-truths were given currency. Next blatant lies were coined. Later still, emissaries of Mírzá Muḥammad-'Alí began to travel extensively, and letters began to pour out of the Holy Land, conveying false reports, injecting the venom of violation.

In Persia, Áqá Jamál-i-Burújirdí—a renowned teacher of the Cause greatly esteemed by the Bahá'ís, who had known imprisonment for the sake of his faith—at odds with the Hands of the Cause, became the chief advocate of Mírzá Muḥammad-'Alí. A story that the present writer heard on several occasions from Ḍíyá'u'lláh Asgharzádih (Ziaullah Asgarzadeh),[45] well illustrates the high regard which Bahá'ís had for the eminent teacher of their Faith. When Ḍíyá'u'lláh was a very young boy, in the village of Mílán near Tabríz in north-western Írán, Áqá Jamál visited the Bahá'ís of that locality. One night Ḍíyá'u'lláh's father invited him and some others to dinner. The young lad's mother told her son, who was particularly fond of a delicacy she was preparing, that should he manage to bring her one of Áqá Jamál's shoes, she would reward him with an extra portion. In those days Persians used to shed their shoes before coming from the street or the courtyard of the house into the carpeted room, and Ḍíyá'u'lláh had no difficulty in getting his mother the prize she coveted. Then he found, to his amazement, that his mother was scraping the earth off the sole of the shoe. This earth, she told him, comes from the footgear of a man holy and exalted in rank. It must of necessity possess curative powers. This was how a devout Bahá'í, simple of heart and unlettered, looked up to Jamál-i-Burújirdí. Of this man 'Abdu'l-Bahá said, in a Tablet addressed to M. and Mme Hippolyte Dreyfus-Barney, that he was foremost among the Bahá'ís.

To another teacher of the Faith, who was as distinguished as Áqá Jamál in his time, and who went the same way at a later date, 'Abdu'l-Bahá wrote one of His most significant Tablets. He tells him that the magnet which attracts bounties and confirmations in this day is the Covenant of God, and that it is the standard against which everything is to be judged. Then he states that should a person become the very personification of the Holy Spirit, and yet hesitate for an instant in the path of the Covenant, he would be truly of the legion of the lost. The fate of Áqá Jamál bore eloquent witness to the truth of 'Abdu'l-Bahá's assertion and stern admonition. Áqá Jamál's desperate efforts to feed the blaze of dissension failed. His rank availed him nothing, and he ended his days in misery and obscurity.

When rebellion came into the open, it was the Centre of the Covenant Who seemed to have been abandoned. Isolated in 'Akká with His sister, His wife, His four daughters, and an old uncle, He was even prevented from entering the Shrine of His Father. There were times when He stood on the plain, and performed the devotionals of visitation from a distance. Mírzá Muḥammad-'Alí and his associates were in full possession of the Mansion, the Shrine, and the adjacent houses. They thronged the upper verandah of the Mansion and hurled insults at 'Abdu'l-Bahá and those faithful to Him whenever they came to pray at the spot where the human temple of Bahá'u'lláh had been laid to rest. 'Abdu'l-Bahá had toiled hard to create a garden adjacent to the Shrine. He had brought fresh soil and water on His own shoulders, assisted by the faithful, to keep the wasteland

ever-verdant, blooming with flowers. His opponents laid
their hands even on that garden, but finding the upkeep
expensive, and requiring hard work and labour, abandoned
it.

Shoghi Effendi has stated that some forty members of
Bahá'u'lláh's family, relatives of the Báb and eminent figures
and teachers of the Cause, were leagued together to refuse
the loyalty due to 'Abdu'l-Bahá, to subvert the Covenant of
Bahá'u'lláh.

Not content with fomenting discord within the community, they began to vilify 'Abdu'l-Bahá in circles outside. They accused Him of having arrogated to Himself the
titles and the rank of a Manifestation of God; of having
attempted to bring the family of Bahá'u'lláh into disrepute—
the Aghsán (Branches) whom the Manifestation of God had
enjoined His followers to love and respect; of giving an
importance out of all proportion to the Testament of
Bahá'u'lláh, which, they contended, was a document solely
concerned with relations within His family; of inventing a
Covenant and vainly praising it as supreme and all-enfolding;
of depriving His brothers and sisters of their heritage; of
acting as a self-aggrandising tyrant. To people who were
not Bahá'ís, they would say that 'Abdu'l-Bahá had disin-
herited His own kith and kin. Bahá'u'lláh, they would tell
them, had never claimed to be a Manifestation of God; He
was a mystic Shaykh seeking to bring men nearer to God,
and it was 'Abbás Effendi, now styling Himself 'Abdu'l-
Bahá, Who was determined to contrive a new religion.

Hájí Mírzá Haydar-'Alí, who was an eyewitness, has left
on record a description of the life which Mírzá Muham-
mad-'Alí and his supporters led in the Mansion of Bahjí.
In vivid contrast to 'Abdu'l-Bahá's simple and constricted
life within 'Akká, His detractors were constantly demanding
vast amounts of choicest provisions, ordering large quantities of goods and clothing, feasting inordinately, inviting

officials to repasts of rich variety. These officials they intended to imbue with hatred of 'Abdu'l-Bahá. They meant
to reduce 'Abdu'l-Bahá to the level of impoverishment, drag
Him down to bankruptcy. But 'Abdu'l-Bahá never refused
them the demands they made. Whenever their requests
came, He told His steward, Áqá Riḍáy-i-Qannád, to comply with them. Whenever gifts arrived 'Abdu'l-Bahá gave
instructions to have them taken to Bahjí. He tried, and
tried hard, to protect those who plotted against Him from
the evil consequences of their deeds. He did all that could
be done to draw a veil over their disloyalty. To malice that
wounded deeply He returned balm and healing. To Mírzá
Muḥammad-'Alí—whose designation 'the Greater Branch'
was the name by which he was known and addressed,
whose station was established in Bahá'u'lláh's Testament as
next to 'Abdu'l-Bahá, taking precedence over every other
Bahá'í with the sole exception of the Centre of the Covenant
—He, a magnanimous and generous Brother, made a fervent appeal. 'Abdu'l-Bahá reminded him that after His
own passing, all that he desired would come to him. To this
appeal Mírzá Muḥammad-'Alí replied that he had no guarantee that he would outlive 'Abdu'l-Bahá. Hankering after
power had destroyed in this son of Bahá'u'lláh every vestige
of trust in His word. He did outlive 'Abdu'l-Bahá by sixteen
miserable years, a broken, dejected man, repudiated by the
world community of Bahá'u'lláh, recalling to the mind of
the beholder the concluding years of the life of Mírzá
Yaḥyá, Ṣubḥ-i-Azal, the uncle of this member of the second
generation of violators.

It was at this period that the Centre of the Covenant, in
order to give proof to the world of the falsity of the accusa-
tion levelled at Him by His detractors that He had placed
Himself on a par with Bahá'u'lláh, declared that hereafter
He was to be known as 'Abdu'l-Bahá—the Servant of Bahá.
He stated that His station was the station of servitude.

Violators, prolific with fantastic invention, retorted that Servitude was an attribute of Godhead, and 'Abdu'l-Bahá was now implicitly identifying Himself with the Creator of the universe. To themselves they applied the epithet 'Muvaḥḥidín' (monotheists, unitarians), and to those who stood firm in the Covenant the epithet 'Mushrikín' (polytheists).

For four years, Mírzá Muḥammad-'Alí and his associates had their way and 'Abdu'l-Bahá suffered in silence. But the time came when concealment was no longer possible. 'Abdu'l-Bahá did not take the initiative in denouncing them to the Bahá'í world. They themselves, feeling desperate, tore the veil which a wise and forgiving Master had drawn over their deeds. Witnessing the gradual ascendancy of the Covenant, and the rallying of the vast majority of the Bahá'ís to the Centre of the Covenant, they rushed into the open. Then separation became inevitable. Their futile attempts at subverting the Covenant continued through the years, but their decline was swift. They stood revealed to all the Bahá'ís as authors of discord.

CHAPTER 6

DISCIPLES IN THE WEST

The years that witnessed the rebellion of Mírzá Muḥammad-'Alí and the near eclipse of the orb of the Covenant, also witnessed the meteoric rise of that orb towards its zenith. The exposure of the true face of violation and the turning of the Bahá'ís to 'Abdu'l-Bahá was paralleled by the introduction of the Faith to the Western world.

The Faith of the Báb and Bahá'u'lláh was not unknown in the West. Travellers, officials, scholars, and students of Eastern thought had written at length of its birth and rise and development. Lady Sheil's *Glimpses of Life and Manners in Persia* had been published as early as 1856, and it carried a vivid account of the events of August 1852.[46] R. B. M. Binning in his *A Journal of Two Years' Travel in Persia, Ceylon, etc.*, published a year later, had referred to the Báb. But undoubtedly it was the famous work of the Comte de Gobineau, *Les Religions et les Philosophies dans l'Asie Centrale*, published in 1865, which made the West aware of the momentous events that had transpired in Persia. It was this very book that inspired Edward Granville Browne, the most distinguished of British orientalists, to take a life-long interest in the new Faith.* Gobineau was a French diplomat who had first gone to Persia in 1855 with a special mission and remained to serve as his country's Chargé d'Affaires. He returned to France in 1858, but had a further term of office in Persia from 1862 to 1863, as the fully accredited

* See H. M. Balyuzi, *Edward Granville Browne and the Bahá'í Faith*.

representative of Napoleon III. The Comte de Gobineau was a bigoted forerunner of the proponents of racialism, an authoritarian who went to Persia elated to be visiting the homestead of the Aryans. But once in Írán he felt downcast, because he did not find a pure race (which was a figment of his imagination) and he was also disquieted that classes merged with ease. Gobineau was also the author of *Essai sur l'Inégalité des Races Humaines* which lesser minds than his would use in future to propound and propagate vicious doctrines of racial superiority. Very strange and startling it seems in retrospect that the pen of a man dedicated to the chimera of racialism should become the vehicle for the dissemination of the knowledge of the Faith of the Báb in the West, for which no less a person than Ernest Renan gave Gobineau pride of place. In Britain, among the leading lights of the literary world, it was Matthew Arnold who was first attracted by Gobineau's dramatic narrative. In an essay entitled *A Persian Passion Play*, which he wrote in 1871, Arnold spoke of the Báb:

> Count Gobineau, formerly Minister of France at Teheran and at Athens, published, a few years ago, an interesting book on the present state of religion and philosophy in Central Asia . . . The chief purpose of his book is to give a history of the career of Mirza Ali Mohammed . . . the founder of *Bâbism*, of which most people in England have at least heard the name.[47]

As strange and remarkable as the role of the Comte de Gobineau, was the part played by a Presbyterian minister, a missionary to the Near East, in being the first person to mention the name of Bahá'u'lláh and to quote His words amidst a large and representative gathering of the people of the West. The year was 1893, the city Chicago, and the occasion the Columbian Exposition celebrating the fourth centenary of the discovery of America. On the twenty-third

of September, in a session of the World's Parliament of
Religions, the Reverend George A. Ford, whose missionary
field lay in Syria, read a paper prepared by the Reverend
Henry H. Jessup, also a missionary serving in the same area.
It closed with these words:

> In the Palace of Bahjí, or Delight, just outside the Fortress
> of 'Akká, on the Syrian coast, there died a few months
> since, a famous Persian sage, the Bábí Saint, named
> Bahá'u'lláh—the 'Glory of God'—the head of that vast
> reform party of Persian Muslims, who accept the New
> Testament as the Word of God and Christ as the Deliverer
> of men, who regard all nations as one, and all men as
> brothers. Three years ago he was visited by a Cambridge
> scholar* and gave utterance to sentiments so noble, so
> Christlike, that we repeat them as our closing words:
>
> 'That all nations should become one in faith and all
> men as brothers; that the bond of affection and unity
> between the sons of men should be strengthened; that
> diversity of religions should cease and differences of race
> be annulled. What harm is there in this? Yet so it shall be.
> These fruitless strifes, these ruinous wars shall pass away,
> and "the Most Great Peace" shall come. Do not you in
> Europe need this also? Let not a man glory in this, that he
> loves his country; let him rather glory in this, that he
> loves his kind.'[48]

The Reverend George Ford and the Reverend Henry
Jessup, Director of Presbyterian Missionary Operations in
North Syria, did not know that on that day—September
23rd 1893—they had opened a new page in the history of the
West. The portent of that day was barely noticed when it
came to pass, and is, as yet, unrecognized.

However, at that fate-laden session of the World's Parliament of Religions were a few who, having heard the name

* Edward Granville Browne. His visit took place in April
1890.

of Bahá'u'lláh, were destined to blaze the trail of His Faith on the American continent.

Ibráhím George Khayru'lláh was a Christian Arab born in a mountain village in the Lebanon and educated in the Syrian Protestant College.* He was one of the first medical graduates of that well-famed institution. From Syria he made his way to Egypt, and in Cairo chanced upon the Bahá'ís. The one who taught him the Faith was Hájí 'Abdu'l-Karím, a merchant of Ṭihrán, resident in Egypt. Khayru'lláh accepted the Faith in the lifetime of Bahá'u'lláh, and was honoured with a Tablet from Him. Emigration of the Levantines and particularly Christian Arabs of the Lebanon to the Americas, notably to the United States, was then a continuous process. Apart from the impelling force of poverty and the desire for a better standard of living, the oppressive régime of the Ottoman Empire was also responsible for this urge to seek new horizons. However, for Dr Khayru'lláh, newly enrolled in the ranks of a world Faith that was still confined to the Near and Middle East, crossing the Atlantic meant eager response to a calling not dissimilar to that inner compulsion which had brought his former teachers in the Syrian Protestant College from the United States to his native Syria. Hájí 'Abdu'l-Karím-i-Ṭihrání, who stood in place of a spiritual guide to him, gave him every encouragement and support. Then Khayru'lláh wrote to 'Abdu'l-Bahá and received His approval.

Dr Ibráhím George Khayru'lláh arrived at New York in December 1892. In February 1894 he moved to Chicago, the city where some months before the name of Bahá'u'lláh had been mentioned in public. There he searched hard and found a number of people interested in the Message which he had to impart. In that same year the first man of the Christian West to respond to the Cause of Bahá'u'lláh gave it his allegiance. That man was Thornton Chase to

* Since 1920, the American University of Beirut.

whom 'Abdu'l-Bahá gave a new name: T͟hábit (Steadfast).
He did not live to behold 'Abdu'l-Bahá in the lands of
the far West, triumphant. But he had seen 'Abdu'l-Bahá,
during the early years of the century, immured within
the walls of 'Akká, His life in peril. On his return to his
homeland, Chase wrote a remarkable book, to which he
gave the title *In Galilee*. 'He is the Master!' said Chase
in another connection. 'He is the Christ-Spirit of this Great
Age! He is the Anointed One! The Appointed of His
Father! That Father was the Greatest Manifestation of God
—Bahá'u'lláh. He is the Center of the Covenant; the Healer
and Satisfier of longing hearts! The King of servitude to
Humanity!'[49]

Years later, as 'Abdu'l-Bahá crossed America from east to
west in 1912, Thornton Chase lay on his death-bed, and
when the Master reached the shores of the Pacific, Chase was
dead. When 'Abdu'l-Bahá learned of his death in San Francisco, and a fortnight later stood at the graveside of this
steadfast disciple in Inglewood Cemetery, Los Angeles, He
said:

> This revered personage was the first Baha'i in America.
> He served the Cause faithfully and his services will ever
> be remembered throughout future ages and cycles . . .
> For the present his worth is not known, but in the future
> it will be inestimably dear. His sun will ever be shining,
> his star will ever bestow the light. The people will honor
> this grave. Therefore, the friends of God must visit
> this grave and on my behalf bring flowers and seek the
> sublimity of the spiritual station for him . . . This per-
> sonage will not be forgotten.[50]

'Thornton Chase is unique and peerless,' 'Abdu'l-Bahá
said on another occasion.

Thornton Chase, who rose to such heights, was not a man
of great intellect and deep learning. He was in the employ-

ment of a well-known life insurance company. In the Middle West, where he learned of the Faith and accepted it, he gave so much of his time to the service of the Cause that his company deemed it advisable to transfer him to a distant region. He was sent to California, but his dedication to the Faith, far from slackening, grew more intense. Duties devolving upon him in the pursuit of his profession took him from city to city, and wherever he went he taught and served the Cause, not only by speech and dissertation, but even more validly, by the radiance of his person. A secretary in an office which he had to visit from time to time, spoke in later years of the electrifying presence of Thornton Chase. She recalled that whenever he came into the room, people felt elated; joy wafted in with him; his face radiated light. Thornton Chase once wrote that he, himself, was a man re-created.

Louisa A. Moore, to whom 'Abdu'l-Bahá gave the name Livá (Banner)—Banner of the Cause—and whom the Guardian of the Faith designated 'the mother teacher of the West', was another distinguished member of the first group of Bahá'ís on the American continent—a group that included such outstanding women and men as Helen S. Goodall, Isabella D. Brittingham, Lillian F. Kappes, Arthur P. Dodge, Dr Edward Getsinger, Howard MacNutt, Paul K. Dealy, Chester I. Thatcher. Edward Getsinger married Louisa Moore, and Lua Getsinger, as this notable and devoted woman came to be known, was truly a torchbearer. Among those who heard of the Faith of Bahá'u'lláh from Lua Getsinger, and who, in their turn, shone in its service, was May Ellis Bolles, young in years, endowed with wisdom and insight. Mrs Phoebe Hearst, the wife of Senator George F. Hearst, also heard of the Faith of Bahá'u'lláh from Lua Getsinger. In 1898 Mrs Hearst decided to go to the Holy Land to meet 'Abdu'l-Bahá. She asked a number of Bahá'ís to accompany her on this historic pilgrimage.

Edward and Lua Getsinger and Dr Ibráhím Khayru'lláh, together with his wife, were among those invited by Phoebe Hearst.

During those five years Dr Khayru'lláh had been assiduously teaching the Faith, not only in Chicago, but notably in Kenosha, as well as in Kansas City, Philadelphia, Ithaca, and New York City. The number of the American Bahá'ís raised by the power of the Covenant to compensate for the dishonour brought upon the Cause, and the confusion engendered among friend and foe alike by the violators of the Covenant, could then be counted in hundreds. But soon the same man who had ventured into the American field with the tidings of the advent of Bahá'u'lláh, was to betray the Faith which he had so boldly and effectively championed.

In Paris a number of Americans who lived in the French capital joined the pilgrims. Among them were two nieces of Mrs Hearst, Mrs Thornburgh and her daughter Miriam Thornburgh-Cropper, the first Bahá'í of the British Isles (though not the first British Bahá'í), also May Bolles. There were further additions in Egypt, making a total of fifteen. Because of the exigencies of the time they divided themselves into three groups. The first arrived at 'Akká on December 10th 1898.

This was a historic day in the annals of the Faith of Bahá'u'lláh. It was also a day unparalleled in the chronicles of the Christian West. Never before had the East, where the Manifestation of God had always appeared, witnessed men and women of the West, wishing to offer their homage, come to the doors of the One to whom the Manifestation of God had entrusted His authority. Never before had the Centre of the Covenant of a Manifestation of God stood guard, thus invincible, over the integrity of the Faith.

It was the first time that Bahá'ís raised up in the Christian West were coming face to face with the Master. What was

the impact of this meeting? How did the pilgrims respond?
More than three decades later Mrs Thornburgh-Cropper
wrote:

We then took a small, miserable boat to Haifa.* There
was a storm here also, and we were beaten about un-
mercifully in our all too inadequate steamer. Upon
arrival we went to an hotel, where we remained until
nightfall as it was too dangerous for us, and for 'Abdu'l-
Bahá, . . . for strangers to be seen entering the city of
sorrow.

We took a carriage after the night had fallen, and drove
along the hard sand by 'way of the sea beyond Jordan',
which led us to the gates of the prison city. There our
trusted driver arranged for us to enter. Once inside we
found the friends who were awaiting us, and we started
up the uneven stairs that led to Him. Someone went
before us with a small piece of candle, which cast strange
shadows on the walls of this silent place.

Suddenly the light caught a form that at first seemed
a vision of mist and light. It was the Master which the
candle-light had revealed to us. His white robe, and silver,
flowing hair, and shining blue eyes gave the impression
of a spirit, rather than of a human being. We tried to tell
Him how deeply grateful we were at His receiving us.
'No,' He answered, 'you are kind to come . . . '

Then He smiled, and we recognized the Light which
He possessed in the radiance which moved over His fine
and noble face. It was an amazing experience. We four
visitors from the Western world felt that our voyage,
with all its accompanying inconvenience was a small price
to pay for such treasure as we received from the spirit
and words of the Master, Whom we had crossed mountain
and seas and nations to meet. This began our work to
'spread the teachings', to 'mention the Name of Bahá'u'-
lláh, and acquaint the world with the Message.'[51]

* From Egypt.

Phoebe Hearst, who had originally planned the pilgrimage, wrote a year later in answer to an enquiry:

Altho my stay in Acca was very short, as I was there only three days, yet I assure you those three days were the most memorable days of my life, still I feel incapable of describing them in the slightest degree.

From a material standpoint everything was very simple and plain, but the spiritual atmosphere which pervaded the place and was manifested in the lives and actions among the Believers, was truly wonderful and something I had never before experienced. One needs but to see them to know that they are a Holy people.

The Master I will not attempt to describe: I will only state that I believe with all my heart that He is the Master and my greatest blessing in this world is that I have been privileged to be in His presence and look upon His sanctified face. His life is truly the Christlife and His whole being radiates purity and holiness!

Without a doubt 'Abbás Effendi is the Messiah of this day and generation and we need not look for another.[52]

Again at the close of 1899 she wrote in reply to another correspondent who enquired about her journey to the Holy Land:

. . . if a statement from me regarding my visit to Acca, also my privilege of being in the Master's presence, and my impressions of the Holy Household, will in the slightest degree confirm anyone in the faith, then I am most happy to render it . . .

It seems to me a real Truthseeker would know at a glance that He is the Master! Withal, I must say He is the Most Wonderful Being I have ever met or ever expect to meet in this world. Tho He does not seek to impress one at all, strength, power, purity, love and holiness are radiated from His majestic, yet humble, personality, and the spiritual atmosphere which surrounds Him and most powerfully affects all those who are blest by being near Him, is indescribable . . . I believe in Him with all my heart and soul, and I hope all who call themselves Believers will concede to Him all the greatness, all the glory, and all the praise, for surely He is the Son of God—and 'the spirit of the Father abideth in Him'.[53]

And here is the testimony of a younger member of that first body of Western pilgrims—a woman of high courage and high resolve, who, throughout four decades, served the Faith of Bahá'u'lláh with greatest distinction—the testimony of May Ellis Bolles:

In a moment I stood on the threshold and dimly saw a room full of people sitting quietly about the walls, and then I beheld my Beloved. I found myself at His feet, and He gently raised me and seated me beside Him, all the while saying some loving words in Persian in a voice that shook my heart. Of that first meeting I can remember neither joy nor pain nor anything that I can name. I had been carried suddenly to too great a height; my soul had come in contact with the Divine Spirit; and this force so pure, so holy, so mighty, had overwhelmed me. He spoke to each one of us in turn of ourselves and our lives and those whom we loved, and although His Words were so few and so simple they breathed the Spirit of Life to our souls . . .

We could not remove our eyes from His glorious face: we heard all He said; we drank tea with Him at His bidding; but existence seemed suspended, and when He arose and suddenly left us we came back with a start to life: but never again, thank God, to the same life on this earth! We had 'beheld the King in His beauty. We had seen the land which is very far off.'

'Abdu'l-Bahá told the pilgrims that on Sunday morning He would meet them on Mount Carmel, under the shade

of the trees where Bahá'u'lláh had sat and rested. But May
Bolles fell ill, and the Master went to visit her on that
Sunday. He felt her pulse and then said:

'There will be no meeting on Mount Carmel to-day . . .
we could not go and leave one of the beloved of God
alone and sick. We could none of us be happy unless
all the beloved were happy.' We were astonished. That
anything so important as this meeting in that blessed
spot should be cancelled because one person was ill and
could not go seemed incredible. It was so contrary to all
ordinary habits of thought and action, so different from
the life of the world where daily events and material
circumstances are supreme in importance that it gave us a
genuine shock of surprise, and in that shock the foundations of the old order began to totter and fall. The
Master's words had opened wide the door of God's
Kingdom and given us a vision of that infinite world
whose only law is love. This was but one of many times
that we saw 'Abdu'l-Bahá place above every other consideration the love and kindness, the sympathy and compassion due to every soul.[54]

Included in this party of pilgrims was Robert Turner,
Mrs Hearst's Negro butler. He was destined to be the first
of his race on the American continent to accept the Faith
of Bahá'u'lláh. One day as the Master sat with the pilgrims,
He asked whether everybody was there, and then He noticed
that the butler was absent. 'Where is Robert?' He enquired,
and as soon as that simple, devoted man came into the room,
'Abdu'l-Bahá rose to His feet and greeted Him affectionately. He made Robert, a servant, sit down with the rest,
and said: 'Robert, your Lord loves you. God gave you a
black skin, but a heart white as snow.'
The sojourn of the pilgrims could not but be very short,
and swiftly came the day when they had to leave. The thought

was unbearable, the wrench shattering. The compassionate Master told them:

And now I give you a commandment which shall be for a covenant between you and Me—that ye have faith; that your faith be steadfast as a rock that no storms can move, that nothing can disturb, and that it endure through all things even to the end; even should ye hear that your Lord has been crucified, be not shaken in your faith; for I am with you always, whether living or dead, I am with you to the end. As ye have faith so shall your powers and blessings be. This is the balance—this is the balance—this is the balance.

And at the hour of parting He told them:

. . . separation is only of our bodies, in spirit we are united. Ye are the lights which shall be diffused; ye are the waves of that sea which shall spread and overflow the world . . . Another commandment I give unto you, that ye love one another even as I love you . . . look at one another with the eye of perfection; look at Me, follow Me, be as I am; take no thought for yourselves or your lives, whether ye eat or whether ye sleep, whether ye are comfortable, whether ye are well or ill, whether ye are with friends or foes, whether ye receive praise or blame . . . Look at Me and be as I am; ye must die to yourselves and to the world, so shall ye be born again and enter the Kingdom of Heaven. Behold a candle how it gives its light. It weeps its life away drop by drop in order to give forth its flame of light.[55]

To May Bolles 'Abdu'l-Bahá gave a specific task. He told her to remain in Paris and teach the Faith there. Within a few months she established the first Bahá'í centre of the European continent. And in Britain, Miriam Thornburgh-Cropper, fellow-pilgrim with May Bolles, an American domiciled in London, helped in the summer of 1899 to bring the second Bahá'í of the British Isles into the fold of the Faith. She was Ethel Jenner Rosenberg, an accomplished miniature painter,* a very remarkable woman who served and promoted the Cause of Bahá'u'lláh with exemplary devotion for the next thirty years.†

But it was May Ellis Bolles who confirmed the first Englishman, in Paris. The story of Thomas Breakwell is dramatic and thrilling. May Bolles herself has recounted it.[56]

It was the summer of the year 1901. Thomas Breakwell, a young Englishman in his twenties, who held a responsible and lucrative post in a cotton mill in the south of the United States, was on holiday in Europe. May Bolles had stayed in Paris. Her mother wished to take her during the summer season to Brittany, but 'Abdu'l-Bahá had told her that she 'must on no account' absent herself from Paris. ' . . . my unhappy and indignant mother,' she writes, 'had closed our home and left me alone.'

A mutual friend who had noticed that Thomas Breakwell was attracted to themes of mysticism and esoteric thought, brought him to meet May Bolles. One morning she found them outside her door.

' . . . my attention,' she has recorded, 'was riveted on this youth; of medium height, slender, erect and graceful, with intense eyes and an indescribable charm.' At that first meeting no mention was made of the Faith which May Bolles was serving with the full ardour of her great heart. They talked of Theosophy and Breakwell thought that his hostess's interest centred round that movement. But May had seen in him, in her own words, 'a very rare person of high standing and culture, simple, natural, intensely real in his attitude toward life and his fellowmen'. Breakwell

* A miniature portrait of Bahá'íyyih Khánum, the Greatest Holy Leaf, executed by Ethel Rosenberg, exists in the Bahá'í Archives of the British Isles.
† Died November 17th 1930.

asked whether he would be permitted to call again the next day, and he came the following morning. When he arrived he was in a state of exultation, and immediately asked May Bolles whether she could see anything 'strange' about him. Then he went on to say:

> When I was here yesterday I felt a power, an influence that I had felt once before in my life, when for a period of three months I was continually in communion with God. I felt during that time like one moving in a rarefied atmosphere of light and beauty. My heart was afire with love for the supreme Beloved, I felt at peace, at one with all my fellowmen. Yesterday when I left you I went alone down the Champs-Élysées, the air was warm and heavy, not a leaf was stirring, when suddenly a wind struck me and whirled around me, and in that wind a voice said, with an indescribable sweetness and penetration, 'Christ has come again! Christ has come again!'

Breakwell next asked whether she thought that he was parting with his senses, to which she replied: 'No, you are just becoming sane.' And she told him of the advent of Bahá'u'lláh.

There and then Thomas Breakwell became a Bahá'í.

But the story of Thomas Breakwell does not end there. His burning desire was to find his way into the presence of 'Abdu'l-Bahá. 'My Lord, I believe, forgive me, Thy servant Thomas Breakwell,' were the words which conveyed his hope and his allegiance to the Master.

> That evening (writes his teacher) I went to the Concierge of our apartment to get my mail, and there lay a little blue cablegram from 'Abdu'l-Bahá! With what wonder and awe I read His Words. 'You may leave Paris at any time' . . .
>
> How gratefully my heart dwells on the divine compassion of the Master, on the joy and wonder of my

mother as I told her everything, and when she read the Master's cablegram she burst into tears and exclaimed, 'You have, indeed, a wonderful Master'.

'Abdu'l-Bahá's permission for pilgrimage came and, within a short time, Thomas Breakwell was in 'Akká in the company of Herbert Hopper, a young American Bahá'í, who was also taught by May Bolles. As she relates,

... they were ushered into a spacious room, at one end of which stood a group of men in oriental garb. Herbert Hopper's face became irradiated with the joy of instant recognition, but Breakwell discerned no one in particular among these men. Feeling suddenly ill and weak, he seated himself near a table, with a sense of crushing defeat ...

Sitting thus he bitterly lamented: Why had he come here? Why had he abandoned his projected journey and come to this remote prison, seeking—he knew not what?

Sunk in utter gloom, he was in an instant rescued from his darksome world. The floodgates of light opened upon him. 'Abdu'l-Bahá entered the room and Thomas Breakwell became a changed man. From that moment Breakwell never looked back. He told 'Abdu'l-Bahá the nature of his profession, that his work was worth while and his earnings were considerable, but he added that now he had misgivings because the organisation that he served was buttressed by child labour. 'Abdu'l-Bahá advised him: 'Cable your resignation.' He did. He went back to Paris and made it his home. The Master wished it.

His teacher further relates:

He seemed to have no care for the future; burning like a white light in the darkness of Paris, he served his fellowmen with a power and passion to the last breath of his life.

That last breath was not long delayed, for he succumbed to consumption. The world could contain him no longer.

An eyewitness of those two memorable days that Breakwell spent in the prison city of 'Akká, recorded this account of the first Englishman to come as a pilgrim:*

The fervour and the faith of this young man were so sublime in character that his blessed name shall ring throughout centuries, and shall be remembered with deep affection in many chronicles. Verses from the Gospels which attest to the glories of the Kingdom were always on his lips. His sojourn was too short, but so intense was his love, and so ardent his zeal that he touched the depths of the hearts of those who heard him. Whenever he was in the presence of our peerless Master he was rapt in wonderment. At other times his bearing and all that he did bore witness to his dedication. It was not possible for him to meet all the friends in 'Akká.† The day he left the Master told him: 'Stay in Paris.' As bidden by the Master, I accompanied him on his return journey to Haifa, and the point of embarkation. Away from 'Akká, it was possible to entertain him for an hour or two, in the home of one of the believers, before his boat was ready to sail. In that house we were in a room that looked towards 'Akká. There he would stand, every now and then, perfectly still, facing 'Akká in a state of communion. Whilst his eyes welled with tears, his tongue uttered words of supplication. All those who were there were greatly moved. In that state of ecstasy he asked me whether he could correspond with me from time to time. My letters in answer to his, he said, would convey to him the fragrances of the effulgent city of 'Akká. We were all in tears when we bade farewell to him.

* Dr Yúnis Khán Afrúkhtih, in *Memories of Nine Years in 'Akká*, pp. 180–7.
† Owing to the reimposition of restrictions by the authorities.

Dr Yúnis Khán, who served 'Abdu'l-Bahá as secretary and interpreter with exemplary devotion during a very critical period of His Ministry, carries further this absorbing story of Thomas Breakwell. He received letters regularly, at fortnightly intervals, from the young Englishman in Paris, who was then battling with advanced consumption. In one of his letters Breakwell had remarked that he implored God for pain and affliction and suffering, lest he forget his Beloved. The more pronounced the ravages of the disease became, the more eloquent and the more fervent became Breakwell's paeans of joy. His correspondent recounts:

> Everything he wrote I presented to the Master. Sometimes He would say: 'Send him my greetings.' Whenever He made no comment I knew that the mysterious communion between the lover and the Beloved had no need of the spoken word. Then came his last letter. He wrote: 'Suffering is a heady wine; I am prepared to receive that bounty which is the greatest of all; torments of the flesh have enabled me to draw much nearer to my Lord. All agony notwithstanding, I wish life to endure longer, so that I may taste more of pain. That which I desire is the good-pleasure of my Lord; mention me in His presence.' A few days later, together with the late Dr Arastú Khán,* I was accompanying the Master in the evening from the house where He received His visitors to His home by the seaside. All of a sudden He turned to me and said: 'Have you heard?' 'No, Master,' I replied, and He said: 'Breakwell has passed away. I am grieved, very grieved. I have written a prayer of visitation for him. It is very moving, so moving that twice I could not withhold my tears, when I was writing it. You must translate it well, so that whoever reads it will weep.' I never knew

---

* Brother of the late Dr Luṭfu'lláh Ḥakím. The latter was a member of the first Universal House of Justice. Breakwell died in Paris on 13 June 1902.

who had given the Master the news of Breakwell's death. If anyone had written or cabled either in English or French, that communication would have passed through my hands. Two days later the prayer of visitation was given to me. It wrung one's heart, and I could not hold back my tears. I translated it into French, and later, with the help of Lua Getsinger, into English.

Here are some extracts from that eulogy:

O Breakwell, my beloved! Where is thy beautiful countenance and where is thy eloquent tongue? Where is thy radiant brow and where is thy brilliant face? . . .

O my dear, O Breakwell! Where are thy bright eyes and where are thy smiling lips? Where are thy gentle cheeks and where is thy graceful stature?

O my dear, O Breakwell! Verily thou hast abandoned this transitory world and soared upward to the Kingdom, hast attained to the grace of the Invisible Realm and sacrificed thyself at the Threshold of the Lord of Might! . . .

O my adored one, O Breakwell! Then thou hast ignited a light in the glass of the Supreme Concourse, hast entered the Paradise of Abhá, art protected under the shade of the Blessed Tree and hast attained to the meeting (of the Lord of Truth) in the Abode of Heaven! . . .

O my beloved, O Breakwell! Verily, thy Lord hath chosen thee for His love, guided thee to the court of His Holiness, caused thee to enter into the Riḍván of His company and granted thee to behold His Beauty! . . .

O my beloved, O Breakwell! Thou hast become a star in the most exalted horizon, a lamp among the angels of heaven, a living spirit in the Supreme World, and art established upon the throne of immortality! . . .

O my adored one, O Breakwell! I mention thy name continually, I never forget thee, I pray for thee day and night, and I see thee clearly and manifestly, O my adored one, O Breakwell![57]

Dr Yúnis Khán, this faithful chronicler, has still more to tell us about Thomas Breakwell. 'A year later,' he writes,

'Abdu'l-Bahá called me one day to His presence, to give me letters to translate. There were many envelopes sent from various places. While examining them still sealed, He, all of a sudden, picked out one and said: 'How pleasing is the fragrance that emanates from this envelope. Make haste, open it and see where it comes from. Make haste.' Previously it had happened many a time that the Master had picked up a particular envelope to be opened first, and of a certainty the letter therein had contained news of great spiritual import. Now I hurried to open this particular envelope selected by the Master. In it there was a postcard . . . The postcard was coloured a beautiful shade, and attached to it was one solitary flower—a violet. Written in letters of gold were these words: 'He is not dead. He lives on in the Kingdom of God.' Further, there was this sentence: 'This flower was picked from Breakwell's grave.' When I told the Master what the message of the postcard was, He at once rose up from His seat, took the card, put it on His blessed brow, and tears flowed down His cheeks.

Thomas Breakwell is a luminary* in the firmament of the Faith of Bahá'u'lláh.[58]

The first French Bahá'í was also introduced to the Faith by May Ellis Bolles. He was Hippolyte Dreyfus, who, after his marriage to Laura Clifford Barney, another renowned Bahá'í taught by the same tireless founder of the Paris group, adopted the surname, Dreyfus-Barney. This French scholar, too, heard of the Faith of Bahá'u'lláh in the summer of 1901. May Bolles Maxwell wrote of him:

He was at the time an agnostic who believed that life and character are above dogma and creed. Although he

* Thus specified by the Guardian of the Faith.

THE FIRST BAHÁ'Í GROUP IN EUROPE

Paris, *circa* 1901

THE SHRINE OF THE BÁB ON MOUNT CARMEL IN EARLY YEARS
On one of His visits to Mount Carmel, Bahá'u'lláh sat under the cypress trees shown in the left background

had never believed in any force transcending nature, nor had he received intimations of the possible existence of a Supreme Being, yet after hearing of the advent of Bahá'u'lláh his inner susceptibilities became unfolded and in his subsequent study of the teachings and his visit to 'Abdu'l-Bahá in the prison of 'Akká, he attained a supreme realization of the significance and importance of this message to the world.[59]

Hippolyte Dreyfus was the first European Bahá'í to visit Írán, the cradle of the Faith. He learned Persian and Arabic to enable him to translate the Writings of Bahá'u'lláh and 'Abdu'l-Bahá. He undertook extensive journeys to Canada and the United States and as far east as Japan, in the interests of the Faith which he had zealously embraced. His translations of the Scriptures, and his own book* on the history and the teachings of the Cause, are of high merit. In later years he attended 'Abdu'l-Bahá during His travels in Europe and served Him with devotion and distinction. Hippolyte Dreyfus died in 1929.

Laura Clifford Barney belonged to an American family established in Paris and well-known among its *literati*. At the dawn of the century she accepted the Revelation of Bahá'u'lláh. Soon after, she went on pilgrimage to 'Akká. Then she went a second time, and in 1904 a third time in the company of Ethel Rosenberg.† These, as we shall see, were perilous years in the ministry of 'Abdu'l-Bahá. Then came a short visit to Egypt and a lightning visit to Europe during the spring. She returned to the Holy Land and took her mother with her. During the summer of 1906 Hippolyte Dreyfus accompanied Laura Clifford Barney and her travelling companion to the native land of Bahá'u'lláh. That autumn she was once again in 'Akká, where her sojourn

* *Essai Sur Le Baháisme*. See bibliography.
† Ethel Rosenberg's first pilgrimage was in 1900.

extended into the year 1906. In 1908 she made yet another pilgrimage.

It is of particular interest to know the details of Laura Clifford Barney's repeated and extended visits to the Holy Land, because it was during those months, stretched over several years, that a book unique in the entire range of the Writings of the Founders of the Faith took shape. The book was *Some Answered Questions*. Questions came from Laura Barney and 'Abdu'l-Bahá answered them. In her own words, taken from the introduction to the book:

> . . . these answers were written down in Persian while 'Abdu'l-Bahá spoke, not with a view to publication, but simply that I might have them for future study . . . But I believe that what has been so valuable to me may be of use to others, since all men, notwithstanding their differences, are united in their search for reality; and I have therefore asked 'Abdu'l-Bahá's permission to publish these talks.

That permission was granted in the year 1906. The English edition appeared in 1908, and the Persian text was published in the same year. Hippolyte Dreyfus translated it into French under the title, *Les Leçons de Saint Jean-d'Acre*. By the generosity of the compiler herself, the original Persian manuscript containing 'Abdu'l-Bahá's occasional corrections and emendations is deposited and preserved in the International Archives of the Bahá'í Faith.

The Persian text has a sub-title: 'Talks During Luncheon'. ' "I have given to you my tired moments," ' Laura Barney recalls that 'Abdu'l-Bahá told her, 'as he rose from table after answering one of my questions.' Weighed down with the oppression of the times; facing hostile officials resolved to destroy Him—officials dispatched under the guise of a 'Commission of Enquiry' from the seat of Ottoman autocracy, 'the Enquiry' set afoot by the treachery of His own kith and kin; baulked momentarily in the greatest enterprise He had undertaken—raising the mausoleum of the Báb on Mount Carmel; every minute of the life of 'Abdu'l-Bahá was filled with sorrow, demanding vigilant action and unflinching fortitude. Such were the moments that He gave to Laura Clifford Barney as she sought knowledge and understanding.

Yet, in this book, *Some Answered Questions*, the supreme genius of 'Abdu'l-Bahá is overwhelmingly manifest. Men who have devoted precious years of their lives to study and research—to the building of arguments, the laying of premises, and the marshalling of facts—have never presented the fundamentals of life and belief, the basic truths of the universe around them, and the mainsprings of action, with such lucidity and coherence as are here apparent. Nor can they hope to rival, much less to match 'Abdu'l-Bahá's all-encompassing wisdom. And these were words spoken without previous intimation of the nature and purport of the query. Not only do His answers arrest attention and compel thought, the strength wedded to the crystal clarity of the language enchant the mind. His statements are unencumbered, His similes most apt. His reasoning is flawless. His conclusions are unhedged and emphatic, informed with authority. *Some Answered Questions* has no equal, and the service rendered by its compiler has been characterized by the Guardian of the Faith as 'imperishable'.

Dr Yúnis Khán Afrúkhtih, from whose memoirs valuable excerpts have been quoted in this narrative, recalls a delightful occasion when 'Abdu'l-Bahá was answering Miss Barney's questions on the theme of 'Evil'. 'Abdu'l-Bahá had said: 'There is no evil in existence.' Then He turned to Yúnis Khán who was acting as His interpreter and said with a smile: 'Next she will ask, how is it then that God has created the scorpion.' In a moment Laura Barney posed this very question. The Master remarked: 'Did I not say so?'

and proceeded to explain that the venom of the scorpion's sting is its means of defence, and does not constitute evil in its own milieu.

May Ellis Bolles, whose outstanding work in the French capital we have already noted, married William Sutherland Maxwell in 1902. He was a young Canadian architect, then at the threshold of a brilliant career which culminated in the designing of the beautiful and majestic superstructure of the mausoleum of the Báb on Mount Carmel. They established their home in Montreal where they founded the first centre of the Faith on Canadian soil. That home became a haven. In 1912 'Abdu'l-Bahá spent some days under its roof. Today it is a cherished Shrine for the Bahá'ís of Canada.

May Maxwell served assiduously and selflessly for forty years as a teacher and administrator of the Faith. She helped many on the American continent to see the truth of the Message of Bahá'u'lláh. No one ever came across her path who was not in some measure enriched and invigorated by that contact. When advanced in years and poor in health, she unhesitatingly responded to the call that came from the Guardian of the Faith, and turned to fresh fields of pioneering. She went to South America. Her spirit shone brighter than ever, but the physical frame was spent. The end came in Buenos Aires in 1940. Shoghi Effendi told the Bahá'í world that May Maxwell had attained the station of a martyr. Glorious was her life, and glorious her end.

Her husband, Sutherland Maxwell, was elevated to the rank of Hand of the Cause of God in 1951. Soon after, he passed away, and 'his mantle', in the words of the Guardian of the Cause, came to rest upon the shoulders of his daughter, Mary, named Rúḥíyyih by the Guardian at the time of her marriage to him in 1937. She was also accorded the title of Amatu'l-Bahá—the Handmaiden of Bahá—by Shoghi Effendi. Rúḥíyyih Khánum served as the Guardian's secretary, also as a member of the International Bahá'í Council appointed by him in 1951, and as liaison between him and the Council. In those years, and after the passing of Shoghi Effendi in November 1957, in her capacity as a Hand of the Cause of God in the Holy Land, Amatu'l-Bahá Rúḥíyyih Khánum followed the example set by her valiant mother.

While the disciples of 'Abdu'l-Bahá were blazing the trail in the West, a hurricane was gathering force to sweep over the scene of their labours—a hurricane that threatened to extinguish the light which they had lit and kept shining with exemplary devotion. The same person who had taken the Message of Bahá'u'lláh across the ocean, who had established the first Bahá'í centre in the Christian West, who had, over a period of six years, taught the Faith and nursed it in a distant land, became the vehicle of that storm. He, whose services 'Abdu'l-Bahá had highly extolled, whom He had addressed as 'Bahá's Peter', chose to join the ranks of the violators of the Covenant. The success which attended Dr Khayru'lláh's endeavours became eventually the instrument of his downfall. He became vainglorious and introduced tenets and interpretations which were of his own invention. His case is not unique in the annals of the Faith of Bahá'u'lláh, nor in the chronicles of the other great religious systems of mankind.

Khayru'lláh dreamt of sharing 'Abdu'l-Bahá's authority. Let 'Abdu'l-Bahá, he conjured in a mind dangerously distorted, have the East to guide and administer; he, Khayru'lláh, by virtue of his brilliant achievement, would lead and shepherd the West. Until he went in Mrs Hearst's party on pilgrimage to 'Akká, he had not met 'Abdu'l-Bahá. It was then that he saw how appallingly he had miscalculated. The integrity of 'Abdu'l-Bahá's stewardship could not be breached. But having become enamoured of power and having followed the mirage of leadership, Dr Khayru'lláh decided to turn to Mírzá Muḥammad-'Alí. In secret he established relations with the violators. Soon it became apparent that he was seriously disaffected. Mírzá Muḥammad-'Alí sent his eldest son, Mírzá Shu'áu'lláh, to America to lend him his support. Shu'áu'lláh was followed by Mírzá Ghulámu'lláh, son of Áqá Muḥammad-Javád-i-Qazvíní, one of the most inveterate adversaries of 'Abdu'l-Bahá. On his way to the United States, Ghulámu'lláh visited Professor Edward Browne at Cambridge.

'Abdu'l-Bahá tried hard to rescue Dr Khayru'lláh. Ḥájí 'Abdu'l-Karím, the Ṭihrání merchant in Cairo who had taught the Syrian doctor the Faith, and had made it possible for him to embark on his mission in America, was instructed by 'Abdu'l-Bahá to go to the United States, both to protect the nascent community there from the intrigues and insinuations of the violators, and to endeavour to make Khayru'lláh see the error of his ways.

The year was 1900. Contrary to what Edward Granville Browne has stated in his *Materials for the Study of the Bábí Religion*, no schism occurred in the American Bahá'í community. The very people whom Khayru'lláh had helped to come into the Faith now refused to stand by him. He was repudiated by all, except a few. The presence of Mírzá Shu'áu'lláh had no appreciable effect.[60] Violation failed to strike root in the American soil. But the strain to which the infant community was subjected was titanic and truly testing.

In the same year, 1900, upon the return of Ḥájí 'Abdu'l-Karím to Egypt, 'Abdu'l-Bahá sent another Persian Bahá'í, resident in the same country, to the United States. Ḥájí Mírzá Ḥasan-i-Khurásání also tried to bring Dr Khayru'lláh to his senses. But Khayru'lláh could not be saved. He published his book *Beháullah* (the Glory of God)[61] in which he drew particular attention to Mírzá Muḥammad-'Alí and his brothers, Mírzá Ḍíyá'u'lláh and Mírzá Badí'u'lláh, and tried to present them as equals of 'Abdu'l-Bahá. He gave to Mírzá Díyá'u'lláh, who had recently died, the designation 'Ghuṣn-i-Aṭhar' (the Purest Branch)[62] which properly belonged to Mírzá Mihdí, that son of Bahá'u'lláh who met his death in the citadel of 'Akká. Furthermore, Dr Khayru'lláh invented the designation 'Ghuṣn-i-Anvar' (the Most Luminous Branch) and applied it to Mírzá Badí'u'lláh. It was stated that Howard MacNutt had 'assisted' the author in writing his book. Howard MacNutt, however, did not follow Ibráhím Khayru'lláh into the wilderness and, after 'Abdu'l-Bahá's visit to America in 1912, compiled two volumes of His discourses, under the title *The Promulgation of Universal Peace*.

After the return of the Khurásání merchant, Mírzá Asadu'lláh-i-Iṣfahání was sent on the same errand. He was the emissary who, at the bidding of 'Abdu'l-Bahá, had safely taken the remains of the Báb from Írán to the Holy Land. Mírzá Asadu'lláh was assisted by Ḥusayn Rúḥí, the capable and devoted son of a Bahá'í of Tabríz.[63] And finally, the most erudite and accomplished scholar and divine that the Cause of Bahá'u'lláh has ever won to its side, Mírzá Abu'l-Faḍl of Gulpáygán, was directed to America by a vigilant Master. This great teacher's visit extended from 1901 to 1902. Dr Ali-Kuli Khan, who was later given the title of Nabíli-'d-Dawlih by the Government of Írán, and served as its Chargé d'Affaires in Washington, D.C., acted as his interpreter. Ali-Kuli Khan's services were invaluable, as he also contributed to the compendium of the Scriptures of the Faith available in English, by undertaking copious translations.[64]

A Bahá'í publication, first of its kind, that bore the title *Prayers, Tablets, Instructions and Miscellany*, appeared at the time when Khayru'lláh's total alienation was no longer in doubt. It was stated that materials for that publication were 'Gathered by American Visitors to the Holy City During the Summer of 1900'. Ali-Kuli Khan was with that group of pilgrims. When one looks at this small book of only 91 pages, one is amazed at how little these early Western Bahá'ís had of the Words and the Writings of Bahá'u'lláh and 'Abdu'l-Bahá, and how deep their faith was that so little sufficed.

Tribulations which afflicted the newly-born community of American Bahá'ís were severe, and the gales of violation that swept over it were tempestuous. But the Bahá'ís of America proved their mettle. Their superb loyalty attested to their maturity. Their ranks could not be breached.

Thus Dr Ibráhím Khayru'lláh, defeated and disowned, passed from the scene. Occasionally, his feeble efforts caused a ripple, hardly perceptible, that died out quickly. A letter which he wrote to Professor Edward Browne, on April 4th 1917, and which the eminent orientalist included in *Materials for the Study of the Bábí Religion*, his last book on the Faith of Bahá'u'lláh, is the best indication of the depths to which Dr Khayru'lláh had sunk. He wrote:

> The Bahá'í movement in America became slow and dull since the sad dissension reached the West nineteen years ago. I thought then that to call the people to this Great Truth was equivalent to inviting them into a quarrel. But the visit of 'Abbás Efendi 'Abdu'l-Bahá to this country, his false teachings, his misrepresentation of Bahá'ísm, his dissimulation, and the knowledge that his end is nigh, aroused me to rise up for helping the work of God, declaring the Truth, and refuting the false attacks of theologians and missionaries. Now I am struggling hard to vivify the Cause of God, after its having received by the visit of 'Abbás Efendi a death-blow.[65]

It is of positive value that Edward Browne gave wide publicity to Khayru'lláh's letter, because therein the man who was once known as 'the conqueror of America' and 'the second Columbus', condemned and exposed his own delusions. Not one person did he lead to the Faith of Bahá'u'lláh in those long, long years of treading the wilderness. And he was the same man who established this Faith in the American continent in the days when he walked the high-road of the Covenant.

CHAPTER 7

YEARS OF PERIL

When the Báb, the Martyr-Prophet and the Herald of the
Faith of Bahá'u'lláh, fell* before a firing squad in the public
square of Tabríz, His remains, inextricably joined with the
flesh of the unflinching disciple † who died with Him, were
thrown on the edge of the moat surrounding the city, to
be consumed by beasts and birds of prey. Through the
courageous efforts of one of His followers, Sulaymán Khán
(who was himself later engulfed by the holocaust of 1852),
those remains were rescued in the dead of night and removed
to a silk factory that belonged to Ḥájí Aḥmad, a Bábí of
Mílán.‡ There they were enshrouded and secreted under
bales of silk. Then on the instructions of Bahá'u'lláh, Who
had, in the first instance, sent Sulaymán Khán on this
mission to Tabríz, the remains of the Báb were taken to
Ṭihrán and kept in a safe place within a Muslim shrine. Next
followed fifty years, in lunar reckoning, during which,
time after time, they had to be moved from place to place—
from the precincts of shrines to the shelter of humble
homes—until the last year of the nineteenth century.

In the same year that the first Western pilgrims reached
'Akká, the hazardous task of the conveyance of the remains
of the Báb from Írán to the Holy Land, a task which 'Abdu'l-
Bahá had planned with greatest care and entrusted to Mírzá
Asadu'lláh-i-Iṣfahání, was accomplished. Of the details of

* July 9th 1850.
† Mírzá Muḥammad-'Alíy-i-Zunúzí.
‡ A village in the vicinity of Tabríz.

that long and perilous journey our knowledge is scant. However, we know that the casket had to be moved first from Ṭihrán to Iṣfahán, and thence to Kirmánsháh. Then over the same route that Bahá'u'lláh had travelled when banished from His native land, the remains of the Martyr-Prophet were taken out of Írán to Baghdád, the city where Bahá'u'lláh had sojourned for a decade, where He had revealed His Mission. Next, the road lay over the wastes of the Syrian desert to Damascus, the most ancient inhabited city in the world. Finally on the last day of January 1899, the end of the long trail was reached, by way of the sea, from Beirut. A miraculous feat had been achieved; the first stage of one of the cardinal acts in the ministry of 'Abdu'l-Bahá had been concluded.

But as yet there was no mausoleum in the heart of Carmel to receive and harbour the shattered human temple of a Manifestation of God. The purchase of the land—the site chosen by Bahá'u'lláh, on which this mausoleum was to be raised; the construction of the edifice and the safeguarding of uninterrupted access to it; the deposition of the sarcophagus in the vault beneath the building—these took another decade. This long and significant period was fraught with fresh dangers and tribulations. And 'Abdu'l-Bahá was subjected to pains and heartaches beyond human endurance. Movements were afoot to bring about His death. An attempt was made on His life in the streets of Haifa, which remained unexplained. But the decade culminated in the total rout of the forces of sedition and tyranny.

The prime movers of mischief, who were determined to wreck an enterprise enjoined by Bahá'u'lláh, were the members of His family. They were the fountain-head of the violation of the Covenant, and they plotted recklessly. Every means was employed, base and treacherous and degrading, to prevent 'Abdu'l-Bahá from building a shrine for the Martyr-Prophet. It is said that even a man as disaffected as Mírzá Áqá Ján, was alarmed and told them not to try to block this enterprise, because the prophets of the Old Testament had foretold its consummation. But they turned a deaf ear to any such advice. They continued to plot, cajole, and bribe, in their constant efforts to incite the Ottoman officials against 'Abdu'l-Bahá.

When the first group of Western pilgrims arrived in the Holy Land, 'Abdu'l-Bahá had already purchased the site for the Shrine of the Báb. One day He took Ibráhím Khayru'lláh with Him to Mount Carmel, and there He laid the foundation-stone of the mausoleum which today adorns the mountain. Not long after, a marble sarcophagus, the offering of the Bahá'ís of Rangoon, reached Haifa. A few months later, as the new century dawned, work began on the construction of the building. The violators of the Covenant, already rejected by the Bahá'ís, were then stung to fresh and feverish activity. Here were pilgrims coming from the West—the Christian West—and here was a structure in the process of being raised on a commanding height. And here the violators of the Covenant saw their opportunity. They would represent to the rulers of an archaic Empire, plagued by the unrest of a multitude of oppressed peoples, that 'Abdu'l-Bahá was laying the ground for rebellion, that He was gathering together a band of malcontents, that He was enlisting the support of Christians from the West, that He was building a strong fortress on Mount Carmel which dominated the city and the plain of 'Akká, that He was biding His time to raise the banner of rebellion and defy the august person of the Sulṭán—the Caliph of Islám. To obtain the support of a corrupt officialdom they needed a large sum of money. To obtain the money they mortgaged the Mansion of Bahjí, holy ground to the Bahá'ís, the home of Bahá'u'lláh where He had found peace in the evening of His life, next to which stood His Shrine. They even gave away the garments and personal effects of Bahá'u'lláh to government functionaries, to serve as chattels of bribery and to provide as well the means of humiliating 'Abdu'l-Bahá. At their instigation the Deputy-Governor of Haifa would, whilst visiting 'Abdu'l-Bahá, ostentatiously wear Bahá'u'lláh's cloak and brazenly use His spectacles. Before long this man was dismissed from his post and fell on evil days. Then he went to 'Abdu'l-Bahá and begged His forgiveness. He had acted, he said, in the manner he did, because he was prompted by 'Abdu'l-Bahá's own relatives. The Master showed him utmost kindness and generosity, as He always did towards those who had wronged Him and had been overtaken by adversity.

There exists, as already mentioned, the testimony of Mírzá Badí'u'lláh, the youngest son of Bahá'u'lláh, who, for a short period, renounced all connections with the centre of sedition—his brother, Mírzá Muḥammad-'Alí—and turned to 'Abdu'l-Bahá, apparently contrite and repentant. Of his own accord he wrote a long letter addressed to the Bahá'ís of the world, in which he detailed the perfidious acts of the violators of the Covenant. He stated that Mírzá Majdi'd-Dín went to Damascus armed with the money obtained through mortgaging the Mansion of Bahjí, in order to win over Náẓim Páshá, the Válí of the province of Syria, and to lay before him accusations against 'Abdu'l-Bahá—accusations which would inevitably arouse the wrath of the rulers of the Ottoman Empire. When these rulers took action, the violators blamed Mírzá Abu'l-Faḍl who, at that time, resided in Cairo. They fabricated the story that that eminent scholar had written a pamphlet to glorify 'Abdu'l-Bahá, in which wild and exaggerated claims had been made, and since it had fallen into the hands of the officials, these had been alarmed and forced to act. It was the in-discretion of Mírzá Abu'l-Faḍl, they alleged, that had put 'Abdu'l-Bahá under restraint and had brought fresh hard-ships to the Bahá'ís of 'Akká and its neighbourhood. In

'Akká there was a certain Yaḥyá Bey, notorious for his avarice, who held an influential post in the government. Well-bribed, he became an enthusiastic champion and accomplice of the violators.

On August 20th 1901, 'Abdu'l-Bahá celebrated the Anniversary of the Declaration of the Báb (in accordance with the lunar calendar). He observed the festival in the precincts of the Shrine of Bahá'u'lláh. When He returned to 'Akká at nightfall, He learned from the Governor that, by decree of the Sulṭán, He and His brothers would be confined within the city limits of 'Akká and forbidden the freedom of the countryside. Mírzá Muḥammad-'Alí and Mírzá Badí'u'lláh were brought in from the Mansion of Bahjí, and Mírzá Majdi-'d-Dín was fetched from Tiberias where he resided.

Just as Mírzá Yaḥyá, at an earlier time, had enmeshed himself in his own intrigues, so now Mírzá Muḥammad-'Alí fell into the same self-laid trap. The written and published testimony of Mírzá Badí'u'lláh leaves no doubt that it had been the visit of Mírzá Majdi'd-Dín to Náẓim Páshá, provided as he was with Mírzá Muḥammad-'Alí's denunciatory letter and with ample money to buy his way in, that now led to the arousal of the fear and anger of Sulṭán 'Abdu'l-Ḥamíd. Mírzá Badí'u'lláh also records Náẓim Páshá's contemptuous treatment of Mírzá Muḥammad-'Alí thereafter. Finding himself removed from the Mansion of Bahjí and kept within the walls of 'Akká, Mírzá Muḥammad-'Alí wrote two more letters to the crafty Válí at Damascus. Neither was acknowledged. It was 'Abdu'l-Bahá Who interceded for Mírzá Muḥammad-'Alí and Mírzá Badí'u'lláh and Mírzá Majdi'd-Dín. It was He Who asked the Governor of 'Akká that they should not suffer incarceration within the city walls.

The most grievous deprivation which 'Abdu'l-Ḥamíd's edict inflicted upon 'Abdu'l-Bahá was separation from the

Shrine of His Father. 'Abdu'l-Bahá was once again a prisoner within the walls of 'Akká. He is reported to have said: I toiled for thirty years to change the prison into a pavilion. The violators of the Covenant have reversed the situation in so short a time.

Now began the most perilous period in the ministry of 'Abdu'l-Bahá.

The Governor of 'Akká was loth to see 'Abdu'l-Bahá placed under restriction. Nevertheless, 'Abdu'l-Bahá was subjected to long interviews and detailed questioning. He faced the officials alone, with dignity and composure, while the Bahá'ís of 'Akká also felt the impact of galling restrictions.

But before long the first storm subsided. 'Abdu'l-Bahá's intercession for Mírzá Muḥammad-'Alí and others with him, as well as His pleas for His followers, achieved their end. Mírzá Muḥammad-'Alí and his supporters went back to the Mansion of Bahjí. The Bahá'ís of 'Akká went about their daily tasks, free to attend to their means of living.

Then the Governor asked 'Abdu'l-Bahá to take him to visit the Shrine of Bahá'u'lláh. In his company 'Abdu'l-Bahá came out of 'Akká. Still ill at ease and still trying to circumvent the strict orders of the Sublime Porte, the Governor requested another conducted visit to the Shrine, this time accompanied by other high-ranking officials. From the verandahs of the Mansion, Mírzá Muḥammad-'Alí and his partisans, gathered there in force, could witness the marks of respect shown towards 'Abdu'l-Bahá by the élite of officialdom. Enraged by what they saw, the violators were stung to fresh action and followed another line of intrigue which led them to Shaykh Abu'l-Hudá, the evil genius of Sulṭán 'Abdu'l-Ḥamíd.

Shaykh Abu'l-Hudá was an ignorant obscurantist, and his

baneful influence eventually ruined 'Abdul the Damned'.*
But he had his day. Guided and instructed by him his royal
master wronged a host of people and blocked all reform.
To this man Mírzá Muḥammad-'Alí and his lieutenants
turned to solicit aid.

But as the year 1902 went by the situation was greatly
eased. Pilgrims came, and although 'Abdu'l-Bahá was confined to 'Akká the work of the construction of the sepulchre
of the Báb made steady progress. Whatever else suffered
eclipse or deferment during the eight long years of peril, the
task of raising the edifice on Mount Carmel was never
halted. Whatever happened 'Abdu'l-Bahá was determined
that this command and behest of Bahá'u'lláh should be
fulfilled. One of the pilgrims of those opening years of the
new century was Isabella D. Brittingham (1852–1924).
Mrs Brittingham was one of the first Bahá'ís of the United
States. The life of the Master and the conditions under
which He lived and laboured touched the core of her being.
Returned to America, she set out with renewed zeal and
dedication to share her faith with others. Week after week
her letters would come to 'Abdu'l-Bahá, enclosing declara-
tions of belief from people to whom she had taught the
Faith of Bahá'u'lláh. One of these was Dr Susan Moody.
Before the close of the decade Dr Moody was dispensing
much-needed medical aid in the native land of Bahá'u'lláh.[66]
'Abdu'l-Bahá said laughingly that Mrs Brittingham was our
Bahá'í-maker, and He recalled that Bahá'u'lláh had spoken
of Shaykh Salmán as the Bábí-maker. (Salmán was the tireless courier who walked back and forth between 'Akká
and Írán. He always had letters from new believers to present
to Bahá'u'lláh.)

Lua Getsinger came again on pilgrimage and stayed for
more than a year, to teach English in the household of

* The British public had conferred this epithet on Sulṭán
'Abdu'l-Ḥamíd.

'Abdu'l-Bahá. One day she came face to face with Mírzá Ḥusayn-'Alí-i-Jahrumí, a staunch supporter of Mírzá Muḥammad-'Alí. She told him that she was not concerned with the rank or station of Mírzá Muḥammad-'Alí, but she wanted to know why he would not do what she, an American woman, had done. She had given the Message of Bahá'u'lláh to more than two score eager seekers.

Lua Getsinger sang well, and whenever she sang the famous hymn, 'Nearer my God to Thee', her gaze directed towards the Shrine of Bahá'u'lláh, it brought tears to the eyes of 'Abdu'l-Bahá. Cut off from that sacred Shrine, 'Abdu'l-Bahá had a wooden cabin built on the roof of His house in 'Akká, where a commanding view could be had of the vast plain extending as far as Bahjí; and there many a dawn saw Him, during those years of oppression, rapt in prayer.

When the time came for her to leave, Lua Getsinger wrote a poem addressed to 'Abdu'l-Bahá. Unfortunately the original is not available, but there is a rendition into Persian verse, the work of Dr Yúnis Khán. It is a very moving poem. Retranslated from the Persian, the opening line reads: 'Stay with me, O Lord, in this my journey far'. In Cairo the grave of Lua Getsinger lies next to the grave of the celebrated Mírzá Abu'l-Faḍl. There East and West meet.

In December 1902, Myron H. Phelps, a prominent member of the New York Bar, and Countess M. A. de S. Canavarro spent the whole month in 'Akká, at the invitation of 'Abdu'l-Bahá. 'This month,' writes Myron Phelps, 'was one of the most memorable in my life; for not only was I able to gain a satisfactory general view of this religion, but I made the acquaintance of Abbas Effendi, who is easily the most remarkable man whom it has ever been my fortune to meet.' Phelps witnessed at close quarters the way 'Abdu'l-Bahá lived. We can do no better than to quote extensively from his book: *Abbas Effendi, His Life And Teachings.*

Imagine that we are in the ancient house of the still more ancient city of Akka [writes Myron Phelps], which was for a month my home. The room in which we are faces the opposite wall of a narrow paved street, which an active man might clear at a single bound. Above is the bright sun of Palestine; to the right a glimpse of the old sea-wall and the blue Mediterranean. As we sit we hear a singular sound rising from the pavement, thirty feet below—faint at first, and increasing. It is like the murmur of human voices. We open the window and look down. We see a crowd of human beings with patched and tattered garments. Let us descend to the street and see who these are.

It is a noteworthy gathering. Many of these men are blind; many more are pale, emaciated, or aged . . . Most of the women are closely veiled, but enough are uncovered to cause us well to believe that, if the veils were lifted, more pain and misery would be seen. Some of them carry babes with pinched and sallow faces. There are perhaps a hundred in this gathering, and besides, many children. They are of all the races one meets in these streets—Syrians, Arabs, Ethiopians, and many others.

These people are ranged against the walls or seated on the ground, apparently in an attitude of expectation; —for what do they wait? Let us wait with them.

We have not to wait long. A door opens and a man comes out. He is of middle stature, strongly built. He wears flowing light-coloured robes. On his head is a light buff fez with a white cloth wound about it. He is perhaps sixty years of age. His long grey hair rests on his shoulders. His forehead is broad, full, and high, his nose slightly aquiline, his moustaches and beard, the latter full though not heavy, nearly white. His eyes are grey and blue, large, and both soft and penetrating. His bearing is simple, but there is grace, dignity, and even majesty about his movements. He passes through the crowd, and as he goes utters words of salutation. We do not understand them, but we see the benignity and the kindliness of his countenance. He stations himself at a narrow angle of the street and motions to the people to come towards him. They crowd up a little too insistently. He pushes them gently back and lets them pass him one by one. As they come they hold their hands extended. In each open palm he places some small coins. He knows them all. He caresses them with his hands on the face, on the shoulders, on the head. Some he stops and questions. An aged negro who hobbles up, he greets with some kindly inquiry; the old man's broad face breaks into a sunny smile, his white teeth glistening against his ebony skin as he replies. He stops a woman with a babe and fondly strokes the child. As they pass, some kiss his hand. To all he says, '*Marhabbah*, *marhabbah*'*—'Well done, well done!'

So they all pass him. The children have been crowding around him with extended hands, but to them he has not given. However, at the end, as he turns to go, he throws a handful of coppers over his shoulder, for which they scramble.

During this time this friend of the poor has not been unattended. Several men wearing red fezes, and with earnest and kindly faces, followed him from the house, stood near him and aided in regulating the crowd, and now, with reverent manner and at a respectful distance, follow him away. When they address him they call him 'Master'.

This scene you may see almost any day of the year in the streets of Akka. There are other scenes like it, which come only at the beginning of the winter season. In the cold weather which is approaching, the poor will suffer, for, as in all cities, they are thinly clad. Some day at this season, if you are advised of the place and time, you may see the poor of Akka gathered at one of the shops where clothes

* Marḥabá—a form of greeting.

are sold, receiving cloaks from the Master. Upon many, especially the most infirm or crippled, he himself places the garment, adjusts it with his own hands, and strokes it approvingly, as if to say, 'There! Now you will do well.' There are five or six hundred poor in Akka, to all of whom he gives a warm garment each year.

On feast days he visits the poor at their homes. He chats with them, inquires into their health and comfort, mentions by name those who are absent, and leaves gifts for all.

Nor is it the beggars only that he remembers. Those respectable poor who cannot beg, but must suffer in silence—those whose daily labour will not support their families—to these he sends bread secretly. His left hand knoweth not what his right hand doeth.

All the people know him and love him—the rich and the poor, the young and the old—even the babe leaping in its mother's arms. If he hears of any one sick in the city—Moslem or Christian, or of any other sect, it matters not—he is each day at their bedside, or sends a trusty messenger. If a physician is needed, and the patient poor, he brings or sends one, and also the necessary medicine. If he finds a leaking roof or a broken window menacing health, he summons a workman, and waits himself to see the breach repaired. If any one is in trouble,—if a son or a brother is thrown into prison, or he is threatened at law, or falls into any difficulty too heavy for him,—it is to the Master that he straightway makes appeal for counsel or for aid. Indeed, for counsel all come to him, rich as well as poor. He is the kind father of all the people . . .

For more than thirty-four years this man has been a prisoner at Akka. But his jailors have become his friends. The Governor of the city, the Commander of the Army Corps, respect and honour him as though he were their brother. No man's opinion or recommendation has greater weight with them. He is the beloved of all the city, high and low. And how could it be otherwise? For to this man it is the law, as it was to Jesus of Nazareth, to do good to those who injure him. Have we yet heard of any one in lands which boast the name of Christ who lived that life?

Hear how he treats his enemies. One instance of many I have heard will suffice.

When the Master came to Akka there lived there a certain man* from Afghanistan, an austere and rigid Mussulman.† To him the Master was a heretic. He felt and nourished a great enmity towards the Master, and roused up others against him. When opportunity offered in gatherings of the people, as in the Mosque, he denounced him with bitter words.

'This man,' he said to all, 'is an imposter. Why do you speak to him? Why do you have dealings with him?' And when he passed the Master on the street he was careful to hold his robe before his face that his sight might not be defiled.

Thus did the Afghan. The Master, however, did thus: The Afghan was poor and lived in a mosque; he was frequently in need of food and clothing. The Master sent him both. These he accepted, but without thanks. He fell sick. The Master took him a physician, food, medicine, money. These, also, he accepted; but as he held out one hand that the physician might take his pulse, with the other he held his cloak before his face that he might not look upon the Master. *For twenty-four years* the Master continued his kindnesses and the Afghan persisted in his enmity. Then at last one day the Afghan came to the Master's door, and fell down, penitent and weeping, at his feet.

'Forgive me, sir!' he cried. 'For twenty-four years I have done evil to you, for twenty-four years you have done good to me. Now I know that I have been in the wrong.'

The Master bade him rise, and they became friends.

This Master is as simple as his soul is great. He claims nothing for himself—neither comfort, nor honour, nor

---

* His name was Ḥájí Ṣiddíq.
† Musalmán (Muslim).

repose. Three or four hours of sleep suffice him; all the remainder of his time and all his strength are given to the succour of those who suffer, in spirit or in body. 'I am,' he says, 'the servant of God.'

Such is Abbas Effendi, the Master of Akka.[67]

In February 1903, Mírzá Badí'u'lláh addressed his letter to the Bahá'ís, announcing his break with Mírzá Muḥammad-'Alí and his adherence to 'Abdu'l-Bahá. So did, in a separate letter, Ḥájí Siyyid 'Alíy-i-Afnán, a son of the Great Afnán, and a son-in-law of Bahá'u'lláh. The booklet written by Mírzá Badí'u'lláh, in which he gave details of the plots and machinations of the violators, was later printed in Cairo. Professor Edward Browne was in Cairo in the spring of 1903. On hearing of his arrival in Egypt, Mírzá Badí'u'lláh sent him a letter, dated March 11th, in which he stated, of a certainty, that whatever Mírzá Muḥammad-'Alí had been circulating about 'Abdu'l-Bahá was sheer fabrication, and that Mírzá Muḥammad-'Alí was motivated only by malice and desire for personal gain. Mírzá Badí'u'-lláh further declared to Professor Browne that he had given his own allegiance to 'Abdu'l-Bahá, the one appointed by Bahá'u'lláh. But Mírzá Badí'u'lláh did not remain faithful.

The summer of 1903 witnessed a vicious outbreak of persecutions in Persia. Amínu's-Sulṭán,[68] the resourceful, capable, but unprincipled Ṣadr-i-A'ẓam (prime minister), had held power for more than a decade, under two Sháhs: Náṣiri'd-Dín (reigned 1848–1896) and his son, Muẓaffari'd-Dín (reigned 1896–1907). Pressure was mounting against Amínu's-Sulṭán, both from inside and outside the country. Intrigues, open and covert, led to agitation, at first directed mainly against foreigners, Jews, and Zoroastrians. The calm was first shattered in the north-west, in Tabríz, but it was in the south that the worst barbarities were perpetrated, the victims being the Bahá'ís. As usual, they were made the scapegoats. Sir Arthur Hardinge, the British Minister in Ṭihrán, reported to the Foreign Secretary, Lord Lansdowne, that Amínu's-Sulṭán had expressed his satisfaction at the turn of events 'since attacks upon Christian schools and officials might have greater results than a mere outcry against the Babis'.[69] Shaykh Muḥammad-Taqí, better known as Áqá Najafí, an influential divine of Iṣfahán, to whom Bahá'u'lláh had addressed His 'last outstanding Tablet', the *Epistle to the Son of the Wolf*, brought the mob into the streets and let them loose in his town.[70] Not only did he commit Iṣfahán to anarchy, but both by his example and by direct incitement he drove the people of Yazd to frenzy. The Governor of Yazd, Maḥmúd Mírzá, the Jalálu'd-Dawlih, was a mere cypher, only too glad to save his own skin at the price of dereliction of duty. The madness that gripped the fanatics, and the extravagances of individuals bent on securing personal gain, were intentionally not contained. The virus soon spread to small townships and villages surrounding Yazd. The horrors that ensued paralleled the atrocities of August 1852.

In Iṣfahán, Bahá'ís sought safety in the precincts of the Russian consulate. This move was rather ill-advised, but the threats and inflammatory harangues of Áqá Najafí and the apparent helplessness of the Prince-Governor had made their plight desperate. They were given assurances and persuaded to leave the consulate, but once outside they were attacked in the course of the night. Siyyid Abu'l-Qásim-i-Márnúní, a man of eighty years of age and highly respected in Iṣfahán, was brutally murdered. Mírzá Asadu'lláh Khán, Vizier of Iṣfahán, in charge of its finances for nearly thirty years, and a life-long Bahá'í, could do nothing to avert disaster; and he himself did not escape unscathed, in spite of his high position. However nothing happened in Iṣfahán to approximate what transpired in Yazd and its vicinity.

The first martyr of Yazd was an artisan, Ḥájí Mírzáy-i-Ḥalabí-Sáz,* who, on becoming a Bahá'í, had taken up a trade and abandoned the practice of receiving money from the well-to-do, in return for performing on their behalf the pilgrimage to Mecca. Refusing to be any longer a proxy on such an errand had angered many. The mob broke into his modest house, wrecked it, beat him and his wife, hauled him into the bazar where with a cleaver they slashed his skull open and hacked off an arm. His wife was left helpless, covered with severe wounds. None but a prostitute took pity on her to provide her with medicaments and clothing. Their eleven-year-old son was ordered by the schoolmaster to recant and to abuse the Faith of his parents. The child replied that he was not old enough to pass judgment, and in any case he could not utter imprecations; whereupon, prompted and aided by the teacher, other boys assailed him with stick and penknife. Later, they who murdered him attested that as they stifled that young life, the child was calling out: 'Yá Bahá'u'l-Abhá'—O Glory, the Most Glorious.

In that same city of Yazd, Áqá Muḥammad, a young man of twenty-seven, was butchered in the presence of his mother. His throat was partly cut, but he stayed alive. Then the mob pulled him about for hours in the streets, before giving him the *coup de grâce*. Such were his sufferings that the Prince-Governor wept over his story.

In the village of Taft, Áqá Ḥusayn, a youth of eighteen, was denounced by his own father and handed to the mob. They tore him to pieces in front of a bewailing mother who was holding aloft a copy of the Qur'án, pleading for the life of her son.

In the village of Hanzá, a woman named Fáṭimih Bagum had succeeded in hiding her brother, Siyyid Muḥammad-'Alíy-i-Gázir. Amidst jeers she was dragged out of her home,

* Tinsmith.

and with the thrust of a dagger her chest and abdomen were slit open. Then her body was trussed up and left hanging from a tree over a blazing fire. The cords were consumed by the flames, and the suspended corpse fell down. But strangely, when the fire was burnt out, and the village cleric allowed her mother to see what could be retrieved of the corpse, it was found that fire had not harmed it. Villagers were astounded, but it did not stop them tricking the aged mother to reveal the hiding-place of her son. Siyyid Muḥammad-'Alí was found and, while being beaten, he was driven mercilessly over open fields. Overcome by thirst, he begged for water. A brook was pointed to him to drink from, but before he had the chance to drink, he went down before a volley of bullets.

Thus did scores of Bahá'ís, young and old, men and women, perish in Yazd and its environs.

Áqá 'Alí-Riḍáy-i-Sha'r-Báf was the last of these martyrs. He had left Yazd to stay with his niece on a farm. Once traced there, seven men went out in search of him, two of whom were young men apprenticed to him. They told him that they had come to take him back to town, to help to dispel suspicions lurking around him. Áqá 'Alí-Riḍá was not unaware of their purpose. He offered them refreshments and lunch. 'Linger awhile,' he said, 'no need to hurry, your quarry will not escape you.' After luncheon, he said farewell to his niece, and set out with his uninvited guests. Away from the farm, one of them shot him, though not fatally. Áqá 'Alí-Riḍá sat down and covered his eyes. He had done so, he said, that his apprentices might not feel deterred; let them shoot if they wished. His severed head was carried in a bag to Yazd and delivered to his wife. She was told that it was a gift from her husband.

Central provinces being so convulsed, other areas of Írán were naturally not left undisturbed. To the north of Iṣfahán, in the city of Káshán, Muslim divines were joined by Jewish leaders in their denunciations. A large number of Bahá'ís took sanctuary in the telegraph office.* The Governor, Muḥammad-Ja'far Khán, telegraphed the Ṣadr-i-A'ẓam to the effect that Bahá'ís must be suppressed as they constituted a danger to the Jewish Faith. The wily and astute Amínu's-Sulṭán was highly amused. This outcry resulted in the imposition of heavy fines on Bahá'ís of Jewish background, and the infliction of corporal punishment on others. To the west, in Hamadán, Riḍá-Qulí Sulṭán, a military commander sent from Ṭihrán, was assassinated. Not far away, in Maláyir, a dervish created such turmoil that many had to leave the town, and Mírzá Ismá'íl-i-Khayyát (Tailor), a Bahá'í well-known and well-liked in the locality, was murdered. 'Abdu'l-Bahá honoured him with the title Siráju'-sh-Shuhadá—The Lamp of the Martyrs.

By the middle of September the position of Amínu's-Sulṭán was untenable. He either resigned (perhaps hoping it would not be accepted), or was dismissed, and went abroad. With his downfall, all agitation ceased and a deceptive calm settled over Írán.

In future years 'Abdu'l-Bahá was to speak of the agony He experienced when the blood of the Bahá'ís flowed so freely in the centre of Persia. At the time, a remarkable Tablet came from His pen, in which He described the course of the persecutions. The previous year He had told the Bahá'ís of 'Akká to pray for their fellow-believers in Yazd, because danger threatened them. What He foresaw had come to pass. 'Abdu'l-Bahá says in the same Tablet (mark also these words):

Decreed by God, the veil will be lifted from the visage of the Cause, and this Light will illumine the horizons

* This was common practice for individuals and groups to seek 'bast' (sanctuary) in the telegraph office, and communicate with the authorities in the capital.

of all lands. Evidences of the Faith of God will prevail, and the standards of your Lord, the Exalted, will wave aloft mighty heights. Foundations of doubt will crumble, and clouds of darkness will be riven apart. The morn of certainty will break, and the resplendence of wondrous signs will suffuse the Kingdom of earth and heaven. Then will be seen the banners of factions cast down, the faces of foes transmogrified, the edicts of false leaders discarded, believers immeasurably blissful, deniers in manifest loss.[71]

The intrigues of Mírzá Muḥammad-'Alí and his associates were ceaseless. Their attempts to stop or delay the construction of the mausoleum on Mount Carmel were particularly abhorrent. Some Bahá'ís, feeling outraged, requested 'Abdu'l-Bahá to expose the misdeeds of the violators, and lay the case before the Ottoman authorities. 'Abdu'l-Bahá did not accede to their request; He would not, He said, present to the world at large the family of Bahá'u'lláh, Whose mission is to unify the entire human race, as the wreckers of the edifice of that unity.

In the West, Bahá'ís were seeking ways and means of liberating 'Abdu'l-Bahá from the yoke of Ottoman tyranny. An appreciable sum of money was collected in Paris by Mme Jackson and Hippolyte Dreyfus with the aid of two other Bahá'ís. They intended to go to Constantinople and arrange 'Abdu'l-Bahá's release. As soon as 'Abdu'l-Bahá was informed, He cabled them not to proceed with their plans. Somehow the news leaked out and the violators heard of it. It provided them with a weapon to use against 'Abdu'l-Bahá. Káẓim Páshá, the Válí of Beirut, was told that if the Paris scheme had gone forward, he would have benefited to the extent of thirty thousand pounds. 'Abdu'l-Bahá, they insinuated, had placed the ban because He was unfriendly towards the Válí. Káẓim Páshá was infuriated and his hostility increased.

By the year 1904, 'Abdu'l-Bahá had planned and put into execution two undertakings of great significance: the restoration of the house of the Báb in S͟híráz, and the construction of the first Mas͟hriqu'l-Ad͟hkár of the Bahá'í world in the city of 'Is͟hqábád. (Askabad). During the very period when Persia was witnessing a sustained and barbaric persecution of the Bahá'ís, 'Abdu'l-Bahá sent an urgent call to Áqá Mírzá Áqá, an outstanding member of the family of the Báb and a nephew of His wife, to start immediately the work of restoration. That house—in which the Báb had declared His mission to Mullá Ḥusayn-i-Bus͟hrú'í, and the custodianship of which Bahá'u'lláh had placed in perpetuity in the care of Áqá Mírzá Áqá and his descendants—had been altered in the course of years, and the passage of time had thinned the ranks of those who remembered its original form and design. Under 'Abdu'l-Bahá's direction Áqá Mírzá Áqá prepared a plan, which included every detail of the house as it had stood in the days of the Báb. Despite difficulties and dangers the house was renovated and restored. Soon after, Áqá Mírzá Áqá, whose intimate knowledge and close supervision had been of inestimable value, passed away. 'Abdu'l-Bahá's foresight had guided an important and necessary task to a successful conclusion before it was too late.

During the eighties of the last century, a new town, which came to be called 'Is͟hqábád, sprang up and flourished in the then Russian Turkistán. 'Is͟hqábád* is close to the Iranian province of K͟hurásán, only a short distance from the border. Persian Bahá'ís, harassed in their native land, were attracted to 'Is͟hqábád, as were others of their countrymen. Among the latter were men who intensely disliked the Bahá'ís, some motivated by prejudice, some by envy. There was also no lack of hirelings and adventurers. Their plot-

* 'Is͟hqábád or Askabad is situated in the present-day Soviet Republic of Turkmenistan.

tings led, in September 1889, to the murder of Ḥájí Muḥam-mad-Riḍáy-i-Iṣfahání. In broad daylight and in the middle of the bazar he was attacked and stabbed to death by two hired assassins. The police arrested those men, but the lives of other Bahá'ís were in jeopardy. Accusation had been levelled against the martyred Ḥájí Muḥammad Riḍá that he had spoken disparagingly of the Imáms. His lamentable language, it was claimed, had aroused the ire of men who were deeply religious. Mírzá Abu'l-Faḍl happened to be in 'Ishqábád. He sought a meeting with the Russian Governor and presented the case for the Bahá'ís: they believed in and honoured all the Manifestations of God; their Faith enjoined upon them to live in harmony with the followers of all religions; they too revered the Imáms * whom the Shí'ahs revered.

The Czar, Alexander III, sent a military commission from St Petersburg to conduct the trial. The two assailants were found guilty of murder and sentenced to death. Six others, proved to have been involved in the murder plot, were ordered to be transported to Siberia. Strenuous efforts were made to have the verdict altered, but to no avail. However, right at the foot of the scaffold it was announced that the Bahá'ís had magnanimously interceded for the murderers, who were banished to Siberia. Bahá'ís gained greatly in prestige. Furthermore, the ground was now prepared for the initiation of enterprises, such as the establishment of schools, libraries and the construction of a House of Worship—the Mashriqu'l-Adhkár.

The task of raising that edifice in 'Ishqábád was entrusted by 'Abdu'l-Bahá to Ḥájí Mírzá Muḥammad-Taqí, the Vakíl-u'd-Dawlih, son of Ḥájí Siyyid Muḥammad, the uncle of the Báb, for whom Bahá'u'lláh had revealed the *Kitáb-i-Íqán* (The Book of Certitude), in answer to his questions. The general design of that House of Worship was delineated

* Apostolic successors to Muḥammad.

by 'Abdu'l-Bahá Himself; and a Russian architect, Volkov, planned and executed the details of construction.

Ḥájí Mírzá Muḥammad-Taqí resided in Yazd. On his way to 'Iṣhqábád, where he and his relatives already owned extensive properties, he stopped at Maṣhhad, the holy city that holds the Shrine of Imám Riḍá, the eighth Imám. Ḥájí Mírzá Muḥammad-Taqí was well known and his arrival at Maṣhhad caused a stir. A plot was hatched to deny him entry to the Shrine. Naṣíri'd-Dawlih, a native of Shíráz, custodian of the Shrine and its vast endowments and institutions, was a personal friend of Ḥájí Mírzá Muḥammad-Taqí. Together they visited the Shrine and performed the required ceremonies. This event also redounded to the prestige of the Cause.

The corner-stone of the Maṣhriqu'l-Adhkár was laid in December 1902, in the presence of leading officials. Thereafter the work went ahead without interruption. By the year 1907 the dome of the Temple was in place, and Ḥájí Mírzá Muḥammad-Taqí had used the larger part of his own fortune to rear that noble building. Now 'Abdu'l-Bahá invited him to visit 'Akká. He reached the Holy Land at the close of the year. An eyewitness, Dr Ḥabíb Mu'ayyad,* has given us a picture of the meeting between 'Abdu'l-Bahá and Ḥájí Mírzá Muḥammad-Taqí. The small boat bringing the latter ashore had been overwhelmed by high waves, and he had been thrown into the sea. At his advanced age the experience was alarming and had left him very weak. 'Abdu'l-Bahá, much concerned about his health and comfort, told the pilgrims that He and they would all go together and call on the Afnán. All that he could return to 'Abdu'l-Bahá's tender enquiries was to recite the first line of a famous couplet, unable to complete it: 'Thy presence I craved, to open to Thee my heart.'

Ḥájí Mírzá Muḥammad-Taqí lived the rest of his life in

* In his *Khátirát-i-Ḥabíb* (Memoirs of Ḥabíb), 1961.

the Holy Land. He died in Haifa in the year 1911. His grave, at the foot of Mount Carmel, lies next to the grave of John Ebenezer Esslemont,* the Scottish disciple of 'Abdu'l-Bahá, and the distinguished author of *Bahá'u'lláh and the New Era*. There too, as in Cairo, where the graves of Mírzá Abu'l-Faḍl and Lua Getsinger adjoin each other, the East and the West meet.

It was to this cousin of the Báb that 'Abdu'l-Bahá had addressed these prophetic words, when He Himself stood in grave peril:

> How great, how very great is the Cause! How very fierce the onslaught of all the peoples and kindreds of the earth. Ere long shall the clamour of the multitude throughout Africa, throughout America, the cry of the European and of the Turk, the groaning of India and China, be heard from far and near. One and all, they shall arise with all their power to resist His Cause. Then shall the knights of the Lord, assisted by His grace from on high, strengthened by faith, aided by the power of understanding, and reinforced by the legions of the Covenant, arise and make manifest the truth of the verse: 'Behold the confusion that hath befallen the tribes of the defeated!'[72]

The year 1904 brought fresh tribulations. Wild rumours, fed to the public by the partisans of Mírzá Muḥammad-'Alí, created confusion and unrest within 'Akká. Newly-appointed officials were unfriendly, even hostile. Their attitude, and the attitude of certain sections of the inhabitants of 'Akká and Haifa, became more and more menacing. Disturbing reports about 'Abdu'l-Bahá appeared in the newspapers of Syria and Egypt. Dr Mírzá Muḥammad-Mihdí Khán, the Za'ímu'd-Dawlih, owner and editor of a Persian newspaper in Cairo, had already published his book, *Miftáḥu Bábi'l-Abwáb*[73] (The Key to the Gate of Gates). Ostensibly

* Died November 1925.

it was a straightforward and sober account of the Faith of the
Báb and Bahá'u'lláh, but in fact a distortion of truth, and in
effect, as attested by 'Abdu'l-Bahá, it was intended to arouse
passions against the Bahá'ís.

The violators now proceeded to draw up an indictment
against 'Abdu'l-Bahá, replete with absurd and baseless
accusations. Witnesses were sought and found among the
people of 'Akká, willing and ready to append their signatures to false documents. These papers the supporters of
Mírzá Muḥammad-'Alí sent to Constantinople through
channels known to them, in the sure hope that the tyrant
'Abdu'l-Ḥamíd would be alarmed and would take measures
to destroy 'Abdu'l-Bahá. In due course a Commission of
Enquiry arrived, dispatched by order of the Sulṭán.

Spies were planted around the house of 'Abdu'l-Bahá.
They kept close watch throughout the day, and could be
seen stealing about at night. Fright seized many who had
previously frequented that house. Now, they kept away.
The Bahá'ís of 'Akká were made to feel that their presence
there was not desired. To ease their burdens and to forestall
uglier scenes, 'Abdu'l-Bahá decided that they should seek
temporary residence elsewhere. The redoubtable Ḥájí
Mírzá Ḥaydar-'Alí had already left to undertake another of
his historic journeys through Írán. He was in 'Ishqábád
when the crisis heightened in the Holy Land. Many of the
Bahá'ís of 'Akká needed financial support to be able to
abandon, even for a short while, their homes and their means
of living. 'Abdu'l-Bahá Himself borrowed a large sum of
money from an American in Paris, to facilitate their move to
Egypt. Some seventy of them went. At the same time the
number of pilgrims was drastically reduced, and then all
pilgrimage, either from the East or the West, was totally
halted. 'Andalíb,[74] learned and versatile poet, voiced emotions shared by the Bahá'ís. For years, he wrote, referring
to the violators, they, out of envy, flung every door wide

open upon calumny; and now, because of them, the doors of bounty are shut upon the faces of all.

The Commission summoned 'Abdu'l-Bahá to answer the accusations levelled against Him. He met the members of the Commission several times. In no uncertain terms He told them that the charges preferred were patently threadbare, that the Writings of Bahá'u'lláh, which were shown to them, made it inconceivable that He, the Son of Bahá'u'lláh and His Successor, could ever be implicated in any nefarious design to overthrow the Ottoman rule, that He was ready to meet any insult, any injury, any harm which they might devise to inflict upon Him. Mírzá Muḥammad-'Alí, a superb calligraphist of the first rank, had written the emblem: Yá Bahá'u'l-Abhá (O Glory, the Most Glorious) on a piece of cloth, and had sent it to the authorities with the statement that this was the standard which 'Abdu'l-Bahá had contrived. It was also alleged that Mírzá Dhikru'lláh, the son of Mírzá Muḥammad-Qulí,* had hoisted this standard in Galilee to invite support, and furthermore, that Shaykh Maḥmúd of 'Akká had gone with it among the Bedouin beyond Jordan to incite them to revolt. To this preposterous charge 'Abdu'l-Bahá observed that it was miraculous that a standard so prominently displayed had not been noticed by the numerous agents of the Válí, Rashíd Páshá. Another charge against 'Abdu'l-Bahá was that He had acquired vast tracts of land, to serve as the base for the kingdom He craved. It would be nothing short of a miracle, 'Abdu'l-Bahá replied, if He, a prisoner of the Turkish Empire, Who was kept under surveillance, Whose movements were closely watched and scrutinized, had succeeded in establishing the base for a kingdom; in any case He was willing to sell all those huge acres for only two thousand pounds.

* The faithful half-brother of Bahá'u'lláh who had staunchly upheld His Covenant and stood loyally by the side of 'Abdu'l-Bahá. At this date he was deceased.

All the charges were demolished. Then the Commission asked for what reason the Americans came to 'Akká. 'Abdu'l-Bahá replied that they came to visit the Shrine of Bahá'u'lláh and to learn of spiritual matters. The Commission then asked what 'Abdu'l-Bahá had to say to the charge that He had distributed seditious literature, seen to be in His possession. Such material, He answered, had not been in His possession and no one could have seen it. The Commission had cajoled, bribed, or forced a number of people to come and give evidence to the contrary. Now these witnesses were mentioned. At that 'Abdu'l-Bahá rose up, majestic and commanding, declared emphatically that no seditious literature could ever have been in His possession, and walked out of the room unhindered. Thereafter the whole enquiry collapsed.

'Abdu'l-Bahá's mail was, as a rule, directed to Haifa, where a resident Bahá'í, Ḥájí Siyyid Muḥammad-Taqíy-i-Manshádí, received it and took it to 'Akká. Developments in the course of 1904 made it imperative that mail should be diverted. It went instead to Port Said. During a very critical period, 'Abdu'l-Bahá decided that the mail directed to Port Said should be held there and not be re-routed to the Holy Land. But neither was the pen of 'Abdu'l-Bahá stilled, nor the stream of letters addressed to Him checked. On the contrary those very months of exacting strain constituted a particularly fertile and creative period in the ministry of 'Abdu'l-Bahá. Oftentimes the light in His room could be seen burning to the hour of sunrise, as He wrote steadily throughout the night. As many as ninety Tablets flowed from His pen in one day. His followers and others who bore no allegiance to Him, both in the East and in the West, wrote to Him in ever-increasing volume. Eventually they all received answers from Him.

As the year 1904 drew to its close, normality gradually

returned. Pilgrims and visitors came once again. Bahá'ís who had gone to Egypt and elsewhere could also return. Friendly officials replaced those who were hostile. The most notable displacement was that of the Chief of Police, Yaḥyá Bey, who had become an accomplice of the violators. His reports and telegrams had inflamed the situation and strengthened the suspicions of the authorities in Constantinople. But when he tried to implicate another Ottoman official, of a rank higher than his own, he was ordered to Damascus. In despair, Yaḥyá Bey went to 'Abdu'l-Bahá to seek protection for his family in his absence. 'Abdu'l-Bahá assured him that he could go away with an easy mind and have no anxiety for the safety and welfare of his family. As He had promised, 'Abdu'l-Bahá saw generously to the needs of Yaḥyá Bey's family, but the ex-Chief of Police did not give up his previous associations. The violators had produced an apologia in English, ostensibly the work of a Bahá'í, written to extol 'Abdu'l-Bahá as Christ incarnate, and to assert that He, being the Lord of the Kingdom, could and did command the submission of all the sovereign authorities of the world. Their purpose was evident: to misrepresent the nature and purport of Bahá'í teaching in the Western world. Furthermore, the image of 'Abdu'l-Bahá as one seeking temporal power was bound to incense Sulṭán 'Abdu'l-Ḥamíd, whose realms, particularly in the Balkans, were plagued with unrest. The violators sent a copy of their forgery to Yaḥyá Bey in Damascus, and persuaded him to translate it into Arabic and Turkish, and publish the two versions as a warning to the powers in the land. These translations reached Constantinople. But 'Abdu'l-Bahá still extended His aid to the family of the ex-Chief of Police.

Many years before, in the days of Bahá'u'lláh, 'Akká had had an official, in charge of the secretariat, named Muṣṭafá Effendi, who constantly incited the Governor to make life unbearable for the Bahá'ís. And the Governor was not averse to using the occasion for personal gain. To his various stratagems 'Abdu'l-Bahá paid no attention. The Governor hit upon the idea of forcing the Bahá'í shopkeepers to close down. 'Abdu'l-Bahá forestalled him and advised them to stop trading. Baulked, the Governor called a meeting in his residence of the notables and the divines who were hostile towards the Bahá'ís. It was intended to concert a plan of action. In the meantime, Sa'da'd-Dín Ramaḍán, the chief of the merchants, hurried to see 'Abdu'l-Bahá. He begged for money. Only money, he pleaded, would make the Governor give up his machinations; there was no time to lose. 'Abdu'l-Bahá kept him waiting, while he thought that 'Abdu'l-Bahá was filling a purse with gold that he might take it to the Governor. For his pains he had only a hard slap in the face from 'Abdu'l-Bahá, and was told not to tarry there, as money had already been sent to the Governor. But what the Governor of 'Akká received was a telegram from the Válí in Beirut, dismissing him and other officials. Three months later this ex-Governor was further humiliated and banished to Damascus. He had to leave his family behind in 'Akká. 'Abdu'l-Bahá provided both for him and his family; and in due time, meeting all the expenses, He arranged to reunite them. Thus did 'Abdu'l-Bahá treat the fallen adversary.

The years 1905 and 1906 were relatively free of pressures and impositions. Pilgrims and resident Bahá'ís alike found the environment of 'Akká more relaxed. On the other hand, the Ottoman domains and Persia were in the throes of rising discontent. The extravagances of Muẓaffari'd-Dín S̲h̲áh had propelled Persia from one disastrous foreign loan to another. She was beholden to Russia and to Britain as well. As the Russian influence was in the ascendant, Britain was unhappy. On the other hand, Kaiser Wilhelm II was trying to throw Germany's protecting arm round the 'Sick Man of Europe',* which made both Russia and Britain unhappy. The autocracy and stubborn unreasonableness of Prince 'Aynu'd-Dawlih, the ailing Sháh's grand vizier, was driving almost everybody to despair. And Sulṭán 'Abdu'l-Ḥamíd had, throughout his reign, resorted to every ruse to keep everyone at loggerheads. After a quarter of a century of ceaseless chicanery he was weary, but still ruthless.

In August 1906, chiefly through the active support of Mr Grant Duff, the British Chargé d'Affaires in Ṭihrán, the Persian reformists, who had taken sanctuary in the grounds of the British Legation, got the ear of Muẓaffari'd-Dín Sháh, and the monarch, no more than four months from his death, promised the grant of a constitution and the election of a national assembly. 'Abdu'l-Ḥamíd, aware of ominous rumblings throughout his own ramshackle empire, was thoroughly alarmed. Frenziedly he tried to tighten his hold, but the iron grip of yore had turned feeble and his grasp was unsure. Persians arriving at Istanbul, if taking boat from there, were not allowed to land at any of the ports of the Eastern Mediterranean, lest the contagion of their revolutionary thought should spread. They had to go instead to Jeddah in Arabia, the port of Mecca. Mírzá Muḥammad-Taqí, the Vakílu'd-Dawlih, was nearly sent on to Arabia. But Bahá'í pilgrims coming through Istanbul found a way to circumvent 'Abdu'l-Ḥamíd's ordinance. They went to Greece or Italy, then on to Egypt where they had no difficulty in embarking for the port of Haifa.

'Abdu'l-Ḥamíd was frightened, and the violators realized that the chance to play on his fears was too good to miss. Although a good deal of their strength had gone from them, they rallied their forces for what proved to be their final, concerted but futile assault. True, a decade later, in the course of the Great War, they made another move which could have been calamitous, but it was of local proportions. For

* The Ottoman Empire.

that matter, over the next fifty years, their remnants continued their opposition, until time obliterated the traces of
their mischief.

As a consequence of their intrigues, a Commission of four,
under the chairmanship of 'Árif Bey, arrived in the winter
of 1907 post-haste from the seat of the Empire. They came
bringing with them documents and papers which a previous
Commission of Enquiry had found unsubstantiated and had
discarded.* For their residence they chose the house of
'Abdu'l-Ghaní Baydún, a local magnate and a close associate of the violators. Their first act was to stamp their own
authority upon the administration of 'Akká. Officials, including the Governor, who were regarded as friendly
towards 'Abdu'l-Bahá, were instantly dismissed; both the
post and the telegraph were placed under strict scrutiny; the
time-honoured overlordship of the Válí at Damascus was
explicitly ignored, and direct communication was established with the ministers of the Sultán in Istanbul. Spies
were once again planted around the house of 'Abdu'l-
Bahá, and once again people were kept away. Even the poor
of 'Akká dared not come, as was their wont on Fridays, to
receive alms.

Rumours were rife that 'Abdu'l-Bahá would be forcibly
removed to Fízán in Tripolitania, a vast expanse of desert,
totally cut off from the rest of the world. However, to the
astonishment of the inhabitants of 'Akká, 'Abdu'l-Bahá
could be seen engaged in normal activities, apparently unconscious of rumours and completely indifferent to the
presence of the powerful and high-handed Commission of
Enquiry. He attended to repairs of His house, which He
rented. The agent of the landlord was puzzled. He could not
understand why all that care and expense were bestowed on
repairs and improvements, since he was certain, as was
almost everyone, that before long 'Abdu'l-Bahá would be

* See p. 114.

banished from 'Akká. 'Abdu'l-Bahá told the agent that it
was surely commendable to repair and construct. One of the
notables of 'Akká visiting Him found Him planting a tree.
For whom do you plant this tree? the notable enquired.
Those who preceded us planted and we have enjoyed the
fruit, replied 'Abdu'l-Bahá; it is our duty to do the same to
benefit those who come after us. The people of 'Akká were
even more astonished to discover that 'Abdu'l-Bahá was
buying and storing fuel for the winter.

A few days before the arrival of the Commission of Enquiry 'Abdu'l-Bahá had a dream which He related to the
Bahá'ís. He dreamt that a ship sailed into the bay of Haifa,
and birds resembling dynamite flew inland from it. The
people of 'Akká were terrified, and He stood among them,
calm and collected, watching these birds. They circled and
circled over the town and then went back whence they
had come. There was no explosion. 'Abdu'l-Bahá said that
danger loomed, but it would pass and no harm would
result.

The violators were naturally jubilant. The residence of the
members of the Commission was close to theirs. They could
obtain all the news they wanted. The day the Commission
arrived Mírzá Muhammad-'Alí and his party forgathered in
the shop of Áqá Muhammad-Javád-i-Qazvíní to celebrate
the occasion. At long last what they had striven and toiled,
borrowed and bribed to bring about, was now tantalizingly
within their reach. 'Abdu'l-Bahá's doom was as clear to
them as the blue of the Mediterranean. Extinction awaited
Him in the landlocked sandy wastes of Fízán. He could
surely never come away alive from those torrid, inhospitable
regions. Such was their alluring vision of the immediate
future. Their euphoria lasted for nearly a month.

But 'Abdu'l-Bahá categorically refused to call on the
members of the Commission of Enquiry. Should He do so,
He maintained, and the Commission acquitted Him of all

charges, people would say that He had bribed His way out
of His trouble. Had these distinguished men been merely
visitors to 'Akká, He added, He would unhesitatingly have
called on them. A certain Shaykh Muḥammad, who presided over the Criminal Court, was sent to persuade 'Abdu'l-Bahá to change His mind. This Shaykh feigned friendship. The members of the Commission, he said, had had
visits from everyone of note in the city of 'Akká except
'Abdu'l-Bahá; they were furious and nothing but a personal call on them would assuage their anger. The Shaykh
insisted that for the sake of His own safety 'Abdu'l-Bahá
should do what all the leading men of 'Akká had done.
Were He to do so, 'Abdu'l-Bahá calmly replied, it would
look as if He were currying favour, and He had nothing
to answer for, no favours to seek. The Shaykh went away
crest-fallen.

Not to be outdone, Khalíl Páshá, the Válí in Beirut, told
his deputy 'Abda'r-Raḥmán al-Ḥút to write to the Governor
of 'Akká that 'Abdu'l-Bahá must be put on trial. The
deputy spoke in that letter of ' 'Abbás Bahá'í'. 'Abdu'l-
Bahá remarked to the Governor that He was grateful for
having been called simply 'Abbás, thereby placing Him in the
ranks of the Prophets. Had one ever heard of Moses Bey,
Jesus Effendi, Muḥammad Áqá? And at the same time He
challenged His oppressors: they should know that God
had not created Him to be abased because, contrary to their
belief, humiliating Him, chaining Him, dragging Him in the
mire, crucifying Him, would not bring Him degradation,
but radiant glory.

Newspapers in Beirut and Cairo reported the molestation
of Persians in 'Akká. Indeed, well-established Bahá'í merchants trading in Egypt had been prevented from leaving
'Akká, and Bahá'ís in 'Akká had been put under heavy
restraint. Írán's Ambassador in Istanbul, perturbed by what
he read in the newspapers, sent a representative, Muḥam-

mad-Ibráhím Big, to protect the interests of Persian sub-jects. However, the authorities in 'Akká were adamant and the Ambassador's representative proposed to lodge a strong protest in Beirut and Istanbul. 'Abdu'l-Bahá advised him to wait: these troubles would not last long. And they did not.

One night a man drove from Haifa to 'Akká in a covered carriage. He was an Italian who acted as Consul for Spain. Members of his family had the agency for an Italian steam-ship company. Taking great care not to be noticed and recog-nized, he managed to reach the house of 'Abdu'l-Bahá and asked to meet Him immediately. In the bay was an Italian cargo boat which this man, in his great love and regard for 'Abdu'l-Bahá, had kept waiting, moving it from one end of the bay to the other to avert suspicion; and now he had come to offer Him a safe passage to any port He might desire. Time was running out. 'Abdu'l-Bahá asked Ḥájí Mírzá Ḥaydar-'Alí, Áqá Riḍáy-i-Qannád, Mírzá Maḥ-múd-i-Káshí, Siyyid Yaḥyá (His brother-in-law), and Mírzá Asadu'lláh to consult, and give Him their opinion. They unanimously resolved to request 'Abdu'l-Bahá to accept the Consul's offer. But His response was: The Báb did not run away, and I shall not run away.

In the meantime the Commission of Enquiry was receiving evidence from the very people who had signed the letters of indictment, and was being bombarded by cables from 'Abdu'l-Ḥamíd. They also visited the mausoleum on Mount Carmel which was nearing completion. It was, it is, a very solid building; it had to be to serve its purpose. But the Commission ignored that purpose. There were vaults under the building, a fact they considered to be very significant, as they had been told that 'Abdu'l-Bahá was constructing a fortress.

Soon after this visit they boarded the boat which had brought them from Constantinople and now lay anchored off Haifa. The sun was westering. The boat turned towards 'Akká. The whole populace of the two cities could see it set on this menacing course. They believed that 'Abdu'l-Bahá was about to be arrested and taken on board. They were convinced that He would be transported to Fízán, or to some other remote and dreary region where he would surely perish. The family of 'Abdu'l-Bahá and other Bahá'ís were in despair. But 'Abdu'l-Bahá, calm and serene, was walking all alone in the courtyard of His house. Here and there, at vantage points along the shores of 'Akká, anxious Bahá'ís were watching the movement of that boat of ill omen. The sun sank in the Mediterranean, and the boat kept its course. It came very close to 'Akká, but then, all of a sudden, changed direction and made for the open sea. In an instant danger had vanished. 'Abdu'l-Bahá was safe. When the news was brought to Him dusk had fallen, and He was still calmly walking in His courtyard—with 'radiant acquiescence'.

In the wake of the hurried departure of the Commission news came from Istanbul that 'Abdu'l-Hamíd had narrowly escaped death. A bomb meant for him had exploded, killing and injuring others. An attempt of this nature on a Friday, when the Caliph surrounded by the pomp of 'Selamlik'* was returning from the mosque, was not only outrageous but, more than that, blasphemous, an obscenity in the eyes of the orthodox. The Commission of Enquiry reached Istanbul at a time most unpropitious. 'Abdu'l-Hamíd was now wide awake to the threat of impending revolution. All his thought and action were focused on discovering and destroying the revolutionaries in and around his capital. Despite the expenditure of vast sums of money and the activities of a large number of spies, Munír Páshá, his ambassador to Paris—where for years refugees from his tyranny

* A public appearance of the Sultán, who was also Caliph, with both religious and imperial overtones.

had been conspiring and plotting to overthrow him—had failed to uncover the identity of the leaders of the Committee of Union and Progress. When the Commission of Enquiry presented its voluminous report, packed with untruth, to 'Abdu'l-Ḥamíd, he pushed it aside. Another time will do, he said. And so the report on which the adversaries of 'Abdu'l-Bahá had pinned their hopes was set aside to gather dust. Months later, when 'Abdu'l-Ḥamíd's attention was drawn to it, it was too late. In Monastir and Salonika, both of which were soon to be wrested from Ottoman rule, Young Turks of the Committee of Union and Progress had raised the banner of revolt; and 'Abdu'l-Ḥamíd knew that the days of his despotism were numbered. He had no alternative but to submit. The Central Committee in Monastir issued a declaration on July 23rd 1908, demanding the restoration of the constitution, dead for thirty years, within twenty-four hours. This was Midḥat Páshá's old constitution which 'Abdu'l-Ḥamíd himself had suspended. The Sulṭán was told, in no uncertain terms, that should he fail to comply with the Committee's demands the Second and Third Army Corps would bring him down. They were ready and poised for action. Apparently the Grand Orient had done its work well. The next day the 'Iradé'—royal rescript—gave the constitution back to the people of the Empire. And all the political and religious prisoners of 'Abdu'l-Ḥamíd were set free. Notwithstanding, such were the fears and opposition engendered in 'Akká that officials sent a cable to Constantinople, enquiring whether 'Abdu'l-Bahá, too, was to be given His liberty. They were instructed to do so.

'Abdu'l-Ḥamíd was anxious to safeguard his position as a constitutional monarch, but within nine months he fell into the trap of a counter-revolution. The Committee of Union and Progress, so vociferously hailed in liberal quarters in Europe, was both arrogant and inept. The shameless and

cynical behaviour of European Powers, and the clamourings
of the still subjugated Macedonians, Greeks and Albanians,
made the tasks of the new régime even more difficult.
In October, Aehrenthal, the Austrian Foreign Minister,
having duped Isvolsky, the ambitious Foreign Minister
of the Czar, annexed Bosnia and Herzegovina, provinces
which Austria-Hungary had administered since 1878 on trust
from Turkey. Immediately the 'old fox', Ferdinand of Bulgaria, annexed Eastern Roumelia and declared his independence. On April 13th 1909 troops mutinied in Istanbul
and the Young Turks were overthrown, but within a week
the Arab General, Maḥmúd Shawkat Páshá, arrived with
troops from Salonika, and within a fortnight 'Abdu'l-
Ḥamíd was deposed. He died nine years later, and all those
years he was under close surveillance.

Murders go hand in hand with political upheavals. The
restored régime of Young Turks put to death, in one day,
thirty-one of the ministers and functionaries of the old
régime. Among them were a number of the adversaries
of the Faith of Bahá'u'lláh. 'Árif Bey, who had headed that
notorious Commission of Enquiry, was shot by a sentry.
Two of his colleagues also perished. The fourth, Adham
Bey, the Damascene, fled to Egypt and one day presented
himself at the business-house of Ḥájí Mírzá Ḥasan-i-
Khurásání in Alexandria. His servant had stolen all he had.
He could not even take himself to Cairo. He was given a
small sum of money. When 'Abdu'l-Bahá was informed He
sent Adham Bey ten pounds. Thereafter nothing was heard
of him. The ex-police chief of 'Akká, now totally discredited
and reduced to penury, also received special consideration
from 'Abdu'l-Bahá; so did others, foes of yesteryear, now
fallen on evil days.

It was in the course of those years of peril that 'Abdu'l-
Bahá wrote, at intervals, His Will and Testament, charac-

terized by Shoghi Effendi, His grandson and the Guardian
of the Faith, as the 'Charter of the New World Order':

O dearly beloved friends! [He wrote] I am now in very
great danger and the hope of even an hour's life is lost to
me. I am thus constrained to write these lines for the protection of the Cause of God, the preservation of His Law,
the safeguarding of His Word and the safety of His
Teachings. By the Ancient Beauty! This wronged one
hath in no wise borne nor doth he bear a grudge against
any one; towards none doth he entertain any ill-feeling
and uttereth no word save for the good of the world.
My supreme obligation, however, of necessity, prompteth
me to guard and preserve the Cause of God.[75]

CHAPTER 8

RAISING THE TABERNACLE OF THE LORD

On March 21st 1909, one month prior to the fall of 'Abdu'l-Ḥamíd, 'Abdu'l-Bahá placed the remains of the Báb in a central vault beneath the mausoleum, then completed, in the heart of Mount Carmel. To the Bahá'ís He wrote:

> The most joyful tidings is this, that the holy, the luminous body of the Báb . . . after having for sixty years been transferred from place to place, by reason of the ascendancy of the enemy, and from fear of the malevolent, and having known neither rest nor tranquillity has, through the mercy of the Abhá Beauty, been ceremoniously deposited, on the day of Naw-Rúz, within the sacred casket, in the exalted Shrine on Mt. Carmel . . . By a strange coincidence, on that same day of Naw-Rúz, a cablegram was received from Chicago, announcing that the believers in each of the American centers had elected a delegate and sent to that city . . . and definitely decided on the site and construction of the Maṣẖriqu'l-Adẖkár.[76]

But between that joyous, triumphant consummation and the day 'Abdu'l-Bahá took the first step to carry out the command of Bahá'u'lláh, and obtain the land specified by Him as the site of the Shrine for the Martyr-Prophet, lay a decade of heartache. 'Every stone of that building, every stone of the road leading to it,' 'Abdu'l-Bahá is known to have said, 'I have with infinite tears and at tremendous cost, raised and placed in position.'

We have already seen that opposition was mainly engineered by Mírzá Muḥammad-'Alí and his associates. A German businessman, resident in Haifa, who was negotiating with the owner of the land on behalf of 'Abdu'l-Bahá, was forced, reluctantly and disgustedly, to take the case back to Him, asking bluntly how he could bring the deal to a satisfactory conclusion when 'Abdu'l-Bahá's own brother provided the stumbling-block. And when, at last, the owner agreed to sell at a reasonable price, the violators incited a number of people to petition the government and lay claim to the ownership of the land. Another six months passed before the falsity of their claims was established. The land was purchased, and 'Abdu'l-Bahá laid the foundation-stone of the mausoleum.

Construction then began according to the plan He had envisaged. The path leading to the building-site was very rocky and difficult to negotiate. Efforts were made to acquire better means of access. It would have been an easy transaction to obtain the strip of land required had it not been for fresh machinations. The violators incited the owner not to sell, but to hold on for a much higher price. The Qá'im-Maqám (deputy-governor) of Haifa was also proving disputatious. The building being reared on Mount Carmel, he contended, was distant from the town, in a position not desirable; its construction must have the sanction of the Sulṭán. The head of the Land Registry, acting in accordance with his advice, stated that political considerations intervened and construction should be halted. Therefore, the matter was laid before the Governor of 'Akká. He appointed Ṣáliḥ Effendi, his city architect, and another official in Haifa to examine the case and report: their report was favourable. There could not possibly be any political or strategic consideration; the building consisted only of six rooms, it was not isolated on Mount Carmel, there was a great monastery on the shoulder of the mountain, and the Germans also had buildings in the neighbourhood. The Qá'im-Maqám refused to accept the report and insisted that the whole case be referred to the Sulṭán. 'Abdu'l-Bahá knew that in that event 'Abdu'l-Ḥamíd's suspicions would be thoroughly aroused, as later developments amply bore out. He went in person to see the Deputy-Governor. When pressed to state his reasons for opposing the project, the Qá'im-Maqám had to confess that he was afraid to shoulder the responsibility and permit the work to go ahead. 'Abdu'l-Bahá walked with him from his office to his home. At the threshold of his house, the Qá'im-Maqám collapsed and died. His death brought a sorrowful chapter to its close.

The building work proceeded, but the question of an access road remained unresolved. In the space of five months, the owner of that strip of land changed his mind twice, after having agreed to sell. All the time, adversaries were bringing pressure to bear upon him, enticing him to hold on, dangling in front of him the prospect of exorbitant profits. The second time he broke his word on the plea that he wished to keep the trees on his land. 'Abdu'l-Bahá told him that he could have them all. Next he said that he required a partition of barbed wire, in order to protect the rest of his property. 'Abdu'l-Bahá offered to have a wall built as high as he wished. He retorted that he must have a guarantor to assure him that his property would be safe and secure. He named Ṣádiq Páshá, a highly-respected magnate, as the guarantor most acceptable to him. It was arranged that they should all meet in Ṣádiq Páshá's house. But the owner never came, and in rainy weather Ṣádiq Páshá went out himself to find and fetch him. At his house Ṣádiq Páshá was told that he was not at home. The magnate returned, dripping wet, and very angry.

That night 'Abdu'l-Bahá could neither eat nor sleep. In His anguish He recited over and over again a prayer of the Báb, until, soothed and calmed, sleep came to Him at the hour of dawn. When He woke up in the forenoon, He was

informed that the dragoman of the German consulate together with the nephew of the Consul had been waiting for
a long time to see Him. They had come to offer Him the
sale of another piece of land.

Then, in August 1901, fresh orders came from Constantinople, and 'Abdu'l-Bahá was once again incarcerated
within the city walls of 'Akká. He could no longer personally
supervise the construction of the mausoleum for the Báb,
but the work went steadily forward throughout these years
of peril. And when the autocracy of 'Abdu'l-Hamíd
crumbled the mausoleum was completed, ready to receive
the remains of the Martyr-Prophet.

On the morning of March 21st 1909, the day of Naw-Rúz,
'Abdu'l-Bahá had the marble sarcophagus—gift of the
Bahá'ís of Rangoon—carried up the mountain and placed in
the vault.[77] That evening He laid in the sarcophagus the
wooden casket which contained the inseparable remains of
the Báb and the disciple who had died with Him. A solitary
lamp lit the scene, so poignant and yet so exultant. The Báb
had been cruelly maligned, cruelly wronged, cruelly put to
death. His torn and smashed body had had no home for
many long years. Now the heart of Carmel was receiving it
forevermore. Of this event Zechariah had written: 'Thus
speaketh the Lord of hosts, saying, Behold the man whose
name is The Branch; and he shall grow up out of his place,
and he shall build the temple of the Lord'.[78] How mysteri-
ously and indubitably had his prophecy come true. 'The
Branch' had built 'the temple of the Lord', had raised His
'tabernacle' on His Mountain—on Carmel—the Mountain
of God.

With 'Abdu'l-Bahá on that same evening, in the vault of
the Shrine which He had so hardly reared, were Bahá'ís of
both the East and the West. There were veterans of the
Faith, who had passed through its darkest days, among them:
Hájí Mírzá Muhammad-Taqí, the Vakílu'd-Dawlih, cousin

of the Báb, the chief builder of the first Mashriqu'l-Adhkár of the Bahá'í world; and Ḥájí Mírzá Ḥaydar-'Alí, prisoner of Khartúm, stalwart defender of the Covenant.

'When all was finished, and the earthly remains of the Martyr-Prophet of Shíráz were, at long last, safely deposited for their everlasting rest in the bosom of God's holy mountain, 'Abdu'l-Bahá, Who had cast aside His turban, removed His shoes and thrown off His cloak, bent low over the still open sarcophagus, His silver hair waving about His head and His face transfigured and luminous, rested His forehead on the border of the wooden casket, and, sobbing aloud, wept with such a weeping that all those who were present wept with Him.'[79] Sorrows and memories of a lifetime came flooding in His tears. That night, too, sleep parted from His eyes.

The triumph which 'Abdu'l-Bahá achieved on that day in 1909 shines with ever-increasing splendour.

CHAPTER 9

LIBERTY AT LAST

The very first act of 'Abdu'l-Bahá, on hearing that He was free, was to visit the Shrine of His Father. During the years of His renewed incarceration, tribulations, diverse in character, had weighed heavily upon Him, and of them all the hardest to bear was separation from that beloved and sacred spot. How often did He tell the pilgrims, longingly and wistfully, that there was nothing He desired more than liberty to visit the Shrine of Bahá'u'lláh, that He was a prisoner and denied that freedom, that He would ask them to deputize for Him. No sooner was He free to visit Bahjí than He resumed the task which He had so diligently pursued in days past. Since the time He had planned and created a garden adjacent to the Shrine of Bahá'u'lláh, He had, personally, week after week, fetched jars of water for that garden. Now again, every Friday and Sunday, even when notables and officials were visiting Him, He would unfailingly carry water as many as sixty times.

But now He was sixty-five years old, and His health had been taxed to the utmost by the hardships which He had endured. The physical exertion to which He was subjecting Himself brought about fresh bouts of illness. Bahá'ís, resident and pilgrim, became anxious and begged 'Abdu'l-Bahá to spare Himself the task of carrying water, and to permit others to deputize for Him. He acceded to their request, but so sad did He look that the Bahá'ís regretted having made this plea to Him. A fortnight later, 'Abdu'l-Bahá called them together. He had complied with their wishes, He said, but that particular service had always brought Him great joy and peace of heart. Would they now, He asked them, permit Him to take it up once again. He wished them to reply exactly as their consciences dictated. How could they, this group of devoted men, refuse Him their consent, seeing so evidently what happiness would be His.

During the period immediately following the change of the Turkish régime, 'Abdu'l-Bahá continued His residence in 'Akká. But after the entombment of the remains of the Báb, He chose to live in Haifa, where a house was being built for Him. Soon a time came when He ceased to set foot within the city gates of 'Akká. He had been twenty-four years old when led a Prisoner into its citadel, sixty-five years of age when finally liberated from the shackles of that town.

The Shrine of the Báb was now a place of pilgrimage. A Bahá'í of 'Ishqábád, Áqá Mírzá Ja'far-i-Hádíoff, originally a native of Shíráz (to whom 'Abdu'l-Bahá gave the surname Rahmání), was moved to offer to defray the expense of building a pilgrim house in the close vicinity of the Shrine. It was on the balcony of this same Pilgrim House, over-looking the town of Haifa, the bay and the plain of 'Akká beyond, that 'Abdu'l-Bahá stood, soon after its completion, and spoke of the vision He had of the future of Mount Carmel and the bay, of the two towns stretched out there before His gaze. Behind Him stood Mírzá Mahmúd-i-Zarqání, His secretary during His tour of the Western world and the diarist of that tour. Did Mírzá Mahmúd see the splendorous scene, He asked. Poor Mírzá Mahmúd could see nothing but a puny town below, which was Haifa, an almost deserted port that had no harbour facilities, a bare waste of desert and sand round the arc of the bay, in the distance a walled, circumscribed 'Akká, dimly discernible. But 'Abdu'l-Bahá could see the two towns joined round the bay, a fine harbour teeming with the ships of all nations,

Carmel bathed in light at nightfall, shining like a jewel, great institutions serving the needs and the aspirations of the human race. He saw the world metropolis of the future, sited in a land holy since the days of Abraham.

Ḥájí Mírzá Ḥaydar-'Alí writes in the *Bihjatu'ṣ-Ṣudúr* of the hopes of the Bahá'ís that, as the heir to Bahá'u'lláh, 'Abdu'l-Bahá would, with the passage of years, come to resemble Him physically as well; but their hopes did not materialize, because sorrows and tribulations pressed hard upon 'Abdu'l-Bahá, afflictions weakened His frame and made Him a prey to a number of ailments. He goes on to say that 'Abdu'l-Bahá, in order to protect His followers from worry and anxiety, would not expose them to the knowledge of His maladies which at times were severe. However, physicians advised Him that He ought to seek a change of air, and leave the Holy Land. But subsequent events demonstrated the fact that 'Abdu'l-Bahá, when He did this, was not just embarking on a journey to improve His health in a different setting, or to prevent its further deterioration. He was indeed taking the first step to reach the world of the West and deliver, in person, the Message of His Father. There was another purpose evident in 'Abdu'l-Bahá's journey. Mírzá Muḥammad-'Alí and his partisans were now thoroughly discredited. In the absence of 'Abdu'l-Bahá from the Holy Land the violators would have the field entirely to themselves, but their utter inability to make any move to impair the unity of the Bahá'ís would set the final seal on their downfall. 'Abdu'l-Bahá particularly stressed this fact in a Tablet addressed at the time to a Bahá'í of Iskandarún (Alexandretta).

The *Bahai News* of the Bahá'ís of the United States, which had begun its life on March 21st 1910,* carried in its twelfth number of October 16th 1910, a portion of a letter written

* Known later as *Star of the West*.

to Isabella Brittingham from Haifa. It was dated August 29th and read in part:

> I have a very big piece of news to tell you. Abdul-Baha has left this Holy Spot for the first time in forty-two years, and has gone to Egypt. Think of the vast significance and importance of this step! By it many prophecies of the sacred Scriptures are fulfilled . . . Everyone was astounded to hear of Abdul-Baha's departure, for no one knew until the very last minute that he had any idea of leaving. The afternoon of the day he left, he came to Mírzá Assad Ullah's * home to see us and sat with us awhile beside a new well that has just been finished and said that he had come to taste the water. We did not realize that it was a good-bye visit. Then he took a carriage and went up the hill to the Holy Tomb (of the Bab). That night, as usual, the believers gathered before the house of Abdul-Baha to receive that blessing, which every day is ours, of being in his presence, but we waited in vain, for one of the sons-in-law came and told us that Abdul-Baha had taken the Khedivial steamer to Port Said.†

The fifteenth number of the *Bahai News*, dated December 12th 1910, carried a further letter about 'Abdu'l-Bahá's journey to Egypt. It was written by Siyyid Asadu'lláh-i-Qumí who was to be 'Abdu'l-Bahá's attendant during His travels. He said:

> You have asked for an account of Abdul-Baha's departure to the land of Egypt. Abdul-Baha did not inform anyone

---

* Mírzá Asadu'lláh, the man who was in charge of the conveyance of the remains of the Báb from Írán to the Holy Land.

† The writer of the letter was Sydney Sprague, who was married to the daughter of Mírzá Asadu'lláh. Sprague had been one of the early pioneer teachers. His book: *A Year with the Bahais In India and Burma*, was published in London in 1908. Sprague rendered valuable help in the running of the Bahá'í Tarbíyat School in Ṭihrán. We shall have cause to refer to him again.

that he was going to leave Haifa. The day he left he visited
the Holy Tomb of the Bab on Mt. Carmel and when he
came down from the mountain of the Lord, he went direct
to the steamer. This was the first anyone knew about the
matter. Within two days he summoned to his presence,
Mirza Noureddin, Shougi Effendi, Khosro,* and this
servant. The only persons who accompanied Abdul-Baha
to Egypt were Mirza Moneer Zain and Abdul Hossein,†
one of the pilgrims who was leaving at that time. When
Mirza Noureddin arrived in Port Said, his brother Mirza
Moneer returned to Haifa.

For nearly one month Abdul-Baha remained in Port
Said and the friends of God came from Cairo, in turn, to
visit him. One day he called me to accompany him when
taking a walk in the streets of the city. He said: 'Do you
realize now the meaning of my statement when I was
telling the friends that there was a wisdom in my in-
disposition?' I answered, 'Yes, I do remember very well.'
He continued, 'Well, the wisdom was that I must always
move according to the requirements of the Cause. Whatever the Cause requires for its promulgation, I will not
delay in its accomplishment for one moment! Now, the
Cause did require that I travel to these parts, and had I
divulged my intention at that time, many difficulties
would have arisen.

Meanwhile Mírzá Muhammad-'Alí was busy spreading
strange rumours. He told the Metropolitan of 'Akká, a
cleric in league with him, that 'Abdu'l-Bahá had fled the
Holy Land. The Metropolitan telegraphed one of his own
men in Jaffa and instructed him to find out whether or not
'Abdu'l-Bahá was on His way to Egypt. That man boarded

* Mírzá Núri'ddín-i-Zayn, son of Zaynu'l-Muqarrabín;
Shoghi Effendi, grandson of 'Abdu'l-Bahá, appointed by Him
the Guardian of the Cause of God; and K͟husraw, an attendant of
'Abdu'l-Bahá, who was of Burmese origin.

† Mírzá Munír-i-Zayn and 'Abdu'l-Husayn.

the Khedivial steamer and came face to face with 'Abdu'l-Bahá. He had the temerity to ask Him to affirm His identity. Ashore, the Metropolitan's man sent this telegram: 'The said person is aboard.' The same thing happened in Port Said. A man came on behalf of the Metropolitan of 'Akká to make certain that 'Abdu'l-Bahá was there.

After a month's stay in Port Said, 'Abdu'l-Bahá once again took ship, without previous intimation. He intended to go to Europe, but it became evident that the state of His health did not permit the strenuous work involved. He landed in Alexandria. It was in that ancient city that a sudden change occurred. Journalists in Egypt, who had hitherto shown open hostility, asked to meet 'Abdu'l-Bahá and perceptibly changed their tone. Even more, they wrote in terms of high praise. Shaykh 'Alí Yúsuf, the editor of the Arabic paper, al-Mu'ayyad, had previously made harsh attacks on Bahá'ís and the Bahá'í Faith, urging severe counter-measures against them. He visited 'Abdu'l-Bahá, and in the October 16th issue of his paper he published an article under the heading: 'Al-Mírzá 'Abbás Effendi'. These are the opening lines of that remarkable article: 'His Eminence Mírzá 'Abbás Effendi, the learned and erudite Head of the Bahá'ís in 'Akká and the Centre of authority for Bahá'ís throughout the world, has reached the shores of Alexandria.' At first, related the writer, 'Abdu'l-Bahá stayed in the Victoria Hotel, but after a few days moved to a rented house. Then he went on to say:

He is a venerable person, dignified, possessed of profound knowledge, deeply versed in theology, master of the history of Islám, and of its denominations and developments . . . whosoever has consorted with Him has seen in Him a man exceedingly well-informed, Whose speech is captivating, Who attracts minds and souls, Who is dedicated to belief in the oneness of mankind . . .

His teaching and guidance revolve round the axis of relinquishing prejudices: religious, racial, patriotic.

Another notable example of that change of attitude was afforded by the Persian weekly, *Chihrih-Nimá*. Its editor, Mírzá 'Abdu'l-Muḥammad-i-Íráni, the Mu'addibu's-Sulṭán, had in the past, in common with many of his countrymen resident in Egypt, displayed feelings far from friendly. Now he reported 'Abdu'l-Bahá's travels with respect and admiration. Even that antagonist of old, Dr Mírzá Muḥammad-Mihdí Khán, the Za'ímu'd-Dawlih,[80] visited 'Abdu'l-Bahá several times and was not lacking in reverence. 'Abdu'l-Bahá's sojourn in Alexandria coincided with the Muslim lunar month of Muḥarram. This is the month that witnessed the martyrdom of Ḥusayn, the grandson of the Prophet Muḥammad and the third apostolic Imám of His Faith, together with many others of the House of the Prophet. That tragedy occurred on the tenth day of Muḥarram, 61 A.H., which corresponded to October 10th A.D. 680. The Shí'ah world has mourned his martyrdom ever since. Throughout the month of Muḥarram and the succeeding month of Ṣafar, wherever Shí'ahs are, their grief is given some form of expression. They arrange gatherings at which the sufferings and the heroism of the Family [House] of Muḥammad, the treachery and the brutality of the foe are recited. Persians of Alexandria invited 'Abdu'l-Bahá to their meeting. He went and was received with every mark of respect. He gave a robe to the reciter of the heart-rending story of Karbilá,* rewarding him richly for his talent and devotion. He also left money with the hosts to hold a commemorative meeting on His behalf and to feed the poor.

An English admirer, Wellesley Tudor-Pole,† visited

* The spot on the bank of the Euphrates where Ḥusayn was martyred and where his Shrine stands.

† Later, Major Tudor-Pole.

'Abdu'l-Bahá in the autumn of that year. His letter, reporting his visit, appeared in the *Bahai News* of February 7th 1911. He wrote:

> You may be interested in hearing of my recent visit to Abdul-Baha at Ramleh, near Alexandria. I spent nine days at Alexandria and Cairo during the second half of November, 1910. Abdul-Baha's health had very greatly improved since his arrival from Port Said. He was looking strong and vigorous in every way. He spoke much of the work in America, to which he undoubtedly is giving considerable thought. He also spoke a good deal about the work that is going forward in different European centres as well as in London, and he expects great things from England during the coming year ... A Bahai paper is to be read at the Universal Races Congress in London next July.

'Abdu'l-Bahá had been asked to address the Universal Races Congress, but He decided to defer His departure from Egypt. Early in May He moved to Cairo and took residence nearby in Zaytún. As 'Abdu'l-Bahá's sojourn in Egypt lengthened, newspapers showed increasing admiration and friendliness. *Al-Muqaṭṭam*, the most prominent of them, had on November 28th of the preceding year (1910) published a highly appreciative account. Other papers such as *al-Ahrám* and *Wádía'n-Níl* were no less laudatory. In Cairo, Shaykh Muḥammad Bakhit, the Muftí of Egypt, and Shaykh Muḥammad Rishád, the Khedive's Imám, called on 'Abdu'l-Bahá and He returned their call. On a Friday He visited the shrine of Siyyidah Zaynab and said the Friday prayer there. The Khedive, 'Abbás Ḥilmí II,* also met 'Abdu'l-Bahá, and 'Uthmán Páshá, the notable

---

* Deposed by British authorities in November 1914, while absent in Istanbul. The Ottoman Empire had entered the war on the side of Germany.

responsible for arrangements, later attested to the particular reverence which the Khedive had exhibited towards
Him. Their meeting was repeated. Ronald Storrs,* Oriental
Secretary of the British Agency, had first come to know
'Abdu'l-Bahá in 1909, within the prison-city of 'Akká;
and now, in Egypt, in his own words, 'had the honour
of . . . presenting him to Lord Kitchener, who was deeply
impressed by his personality, as who could fail to be?'[81]
George Zaydán, the eminent writer and celebrated editor
of the magazine *al-Hilál*, was another leading figure in the
public life of Egypt who visited 'Abdu'l-Bahá. Indeed
they were many, clerics, aristocrats, administrators, parlia-
mentarians, men of letters, journalists and publicists, Arabs,
Turks and Persians, who sought His presence. The poor
and the deprived also had access to Him and went away
happy.

His personal triumph resounding in Egypt, 'Abdu'l-Bahá
turned His attention to Europe. On August 11th 1911, He
boarded S.S. *Corsica*, bound for Marseilles.

* Later, Sir Ronald Storrs, K.C.M.G., C.B.E.

CHAPTER 10

'A NEW CYCLE OF HUMAN POWER'

'Abdu'l-Bahá rested for a few days at Thonon-les-Bains on the shore of Lake Leman, and then travelled to London, which He reached on Monday, September 4th 1911. He had chosen the metropolis of the British Empire as the scene of His first appearance before the public. One week later He addressed the congregation of the City Temple. That day was indeed historic in the crowded annals of the Christian West, but neither the West nor the rest of the world has, as yet, been aware of it. Never before in pagan or Christian history had the recognized Head of a World Faith come from the East—where all religions have arisen—to stand before and address a Western congregation in public. It is believed that Peter, on whom Christ had conferred supreme authority, visited Rome and spoke to its people. Even so, St Peter was not acclaimed as the Vicar of Christ, and he could not openly and publicly address the citizens of the world's chief capital. Providence ordained this unique distinction for 'Abdu'l-Bahá. When He spoke on that Sunday, September 10th 1911, from the pulpit of the City Temple in Holborn, 'Abdu'l-Bahá was appearing for the first time before any audience anywhere. He had never given a public talk or preached a sermon. These are His words:

O Noble friends; seekers after God! Praise be to God! Today the light of Truth is shining upon the world in its abundance; the breezes of the heavenly garden are blowing throughout all regions; the call of the Kingdom is heard in all lands, and the breath of the Holy Spirit is felt in all hearts that are faithful. The Spirit of God is giving eternal life. In this wonderful age the East is enlightened, the West is fragrant, and everywhere the soul inhales the holy perfume. The sea of the unity of mankind is lifting up its waves with joy, for there is real communication between the hearts and minds of men. The banner of the Holy Spirit is uplifted, and men see it, and are assured with the knowledge that this is a new day.

This is a new cycle of human power. All the horizons of the world are luminous, and the world will become indeed as a garden and a paradise. It is the hour of unity of the sons of men and of the drawing together of all races and all classes. You are loosed from ancient super-stitions which have kept men ignorant, destroying the foundations of true humanity.

The gift of God to this enlightened age is the know-ledge of the oneness of mankind and of the fundamental oneness of religion. War shall cease between nations, and by the will of God the Most Great Peace shall come; the world will be seen as a new world, and all men will live as brothers.

In the days of old an instinct for warfare was developed in the struggle with wild animals; this is no longer neces-sary; nay, rather, co-operation and mutual understanding are seen to produce the greatest welfare of mankind. En-mity is now the result of prejudice only.

In the *Hidden Words* Baha'u'llah says, 'Justice is to be loved above all.' Praise be to God, in this country the standard of justice has been raised; a great effort is being made to give all souls an equal and a true place. This is the desire of all noble natures; this is today the teaching for the East and for the West; therefore the East and the West will understand each other and reverence each other, and embrace like long-parted lovers who have found each other.

There is one God; mankind is one; the foundations of

religion are one. Let us worship Him, and give praise for all His great Prophets and Messengers who have manifested His brightness and glory.

The blessing of the Eternal One be with you in all its richness, that each soul according to his measure may take freely of Him. Amen.[82]

With that discourse 'Abdu'l-Bahá opened a phase of His ministry which must, in every aspect, remain unrivalled. In His sixty-eighth year, in precarious health, He stepped into a crowded, demanding arena to proclaim to the Christian West the essential verities of the Faith of His Father. He addressed meeting after meeting; He met day after day, throughout the day, a stream of visitors; He sat patiently with press reporters; He talked with the eminent and the accomplished; He sought the poor and the under-privileged, and His love went out to them abundantly, as did His munificence. And He refused to curry favour with the powerful, the mighty, and the rich.

When 'Abdu'l-Bahá spoke those words from the pulpit of the City Temple the world was not a peaceful place. Indeed He Himself, time and time again during His tour of the West, gave the warning that Europe was similar to a large arsenal, needing but one spark to set it alight. The Bosnian affair in 1908 had dragged Europe near to war and the Agadir Crisis of that very year 1911 had pushed her further to the brink. At the end of September, Italy, with an avaricious eye on Tripolitania, declared war on the Ottomans, and was soon the master of that territory to the southern extremities of which the minions of the Sultán had intended to banish 'Abdu'l-Bahá. The following year, the Greeks, the Macedonians, the Slavs, and the rest of the small nations of the Balkans, hating one another, but united by the common bond of a greater hatred for the Ottomans, humiliated the new régime of the Young Turks, and Europe was once again poised on the edge of war. But Kaiser Wilhelm and Sir Edward Grey managed to avert the disaster, or rather to postpone it. Monastir and Salonika, towns in which the Young Turks had hatched their plots and from which they had marched to topple 'Abdu'l-Ḥamíd from his throne, were forever lost to the Ottomans. Catastrophe came in 1914 and the five continents were engulfed. In truth Europe committed suicide. Its supremacy was undermined, to be finally demolished in the course of the Second World War. Divisions were multiplied and ancient crowns fell to dust. In between the two world conflagrations, obsessions of racialism that had hitherto mainly tortured and twisted restless intellects afflicted the lives of nations and desecrated their humanity. The War of 1939 not only engendered undreamt-of horrors, but produced fresh animosities to plague and threaten the entire human race.

But on that September day, in the pulpit of the City Temple, 'Abdu'l-Bahá was describing a world that is the inheritance of mankind, to which it must and will come; a world which the advent, the labour and the promise of Bahá'u'lláh have presaged: ' . . . these fruitless strifes, these ruinous wars shall pass away and the "Most Great Peace" shall come' was Bahá'u'lláh's solemn declaration to Edward Granville Browne.

Sara Louisa, Lady Blomfield, whom 'Abdu'l-Bahá called Sitárih* Khánum, put her flat, at 97 Cadogan Gardens, at the disposal of 'Abdu'l-Bahá.

'He arrived, and who shall picture Him?' she writes.

A silence as of love and awe overcame us, as we looked at Him; the gracious figure, clothed in a simple white garment, over which was a light-coloured Persian 'abá; on His head He wore a low-crowned táj, round which was folded a small, fine-linen turban of purest white; His hair

* 'Star'.

and short beard were of that snowy whiteness which had once been black; His eyes were large, blue-grey with long, black lashes and well-marked eyebrows; His face was a beautiful oval with warm, ivory-coloured skin, a straight, finely-modelled nose, and firm, kind mouth. These are merely outside details by which an attempt is made to convey an idea of His arresting personality.

His figure was of such perfect symmetry, and so full of dignity and grace, that the first impression was that of considerable height. He seemed an incarnation of loving understanding, of compassion and power, of wisdom and authority, of strength, and of a buoyant youthfulness, which somehow defied the burden of His years; and such years!

One saw, as in a clear vision, that He had so wrought all good and mercy that the inner grace of Him had grown greater than all outer sign, and the radiance of this inner glory shone in every glance, and word, and movement as He came with hands outstretched.[83]

The Reverend R. J. Campbell, well-known in Britain for his liberal thought and attitude, was the minister of the City Temple who invited 'Abdu'l-Bahá to address his congregation. The *Christian Commonwealth* of September 13th carried a six-column article headed: 'Towards Spiritual Unity. An Interview with Abdul Baha. Dialogue Between Abbas Effendi and Rev. R. J. Campbell, M.A.' This paper always provided ample space to report the visit of 'Abdu'l-Bahá to London. Furthermore, it carried articles on the work, the aims, and the growth of the Bahá'í Faith. The Reverend R. J. Campbell, as reported by the *Christian Commonwealth*, said on that occasion: 'I have long looked forward to this opportunity.' 'Abdu'l-Bahá replied: 'That is proof that both our hearts are at one.' The Reverend R. J. Campbell's comment was: 'I think that is true;' and he further said: 'I am so glad that you took the resolution to come to England, even though you can remain only a short time.' And 'Abdu'l-Bahá replied: 'From the time I left Egypt my purpose was to come here, but I remained a few days on the Lake of Geneva for change of air.'

When 'Abdu'l-Bahá visited the City Temple He wrote three lines in the pulpit Bible which read in translation: 'This book is the Holy Book of God, of celestial Inspiration. It is the Bible of Salvation, the noble Gospel. It is the mystery of the Kingdom and its light. It is the Divine Bounty, the sign of the guidance of God—Abdul-Baha Abbas.' During the Second World War the City Temple received a direct hit, and the pulpit Bible was destroyed. Fortunately the pages of the *Christian Commonwealth* have preserved the facsimile of what 'Abdu'l-Bahá wrote in that Bible.

Soon after His arrival in London [writes Lady Blomfield], 'Abdu'l-Bahá received Archdeacon Wilberforce in audience. This was a remarkable interview. Our dear friend, the Archdeacon, sat on a low chair by the Master. 'Abdu'l-Bahá spoke to him in His beautiful Persian. He placed His hand on the head of the Archdeacon, talked long to him, and answered many questions. Evidently His words penetrated further than the outer ears, for both were deeply moved. On this occasion the invitation was given for 'Abdu'l-Bahá to speak to the congregation of St John the Divine, at Westminster, on the following Sunday.[84]

'Abdu'l-Bahá addressed the congregation of St John's, Westminster* on September 17th. Archdeacon Wilberforce had the Bishop's chair placed on the chancel steps for

* This church in Smith Square was also bombed during the Second World War.

'Abdu'l-Bahá, and stood beside Him to read the translation
of His discourse. In the September 20th issue of the *Christian
Commonwealth* one reads:

Eighteen months ago Archdeacon Wilberforce, who had
been watching the Bahai movement for some time with
interest, sent a message to Abdul Baha. 'We are all one,'
he said, 'there, behind the veil.' And Abdul Baha replied
from his home in Akka, 'Tell him the veil is very thin,
and it will vanish quite.'

All who were present in St. John's, Westminster, last
Sunday evening, could not fail to realise that the veil was
vanishing. Archdeacon Wilberforce's beautiful inter-
cessory service was a means to that end . . . Then Dr.
Wilberforce told of the teacher—'Master' he called him—
who had come to London to emphasise unity, and who was
present that evening at St. John's to proclaim the meaning
of it. 'Whatever our views,' the Archdeacon said, 'we shall,
I am sure, unite in welcoming a man who has been for
forty years a prisoner for the cause of brotherhood and
love' . . . Full of expectation, the congregation waited
when the Archdeacon for a brief moment left the church.
Divested of his white surplice, he returned with Abdul
Baha. All eyes were fixed on the leader of the Bahai
movement. In his customary Eastern robe and head-
dress, walking hand in hand with a leader of the West,
it did indeed seem that the veil was vanishing.

Down the aisle they passed to the bishop's chair, which
had been placed in front of the altar for Abdul Baha.
Standing at the lectern, Archdeacon Wilberforce introduced the 'wonderful' visitor. He told of his life in prison,
of his sufferings and bravery, of his self-sacrifice, of his
clear and shining faith . . . Then Abdul Baha rose.
Speaking very clearly, with wonderful intonations in his
voice and using his hands freely, it seemed to those who
listened almost as if they grasped his meaning, though he
spoke in Persian . . .

Here are extracts from 'Abdu'l-Bahá's second address to a Western audience:

O Noble Friends! O Seekers for the Kingdom of God! Man all over the world is seeking for God. All that exists is God; but the Reality of Divinity is holy above all understanding.

The pictures of Divinity that come to our mind are the product of our fancy; they exist in the realm of our imagination. They are not adequate to the Truth; truth in its essence cannot be put into words.

Divinity cannot be comprehend*ed* because it is comprehend*ing*.

Man, who has also a real existence, is comprehended by God; therefore, the Divinity which man can understand is partial; it is not complete. Divinity is actual Truth and real existence, and not any representation of it. Divinity itself contains All, and is not contained . . .

But the Essence of Divinity, the Sun of Truth, shines forth upon all horizons and is spreading its rays upon all things. Each creature is the recipient of some portion of that power, and man, who contains the perfection of the mineral, the vegetable and animal, as well as his own distinctive qualities, has become the noblest of created beings. It stands written that he is made in the Image of God. Mysteries that were hidden he discovers; and secrets that were concealed he brings into the light. By Science and by Art he brings hidden powers into the region of the visible world. Man perceives the hidden law in created things and co-operates with it . . .

If we claim that the sun is seen in the mirror, we do not mean that the sun itself has descended from the holy heights of his heaven and entered into the mirror! This is impossible. The Divine Nature is seen in the Manifestations and its Light and Splendour are visible in extreme glory.

Therefore, men have always been taught and led by the Prophets of God. The Prophets of God are the

Mediators of God. All the Prophets and Messengers have come from One Holy Spirit and bear the Message of God, fitted to the age in which they appear. The One Light is in them and they are one with each other. But the Eternal does not become phenomenal; neither can the phenomenal become Eternal.

Saint Paul, the great Apostle, said: 'We all, with open face beholding as in a mirror the glory of God, are changed into the same image from glory to glory, as by the Spirit of the Lord.'

Then 'Abdu'l-Bahá lifted up His hands and ended His discourse with a prayer:

O God the Forgiver! O Heavenly Educator! This assembly is adorned with the mention of Thy holy Name. Thy children turn their faces towards Thy Kingdom, hearts are made happy and souls are comforted.

Merciful God! cause us to repent of our shortcomings! Accept us in Thy heavenly Kingdom and give unto us an abode where there shall be no error. Give us peace; give us knowledge, and open unto us the gates of Thy heaven.

Thou art the Giver of all! Thou art the Forgiver! Thou art the Merciful. [85]

Archdeacon Wilberforce asked 'Abdu'l-Bahá to pronounce the benediction, saying: 'I think we should take it kneeling.' Then as the congregation sang the hymn, 'O God, our help in ages past', 'Abdu'l-Bahá and the Archdeacon walked hand in hand down the aisle to the vestry.

In Smith Square members of the Salvation Army were holding a service. 'Abdu'l-Bahá greatly admired their faith and courage.

Lady Blomfield writes:

The history of 'Abdu'l-Bahá's stay in our house lies in the relating of various incidents, connected with individuals, who stand out from amongst the crowd of those persons who eagerly sought His Presence.

Oh, these pilgrims, these guests, these visitors! Remembering those days, our ears are filled with the sound of their footsteps—as they came from every country in the world! Every day, all day long, a constant stream. An interminable procession.[86]

These visitors represented a spectrum of humanity. Among them were leading men of all Faiths. Most of them had broad sympathies, liberal minds. There were also some who were bigoted and had narrow outlooks. Of the latter category was the Reverend Peter Z. Easton. He called to meet 'Abdu'l-Bahá on September 21st. This interview was followed by a virulent and venomous attack on the Bahá'í Faith. Referring to 'Abdu'l-Bahá, he wrote in the *English Churchman*: 'I found him to answer to Dr. H. H. Jessup's description of him as a man of great affability and courtesy. He was glad to meet with an Occidental, who could talk with him in Tartar Turkish, the language of Azerbeigan,* Persia, in which and the adjoining Caucasus I have been labouring as a missionary since 1873.' Then he complained that to his query 'Abdu'l-Bahá had given no answer, that He had changed the subject. And what was his query? What did 'Abdu'l-Bahá have 'to add to the New Testament teaching of repentance toward God and faith toward our Lord Jesus Christ, the Way, the Truth and the Life, through whom alone we can come to the Father.' Apparently the Reverend Peter Z. Easton wanted a slanging match. Having failed to obtain the answer he desired, the irate cleric said that he had to seek it elsewhere. Sydney Sprague in his *Story of the Bahai Movement* had referred to Gobineau. Now, Mr Easton would find his answer. And there it was in the pages of *Religions et Philosophies dans l'Asie Centrale* where

* Ázarbayján.

Gobineau had characterized the Bábí Faith as 'the latest expression of an eclectic evolution, growing out of the innate pantheism of the Iranian mind'; and so Mr Easton was in full gallop: 'Here, then, we have a very important statement in regard to the character of the movement. It is a pantheistic, not a Christian, nor even a Mohammedan movement, one of a long series of such movements, beginning with the very beginning of Persian history and continuing to the present day, a movement akin likewise to the pantheistic sects of other lands, such as Mormons, Spiritists, Theosophists, Christian Scientists, etc.' Mr Easton did have astonishing views. To put Christian Scientists in the category of pantheists is no mean feat. The mind reels. Mr Easton even formulated a definition of pantheism. But he was not a competent theologian. Next he proceeded to defame Bahá'u'lláh, and waxed so bold as to say: 'In short, he was a moral and spiritual monster, who exalted himself against all that is called God or that is worshipped. To become a Bahai means to put this anti-Christ in the place of the God and Father of our Lord Jesus Christ. This is what the people of Great Britain are now invited to do.' Then, after presenting some dubious historical analogies, Mr Easton was moved to express his personal hope and concern for 'Abdu'l-Bahá: 'I am sorry for Abdul Baha. Brought up in this terrible system, he is entangled in its meshes. From what I have heard of late, I would fain hope that some glimmerings of light have dawned upon him. May God in great mercy open his eyes to behold the truth as it is in Jesus . . . '

Mr Easton was not content with this one article. He took his invective to the pages of *Evangelical Christendom*. Mírzá Abu'l-Faḍl was then living in Beirut. He was apprised of the contents of Mr Easton's second article by students at the Syrian Protestant College.* From his sick-bed he wrote one of the most effective treatises that ever came from

* American University of Beirut since 1920.

his powerful pen, in answer to the Reverend Peter Z. Easton. This was *Burhán-i-Lámi'*—*The Brilliant Proof*—translated into English at the instruction of 'Abdu'l-Bahá and published in Chicago. Mírzá Abu'l-Faḍl writes:

His Holiness Abdul-Baha calls the people of Europe to the lofty attributes of humanity, but Peter Z. Easton teaches them libels, execration, falsehood and calumnies!

His Holiness Abdul-Baha summons the dwellers in the world to unity and harmony, but Peter Z. Easton invites men to division and inharmony!

His Holiness Abdul-Baha lifts His blessed hands heavenward in the assemblage of prayer and invokes blessing and mercy for the people of Europe from the Court of the Almighty, but Peter Z. Easton attempts to prove in learned magazines the remoteness of the people of the East from praiseworthy Christian qualities, and desires that torment and punishment should fall upon them!

Abdul-Baha commands: 'Speak evil of no one and wish evil for no one'; but Peter Z. Easton says that no one should wish well for, or consider as worthy of grace, a people whose number he estimates as three millions!

I wonder therefore how we are to distinguish the good and evil fruits of the tree of existence; and how shall we comprehend and interpret the blessed words: 'Ye shall know the tree by its fruits'? To my mind there is no criterion but this, and Peter Z. Easton cannot teach otherwise.[87]

Mr Easton's arguments are well answered and well demolished in *The Brilliant Proof*.

At a later date in Paris, 'Abdu'l-Bahá was visited by a number of Church dignitaries, of the same frame of mind as Mr Easton. Let Lady Blomfield tell their story:

One afternoon, a party of the latter type arrived. They spoke words of bigotry, of intolerance, of sheer cruelty in their bitter condemnation of all who did not accept their own particular dogma, showing themselves obsessed by 'the hate of man, disguised as love of God,' a thin disguise to the penetrating eyes of the Master. Perhaps they were dreading the revealing light of Truth which He sought to shed upon the darkness of their outworn ecclesiasticism. The new revelation was too great for their narrowed souls and fettered minds.

The heart of 'Abdu'l-Bahá was saddened by this interview, which had tired Him exceedingly. When He referred to this visit there was a look in His eyes as if loving pity were blended with profound disapproval, as though He would cleanse the defiled temple of Humanity from the suffocating diseases of the soul. Then He uttered these words in a voice of awe-inspiring authority:

'Jesus Christ is the Lord of Compassion, and these men call themselves by His Name! *Jesus is ashamed of them!*'

He shivered as with cold, drawing His *'abá* closely about Him, with a gesture as if sternly repudiating their misguided outlook.[88]

'Abdu'l-Bahá's last public address in London was delivered at the Theosophical Society on September 30th. Mrs Annie Besant, the renowned president of the Society, had called on 'Abdu'l-Bahá and asked Him to visit and speak in their new headquarters. A. P. Sinnett, another leading Theosophist, was in the chair. Here for the first time 'Abdu'l-Bahá made a systematic presentation of some of the basic principles of the Faith of His Father. 'This is a short summary of the Teachings of Bahá'u'lláh,' He said. 'To establish this Bahá'u'lláh underwent great difficulties and hardships. He was in constant confinement and he suffered great persecution. But in the fortress [of 'Akká] he reared a spiritual palace and from the darkness of his prison he sent out a great light to the world.'[89]

At the invitation of Mrs Thornburgh-Cropper some four hundred and sixty 'representative people' had gathered the previous day in the hall of Passmore Edwards' Settlement,* Tavistock Place, to say farewell to 'Abdu'l-Bahá. His stay in Britain was nearing its close. Professor Michael Sadler presided.

> We have met together [he said] to bid farewell to Abdul Baha, and to thank God for his example and teaching, and for the power of his prayers to bring Light into confused thought, Hope into the place of dread, Faith where doubt was, and into troubled hearts, the Love which overmasters self-seeking and fear.
>
> Though we all, among ourselves, in our devotional allegiance have our own individual loyalties, to all of us Abdul Baha brings, and has brought, a message of Unity, of sympathy and of Peace. [90]

Among the speakers were Sir Richard Stapley and Mr Claude Montefiore, a prominent member of the Jewish Faith. 'Abdu'l-Bahá gave a clear announcement of the advent of His Father:

> He brought the light of guidance to the world; he kindled the fire of love and revealed the great reality of the True Beloved . . .
>
> His mission was to change ignorant fanaticism into Universal love, to establish in the minds of his followers the basis of the unity of humanity and to bring about in practice the equality of mankind . . .
>
> Yet the whole of Baha'u'llah's life was spent in the midst of great trial and cruel tyranny. In Persia he was

* Now known as Mary Ward Centre, named after Mrs Humphry Ward, the author of *Robert Elsmere*, who did much to help to found it.

thrown into prison, put into chains, and lived constantly under the menace of the sword. He was scorned and scourged . . .

As the East and the West are illumined by one sun, so all races, nations, and creeds shall be seen as the servants of the One God. The whole earth is one home, and all peoples, did they but know it, are bathed in the oneness of God's mercy. God created all. He gives sustenance to all. He guides and trains all under the shadow of His bounty. We must follow the example God Himself gives us, and do away with all disputations and quarrels . . .

In the future untrue reports will be spread regarding Baha'u'llah in order to hinder the spread of Truth. I tell you this, that you may be awake and prepared.

I leave you with prayer that all the beauty of the Kingdom may be yours. In deep regret at our separation, I bid you good-bye.[91]

'Abdu'l-Bahá left for Paris on October 3rd. That morning everything was ready for His departure. But He made no effort to leave and was engaged in writing. Let us again hear Lady Blomfield tell the story in her vivid prose:

'Abdu'l-Bahá sat calmly writing. We reminded Him that the hour to leave for the train was at hand. He looked up, saying: 'There are things of more importance than trains,' and He continued to write.

Suddenly in breathless haste a man came in, carrying in his hand a beautiful garland of white flowers. Bowing low before the Master, he said: 'In the name of the disciples of Zoroaster, the Pure One, I hail Thee as the Promised Sháh Bahrám!'

Then the man, for a sign, garlanded 'Abdu'l-Bahá, and proceeded to anoint each and all of the amazed friends who were present with precious oil, which had the odour of fresh roses.

This brief but impressive ceremony concluded, 'Abdu'l-

Bahá, having carefully divested Himself of the garland, departed for the train.*

We had witnessed a solemn act in the Mysterious Sacred Drama of the World.[92]

Nothing has been said, so far, of 'Abdu'l-Bahá's keen sense of humour. A small incident in the course of His last afternoon in London illustrates it. A reporter wished to know what 'Abdu'l-Bahá's future plans were. To that reporter's astonishment, 'Abdu'l-Bahá spoke in English, and said that He was going to Paris, and then back to Egypt. How well 'Abdu'l-Bahá pronounced English, the reporter remarked. Whereupon He rose up and, pacing the room, uttered a number of complicated English words, such as 'hippopotamus', and then laughingly said, 'Very difficult English words I speak.'

One day in the Holy Land He told Harlan Ober, an American Bahá'í, that he was to go to India. Harlan Ober did travel far and wide in the interests of the Faith, but at that particular time he did not cherish making that journey. A few days later 'Abdu'l-Bahá told him to go to America. 'But, Master,' Ober said, 'I thought I was going to India.' 'So did Christopher Columbus,' 'Abdu'l-Bahá replied.

Byfleet in Surrey was a village which 'Abdu'l-Bahá visited twice during His sojourn in London. There, at Vanners, a number of working women from Passmore Edwards' Settlement were staying. 'We gathered round him in a circle,' they wrote, 'and he made us sit beside him in the window seat. One of the members, who was ill, had a specially beautiful greeting from him. Abdul Baha began by saying, as he seated himself: "Are you happy?" and our faces must have shown him that we were. He then said: "I love you all, you are the children of the Kingdom, and you are accepted of God. Though you may be poor here, you are rich in the

* Lady Blomfield preserved that garland.

treasures of the Kingdom. I am the Servant of the poor. Remember how His Holiness Jesus said: 'Blessed are the poor!' If all the queens of the earth were gathered here, I could not be more glad."

'Abdul Baha knew that we had a treasury box from which we try to help people less fortunate than ourselves. Presently he rose, and said: "You are dear to me. I want to do something for you! I cannot cook for you (he had previously seen us busy in the kitchen) but here is something for your fund." He went round the circle to each, with a beautiful smile, shaking hands with all, and giving the Bahai greeting: "Allaho'Abha." '93

The only other city in Britain which 'Abdu'l-Bahá visited during His first English sojourn was Bristol, where He stayed at the Clifton Guest House, Clifton, during the weekend of September 23rd to 25th, 1911. At a reception held for Him in the Guest House, which some ninety well-known citizens of Bristol attended, He spoke of Bahá'u'lláh: 'As day follows night, and after sunset comes the dawn, so Jesus Christ appeared on the horizon of this world like a Sun of Truth; even so when the people—after forgetting the teachings of Christ and His example of love to all humanity—had again grown tired of material things, a heavenly Star shone once more in Persia, a new illumination appeared and now a great light is spreading throughout all lands.'94

In the City of London, at the invitation of the Lord Mayor, 'Abdu'l-Bahá called on him at the Mansion House; during their conversation He said of England: 'It is well with a country when the magistrates are as fathers to the people.'

In addition to the daily assemblage of visitors at 97 Cadogan Gardens where 'Abdu'l-Bahá spoke, other meetings were arranged by Bahá'ís—by Mrs Thornburgh-Cropper, Miss Ethel Rosenberg, Miss Elizabeth Herrick, Miss Marion

Jack* whom 'Abdu'l-Bahá called 'General Jack'—some
being held in their homes. Lady Blomfield writes of a day in
East Sheen at the home of Mr and Mrs Jenner. 'Their three
small children clambered on to His knee,' she relates, 'clung
round His neck, and remained as quiet as wee mice whilst
the Master spoke, He meanwhile stroking the hair of the
tiny ones and saying: "Blessed are the children, of whom His
Holiness Christ said: 'Of such are the Kingdom of Heaven'.
Children have no worldly ambitions. Their hearts are pure.
We must become like children . . . " '95

The home of Mr and Mrs Jenner was near Richmond Park.
'Abdu'l-Bahá loved trees and verdure. He went into the
park. A number of boys and a girl, mounted on ponies,
were racing there. 'Abdu'l-Bahá watched them, and when
the girl won He was delighted. He clapped. 'Bravo, bravo,'
He shouted. In the evening the way back to Cadogan
Gardens led over the Serpentine Bridge. Dusk had fallen and
lights twinkled through the foliage. It was an enchanting
sight, and 'Abdu'l-Bahá said: 'I am very much pleased with
this scene. Light is good, most good. There was much
darkness in the prison at 'Akká.' British Bahá'ís who were
with Him felt deeply the poignancy of His remark and expressed their joy that He had at last gained His freedom.
He replied:

> Freedom is not a matter of place . . . I was happy in that
> prison, for those days were passed in the path of service.
> To me prison was freedom.
> Troubles are a rest to me.
> Death is life.
> To be despised is honour.
> Therefore was I full of happiness all through that
> prison time.

* She was Canadian—a stalwart pioneer to the end; she passed
away in Bulgaria, in March 1954.

When one is released from the prison of self, that is indeed freedom! For self is the greatest prison.

When this release takes place, one can never be imprisoned. Unless one accepts dire vicissitudes, not with dull resignation, but with radiant acquiescence, one cannot attain this freedom.[96]

The day 'Abdu'l-Bahá arrived in London He had said: 'Heaven has blessed this day.' He was at the outset of His tour of the Western world. We have seen and, as the story unfolds in the following pages, we shall see how abundantly blessed that day was.

SOJOURN IN PARIS

Paris has a particular distinction among all the cities in Europe, inasmuch as the first Bahá'í centre of the European continent was instituted there. 'Abdu'l-Bahá's visit to the French metropolis lasted nine weeks. He took His residence at 4 Avenue de Camoëns in the area of Quai de Passy. Monsieur and Madame Dreyfus-Barney were at hand to serve Him. Lady Blomfield, her two daughters—Mary Esther and Rose Ellinor Cecilia—and Miss Beatrice Marion Platt (all of whom had also zealously helped at 97 Cadogan Gardens) had come over from London. It was their assiduous application which produced an invaluable collection of 'Abdu'l-Bahá's Talks: a book that has, since 1912, gone through many editions* on both sides of the Atlantic. Horace Holley, who was an eyewitness, has stated that 'As London emphasized the social and spiritual aspects of Bahaism, so Paris revealed its intellectual content and unparalleled power of definition'.[97]

The Trocadéro Gardens are adjacent to the Avenue de Camoëns. 'Abdu'l-Bahá found relaxation in walks through the gardens. It was natural that His appearance should attract attention. But even more, He commanded reverence. A cabman, noticing Him, stopped his *fiacre* and took off his cap, betokening his respect. His gesture was acknowledged by 'Abdu'l-Bahá with great courtesy. One Sunday 'Abdu'l-Bahá went to a shabby district of Paris which was

* With the title of *Paris Talks* in Britain, and *The Wisdom of 'Abdu'l-Bahá* in the United States.

rather contemptuous of convention. He had been invited
to address a congregation of the poor in a mission hall.
On His way back He came upon a noisy crowd. There was
a giant of a man waving about a large loaf of bread. As soon
as his eyes lighted upon 'Abdu'l-Bahá he became calm and
silent. Then waving once again his loaf of bread, he hastened
to clear a passage for 'Abdu'l-Bahá. 'Make way, make way!
He is my Father, make way,' he told his compatriots. The
boisterous, roysting crowd parted, stood aside, respectful, saluting. Smiling at those men and women, 'Abdu'l-
Bahá called them His dear friends and thanked them profoundly.

The salon of the apartment at the Avenue de Camoëns
witnessed, as did the drawing-room of the flat in Cadogan
Gardens, a daily stream of visitors. However, these gatherings in Paris were more varied in their composition and many
more nationalities were represented. 'Abdu'l-Bahá made a
special plea on behalf of peoples from other lands:

> Let not conventionality cause you to seem cold and un-
> sympathetic when you meet strange people from other
> countries. Do not look at them as though you suspected
> them of being evil-doers, thieves and boors. You think
> it necessary to be very careful, not to expose yourselves
> to the risk of making acquaintance with such, possibly,
> undesirable people.
>
> I ask you not to think only of yourselves. Be kind to the
> strangers . . .
>
> Help to make them feel at home; find out where they
> are staying, ask if you may render them any service; try
> to make their lives a little happier.
>
> In this way, even if, sometimes, what you at first sus-
> pected should be true, still go out of your way to be kind
> to them—this kindness will help them to become better.
>
> After all, why should any foreign people be treated as
> strangers? . . . Put into practice the Teaching of Bahá'u'-

lláh, that of kindness to all nations. Do not be content
with showing friendship in words alone, let your heart
burn with loving kindness for all who may cross your
path . . .

What profit is there in agreeing that universal friendship is good, and talking of the solidarity of the human
race as a grand ideal? Unless these thoughts are translated
into the world of action, they are useless.

The wrong in the world continues to exist just because
people talk only of their ideals, and do not strive to put
them into practice. If actions took the place of words, the
world's misery would very soon be changed into comfort.[98]

Every morning in the salon of His apartment 'Abdu'l-
Bahá spoke in like manner. And every day brought visitors
from near and far. Mírzá Muḥammad-Báqir Khán* of Shíráz
was in Paris, in the entourage of 'Abdu'l-Bahá. Prince
Zillu's-Sulṭán† was also in the French capital, a refugee,
banished by the Constitutionalists. Through the good
offices of the former, the Prince, responsible for the death
and sufferings of Bahá'ís, came into the presence of 'Abdu'l-
Bahá. Lady Blomfield writes:

One day, a certain man, a Persian of high degree, came
to 'Abdu'l-Bahá: 'I have been exiled from my country.
I pray you intercede for me that I may be permitted to
return.'

'You will be allowed to return.'

'Some of my land has been bought by one of the Bahá'í
friends. I desire to possess that property once more.'

'It shall be given back to you and without payment.'

'Who is the young man standing behind you? May he
be presented to me?'

* See p. 53.   † See n. 70.

'He is Mírzá Jalál, son of one of the martyred brothers of Iṣfahán.'

'I had no part in that crime.'

'The part you took in that event, I know. Moreover, your motive I know.'[99]

That 'Persian of high degree' was Prince Zillu's-Sulṭán, who tried to put the blame on his father.

On October 21st 'Abdu'l-Bahá told His audience:

I hope you are all happy and well. I am not happy, but very sad. The news of the Battle of Benghazi grieves my heart. I wonder at the human savagery that still exists in the world! How is it possible for men to fight from morning until evening, killing each other, shedding the blood of their fellow-men: and for what object? To gain possession of a part of the earth! Even the animals, when they fight, have an immediate and more reasonable cause for their attacks! How terrible it is that men, who are of the higher kingdom, can descend to slaying and bringing misery to their fellow-beings, for the possession of a tract of land! . . . Land belongs not to one people, but to all people . . . There is nothing so heart-breaking and terrible as an outburst of human savagery!

I charge you all that each one of you concentrate all the thoughts of your heart on love and unity. When a thought of war comes, oppose it by a stronger thought of peace . . . Do not despair! Work steadily. Sincerity and love will conquer hate . . .

In this room today are members of many races, French, American, English, German, Italian, brothers and sisters meeting in friendship and harmony! Let this gathering be a foreshadowing of what will, in very truth, take place in this world, when every child of God realizes that they are leaves of one tree, flowers in one garden, drops in one ocean, and sons and daughters of one Father, whose name is love![100]

Bahá'u'lláh in His Tablet to Queen Victoria had thus addressed the sovereign authorities of the world:

> Be united, O Kings of the earth, for thereby will the tempest of discord be stilled amongst you, and your people find rest, if ye be of them that comprehend. Should any one among you take up arms against another, rise ye all against him, for this is naught but manifest justice.[101]

And in the *Kitáb-i-Aqdas*—the Most Holy Book—He had counselled the 'Rulers of America and the Presidents of the Republics therein':

> Bind ye the broken with the hands of justice, and crush the oppressor who flourisheth with the rod of the commandments of your Lord, the Ordainer, the All-Wise.[102]

'Abdu'l-Bahá came back to the theme of the slaughter in Tripolitania, on November 24th:

> I have just been told that there has been a terrible accident in this country. A train has fallen into the river and at least twenty people have been killed. This is going to be a matter for discussion in the French Parliament today, and the Director of the State Railway will be called upon to speak . . . I am filled with wonder and surprise to notice what interest and excitement has been aroused throughout the whole country on account of the death of twenty people, while they remain cold and indifferent to the fact that thousands of Italians, Turks, and Arabs are killed in Tripoli! The horror of this wholesale slaughter has not disturbed the Government at all! Yet these unfortunate people are human beings too . . . They are all men, they all belong to the family of mankind, but they are of other lands and races. It is no concern of the disinterested countries if these men are cut to pieces, this wholesale slaughter does not affect them! . . . The people

of these other lands have children and wives, mothers, daughters, and little sons! In these countries today there is hardly a house free from the sound of bitter weeping, scarcely can one find a home untouched by the cruel hand of war . . .

Let us all strive night and day to help in the bringing about of better conditions. My heart is broken by these terrible things and cries aloud—may this cry reach other hearts![103]

On November 4th, 'Abdu'l-Bahá addressed these pregnant words to the people gathered in His salon:

Lift up your hearts above the present and look with eyes of faith into the future! Today the seed is sown, the grain falls upon the earth, but behold the day will come when it shall rise a glorious tree and the branches thereof shall be laden with fruit. Rejoice and be glad that this day has dawned, try to realize its power, for it is indeed wonderful! God has crowned you with honour and in your hearts has He set a radiant star; verily the light thereof shall brighten the whole world![104]

Taking each day one of the basic principles of the Faith of His Father to expound, one day He spoke of the 'Means of Existence':

One of the most important principles of the Teaching of Bahá'u'lláh is the right of every human being to the daily bread whereby they exist, or the equalisation of the means of livelihood.

The arrangements of the circumstances of the people must be such that poverty shall disappear, that everyone, as far as possible, according to his rank and position, shall share in comfort and well-being.

We see amongst us men who are overburdened with

riches on the one hand, and on the other those unfortunate ones who starve with nothing; those who possess several stately palaces, and those who have not where to lay their head . . .

This condition of affairs is wrong, and must be remedied. Now the remedy must be carefully undertaken. It cannot be done by bringing to pass absolute equality between men.

Equality is a chimera! It is entirely impracticable! Even if equality could be achieved it could not continue—and if its existence were possible, the whole order of the world would be destroyed. The law of order must always obtain in the world of humanity. Heaven has so decreed in the creation of man.

Some are full of intelligence, others have an ordinary amount of it, and others again are devoid of intellect. In these three classes of men there is order but not equality. How could it be possible that wisdom and stupidity should be equal? Humanity, like a great army, requires a general, captains, under-officers in their degree, and soldiers, each with their own appointed duties. Degrees are absolutely necessary to ensure an orderly organization . . .

Certainly, some being enormously rich and others lamentably poor, an organization is necessary to control and improve this state of affairs. It is important to limit riches, as it is also of importance to limit poverty . . .

There must be special laws made, dealing with these extremes of riches and of want . . . The general rights of mankind must be guarded and preserved.

The government of the countries should conform to the Divine Law which gives equal justice to all. This is the only way in which the deplorable superfluity of great wealth and miserable, demoralizing, degrading poverty can be abolished. Not until this is done will the Law of God be obeyed.[105]

'Abdu'l-Bahá's addresses were of course not confined to talks at 4 Avenue de Camoëns. He spoke in the homes of

Bahá'ís, in the Theosophical Society headquarters, at *L'Alliance Spiritualiste*, in the Church of Pastor Wagner (*Foyer de l'Âme*). 'Abdu'l-Bahá spoke unequivocally to the congregation of Pastor Wagner's church, on November 26th, of the divine missions of Muḥammad and of Bahá'u'-lláh:

All down the ages the prophets of God have been sent into the world to serve the cause of truth—Moses brought the law of truth, and all the prophets of Israel after Him sought to spread it. When Jesus came He lighted the flaming torch of truth, and carried it aloft so that the whole world might be illumined thereby. After Him came His chosen apostles, and they went far and wide, carrying the light of their Master's teaching into a dark world—and, in their turn, passed on.

Then came Muḥammad, who in His time and way spread the knowledge of truth among a savage people; for this has always been the mission of God's elect.

So, at last, when Bahá'u'lláh arose in Persia, this was His most ardent desire, to rekindle the waning light of truth in all lands . . .

All the Manifestations of God came with the same purpose, and they have all sought to lead men into the paths of virtue. Yet we, their servants, still dispute among ourselves! Why is it thus? Why do we not love one another and live in unity?

It is because we have shut our eyes to the underlying principle of all religions, that God is one, that He is the Father of us all, that we are all immersed in the ocean of His mercy and sheltered and protected by His loving care.

The glorious Sun of Truth shines for all alike, the waters of Divine Mercy immerse each one, and His Divine favour is bestowed on all His children . . . The day is coming when all the religions of the world will unite, for in principle they are one already . . .

Doctors of religion were instituted to bring spiritual healing to the peoples and to be the cause of unity among the nations. If they become the cause of division they had better not exist! A remedy is given to cure a disease, but if it only succeeds in aggravating the complaint, it is better to leave it alone. If religion is only to be a cause of disunion it had better not exist . . .

All down the ages we see how blood has stained the surface of the earth; but now a ray of greater light has come, man's intelligence is greater, spirituality is beginning to grow, and a time is surely coming when the religions of the world will be at peace. Let us leave the discordant arguments concerning outward forms, and let us join together to hasten forward the Divine Cause of unity, until all humanity knows itself to be one family, joined together in love.[106]

The last meeting which 'Abdu'l-Bahá addressed in Paris was held at 15 Rue Greuze, on December 1st. The next day He left for Egypt. 'Abdu'l-Bahá said:

Humanity may be likened to a tree. This tree has branches, leaves, buds and fruit. Think of all men as being flowers, leaves or buds of this tree, and try to help each and all to realize and enjoy God's blessings. God neglects none: He loves all. The only real difference that exists between people is that they are at various stages of development . . . but one and all are the children of God. Love them all with your whole heart; no one is a stranger to the other, all are friends. Tonight I come to say farewell to you—but bear this in your minds, that although our bodies may be far apart, in spirit we shall always be together.

I bear you one and all in my heart, and will forget none of you—and I hope that none of you will forget me.

I in the East, and you in the West, let us try with heart and soul that unity may dwell in the world, that all the peoples may become one people, and that the whole surface of the earth may be like one country—for the Sun of Truth shines on all alike.[107]

'Abdu'l-Bahá's visitors were so varied. One day a social worker came to Him: 'I have come from the French Congo, where I have been engaged in mitigating the hardships of some of the natives. For sixteen years I have worked in that country.' To that 'Abdu'l-Bahá said: 'It was a great comfort to me in the darkness of my prison to know the work which you were doing.'[108]

A visitor, to her great relief, reached the doors of 'Abdu'l-Bahá's house only two days before He left Paris. She had travelled post-haste from the United States, and had a remarkable story to relate. At home her little daughter had asked her what she would do should the Lord Jesus return to the world. She would rush to seek Him, she had said, only to be told that the Lord Jesus was here. How did she know, the mother had enquired. The child replied that the Lord Jesus had told her Himself. Some days later the mother was reproached for not doing what she had said she would do. Twice the Lord Jesus had told her that He was here, the little girl insisted. But she did not know where to look, the mother told her child. And the child was certain that they would discover where to go, where to look. That afternoon, on a walk, the little girl suddenly stopped and, excited and ecstatic, pointed to a shop where magazines were displayed. Prominent there was the photograph of 'Abdu'l-Bahá. There, there, the child shouted, was the Lord Jesus. The magazine which contained the photograph of 'Abdu'l-Bahá led the way to Paris, and the American lady, taking the first available boat to cross the Atlantic, sailed that very night.[109]

PART II

AMERICA, FROM COAST TO COAST

CHAPTER 12

THE FIRST VISITS
April 11th–June 10th

'Abdu'l-Bahá wintered in Egypt. The lavish expenditure of
His energies, during the three months' sojourn in London
and Paris, had heavily taxed His physical strength. A period
of relative rest was necessary before embarking on a tour of
the United States which was bound to be much more
taxing. In the meantime American Bahá'ís were pleading
hard for His presence in their midst. They raised £3,200
sterling for the expenses of His journey. 'Abdu'l-Bahá
thanked them and returned the money. It was suggested
to Him that He might travel in the *Titanic*, about to make
her maiden voyage. But He preferred a slower boat, and a
long sea journey. He chose the S.S. *Cedric* which sailed from
Alexandria on March 25th 1912. With 'Abdu'l-Bahá were
His eldest grandson, Shoghi Effendi; His personal attendants, Siyyid Asadu'lláh-i-Qumí and Áqá Khusraw (who
was of Burmese origin); His secretaries, Mírzá Maḥmúd-i-
Zarqání and Mírzá Munír-i-Zayn; His translator, Dr
Amínu'lláh Faríd. At Naples, Italian physicians who came
aboard insisted that Shoghi Effendi, Mírzá Munír, and Áqá
Khusraw ought to disembark and return to Egypt. They
diagnosed an infection of the eyes which disqualified all
three from entry into the United States. There were strong
reasons to doubt their verdict and their impartiality. Italy
and Turkey were still at war, and the Italians took 'Abdu'l-
Bahá and His entourage to be Turks. Six Western Bahá'ís—
Mr Woodcock of Canada, his wife and daughter, Mr and Mrs

Ashton of Denver, and Miss Matthew of London—had also joined the S.S. *Cedric* at Naples. They tried to persuade the Italian physicians to reconsider their verdict, but the medical men were adamant. This painful episode, at the very start of the journey, greatly saddened 'Abdu'l-Bahá.

The officers of the ship invited 'Abdu'l-Bahá to address a meeting in the main lounge, which they had arranged. It was a large gathering. Also on board were two Consuls of Russia and Italy who, with many others among the passengers, asked to meet 'Abdu'l-Bahá in person. Throughout the sea voyage He held converse with them; their reverence for Him was truly remarkable.

On April 11th S.S. *Cedric* docked in New York. Bahá'ís of New York and its environs had gathered in strength along the shore. But 'Abdu'l-Bahá did not leave His stateroom, and sent word to the Bahá'ís to depart; He would meet them in the afternoon at the home of Mr and Mrs Edward B. Kinney. The press, however, had its immediate demands. Reporters asked 'Abdu'l-Bahá what His purpose was, and what had brought Him to America. He answered that His aim was the establishment of universal peace and the oneness of mankind. He had visited London and Paris, and now He had come to America to meet those who worked for the cause of peace.

After taking His residence at the Hotel Ansonia 'Abdu'l-Bahá went out to meet the hundreds who awaited Him. Juliet Thompson, a talented artist and a faithful Bahá'í of the early years, has written:

> When I arrived Abdul Baha was sitting in the center of the dining-room, near the flower-strewn table . . . At His knees stood Sanford and Howard Kinney* and His arms were around them . . . No words could describe the ineffable peace of Him. The people stood around Him in

* The Kinney children.

rows and circles—several hundred in the rooms; many were sitting on the floor in the dining-room. We made a dark background for His effulgence. Our tears only reflected Him; and there were many, many who were weeping just at the sight of Him . . . just at the sight of that divineness. For at last we saw divineness—incarnate . . . [110]

For long had the Bahá'ís of America hoped and prayed for that day. 'Abdu'l-Bahá told them:

After arriving today, although weary with travel, I had the utmost longing and yearning to see you and could not resist this meeting. Now that I have met you, all my weariness has vanished, for your meeting is the cause of spiritual happiness.

I was in Egypt and was not feeling well; but I wished to come to you in America. My friends said 'This is a long journey; the sea is wide; you should remain here.' But the more they advised and insisted, the greater became my longing to take this trip and now I have come to America to meet the friends of God. This long voyage will prove how great is my love for you. There were many troubles and vicissitudes but in the thought of meeting you, all these things vanished and were forgotten . . .

I am very happy to meet you all here today. Praise be to God! that your faces are shining with the love of Bahá'u'lláh. To behold them is the cause of great spiritual happiness. We have arranged to meet you every day at the homes of the friends.

In the East, people were asking me 'Why do you undertake this long voyage; your body cannot endure such hardships of travel?' When it is necessary, my body can endure everything. It has withstood forty years of imprisonment and can still undergo the utmost trials.

I will see you again. Now I will greet each one of you personally. It is my hope that you will all be happy and that we may meet again and again.[111]

The first public address of 'Abdu'l-Bahá on the American continent was given in New York to the congregation of the Church of the Ascension, on April 14th. This was the central point of His message:

Today the world of humanity is in need of international unity and conciliation. To establish these great fundamental principles a propelling power is needed. It is self-evident that unity of the human world and the 'Most Great Peace' cannot be accomplished through material means. They cannot be established through political power, for the political interests of nations are various and the policies of peoples are divergent and conflicting. They cannot be founded through racial or patriotic power, for these are human powers, selfish and weak. The very nature of racial differences and patriotic prejudices prevents the realization of this unity and agreement. Therefore it is evidenced that the promotion of the oneness of the kingdom of humanity which is the essence of the teachings of all the Manifestations of God is impossible except through the divine power and breaths of the Holy Spirit. Other powers are too weak and are incapable of accomplishing this.

For man, two wings are necessary. One wing is the physical power and material civilization; the other is the spiritual power and divine civilization. With one wing only, flight is impossible. Two wings are essential. Therefore no matter how much material civilization advances it cannot attain to perfection except through uplift of the spiritual civilization.[112]

The church was packed to its capacity, and as 'Abdu'l-Bahá left the building people rushed forward to greet Him. A woman caught hold of His cloak and burst into tears. Sobs drowned her speech. Similar scenes were to be witnessed again and again: the onrush of the public, eager to meet that wondrous visitor from the East; outpouring of deep, genuine emotion. 'Abdu'l-Bahá faced all situations with dignity and composure, with all-embracing kindliness and compassion.

At the home of Mr and Mrs Alexander Morten, on April 13th, such was the press of people that 'Abdu'l-Bahá could not reach the drawing-room, and had to address them from the top of the staircase where He stood. He had arrived at that house, fatigued and exhausted, after a day much occupied with throngs of visitors. Perforce He had gone to an upper floor to rest awhile. And yet, standing, He delivered a talk vibrant with power. He spoke of seasons in the physical world and in the world of spirit, of the advent of Christ and of the advent of Bahá'u'lláh. They both renewed the cycle of seasons in the world of spirit. 'The world spiritual is like unto the world phenomenal. They are the exact counterpart of each other. Whatever objects appear in the world of existence are the outer pictures of the world of heaven,'[113] He said. The translator, in the course of this talk, paused to search for the right word. 'Abdu'l-Bahá Himself provided it. With a smile He said in English: 'Summer'. His discourse over, He had, once again, to retire and rest. But there were hundreds moving up the stairs, towards the room in which He was resting. 'Abdu'l-Bahá would not hear of shutting them out. 'Let them come,' He said, and received them in small groups, one succeeding the other. His boundless love for them sustained Him.

In the opening years of the century, the economic theories of Henry George were fashionable. A young man who believed in his panacea was there on that day, and asked for a message to convey to the 'single-taxers'. 'Abdu'l-Bahá, laughing, gave him this message: 'Tell them to come into the Kingdom of God. There they will find plenty of land—and there are no taxes on it.'[114]

That amazing scene in the home of Mr and Mrs Morten

was to be witnessed time and time again during the eight glorious months of 'Abdu'l-Bahá's American tour.

On April 19th, 'Abdu'l-Bahá spoke at Earl Hall of Columbia University. The task of science and man's mastery over and superiority to nature constituted the central theme of His address:

In brief, man through the possession of this ideal endowment of scientific investigation is the most noble product of creation, the governor of nature. He takes the sword from nature's hand and uses it upon nature's head. According to natural law, night is a period of darkness and obscurity, but man by utilizing the power of electricity, by wielding this electric sword overcomes the darkness and dispels the gloom. Man is superior to nature and makes nature do his bidding. Man is a sensitive being; nature is minus sensation. Man has memory and reason; nature lacks them. Man is nobler than nature. There are powers within him of which nature is devoid. It may be claimed that these powers are from nature itself and that man is a part of nature. In answer to this statement we will say that if nature is the whole and man is a part of that whole, how could it be possible for a part to possess qualities and virtues which are absent in the whole.[115]

There were so many in that vast audience who wished to be presented to 'Abdu'l-Bahá that, due to nightfall and His next engagement, it was not possible to keep to the schedule which included inspection of various departments of the University.

This next engagement was a visit to the Bowery Mission. 'Abdu'l-Bahá had said the previous day: 'I am in love with the poor', and He had given Juliet Thompson and Edward Getsinger a thousand-franc note each to convert to small change, instructing them to bring the money to the Mission

Hall the next night. Some four hundred of society's outcasts were in the hall when 'Abdu'l-Bahá arrived. Addressing
them He said:

Tonight I am very happy for I have come here to meet my
friends. I consider you my relatives, my companions;
and I am your comrade . . .
  When Jesus Christ appeared it was the poor who first
accepted Him, not the rich . . . you are His comrades for
He outwardly was poor not rich. Even this earth's happiness does not depend upon wealth . . . While Bahá'u'lláh
was in Baghdád . . . He left all He had and went alone
from the city, living two years among the poor. They
were His comrades . . . He chose for one of His names
the title of 'The Poor One', and often in His writings
refers to Himself as 'Darvísh' which in Persian means
'poor'; and of this title He was very proud. He ad-
monished all that we must be the servants of the poor,
helpers of the poor, remember the sorrows of the poor,
associate with them for thereby we may inherit the kingdom of heaven . . .
  Jesus was a poor man. One night when He was out in
the fields the rain began to fall. He had no place to go for
shelter so He lifted His eyes toward heaven saying 'O
Father! for the birds of the air Thou hast created nests,
for the sheep a fold, for the animals dens, for the fishes
places of refuge, but for me Thou hast provided no
shelter; there is no place where I may lay my head; my
bed consists of the cold ground, my lamps at night are
the stars and my food is the grass of the field, yet who upon
earth is richer than I? . . .'
  And in conclusion I ask you to accept 'Abdu'l-Bahá
as your servant.[116]

Then 'Abdu'l-Bahá walked to the entrance and, standing
there, shook hands with every one of those four hundred:
the flotsam and jetsam of humanity. At the same time He

put a coin or two in each palm. He had done the same for years, on Fridays, outside His own house in 'Akká—meeting the poor, dispensing aid, imparting to stunted lives the balm of care and affection and love. In the street others had gathered and there were also a number of children. 'Abdu'l-Bahá went forth to greet them and offer them also a coin or two. But what mattered most was not the price of a bed He was giving them, but that balm of love and care which healed the wounds of the spirit.

Back in the Hotel Ansonia 'Abdu'l-Bahá encountered a chambermaid, who had been deeply moved by His gift of roses to her; He emptied into her apron the bag containing the remainder of the coins. A Bahá'í told the chambermaid that 'Abdu'l-Bahá had been giving money to the poor at the Bowery Mission. 'I will do the same with this money. I too will give it,' she said. Later that evening 'Abdu'l-Bahá was seated with a number of visitors to whom He was saying as He laughed: 'Assuredly give to the poor! If you give them only words, when they put their hands into their pockets they will find themselves none the richer for you,' when the chambermaid came in. Her eyes were tear-laden and approaching 'Abdu'l-Bahá she said: 'I came to say good-bye, sir, and to thank you for all your goodness to me . . . I never expected such goodness. And to ask you—to *pray* for me!'[117]

The next day, April 20th, 'Abdu'l-Bahá travelled to Washington, D.C. Mrs Parsons had invited Him to take residence in her house. But 'Abdu'l-Bahá had telegraphed that a house should be rented for Him and His attendants. At the station, when He arrived, the Bahá'ís of Washington asked Him to accept Mrs Parsons' invitation. She had had that house specially built, they said, to receive Him and had eagerly awaited the day when it would be thus honoured. 'Abdu'l-Bahá would not have her sorely disappointed, but stipulated that only He and an interpreter would stay at

1700 18th Street Northwest, the home of Mrs Parsons, while others in His retinue should go to the rented house.

In the evening of the same day 'Abdu'l-Bahá addressed a meeting of the Orient-Occident-Unity Conference at the Public Library Hall. 'May this American democracy,' He said, 'be the first nation to establish the foundation of international agreement. May it be the first nation to proclaim the universality of mankind. May it be the first to upraise the standard of the "Most Great Peace" . . . '[118]

Audiences which 'Abdu'l-Bahá addressed in Washington included the congregations of the Universalist Church and the Metropolitan African Methodist Episcopal Church, also the Theosophists, and the students and members of the faculty of Howard University, perhaps the country's leading institution of higher learning for the Negro people. At the Universalist Church He declared:

The revered minister read from the words of the Gospel 'I have yet many things to say unto you, but ye cannot bear them now. Howbeit when he, the Spirit of truth is come, he shall guide you into all the truth.'* The century has dawned when the Spirit of truth can reveal these verities to mankind, proclaim that very Word, establish the real foundations of Christianity and deliver the nations and peoples from the bondage of forms and imitations . . . You must listen to the admonition of this Spirit of truth.[119]

At Howard University 'Abdu'l-Bahá totally rejected any validity for distinction of colour:

God does not behold differences of hue and complexion; He looks at the hearts . . . In the realm of genesis and creation the question of colour is of least importance . . . I am exceedingly glad that both white and coloured people have gathered here and I hope the time will come when

* See John xvi: 12–13.

they shall live together in the utmost peace, unity and friendship.[120]

But He also gave a solemn warning: To bring about complete reconciliation, effort is required by both the black and the white.

> . . . strive earnestly and put forth your greatest endeavour toward the accomplishment of this fellowship and the cementing of this bond of brotherhood between you. Such an attainment is not possible without will and effort on the part of each . . . Each one should endeavour to develop and assist the other toward mutual advancement. This is possible only by conjoining of effort and inclination. Love and unity will be fostered between you, thereby bringing about the oneness of mankind. For the accomplishment of unity between the coloured and whites will be an assurance of the world's peace.[121]

As usual, in the late afternoon of April 23rd the drawing-room of 1700 18th Street was thronged with visitors. 'Abdu'l-Bahá told them:

> Today I have been speaking from dawn until now, yet because of love, fellowship and desire to be with you, I have come here to speak again briefly. Within the last few days a terrible event has happened in the world; an event saddening to every heart and grieving every spirit. I refer to the 'Titanic' disaster in which many of our fellow human beings were drowned, a number of beautiful souls passed beyond this earthly life. Although such an event is indeed regrettable, we must realize that everything which happens is due to some wisdom and that nothing happens without a reason. Therein is a mystery; but whatever the reason and mystery it was a very sad occurrence, one which brought tears to many eyes and distress to many souls. I was greatly affected by this

disaster. Some of those who were lost, voyaged on the 'Cedric' with us as far as Naples and afterwards sailed upon the other ship. When I think of them I am very sad indeed.[122]

He added that although they had been cut off so abruptly from life in this world there are other worlds beyond, as Christ had said: 'In my Father's house are many mansions.'

On April 24th 'Abdu'l-Bahá's first engagement was a reception for children at Studio Hall, 1219 Connecticut Avenue. When He arrived the children were singing. Seeing them gathered so happily together gave Him great delight. Afterwards 'Abdu'l-Bahá said:

What a wonderful meeting this is! What a wonderful meeting this is! These are the children of the kingdom. The song we have just listened to was very beautiful in melody and words. The art of music is divine and effective. It is the food of the soul and spirit . . . The latent talents with which the hearts of these children are endowed will find expression through the medium of music. Therefore you must exert yourselves to make them proficient; teach them to sing with excellence and effect . . . Likewise it is necessary that the schools teach it in order that the souls and hearts of the pupils may become vivified and exhilarated and their lives be brightened with enjoyment.

. . . Know ye the value of these children for they are all my children.[123]

There were two other meetings to address on April 24th, the third, in the evening, at the home of Mrs Andrew J. Dyer, where both the white and the black had gathered in appreciable numbers. 'Abdu'l-Bahá was greatly fatigued and disinclined to talk at length. But noticing the impressive harmony of the two races in that assemblage, He was particularly moved to speak.

This evening I will speak to you [He said] upon the subject of existence and non-existence, life and death. Existence is the expression and outcome of composition and combination. Non-existence is the expression and outcome of division and disintegration. If we study the forms of existence in the material universe, we find that all created things are the result of composition. Material elements have grouped together in infinite variety and endless forms. Each organism is a compound; each object is an expression of elemental affinity. We find the complex human organism simply an aggregation of cellular structure; the tree is a composite of plant cells; the animal a combination and grouping of cellular atoms or units, and so on. Existence or the expression of being is therefore composition, and non-existence is decomposition, division, disintegration. When elements have been brought together in a certain plan of combination the result is the human organism; when these elements separate and disperse, the outcome is death and non-existence. Life is therefore the product of composition, and death signifies decomposition.

Likewise in the world of minds and souls, fellowship, which is an expression of composition, is conducive to life; whereas discord, which is an expression of decomposition, is the equivalent of death. Without cohesion among the individual elements which compose the body-politic, disintegration and decay must inevitably follow and life be extinguished . . . Therefore in the world of humanity it is wise and seemly that all the individual members should manifest unity and affinity. In the clustered jewels of the races, may the coloured people be as sapphires and rubies, and the whites as diamonds and pearls. The composite beauty of humanity will be witnessed in their unity and blending . . . [124]

The very opening sentence of that talk, so rational, so logical, so instructive, had been: 'A meeting such as this seems like a beautiful cluster of precious jewels—pearls, rubies, diamonds and sapphires.'

'Abdu'l-Bahá had still another engagement that night. He was wonderfully exhilarated. As His automobile sped through the streets of Washington, to take Him to the home of the celebrated inventor of the telephone, Alexander Graham Bell, His voice could be heard, loud and clear, exclaiming: 'O Bahá'u'lláh! What hast Thou done! O Bahá'u'lláh! May my life be sacrificed for Thee! O Bahá'u'-lláh! May my soul be offered up for Thy sake! How full were Thy days with trials and tribulation! How severe the ordeals Thou didst endure! How solid the foundations Thou hast finally laid, and how glorious the banner Thou didst hoist.'

Alexander Bell had personally called the previous day to invite 'Abdu'l-Bahá to the conversazione at his home. A number of the savants present spoke, and then the host asked Ali-Kuli Khan, the Persian Chargé d'Affaires, to tell them of the history of the Bahá'í Faith. Next, he requested 'Abdu'l-Bahá to speak, and when it was the turn of another of those eminent men to address the meeting, he had only this to say: 'Where this Seer from the East has spoken, no room is there for my inadequate speech', and he sat down. It was well past midnight when 'Abdu'l-Bahá departed.

The following evening (April 25th) Yúsuf Díyá Páshá, the Turkish Ambassador, gave a dinner party in honour of 'Abdu'l-Bahá. It was a notable occasion. He, Who for forty years had been a prisoner of the Ottoman Empire, was receiving high tribute from the representative of that Empire in the capital of the great Republic of the West. Díyá Páshá had prepared a written address in Turkish which he presented to 'Abdu'l-Bahá. In it he referred to Him as 'the Unique One of the age, who had come to spread His glory and perfection amongst us', but 'Abdu'l-Bahá said:

'I am not worthy of this.' Juliet Thompson recounts: 'As I bade Zia Pasha good night, looking at me through a mist of tears, he said: "Truly, He is a Saint."'[125]

On April 27th, Lee McClung, Treasurer of the United States, had luncheon with 'Abdu'l-Bahá. Later Juliet Thompson asked Lee McClung: 'In what way did Abdul-Baha impress you?' Miss Thompson writes: 'He began shyly: "I seemed to be in the presence of one of the great old prophets—Isaiah—Elijah—Moses. And yet—it was more than that—He was like Christ . . . No—*now* I have it!—He seemed to me like my Divine Father." '[126]

That evening (April 27th), the last of 'Abdu'l-Bahá's stay in Washington, Mrs Parsons held a farewell reception at her home, attended by some three hundred men and women, prominent in public life. Admiral Peary of North Pole fame was there, as were eminent judges, members of Congress, and foreign representatives, including the Swiss Minister, with whom 'Abdu'l-Bahá talked about His visit to Switzerland. To the distinguished explorer 'Abdu'l-Bahá said: 'I hope you will discover the mysteries of the Kingdom of God.' And to a judge He said: 'Just as there is unity amongst the component parts of the United States, there can be unity amongst all the states of the world.' Theodore Roosevelt was another person prominent in public life who met 'Abdu'l-Bahá.

Mrs Parsons wished to offer 'Abdu'l-Bahá a large sum of money, to defray in part the vast expenses of His Western tour. But once again He declined to accept financial assistance from the Bahá'ís of the West and suggested that Mrs Parsons give the money she was offering to the poor.

In the late afternoon of April 28th 'Abdu'l-Bahá left for Chicago. That morning a number of ambassadors and ministers accredited to Washington had called on Him. The British Ambassador, James Bryce (later Viscount Bryce), was one of them.

As the train wended its way through the verdant and beautiful countryside, 'Abdu'l-Bahá's face showed signs of sorrow. Whenever He saw such green and delectable countryside, He told the Bahá'ís who were with Him, He remembered how Bahá'u'lláh loved verdure and open spaces, and how cruelly they had placed Him in the bleak city of 'Akká, deprived of the joys of natural scenery. Throughout the next day He oftentimes spoke of the days of Bahá'u'lláh, His mind occupied with the memories of His Father. Night had fallen when the train drew into the station in Chicago. A large number of Bahá'ís awaited His arrival. They were fervently calling out: 'Yá Bahá'u'l-Abhá.' 'Abdu'l-Bahá drove to the Hotel Plaza. There He sat down with the Bahá'ís, and told them how particularly pleased He was to be in Chicago. His visit to Washington had been very fruitful, the black and the white had been brought together; but Chicago was the city where the call of Bahá'u'lláh had first been raised on the American continent, and so this city was especially dear to Him.

The Bahá'í Temple Unity, a representative body designated to supervise the construction of the first Bahá'í House of Worship in America, had been conducting a convention in Chicago. Its sessions were ending the following day (April 30th). That morning 'Abdu'l-Bahá received a number of journalists to whom He spoke at length about the fundamentals of the Bahá'í Faith. Later in the day He addressed three meetings: a gathering for the reconciliation of the two races at Hull House; the fourth annual conference of the National Association for the Advancement of Colored People at Handel Hall; and the public concluding session of the convention of the Bahá'í Temple Unity at the Masonic Temple. He also met and conversed with many individuals and groups at His hotel. Such was the range of His activities in a single day. And He was just approaching His sixty-ninth year.

May 1st was a remarkable day, a day of very high distinction: 'Abdu'l-Bahá laid the foundation-stone of the Mother Temple of the West. At Wilmette on the shores of Lake Michigan ample land had been purchased. On the site chosen for the construction of the Temple, a large tent had been raised and here, after inspecting the grounds, 'Abdu'l-Bahá took His place to speak. He said:

The power which has gathered you here today notwithstanding the cold and windy weather is indeed mighty and wonderful. It is the power of God, the divine favour of Bahá'u'lláh which has drawn you together. We praise God that through His constraining love human souls are assembled and associated in this way.

Thousands of Mashriqu'l-Adhkárs, dawning-points of praise and mentionings of God for all religionists will be built in the Orient and Occident, but this being the first one erected in the Occident has great importance. In the future there will be many here and elsewhere; in Asia, Europe, even in Africa, New Zealand and Australia;* but this edifice in Chicago is of especial significance . . . [127]

Next, Irene Holmes handed 'Abdu'l-Bahá a small, gold trowel which she had ordered for this very purpose, and He dug the earth to lay the corner-stone, having chosen for this a fragment of rock brought by Mrs Nettie Tobin as her offering. Having done so, He invited the delegates of various American communities to do likewise. Following them, 'Abdu'l-Bahá asked a number of oriental Bahá'ís present to step forth and take part: Mihtar Ardishír Bahrám Surúsh represented Bahá'ís of Zoroastrian background, Siyyid

* The first Mashriqu'l-Adhkárs in Europe, Africa and Australasia were erected in Frankfurt, Kampala and Sydney; the first-named was dedicated in 1964 and the other two in 1961.

Asadu'lláh stood in for Bahá'ís of Muslim origin, Dr Zia (Ḍíyá) Bagdadi (Baghdádí) represented Arab Bahá'ís, and Ghodsieh (Qudsíyyih) Khánum-i-Ashraf the Bahá'í women of the Orient. Then the corner-stone was laid in place.[128]

A talk which 'Abdu'l-Bahá gave the following day at one of the gatherings in the Hotel Plaza must be particularly noted: the world desperately needs to take its lesson to heart. His theme was consultation:

> In this Cause, consultation is of vital importance; but spiritual conference and not the mere voicing of personal views is intended. In France I was present at a session of the senate but the experience was not impressive. Parliamentary procedure should have for its object the attainment of the light of truth upon questions presented and not furnish a battle-ground for opposition and self-opinion. Antagonism and contradiction are unfortunate and always destructive to truth. In the parliamentary meeting mentioned, altercation and useless quibbling were frequent; the result mostly confusion and turmoil; even in one instance a physical encounter took place between two members. It was not consultation but comedy.
>
> The purpose is to emphasize the statement that consultation must have for its object the investigation of truth. He who expresses an opinion should not voice it as correct and right but set it forth as a contribution to the consensus of opinion; for the light of reality becomes apparent when two opinions coincide. A spark is produced when flint and steel come together. Man should weigh his opinions with the utmost serenity, calmness and composure. Before expressing his own views he should carefully consider the views already advanced by others. If he finds that a previously expressed opinion is more true and worthy, he should accept it immediately and not wilfully hold to an opinion of his own . . . Opposition and division are deplorable.[129]

On May 3rd, members of an association of East Indians waited upon 'Abdu'l-Bahá and presented Him with a formal address. They expressed their gratitude that 'Abdu'l-Bahá had come to visit America, and also their hope that He might visit their homeland as well. From such a visit, they stated, great benefits would accrue to India: Hindus and Muslims were disunited, engaged in strife; 'Abdu'l-Bahá's teachings would bring them together.

The next day a scene was witnessed at the Plymouth Congregational Church which was indeed noteworthy. When Dr Milburne, the pastor of the church, introduced 'Abdu'l-Bahá, the congregation rose to its feet, and oblivious of the place and circumstances of a house of worship, broke into clapping, until 'Abdu'l-Bahá raised His hands and asked for silence. In his introductory remarks Dr Milburne said how eager he had been to meet 'Abdu'l-Bahá, having heard much about Him and His teachings from a friend, and that he had been on the point of journeying to 'Akká for that purpose, when the news came that 'Abdu'l-Bahá Himself would visit the United States. More was yet to come of public acclaim. People so crowded in to shake hands and ask for blessings that 'Abdu'l-Bahá negotiated the aisle to the door of the church with great difficulty. Zarqání, the chronicler of those memorable days, states that on that day many followed 'Abdu'l-Bahá, from meeting to meeting, in their cars.

On May 5th, 'Abdu'l-Bahá said farewell to the Bahá'ís of Chicago:

> I am going away but you must arise to serve the Word of God . . . Be in perfect unity. Never become angry with one another. Let your eyes be directed toward the kingdom of truth and not toward the world of creation. Love the creatures for the sake of God and not for themselves . . . Humanity is not perfect. There are imperfections in

every human being and you will always become unhappy if you look toward the people themselves. But if you look toward God you will love them and be kind to them, for the world of God is the world of perfection and complete mercy. Therefore do not look at the shortcomings of anybody; see with the sight of forgiveness. The imperfect eye beholds imperfections. The eye that covers faults looks toward the Creator of souls. He created them, trains and provides for them, endows them with capacity and life, sight and hearing; therefore they are the signs of His grandeur. You must love and be kind to everybody, care for the poor, protect the weak, heal the sick, teach and educate the ignorant.[130]

'Abdu'l-Bahá's visit to Cleveland, Ohio, was of very short duration. Leaving Chicago in the morning of May 6th, He reached Cleveland in the afternoon, and the next morning He proceeded to Pittsburgh. That one night in Cleveland, He stayed in the Euclid Hotel. In Pittsburgh too He stopped for only one night, at the Hotel Schenley, where He addressed a public meeting. On May 8th He travelled once again to Washington. It was a long train journey lasting from nine o'clock in the morning to nine o'clock in the evening. Some of His attendants begged Him to have a compartment reserved for Himself alone, that He might have adequate rest. 'Abdu'l-Bahá would not comply with their request. There were occasions, He told them, when certain expenses were necessitated in order to serve the true interests of the Faith, or to render aid and assistance; otherwise He had never sought privileges for His own person.

In Washington, He stayed in a rented house, 14 Harvard Street, which was in the vicinity of Mrs Parsons' residence. Some of the Washington clerics, incensed by the fame of 'Abdu'l-Bahá and the reverence which He commanded, had displayed signs of strong disapproval and hostility. On the other hand, there were those who wished 'Abdu'l-Bahá to address their congregations. He told them that He had to return to New York, but would come again to Washington.

On May 11th He left for New York, where an apartment at the Hudson Apartment House, 227 Riverside Drive, had been reserved for Him. Juliet Thompson writes:

A few of us prepared His rooms and filled them with flowers for Him—Carrie Kinney, Lua Getsinger, May Maxwell, Kate Ives, Grace Roberts* and I. Mr Mills and Mr Woodcock were also there waiting. His little apartment . . . was high above the world; its windows framed the sky. Now they were all open and the breeze blew in freshly from the river.[131]

And she further relates:

Lua, May and I, the three closest sisters I believe in this Cause, bound together by our rapturous memories of those early days of the Cause in Paris, when the Faith, the Knowledge and the Love of Abdul Baha were just dawning on the three of us—Lua, May and I, for the first time together in the glory of His Presence, sat in a corner on the floor, gazing through tears at Him, and whenever we could tear our eyes from the sorrowful yet radiant beauty of that Face, silhouetted against the sky, gazing at each other, speechless, in wonder too deep for words . . . still through tears.[132]

'Abdu'l-Bahá, on that late afternoon of May 11th, was telling the Bahá'ís gathered at 227 Riverside Drive of His journeys into the interior of the United States:

It is only three weeks that we have been away from the New York friends, yet so great has been the longing to

* Grace Robarts.

see you that it seems like three months. We have had no rest by day or night since we left you; either traveling, moving about or speaking; yet it was all so pleasantly done and we have been most happy. Praise be to God! everywhere and all the time it has been 'harakat', 'harakat', 'harakat' ('motion', 'motion', 'motion') . . .

Yesterday in Washington we met a group of important people. One prominent in political circles came with a justice of the Supreme Court. There were many ladies of the diplomatic circle present. After we had spoken, the politician* referred to raised the point that the foundation of all religions from time immemorial had been peace, love and accord—principles conducive to fellowship and unification,—yet Jesus, he declared, had been 'the cause of discord and strife and not a factor in the realization of unity'. 'Therefore,' he said, 'I cannot accept your statements and explanations that religion has been the source of human betterment.' After we explained further he said 'What you have stated may cause me to change my views and agree with you.' During this time the justice remained silent. Fearing he might have some feeling of dissatisfaction we asked if anything presented had been objectionable to his opinion. He replied 'Not at all! Not at all! It's all right! It's all right!' This is the characteristic expression of the Occident,—'All right!' 'All right!'[133]

'Abdu'l-Bahá spoke those words, 'All right!' 'All right!' in English, and the way He intoned them in the characteristic manner of the Occident sent a ripple of laughter round the room. The next day He was very fatigued and almost exhausted; yet, He travelled to Montclair, New Jersey, to speak from the pulpit of the Unity Church, and returned the same day to New York, to address that evening the International Peace Forum at Grace Methodist Episcopal Church. The following day (May 13th), 'Abdu'l-Bahá was

* He was a friend and associate of Theodore Roosevelt.

so exhausted that He had to keep to bed the whole day. The New York Peace Society had organized for that day a reception at the Hotel Astor. 'Abdu'l-Bahá was to be the guest of honour and the chief speaker. Juliet Thompson asked Him: 'Must you go to the Hotel Astor when you are so ill?' 'Abdu'l-Bahá replied: 'I work by the confirmations of the Holy Spirit. I do not work by hygienic laws. If I did I would get nothing done.'[134]

At the reception many speakers paid their share of tribute to the towering genius of 'Abdu'l-Bahá. Some spoke in such terms that later He was heard to remark on the use of the word 'Prophet'. He had oftentimes emphasized, He said, that He was 'the servant of Bahá', and yet they still applied such epithets to Him. He greatly wished that they would not. One of the speakers at that memorable meeting, who warmly applauded the person and the teachings of 'Abdu'l-Bahá, was the veteran American orientalist, Professor A. V. Williams Jackson of Columbia University, a scholar of high renown. 'Abdu'l-Bahá told that assemblage that 'no greater glory' is there in this day for man than service to the cause of peace, because 'Peace is light whereas war is darkness . . . Peace is the foundation of God; war is satanic institution'. Then He said:

According to an intrinsic law, all phenomena of being attain to a summit and degree of consummation, after which a new order and condition is established. As the instruments and science of war have reached the degree of thoroughness and proficiency, it is hoped that the transformation of the human world is at hand and that in the coming centuries all the energies and inventions of man will be utilized in promoting the interests of peace and brotherhood. Therefore may this esteemed and worthy society for the establishment of international peace be confirmed in its sincere intentions and empowered by God. Then will it hasten the time when the banner of universal agreement will be raised and international welfare will be proclaimed and consummated so that the darkness which now encompasses the world shall pass away.

Next He spoke of the Báb and Bahá'u'lláh. They, He said, 'devoted Their lives to the foundation of international peace and love among mankind.' Through all His ordeals, Bahá'u'lláh had striven

day and night to proclaim the oneness of humanity and promulgate the message of Universal Peace. From the prison of 'Akká He addressed the kings and rulers of the earth in lengthy letters summoning them to international agreement and explicitly stating that the standard of the 'Most Great Peace' would surely be upraised in the world.
    . . . The powers of earth cannot withstand the privileges and bestowals which God has ordained for this great and glorious century. It is a need and exigency of the time. Man can withstand anything except that which is divinely intended and indicated for the age and its requirements . . . [135]

The next three days, May 14th–16th, 'Abdu'l-Bahá spent by Lake Mohonk, having been invited to attend the Conference on Peace and Arbitration held there. The first evening He delivered an address, and the audience, composed of some of the leading men and women of America as well as representatives from other lands, clapped and clapped, asking for more. But 'Abdu'l-Bahá had to decline, because He was tired and had to rest His voice. When He left to return to New York He made a gift of an exquisite Persian rug to the president of the Conference. In New York, on May 19th, 'Abdu'l-Bahá spoke from the pulpit of the Church of the Divine Paternity. A man, proud of his nineteenth century, matter-of-fact atheism, was persuaded to go and hear Him in that church. The same afternoon he went to

'Abdu'l-Bahá's apartment. Juliet Thompson asked him:
'Did you feel the greatness of Abdul Baha?' His angry
reply was: 'Would you feel the greatness of Niagara?'[136]
On the same day too 'Abdu'l-Bahá addressed the congregation of the Brotherhood Church, at Jersey City, New
Jersey. Let the pastor of that church, Howard Colby Ives,
relate the story:

'It was an impressive, even to me a thrilling sight when
the majestic figure of the Master strode up the aisle of the
Brotherhood Church leading the little company of believers
from various parts of the world. As memory now takes its
backward look I realize how little I understood at that time
the full significance of that memorable scene. Here, in a
setting of Western civilization, almost two thousand years
from the dawn of Christian teaching, stood One whose
Life and Word were the very embodiment of the essence of
the message of good-will to all peoples which those nations
which bear His name had seemingly forgotten. Here stood
the living proof of the falsity of the assumption that East
and West can never meet. Here was martyrdom for Truth
and Love speaking lovingly and humbly to souls engrossed
with self and who knew it not . . .

'But to all such thoughts I, like most of the audience, was
a stranger. Yet there was in that hall that evening an atmosphere of spiritual reality foreign to its past . . .

' 'Abdu'l-Bahá sat in the place of honor immediately
behind the pulpit. Beside Him sat the interpreter, who, as I
spoke, translated rapidly and softly to 'Abdu'l-Bahá the
essence of my words. I stood at one side of the platform so
[as] not to be in front of the Master and able to turn towards
Him at times. One of my keenest remembrances of the
evening is that of His attentive, smiling face while the interpreter murmured his rendering. I spoke of His forty years
in the fortress of 'Akká, that indescribably filthy penal
colony of the Turkish empire; of His sixty years of exile

and suffering; of the living proof He afforded that the only bondage is that of the spirit; of the evidence His presence with us that evening furnished of true spiritual brotherhood and unity. I remember particularly turning to Him apologetically as I made the personal reference to the fact that whereas other Easterners came to America exploiting its people in the name of oriental mysticism, His message bore the living imprint of self-sacrificing love. He gave while others grasped. He manifested what others mouthed. And more clearly still do I see before me that calmly smiling face, the glowing eyes, the understanding gaze with which He returned my glance.

'Then 'Abdu'l-Bahá rose to speak. The interpreter stood beside Him, a little behind. "Because this is called the Church of Brotherhood I wish to speak upon the Brotherhood of Mankind." As that beautifully resonant voice rang through the room, accenting with an emphasis I had never before heard the word Brotherhood, shame crept into my heart. Surely this Man recognized connotations to that word which I, who had named the church, had never known. Who was I to stress this word? What had I ever done besides talk to prove my faith in it as a principle of life? Had I ever suffered a pang as its exponent? But this man had lived a long life in which brotherhood to all mankind had been a ruling motive. Prison nor chains; toil nor privation; hatred nor contumely had been able to turn Him from His appointed task of its exemplification, or to lessen the ardor of His proof that it was a possible goal for the race of Man. To Him all races, colors, creeds were as one. To Him prejudice for or against a soul because of outward wealth or poverty, sin or virtue, was unknown. He was at every moment what in one of His divine Tablets He has told us we all must be, a "thrall of mankind".

'As I write there is brought to memory a story told by Lua Getsinger, she who then sat in the audience before me.

In the very early days of the knowledge of the Cause of Bahá'u'lláh in America Mrs. Getsinger was in 'Akká having made the pilgrimage to the prison city to see the Master. She was with Him one day when He said to her, that He was too busy today to call upon a friend of His who was very ill and poor and He wished her to go in His place. Take him food and care for him as I have been doing, He concluded. He told her where this man was to be found and she went gladly, proud that 'Abdu'l-Bahá should trust her with this mission.

'She returned quickly. "Master," she exclaimed, "surely you cannot realize to what a terrible place you sent me. I almost fainted from the awful stench, the filthy rooms, the degrading condition of that man and his house. I fled lest I contract some terrible disease."

'Sadly and sternly 'Abdu'l-Bahá regarded her. "Dost thou desire to serve God," He said, "serve thy fellow man for in him dost thou see the image and likeness of God." He told her to go back to this man's house. If it is filthy she should clean it; if this brother of yours is dirty, bathe him; if he is hungry, feed him. Do not return until this is done. Many times had He done this for him and cannot she serve him once?

'This was He who was speaking in my Church of Brotherhood. . .

'And as I gazed at the Master as I faced Him from the audience, it was not so difficult to imagine a world transformed by the spirit of divine brotherhood. For He Himself was that spirit incarnate. His flowing 'abá, His creamlike fez, His silvery hair and beard, all set Him apart from the Westerners, to whom He spake. But His smile which seemed to embrace us with an overflowing comradeship; His eyes which flashed about the room as if seeking out each individual; His gestures which combined such authority and humility, such wisdom and humor, all conveyed to me, at least, a true human brotherhood which could never be content with plenty while the least of these little ones had less than enough, and yet still less content until all had that divine plenty only to be bestowed through the breaths of the Holy Spirit, that is, by contact with the Manifestation of God. He closed with the following words, as recorded in the first volume of *The Promulgation of Universal Peace*: *

' "Trust in the favor of God. Look not at your own capacities, for the divine bestowal can transform a drop into an ocean; it can make a tiny seed a lofty tree. Verily divine bestowals are like the sea and we are like the fishes in that sea. The fishes must not look at themselves; they must behold the ocean which is vast and wonderful. Provision for the sustenance of all is in this ocean, therefore the divine bounties encompass all and love eternal shines upon all."

'It was one of the briefest of 'Abdu'l-Bahá's public talks. The latter part, as recorded in *The Promulgation of Universal Peace*, was in answer to a question from the audience, which was a departure from the usual custom.

'I had requested of the Master that He speak rather longer than was His wont as I had the universal obsession that the worth of an address was in proportion to its length. That He spoke so briefly was undoubtedly with the endeavor to illustrate to me that a very few words, inspired by the Holy Spirit and aglow with wisdom celestial, were vastly more powerful than all the volumes of man-made sermons ever printed.

'That I should have had the temerity to make such a request of Him again illustrates how far removed I still was from recognition of His station; nay from any true understanding of spiritual reality . . . And He had in fifteen minutes said more, and shown forth more, and loved more of the true Brotherhood, the heavenly and divine Brotherhood, which could transform this world into a paradise, than I had ever dreamed.'[137]

* p. 127.

The heavy strain on 'Abdu'l-Bahá's physical strength was continuous and unrelieved. There were times in late afternoons when He walked out of His apartment, all alone, to snatch a short rest in the park by the side of the river. He said He wished to be alone, to go and lie down on the grass and relax, both mentally and physically. Were He to be accompanied, He would be engaged in conversation, and that could only increase His fatigue. Other times in the evenings He would find some moments of leisure to pace up and down Riverside Drive, but in the company of Bahá'ís.

On May 22nd, 'Abdu'l-Bahá travelled to Boston, where He stayed until the 26th, visiting also Cambridge and Worcester, Massachusetts. In Boston He called at Denison House, where a society that looked after the poor among Syrian and Greek immigrants had its headquarters. He was entertained to lunch, and donated ten pounds to the funds of the society. He told the members seated round the luncheon table that they were blessed to be serving the poor, and that He would deem it an honour were He Himself to be considered as one of the poor.

'Abdu'l-Bahá's last engagement in Boston was on the morning of the day He returned to New York, and it was a visit to al-Ḥalqatadh-Dhahabíyyah (The Golden Circle), another institution connected with the Syrians, their largest association in the United States. A poet recited a poem in praise of 'Abdu'l-Bahá, which he had specially composed for the occasion, and then 'Abdu'l-Bahá spoke to the Syrians in their own language. The text of His talk is not available because translation into English was not needed, and no notes were taken. So moved were the members of the audience that as soon as 'Abdu'l-Bahá stepped down from the platform they rushed forth to reach Him, to kiss His hands. An Arab woman was seen to be struggling through the milling crowd to get close to Him; and when she did she fell on her knees and bowed her head to touch His feet and cried out: 'I bear witness that in Thee dwells the Spirit of God and the person of Christ.'

The day 'Abdu'l-Bahá drove to Worcester, He once again recalled sadly the love which Bahá'u'lláh had for the natural scenery and verdure of the countryside. He wished that Bahá'u'lláh had been able to visit these lands. Coming in His journeys upon a particularly delectable spot, Bahá'u'lláh would pause, for long, to enjoy it more. Once, passing a beautiful lake, He stopped for several hours and the whole caravan came to a halt.

May 23rd was the anniversary of the Declaration of the Báb as well as the anniversary of the birth of 'Abdu'l-Bahá. Although 'Abdu'l-Bahá had always insisted that this day should be exclusively associated with the Báb, Bahá'ís had planned a double celebration at the home of Mr and Mrs Francis W. Breed in Cambridge. 'Abdu'l-Bahá spoke of the Báb and His supreme sacrifice. Then a cake bearing sixty-eight candles was brought in. 'Abdu'l-Bahá would not disappoint these Bahá'ís who were making this offering with joyous devotion. He lighted one of the candles, and others lighted the rest. And how happy were the Bahá'ís there, to take away, each one, a small portion of that cake.

'Abdu'l-Bahá's address on May 24th at the Unitarian Conference attracted particular notice. That Conference, which also had the name of Free Religious Association, was held at Ford Hall in Boston. Prior to 'Abdu'l-Bahá's visit a speaker had severely criticized all religions and the very concept of 'Religion'. Moreover, it had become known that a Christian minister had made a personal attack on 'Abdu'l-Bahá, stating that a false Christ, a denier of the one true Christ, was in their midst. These were the opening sentences of 'Abdu'l-Bahá's address:

Creation is the expression of motion. Motion is life. A moving object is a living object whereas that which is motionless and inert is as dead. All created forms are progressive in their planes or kingdoms of existence under the stimulus of the power or spirit of life. The universal energy is dynamic. Nothing is stationary in the material world of outer phenomena or in the inner world of intellect and consciousness.

Religion is the outer expression of the divine reality. Therefore it must be living, vitalized, moving and progressive. If it be without motion and non-progressive it is without the divine life; it is dead. The divine institutes are continuously active and evolutionary; therefore the revelation of them must be progressive and continuous. All things are subject to reformation. This is a century of life and renewal.

Then 'Abdu'l-Bahá underlined the truth of the mission of all the Manifestations of God, the oneness of their purpose. 'Therefore,' He said, 'if the nations of the world forsake imitations and investigate the reality underlying the revealed Word of God they will agree and become reconciled. For reality is one and not multiple.' Having shown how blind imitation has obscured those eternal verities, He declared unequivocally: '. . . the fundamental reality of the divine religions must be renewed, reformed, revoiced to mankind.' Next He proceeded to do that 'revoicing' which He had said must be done, and made this very emphatic statement regarding the Manifestations of God: 'They have been the root and fundamental source of all knowledge.' And He ended His address with the assertion:

This is the century of new and universal nationhood. Sciences have advanced, industries have progressed, politics have been reformed, liberty has been proclaimed, justice is awakening. This is the century of motion, divine stimulus and accomplishment; the century of human solidarity and altruistic service; the century of Universal Peace and the reality of the divine kingdom.[138]

That address of 'Abdu'l-Bahá made a deep impression on the minds of His audience, and the next morning, at His hotel, a large number of Unitarian ministers gathered, to put further questions to Him. They went away well satisfied with what they heard. Among the visitors of that morning was also Rabbi Fletcher, a prominent figure of Boston Jewry, who was enchanted by the person and the speech of 'Abdu'l-Bahá. The Unitarians were further impressed by the fact that, although they had invited 'Abdu'l-Bahá to visit Boston and address their church (which He had done on the day of His arrival) and their forum, 'Abdu'l-Bahá would accept no remuneration of any kind.

At a farewell meeting, in the evening of May 25th, which the Bahá'ís had convened at Huntington Chambers, Boston, 'Abdu'l-Bahá told them:

> In your hearts I have beheld the reflection of a great and wonderful love. The Americans have shown me uniform kindness and I entertain a deep spiritual love for them. I am pleased with the susceptibilities of your hearts. I will pray for you asking divine assistance and then say farewell.[139]

And He uttered a very moving prayer.

'Abdu'l-Bahá left Boston at noon on May 26th and arrived back in New York at 6 p.m. Then, having had no rest, He went straight from the home of Mr and Mrs Kinney to address the congregation of Mount Morris Baptist Church.

'Abdu'l-Bahá was very tired and had to lean on a pillar when He stood up to speak. And in that state of exhaustion He delivered an address vibrant with power, the profundity of which, matched with the simplicity of expression, made the congregation marvel. He said:

> As I entered the church this evening I heard the hymn 'Nearer my God, to Thee'. The greatest attainment in the

world of humanity is nearness to God. Every lasting glory, honour, grace and beauty which comes to man comes through nearness to God. All the prophets and apostles longed and prayed for nearness to the Creator. How many nights they passed in sleepless yearning for this station; how many days they devoted to supplication for this attainment, seeking ever to draw nigh unto Him! . . . Divine nearness is dependent upon attainment to the knowledge of God, upon severance from all else save God. It is contingent upon self-sacrifice . . . It is made possible through the baptism of water and fire revealed in the Gospels . . . In a word, nearness to God necessitates sacrifice of self, severance and the giving up of all to Him. Nearness is likeness.[140]

Two days later (May 28th) at the Metropolitan Temple, a concourse of people, estimated by Zarqání to have numbered more than a thousand, heard 'Abdu'l-Bahá expound the truth of the Oneness of Religion:

. . . The divine Manifestations since the day of Adam have striven to unite humanity so that all may be accounted as one soul. The function and purpose of a shepherd is to gather and not disperse his flock. The Prophets of God have been divine shepherds of humanity. They have established a bond of love and unity among mankind, made scattered peoples one nation and wandering tribes a mighty kingdom. They have laid the foundation of the oneness of God and summoned all to Universal Peace. All these holy, divine Manifestations are one. They have served one God, promulgated the same truth, founded the same institutions and reflected the same light. Their appearances have been successive and correlated; each One has announced and extolled the One who was to follow and all laid the foundation of reality. They summoned and invited the people to love and made the human world a mirror of the Word of God. Therefore the divine religions they established have one foundation; their teachings, proofs and evidences are one; in name and form they differ but in reality they agree and are the same. These holy Manifestations have been as the coming of spring-time in the world. Although the springtime of this year is designated by another name according to the changing calendar, yet as regards its life and quickening it is the same as the springtime of last year. For each spring is the time of a new creation, the effects, bestowals, perfections and life-giving forces of which are the same as those of the former vernal seasons although the names are many and various. This is 1912, last year's was 1911 and so on, but in fundamental reality no difference is apparent. The sun is one but the dawning-points of the sun are numerous and changing. The ocean is one body of water but different parts of it have particular designation, Atlantic, Pacific, Mediterranean, Antarctic, etc. If we consider the names, there is differentiation, but the water, the ocean itself is one reality.

Likewise the divine religions of the holy Manifestations of God are in reality one though in name and nomen-clature they differ. Man must be a lover of the light no matter from what day-spring it may appear. He must be a lover of the rose no matter in what soil it may be growing . . . Attachment to the lantern is not loving the light . . .[141]

In the audience was Rabbi Silverman who had once assumed an unfriendly attitude towards 'Abdu'l-Bahá. He rose up as soon as 'Abdu'l-Bahá had ended His address, and said that that day he had seen the Light which always dawned in the East and illumined the West. He appealed to the people to heed the words of 'Abdu'l-Bahá: 'Attachment to the lantern is not loving the light.'

The next day at the home of Mr and Mrs Kinney, 'Abdu'l-Bahá returned to the same theme: the essential oneness of religion, but in a different fashion.

The divine Manifestations have been iconoclastic in Their teachings, uprooting error, destroying false religious beliefs and summoning mankind anew to the fundamental oneness of God. All of Them have likewise proclaimed the oneness of the world of humanity . . . Each One is an evident proof sufficient for mankind; each One from foundation to apex proclaims the essential unity of God and humanity, the love of God, abolition of war and the divine standard of peace . . . For the Word of God is collective wisdom, absolute knowledge and eternal truth.

Consider the statement recorded in the first chapter of the book of John: 'In the beginning was the Word, and the Word was with God, and the Word was God.'* This is a brief statement but replete with greatest meanings. Its applications are illimitable and beyond the power of books or words to contain and express. Heretofore the doctors of theology have not expounded it but have restricted it to Jesus as 'The Word made flesh' . . . The essential oneness of Father, Son and Spirit has many meanings and constitutes the foundation of Christianity . . . Why was Jesus the Word?

In the universe of creation, all phenomenal beings are as letters. Letters in themselves are meaningless and express nothing of thought or ideal; as for instance 'a', 'b', etc. Likewise all phenomenal beings are without independent meaning. But a word is composed of letters and has independent sense and meaning. Therefore as Christ conveyed the perfect meaning of divine reality and embodied independent significance He was the Word. He was as the station of reality compared to the station of metaphor. There is no intrinsic meaning in the leaves of a book but the thought they convey leads you to reflect upon the reality. The reality of Jesus was the perfect meaning, the Christhood in Him which in the holy books is symbolized as the Word . . . The Christhood means not the body of Jesus but the perfection of divine virtues manifest in Him . . . The reality of Christ was the embodiment of divine virtues and attributes of God . . . [142]

* John 1: 1.

On May 30th 'Abdu'l-Bahá spoke to the Theosophists at their Lodge (79th Street), and on the 31st He visited Fanwood, New Jersey, at the request of William H. Hoar, a stalwart veteran of the Bahá'í Faith in America. Fanwood, little more than a village, was well endowed with natural beauty. Mr Hoar and his family begged 'Abdu'l-Bahá to stay there a few days and rest; the heat of New York was too oppressive, they said. But 'Abdu'l-Bahá could not stay just to rest. Service called Him. That very day He addressed a meeting at the Town Hall. It was an address of particular significance. He showed how the leaders of religion have contributed to the weakening of its foundations.

> ... materialists are advancing and aggressive while divine forces are waning and vanishing. Irreligion has conquered religion. The cause of the chaotic condition lies in the differences among the religions, and finds its origin in the animosity and hatred existing between sects and denominations. The materialists have availed themselves of this dissension amongst the religions and are constantly attacking them, intending to uproot the tree of divine planting ... If a commander is at variance with his army in the execution of military tactics there is no doubt he will be defeated by the enemy. Today the religions are at variance; enmity, strife and recrimination prevail among them; they refuse to associate, nay, rather, if necessary they shed each other's blood. Read history and record to see what dreadful events have happened in the name of religion ...
>
> Imitation destroys the foundation of religion, extinguishes the spirituality of the human world, transforms heavenly illumination into darkness and deprives man of the knowledge of God. It is the cause of the victory of materialism and unbelief over religion ... When materialists subject imitations to the intellectual analysis of reason they find them to be mere superstitions; therefore they deny religion ...

Then 'Abdu'l-Bahá spoke of the bounties of the past, of the guidance which Moses and Christ brought to mankind, and continued:

Could it be possible that this present period has been deprived of divine bounties while past ages of tyranny and barbarism received an inexhaustible portion of them? The same merciful God Who bestowed His favours in the past has opened the doors of His Kingdom to us. The rays of His Sun are shining, the breath of the Holy Spirit is quickening. The omniscient God still assists and confirms us, illumines our hearts, gladdens our souls and perfumes our nostrils with the fragrances of holiness. Divine wisdom and providence have encircled all and spread the heavenly table before us. We must take a bountiful share of this generous favour.[143]

The next day 'Abdu'l-Bahá returned to New York, and on June 2nd He addressed, for the second time, the congregation of the Church of the Ascension. He began by explaining the significance of a church as a house of worship.

In the terminology of the holy books, the church has been called the 'house of the covenant' for the reason that the church is a place where people of different thoughts and divergent tendencies—where all races and nations—may come together in a covenant of permanent fellowship. In the temple of the Lord, in the house of God, man must be submissive to God . . . He must not consider divergence of races nor difference of nationalities; he must not view variation in denomination and creed nor should he take into account the differing degrees of thoughts; nay, rather, he should look upon all as mankind and realize that all must become united and agreed. He must recognize all as one family, one race, one nativity; see all as the servants of one God, dwelling beneath the shelter of His mercy. The purport of this is that the church is a

collective centre. Temples are symbols of the reality and
divinity of God; the collective centre of mankind . . . but
the real collective centres are the Manifestations of God,
of Whom the church or temple is a symbol and expression. That is to say, the Manifestation of God is the
real divine Temple and Collective Centre of which the
outer church is but a symbol.

Then He spoke of the work of unification achieved by the
Manifestations of God, by Abraham and Moses and Jesus
and Muḥammad, as He named Them, who 'were Collective
Centres of Their day and time, and all arose in the East.'
And today, He told His audience, Bahá'u'lláh 'is the Collec-
tive Centre of unity for all mankind and the splendour of
His light has likewise dawned from the East.' Finally He
directed His attention to the roles of the East and the West:

In the Western world material civilization has attained
the highest point of development but divine civilization
was founded in the lands of the East. The East must
acquire material civilization from the West, and the West
must receive spiritual civilization from the East. This will
establish a mutual bond. When these two come together,
the world of humanity will present a glorious aspect and
extraordinary progress will be achieved . . . Therefore
you must assist the East in order that it may attain material
progress. The East must likewise promulgate the principles of spiritual civilization in the Western world . . .
We pray that God will unite the East and the West in
order that these two civilizations may be exchanged and
mutually enjoyed. I am sure it will come to pass for this is
the radiant century. This is an age for the outpouring of
divine mercy upon the exigency of this new century—the
unity of the East and the West. It will surely be accomplished.

The audience presented a variety of written questions. To
the question: 'What relation do you sustain to the Founder

of your belief? Are you His successor in the same manner as the Pope of Rome?' 'Abdu'l-Bahá replied: 'I am the servant of Bahá'u'lláh the Founder and in this I glory. No honour do I consider greater than this and it is my hope that I may be confirmed in servitude to Bahá'u'lláh. This is my station.' Another question read: 'Is peace a greater word than love?' And 'Abdu'l-Bahá said: 'No! love is greater than peace, for peace is founded upon love. Love is the objective point of peace and peace is an outcome of love. Until love is attained, peace cannot be; but there is a so-called peace without love. The love which is from God is the fundamental. This love is the object of all human attainment, the radiance of heaven, the light of man.'[144]

The following day (June 3rd), 'Abdu'l-Bahá travelled to Milford, Pennsylvania, where He stayed one night. In the train returning to New York, the members of His retinue were concerned to see tears, all of a sudden, coursing down His cheeks. He had been watching the charming scenery, as the train sped through the countryside, and once again the vivid contrast had forced the memory of His Father's sufferings and deprivations to plunge Him in deep sorrow.

A house at 309 West 78th Street (which belonged to Mrs Champney) had been newly rented for Him, and that is where He resided for the rest of His sojourn in New York: a house it was 'whose door', in the words of Juliet Thompson, 'was opened about eight in the morning, or earlier, and kept open all day, with no one to guard it, till midnight.'[145]

Admiral Peary, who had met 'Abdu'l-Bahá in Washington, was now in New York, and when, on June 5th, 'Abdu'l-Bahá visited the Unity Club at Brooklyn, they met again. It was a gala schools' day for the children. At the luncheon which followed, the Admiral was one of the speakers. He talked of his journey to the North Pole, and then he expressed his admiration for 'Abdu'l-Bahá, asking Him, at the same time, to speak to them. Seated at the luncheon table

'Abdu'l-Bahá spoke briefly on the theme of education. The audience was enchanted.

The incessant demands of a long tour had not diminished; rather, they had increased with the passage of weeks. 'Abdu'l-Bahá's physical strength was being sapped to an alarming degree, but He would admit of no pause. The work was too imperative and the time too short. However, when He reached Philadelphia from New York, in the afternoon of Saturday, June 8th, His fatigue was so extreme that He had to cancel some of His engagements. Notwithstanding, He addressed two congregations the following day: that of the Unitarian Church, 15th Street and Girard Avenue, and that of the Baptist Temple, Broad and Berks Streets. Zarqání records that the minister of the Baptist Temple had sent out notices and invitations to prominent people as far away as Washington. 'Abdu'l-Bahá's address to the congregation of the Baptist Temple of Philadelphia is one of the longest He delivered in the whole course of His American tour. He drew a compelling picture of the way of nature and the way of spirit:

> ... The pathway of nature is the pathway of the animal realm. The animal acts in accordance with the requirements of nature, follows its own instincts and desires. Whatever its impulses and proclivities may be it has the liberty to gratify them; yet it is a captive of nature ... The animal possesses no power of ideation or conscious intelligence; it is a captive of the senses and deprived of that which lies beyond them ...
>
> One of the strangest things witnessed is that the materialists of today are proud of their natural instincts and bondage. They state that nothing is entitled to belief and acceptance except that which is sensible or tangible ... If this be a virtue the animal has attained it to a superlative degree, for the animal is absolutely ignorant of the realm of spirit and out of touch with the inner

world of conscious realization. The animal would agree with the materialist in denying the existence of that which transcends the senses. If we admit that being limited to the plane of the senses is a virtue the animal is indeed more virtuous than man, for it is entirely bereft of that which lies beyond, absolutely oblivious of the Kingdom of God and its traces whereas God has deposited within the human creature an illimitable power by which he can rule the world of nature.

Consider how all other phenomenal existence and beings are captives of nature. The sun, that colossal centre of our solar system, the giant stars and planets, the towering mountains, the earth itself and its kingdoms of life lower than the human—all are captives of nature except man. No other created thing can deviate in the slightest degree from obedience to natural law . . . Man is the ruler of nature. According to natural law and limitation he should remain upon the earth, but behold how he violates this command and soars above the mountains in aeroplanes. He sails in ships upon the surface of the ocean and dives into its depths in submarines . . . Though he is a dweller upon earth he penetrates the mysteries of starry worlds inconceivably distant. He discovers latent realities within the bosom of the earth, uncovers treasures, penetrates secrets and mysteries of the phenomenal world and brings to light that which according to nature's jealous laws should remain hidden, unknown and unfathomable. Through an ideal inner power man brings these realities forth from the invisible plane to the visible . . .

How strange then it seems that man, notwithstanding his endowment with this ideal power, will descend to a level beneath him and declare himself no greater than that which is manifestly inferior to his real station. God has created such a conscious spirit within him that he is the most wonderful of all contingent beings. In ignoring these virtues he descends to the material plane, considers matter the ruler of existence and denies that which lies beyond

. . . In fact from this standpoint the animal is the greater philosopher because it is completely ignorant of the Kingdom of God, possesses no spiritual susceptibilities and is uninformed of the heavenly world . . .

Then 'Abdu'l-Bahá turned His attention to the other pathway: the way of spirit. 'This pathway,' He said, 'is conducive to the progress and uplift of the world.' But it has been obscured.

Alas! that humanity is completely submerged in imitations and unrealities notwithstanding the truth of divine religion has ever remained the same. Superstitions have obscured the fundamental reality, the world is darkened and the light of religion is not apparent. This darkness is conducive to differences and dissensions; rites and dogmas are many and various . . . True religion is the source of love and agreement amongst men, the cause of the development of praiseworthy qualities; but the people are holding to the counterfeit and imitation, negligent of the reality which unifies . . . They follow superstitions inherited from their fathers and ancestors . . . Therefore the realm of the religionist has gradually narrowed and darkened and the sphere of the materialist has widened and advanced . . . When the sun sets it is the time for bats to fly. They come forth because they are creatures of the night. When the lights of religion become darkened the materialists appear. They are the bats of night . . . [146]

Finally, 'Abdu'l-Bahá spoke of the advent of Bahá'u'lláh and the principles He enunciated, upon which depend the salvation of the world.

'Abdu'l-Bahá's visit to Philadelphia was, perforce, short. He returned to New York in the afternoon of June 10th. But so scintillating had been the zeal of the few Bahá'ís of that city and so fervently appreciative the response of others that 'Abdu'l-Bahá frequently recalled that short visit, with particular warmth and affection. The next day He told the Bahá'ís of New York, gathered in His house:

> We have just returned from a visit to Philadelphia, spending two nights there and speaking in two large churches. The weather proved unpleasant and affected my health. The purpose in these movements here and there is a single purpose; it is to spread the light of truth in this dark world. On account of my age it is difficult to journey. Sometimes the difficulties are arduous but out of love for the friends of God and with desire to sacrifice myself in the pathway of God, I bear them in gladness. The purpose is the result which is accomplished, love and unity among mankind . . . [147]

The same day that He returned to New York 'Abdu'l-Bahá told Hippolyte Dreyfus in a Tablet addressed to him:

> I visited Philadelphia, for a few days, at the invitation of two ministers and at the request of the friends of God. Two large congregations gathered in the two churches, and I spoke within the measure of my incapacity. But the confirmations of the Abhá Kingdom, as evident as the sun, descended and enfolded us. Although we are powerless He is Mighty. Although we are poor He is All-Sufficient. The import of this blessed verse became truly manifest: 'We shall aid whosoever will arise for the triumph of Our Cause with the Concourse on high and a company of Our favoured angels.'[148]

The wonderful humility of 'Abdu'l-Bahá! He speaks of 'the measure of my incapacity'.

CHAPTER 13

THE CITY OF THE COVENANT
June 11th–July 22nd

In the days that followed 'Abdu'l-Bahá spoke every day
at the meetings held in His residence. There were by far too
many who wished to meet Him separately, but neither the
state of His health nor the time available would permit un-
restricted individual access to Him. Reluctantly He had to
institute a system whereby He would meet in private
only those whom He had not previously met, or who had a
particularly urgent problem. All the rest He would meet
together in His drawing-room.

Juliet Thompson relates an incident of this period of
'Abdu'l-Bahá's sojourn in New York which must have been
one of the many similar to it. It is indicative of the urgent
problems that were brought to 'Abdu'l-Bahá, as well as
the healing which He imparted to the distressed and the
broken in spirit:

> . . . Miss Buckton* had arrived . . . and a poor little
> waif of humanity, a Jewess. She was all in black, this poor
> child, with a little, pale face, careworn and tearworn.
> I had been in the kitchen with Lua. I came out upon
> a scene dominated by the Master. He was sitting, as usual,
> at the window, the strong carving of his face thrown
> into relief by masses of shadow, his turban and white
> aba ['abá] bright in the sunlight. On one side sat Miss

* Alice Buckton, from England, the author of the Christmas
mystery play, *Eager Heart*, *The Dawn of Day*, and other plays.

Buckton, on the other, this poor, stricken child. While the biggest tears I have ever seen splashed from her eyes she told him her hopelessly dismal story.

'Don't grieve now, don't grieve,' he said. He was very, very still . . .

'My brother has been in prison for three years. He was imprisoned unjustly. It was not his fault; he was led; he was weak, a victim of others. He has four more years to serve. My father and mother are depressed all the time. My brother-in-law who was our support has just died' . . .

'You must trust in God,' said Abdul Baha.

'But the more I trust the worse things become!' she sobbed.

'You have never trusted.'

'But my mother is reading the psalms all the time. She does not deserve that God should so abandon her! I read the psalms myself, the ninety-first psalm and the twenty-third psalm every night before I go to bed. I pray, too.'

'To pray is not to read psalms. To pray is to trust in God and to be submissive in all things to Him. Be submissive, then things will change for you. Put your family in God's hands. Love God's will. Strong ships are not conquered by the sea; they ride the waves! Now be a strong ship, not a battered one.'[149]

'Abdu'l-Bahá was in Brooklyn on Sunday June 16th. He addressed the congregation of the Fourth Unitarian Church, Beverly Road, Flatbush, in the morning, and then lunched at the home of Mr and Mrs Howard MacNutt, where a meeting for the Bahá'ís was held later in the day. 'Abdu'l-Bahá spoke to that assemblage and finally, in the evening, He spoke from the pulpit of the Central Congregational Church, Hancock Street. In the Unitarian Church 'Abdu'l-Bahá said:

The unity which is productive of unlimited results is first a unity of mankind which recognizes that all are sheltered beneath the overshadowing glory of the All-Glorious; that all are servants of one God; for all breathe the same atmosphere, live upon the same earth, move beneath the same heavens, receive effulgence from the same sun and are under the protection of one God. This is the most great unity, and its results are lasting if humanity adheres to it; but mankind has hitherto violated it, adhering to sectarian or other limited unities such as racial, patriotic or unity of self-interests . . . Nevertheless it is certain that the radiance and favours of God are encompassing, minds have developed, perceptions have become acute, sciences and arts are widespread and capacity exists for the proclamation and promulgation of the real and ultimate unity of mankind which will bring forth marvelous results. It will reconcile all religions . . . It will cement together the Orient and Occident, remove forever the foundations of war and upraise the ensign of the 'Most Great Peace' . . .

Another unity is the spiritual unity which emanates from the breaths of the Holy Spirit. This is greater than the unity of mankind. Human unity or solidarity may be likened to the body whereas unity from the breaths of the Holy Spirit is the spirit animating the body. This is a perfect unity. It creates such a condition in mankind that each one will make sacrifices for the other and the utmost desire will be to forfeit life and all that pertains to it in behalf of another's good. This is the unity which existed among the disciples of Jesus Christ . . . This is the unity which caused twenty thousand people in Persia to give their lives in love and devotion to it. It made the Báb the target of a thousand arrows and caused Bahá'u'lláh to suffer exile and imprisonment for forty years . . .

In the Word of God there is still another unity, the oneness of the Manifestations of God: Abraham, Moses, Jesus Christ, Muḥammad, the Báb and Bahá'u'lláh. This is a unity divine, heavenly, radiant, merciful; the one Reality appearing in its successive Manifestations . . .

There is also the Divine Unity or Entity which is

sanctified above all concept of humanity. It cannot be comprehended nor conceived because It is infinite Reality and cannot become finite. Human minds are incapable of surrounding that Reality because all thoughts and conceptions of It are finite, intellectual creations and not the reality of Divine Being which alone knows Itself. For example, if we form a conception of Divinity as a living, almighty, self-subsisting, eternal Being, this is only a concept apprehended by a human intellectual reality . . . We ourselves have an external, visible entity but even our concept of it is the product of our own brain and limited comprehension. The reality of Divinity is sanctified above this degree of knowing and realization. It has ever been hidden and secluded in Its own holiness and sanctity above our comprehending. Although It transcends our realization, Its lights, bestowals, traces and virtues have become manifest in the realities of the Prophets, even as the sun becomes resplendent in various mirrors. These holy Realities are as reflectors, and the reality of Divinity is as the sun which although it is reflected from the mirrors, and its virtues and perfections become resplendent therein, does not stoop from its own station of majesty and glory and seek abode in the mirrors; it remains in its heaven of sanctity . . . This is the unity of God; this is oneness—unity of Divinity, holy above ascent or descent, embodiment, comprehension . . . [150]

To the Bahá'ís meeting at the home of Mr and Mrs MacNutt 'Abdu'l-Bahá said:

This is a splendid gathering . . . Whenever such gatherings have taken place in this world the results have been very great . . . Wherever a lamp is lighted in the night, naturally people are attracted and gather around it. When you see such an assemblage as this you may know that a light is illumining the darkness. There are lamps the light of which is limited. There are lamps the light of which is unlimited. There are lamps which illumine small places and lamps which illumine the horizons. The lamp of the guidance of God wherever lighted has shed its radiance throughout the East and the West . . . Consider the days of Christ, how the light of guidance brightened twelve hearts. How limited it seemed, but how expansive it became afterward and illumined the world! You are not a large body of people but because the lamp of guidance has been lighted in your hearts the effects will be wonderful in the years to come . . . The bestowals of the Almighty are descending from the heaven of grace, but capacity to receive them is essential. The fountain of divine generosity is gushing forth, but we must have thirst for the living waters. Unless there be thirst the salutary water will not assuage . . . Unless the eyes of perception be opened the lights of the sun will not be witnessed . . . Unless the heart be filled with longing the favours of the Lord will not be evident . . .

Therefore we must endeavour always, cry, supplicate and invoke the Kingdom of God to grant us full capacity in order that the bestowals of God may become revealed and manifest in us. And as we attain to these heavenly bounties we shall offer thanks unto the threshold of oneness. Then shall we rejoice in the Lord that in this wonderful century and glorious age, under the shelter of the Kingdom of God we have enjoyed these bestowals and will arise in praise and thanksgiving. Therefore I first exhort myself and then I entreat you to appreciate this great bestowal, recognize this most great guidance, accept these bounties of the Lord . . . [151]

At the Central Congregational Church 'Abdu'l-Bahá proclaimed the truth of the mission of the Arabian Prophet. He said:

The holy Manifestations Who have been the Sources or Founders of the various religious systems were united and agreed in purpose and teaching. Abraham, Moses, Zoroaster, Buddha, Jesus, Muḥammad, the Báb and

Bahá'u'lláh are one in spirit and reality. Moreover each Prophet fulfilled the promise of the One Who came before Him and likewise each announced the One Who would follow . . .

If Christians of all denominations and divisions should investigate reality, the foundations of Christ will unite them. No enmity or hatred will remain for they will all be under the one guidance of reality itself. Likewise in the wider field, if all the existing religious systems will turn away from ancestral imitations and investigate the reality, seeking the real meanings of the holy books, they will unite and agree upon the same foundation, the reality itself . . .

Among the great religious systems of the world is Islám. About three hundred millions of people acknowledge it. For more than a thousand years there has been enmity and strife between Muslims and Christians, owing to misunderstanding and spiritual blindness . . .

All Islám considers the Qur'án the Word of God. In this sacred Book there are explicit texts . . . stating that Christ was the Word of God, that He was the Spirit of God, that Jesus Christ came into this world through the quickening breaths of the Holy Spirit, and that Mary His mother was holy and sanctified. In the Qur'án a whole chapter is devoted to the story of Jesus . . . In brief, in the Qur'án there is eulogy and commendation of Christ such as you do not find in the Gospel . . . Furthermore, it is significant and convincing that when Muḥammad proclaimed His work and mission, His first objection to His own followers was: 'Why have you not believed on Jesus Christ? Why have you not accepted the Gospel? Why have you not believed in Moses? Why have you not followed the precepts of the Old Testament? Why have you not understood the Prophets of Israel? Why have you not believed in the disciples of Christ?' . . . Therefore it is evident that ignorance and misunderstanding have caused so much warfare and strife between Christians and Muslims . . . How much blood has flowed in their wars; how many nations have been destroyed; how many children have been made fatherless; how many fathers and mothers have mourned the loss of children and dear ones! All this has been due to prejudice, misunderstanding, and imitations of ancestral beliefs without investigation of the reality. If the holy Books were rightly understood none of this discord and distress would have existed, but love and fellowship would have prevailed instead. This is true with all the other religions as well . . . The essential purpose of the religion of God is to establish unity among mankind. The divine Manifestations were Founders of the means of fellowship and love. They did not come to create discord, strife and hatred in the world. The religion of God is the cause of love, but if it is made to be the source of enmity and bloodshed, surely its absence is preferable to its existence; for then it becomes satanic, detrimental and an obstacle to the human world . . . [152]

He ended His talk in that Congregational Church of Brooklyn with the story of Bahá'u'lláh. Speaking of the invincible power of His Father, 'Abdu'l-Bahá said:

When subjected to banishment by two kings, while a refugee from enemies of all nations and during the days of His long imprisonment He wrote to the kings and rulers of the world in words of wonderful eloquence arraigning them severely and summoning them to the divine standard of unity and justice. He exhorted them to peace and international agreement, making it incumbent upon them to establish a board of international arbitration; that from all nations and governments of the world there should be delegates selected for a congress of nations which should constitute a universal arbitral court of justice to settle international disputes . . . Kings could not withstand Him. They endeavoured to extinguish His light but served only to increase its intensity and illumination . . . [153]

The motion picture that exists of 'Abdu'l-Bahá was taken in Brooklyn, on June 18th, in the grounds of the MacNutt home.

The next day, June 19th, was an historic day for the Bahá'ís of New York, for on that day 'Abdu'l-Bahá named their city the City of the Covenant. He spoke in their gathering of the *Tablet of the Branch*, revealed by Bahá'u'lláh in Adrianople, and declared His own station: the Centre of the Covenant. In New York He had made this emphatic, authoritative statement in public, and therefore New York was invested with that distinction. On the same day He received the manuscript of *The Brilliant Proof** which He greatly admired, and arranged for its translation and publication in the United States.

Zarqání writes that in those days, in the latter part of June 1912, every now and then 'Abdu'l-Bahá evinced a mood similar to the mood that came upon Him during His stay in Zaytún, near Cairo, when He lived in expectation of martyrdom and was particularly desirous of sacrificing Himself. Zarqání quotes in evidence a Tablet addressed to Áqá Riḍáy-i-Qannád, the devout and distinguished veteran of the dawn of the Bahá'í Faith, of the days in Adrianople, and of the earliest times in 'Akká. 'Fidelity,' says 'Abdu'l-Bahá in that Tablet,

> demands roaming over deserts and mountains. True fidelity is attained when a wanderer, nameless and traceless, I become. O Lord! ordain for Thy servant the realization of his utmost wish, this bounty which shines resplendent upon the horizon of fidelity, like unto the sun arisen at dawn. One request I have to put to the loved ones of Bahá, that they prostrate themselves before the holy threshold, lay their heads on the ground and ask that the sinful 'Abdu'l-Bahá be granted the cup of immolation, so that he may, in servitude to the threshold of Bahá,

* See p. 151.

taste the sweet savour of a drop from the ocean of fidelity.[154]

'I am about to leave the city for a few days' rest at Montclair,' 'Abdu'l-Bahá told the Bahá'ís gathered in His home on June 20th; and He continued,

When I return it is my wish to give a large feast of unity. A place for it has not yet been found. It must be outdoors under the trees, in some location away from city noise; like a Persian garden. The food will be Persian food. When the place is arranged all will be informed and we will have a general meeting in which hearts will be bound together, spirits blended and a new foundation for unity established. All the friends will come. They will be my guests. They will be as the parts and members of one body. The spirit of life manifest in that body will be one spirit. The foundation of that temple of unity will be one foundation. Each will be a stone in that foundation, solid and interdependent. Each will be as a leaf, blossom or fruit upon one tree. For the sake of fellowship and unity I desire this feast and spiritual gathering . . . [155]

The next day 'Abdu'l-Bahá travelled to Montclair, New Jersey. The stifling air of New York in midsummer was very trying and 'Abdu'l-Bahá's physical frame was subjected to great strain. The break in Montclair had become imperative, but the week that He spent there was by no means a period of total rest. He visited Newark and stayed the night. He met the Bahá'ís and seekers and admirers every day. He spoke frequently at their gatherings. One day He told them what these words of Christ meant: 'And whosoever doth not bear his cross, and come after me, cannot be my disciple.'[156] Then He talked of the Bábí and Bahá'í martyrs, and particularly of Mírzá 'Abdu'l-Vahháb-i-Shírází. This young man had met Bahá'u'lláh but once, yet had become so devoted to Him that, abandoning everything, he followed

Him to Ṭihrán, only to fall into the hands of officials who, subsequent to the attempt on the life of Náṣiri'd-Dín Sháh, were seeking the Bábís. In the dungeon he reached what he desired: the presence of Bahá'u'lláh. And the day they were to lead him to his martyrdom, he first laid his head on the feet of Bahá'u'lláh and kissed them. Then he embraced his fellow-believers. Having thus made his farewell, he broke into dancing, and snapping his fingers in joy strode out of the dungeon into the arms of martyrdom. Those who heard 'Abdu'l-Bahá relate the inspiriting story of Mírzá 'Abdu'l-Vahháb sat spellbound. Let Juliet Thompson complete the picture:

> Suddenly Abdul Baha's whole aspect changed. It was as though the spirit of the martyr had entered into Him . . . With His head thrillingly erect, snapping His fingers high in the air, beating on the porch with His foot till we could scarcely endure the vibrations set up—such electric power radiated from Him—He sang the martyr's song, ecstatic and tragic beyond anything I had ever heard . . . Another realm opened to me—the realm of Divine Tragedy . . .
>
> He sank back into His chair. Tears swelled in my eyes, blurring everything. When they cleared I saw a yet stranger look on His face. His eyes were unmistakably fixed on the Invisible. They were as brilliant as jewels and so filled with delight that they almost made His vision real to us. A smile of exultation played on His lips. Very low, so that it sounded like an echo, He hummed the martyr's song.
>
> 'See!' He exclaimed, 'the effect that the death of a martyr has in the world. It has changed my condition.'
>
> There was a moment of silence; then He said: 'What is it, Juliet, that you are pondering so deeply?'
>
> 'I was thinking of the look on your face when you said that your condition was changed. I was thinking I had seen a flash of the joy of God over those who die happily for humanity.'[157]

We find another arresting picture from those days in the diary-chronicle of Mírzá Maḥmúd-i-Zarqání. There we see how 'Abdu'l-Bahá used to go to the market, in the company of His attendants, to buy provisions, how He Himself would cook for His guests, how He would see to arrangements in the kitchen. Most of the time He had people sitting down at His table for luncheon or for dinner, and on the rare occasions when there was no guest He contented Himself with bread and cheese, so as not to put extra burdens on the members of His retinue.

June 29th was another memorable day for the Bahá'ís of New York and its environs. The feast, to which 'Abdu'l-Bahá had invited them all, was held on that day at West Englewood, New Jersey. That unforgettable day has been commemorated ever since. 'Abdu'l-Bahá was already greatly fatigued when He reached West Englewood at noon, because the journey from Montclair took a long time and He had to change trains four times. He rested for a short while in the house of Roy Wilhelm,* and then walked to the grove where tables were being laid for the feast. 'There He talked to the people, sitting beneath a great tree, with a poor, old woman on one side—very poor and humble, but with the most shining faith, and on the other side Mrs. Krug,†

---

* This American Bahá'í, who in later years served on the National Spiritual Assembly of the Bahá'ís of the United States and Canada, rendered invaluable services to the Faith, over a period of nearly four decades. After his death in December 1951 he was elevated to the rank of a Hand of the Cause of God by the Guardian of the Faith.

† Mrs Grace Krug was the wife of a famous New York physician. Her husband, Dr Florian Krug, was fiercely opposed to the Faith of Bahá'u'lláh, but once having met 'Abdu'l-Bahá his attitude completely changed. Even more, he himself embraced the Faith which his wife was serving so devotedly. Dr Krug was in Haifa in November 1921, and attended 'Abdu'l-Bahá at His passing.

with her radiant prettiness and rich clothes.'[158] 'Abdu'l-Bahá's guests numbered well over two hundred. He walked among them and anointed them all with attar of rose. Then He spoke these words:

This is a delightful gathering; you have come here with sincere intentions and the purpose of all present is the attainment of the virtues of God. The motive is attraction to the Divine Kingdom. Since the desire of all is unity and agreement it is certain that this meeting will be productive of great results. It will be the cause of attracting a new bounty for we are turning to the Kingdom of Abhá seeking the infinite bestowals of the Lord. This is a new Day and this hour is a new Hour in which we have come together. Surely the Sun of Reality with its full effulgence will illumine us and the darkness of disagreements will disappear. The utmost love and unity will result, the favours of God will encompass us, the pathway of the kingdom will be made easy. Like candles these souls will become ignited and made radiant through the lights of supreme guidance . . .

. . . The efficacy of such meetings as these is permanent throughout the ages. This assembly has a name and significance which will last forever. Hundreds of thousands of meetings shall be held to commemorate this occasion and the very words I speak to you today shall be repeated in them for ages to come. Therefore be ye rejoiced for ye are sheltered beneath the providence of God. Be happy and joyous because the bestowals of God are intended for you and the life of the Holy Spirit is breathing upon you.

Rejoice, for the heavenly table is prepared for you.

Rejoice, for the angels of heaven are your assistants and helpers.

Rejoice, for the glance of the Blessed Beauty, Bahá'u'-lláh, is directed upon you.

Rejoice, for Bahá'u'lláh is your protector.

Rejoice, for the glory everlasting is destined for you.

Rejoice, for the life eternal is awaiting you.

... May you become as the waves of one sea, stars of the same heaven, fruits adorning the same tree, roses of one garden; in order that through you the oneness of humanity may establish its temple in the world of mankind, for you are the ones who are called to uplift the cause of unity among the nations of the earth ... [159]

Juliet Thompson writes:

But the wonderful—the indescribably wonderful time came later. The Master went out alone and remained away hours. When He returned it was dark. A few of us were sitting on the porch* ... Below us on the grass sat the people—that is, those who had lingered—who could not tear themselves away. Their white clothes in the dusk were as soft as moth wings. In their hands they held burning tapers—really to keep off the mosquitoes!— but the effect was of tiny wands tipped with red stars and the incense was like some Eastern temple. It was a fairy-like picture. The Master took a chair in the center of the step, and delicately holding a taper Himself, He spoke in words of flame! I can see it all vividly still—and shall through my life—those trembling red stars among the dim white figures on the grass; behind them a most wonderful tall tree, luxuriant, with rolling outlines—now a great black cloud against the silver stars ...

Before He had finished He rose from His chair and started down the path ...

'Peace be with you,' He said as He receded into the darkness, the rich liquid Persian and the quivering translation floating back to us from His invisibility, 'I will pray for you'.[160]

The night of that memorable day 'Abdu'l-Bahá stayed in West Englewood. The next day He motored to Morristown, also in New Jersey, where the Consul-General for Persia in

* The porch of Roy Wilhelm's house.

New York, Mr Topakiyan, had a home, and had invited Him and His retinue to luncheon. Mr Topakiyan had arranged, as well, for some notabilities to meet 'Abdu'l-Bahá and some newspapermen to interview Him. In the evening 'Abdu'l-Bahá left for New York. His sojourn in that city lasted another three weeks. He was prolonging His stay, He said, because New York occupied a central position, and a strong foundation should be laid there. On July 1st He told the Bahá'ís gathered in His house:

> I desire to make manifest among the friends in America a new light that they may become a new people, that a new foundation may be established and complete harmony be realized; for the foundation of Bahá'u'lláh is love.[161]

One day 'Abdu'l-Bahá was invited to the Hotel Plaza. He chose to sit in one of the smallest rooms and declined to inspect the palatial rooms of the hotel. He told the members of His retinue that whenever He encountered magnificent buildings and enchanting scenery He was immediately reminded of the dark pit of Ṭihrán and the desolate barracks of 'Akká, of the sufferings of Bahá'u'lláh. He was then overcome by sorrow and had no heart for sightseeing.

A talk which 'Abdu'l-Bahá gave at His home on July 5th ought to be particularly noted. Someone had asked Him about past cycles and His own references to them. He said in reply:

> The divine sovereignty is an ancient sovereignty not an accidental sovereignty.
> If we imagine this world of existence has a beginning we can say the divine sovereignty is accidental, that is, there was a time when it did not exist. A king without a kingdom is impossible. He cannot be without a country,

without subjects, without an army, without dominion, or he would be without kingship. All these exigencies or requirements of sovereignty must exist for a king. When they do exist we can apply the word sovereignty to him. Otherwise his sovereignty is imperfect, incomplete. If none of these conditions exist, sovereignty does not exist.

If we acknowledge there is a beginning for this world of creation, we acknowledge the sovereignty of God is accidental; that is, we admit a time when the reality of Divinity has been without dominion . . . The names and attributes of Divinity are requirements of this world. The names 'Powerful', the 'Living', the 'Provider', the 'Creator', require and necessitate the existence of creatures. If there were no creatures 'Creator' would be meaningless. If there were none to provide for, we could not think of the 'Provider'. If there were no life, the 'Living' would be beyond the power of conception. Therefore all the names and attributes of God require the existence of objects or creatures upon which they have been bestowed and in which they have become manifest . . . Therefore the requirements of the attributes of God do not admit of cessation or interruption, for the names of God are actually and forever existing and not potential. Because they convey life they are called Life-Giving; because they provide they are called Bountiful, the Provider; because they create they are called Creator; because they educate and govern, the name Lord God is applied. That is to say, the divine names emanate from the eternal attributes of Divinity. Therefore it is proved that the divine names presuppose the existence of objects or beings.

How then is a time conceivable when this sovereignty has not been existent? This divine sovereignty is not to be measured by six thousand years. This interminable, illimitable universe is not the result of that measured period. This stupendous laboratory and workshop has not been limited to six thousand revolutions of the earth about the sun, in its production. With the slightest

reflection man can be assured that this calculation and
announcement is childish, especially in view of the fact
that it is scientifically proved that the terrestrial globe has
been the habitation of man long prior to such limited
estimate.

... The texts of the holy Books are all symbolical
needing authoritative interpretation ... Bahá'u'lláh says
'the universe hath neither beginning nor ending' ... [162]

'Abdu'l-Bahá's next public engagement in New York was
at another Unitarian Church: All Souls, Fourth Avenue
and 20th Street. He spoke there on July 14th and said in the
course of His talk:

... Bahá'u'lláh has proclaimed and provided the way
by which hostility and dissension may be removed from
the human world. He has left no ground or possibility
for strife and disagreement.

First, He has proclaimed the oneness of mankind and
specialized religious teachings for existing human conditions. The first form of dissension arises from religious
differences. Bahá'u'lláh has given full teachings to the
world which are conducive to fellowship and unity in
religion. Throughout past centuries each system of
religious belief has boasted of its own superiority and
excellence, abasing and scorning the validity of all others.
Each has proclaimed its own belief as the light and all
others as darkness. Religionists have considered the world
of humanity as two trees, one divine and merciful, the
other satanic; they themselves the branches, leaves and
fruit of the divine tree and all others who differ from them
in belief, the product of the tree which is satanic ...

The teachings specialized by Bahá'u'lláh are addressed
to humanity, saying 'Ye are all the leaves of one tree.'
He does not say 'Ye are the leaves of two trees—one
divine, the other satanic.' He has declared that each individual member of the human family is a leaf or branch

upon the Adamic tree; that all are sheltered beneath the
protecting mercy and providence of God; that all are the
children of God; fruit upon the one tree of His love. God
is equally compassionate and kind to all the leaves,
branches and fruit of this tree. Therefore there is no
satanic tree whatever; 'satan' being a product of human
minds and of instinctive human tendencies toward error.
God alone is Creator and all are creatures of His might.
Therefore we must love mankind as His creatures,
realizing that all are growing upon the tree of His mercy,
servants of His omnipotent will and manifestations of His
good-pleasure.

Even though we find a branch or leaf upon this tree
of humanity defective or a blossom imperfect it nevertheless belongs to this tree and not to another. Therefore it is
our duty to protect and cultivate this tree until it reaches
perfection. If we examine its fruit and find it imperfect
we must strive to make it perfect. There are souls in the
human world who are ignorant; we must make them
knowing. Some growing upon the tree are weak and
ailing; we must assist them toward health and recovery.
If they are as infants in development we must minister
to them until they attain maturity. We should never detest
and shun them as objectionable and unworthy. We must
treat them with honour, respect and kindness, for God has
created them and not satan. They are not manifestations
of the wrath of God but evidences of His divine favour.
God the Creator has endowed them with physical, mental
and spiritual qualities that they may seek to know and do
His will; therefore they are not objects of His wrath
and condemnation. In brief, all humanity must be looked
upon with love, kindness and respect, for what we behold
in them are none other than the signs and traces of God
Himself. All are evidences of God; therefore how shall
we be justified in debasing and belittling them, uttering
anathema and preventing them from drawing near to
His mercy. This is ignorance and injustice, displeasing
to God, for in His sight all are His servants.[163]

The same day, in order to meet a group of seekers at the home of Roy Wilhelm, 'Abdu'l-Bahá visited West Englewood, where He stayed the night, and was a guest for dinner at the home of Louis Bourgeois, the future architect of the Mother Temple of the West.

On July 17th 'Abdu'l-Bahá presided over the marriage of Grace Robarts and Harlan Ober,[164] both of whom were destined to render invaluable services to the Faith. Howard Colby Ives (then still a Unitarian minister) was also present, and 'Abdu'l-Bahá asked him to perform the ceremony according to the Christian rites as well. He and Howard Ives both signed the marriage certificate.

There were many Bahá'ís in California, and they were anxiously awaiting the news of 'Abdu'l-Bahá's travel westwards. But the distance was great, long train journeys were taxing, and 'Abdu'l-Bahá's strength was already fully stretched. Furthermore, the erratic and damaging behaviour of Dr Amínu'lláh Faríd,* a member of His retinue and one of His translators, was causing Him great concern and sorrow; Dr Faríd's secret soliciting of money was particularly galling because he was related to the person of 'Abdu'l-Bahá. In the end 'Abdu'l-Bahá decided to undertake the journey to the West. But He still had other localities to visit in the Eastern states. He delayed His departure from New York one more day in order to meet Prince Muḥammad-'Alí Páshá, the brother of the Khedive of Egypt. In the memoirs of his travels the Prince writes:

On the morning of July 22nd . . . I learned that the highly-esteemed Eastern savant, 'Abbás Effendi, the

* Dr Faríd's name was usually spelt as such: Fareed. His mother was the sister of Muнírih Khánum, the wife of 'Abdu'l-Bahá; and his father, Mírzá Asadu'lláh-i-Iṣfahání, was the emissary who had taken the remains of the Báb from Írán to the Holy Land.

Head of the Bahá'ís, intended to meet me. I appointed the hour of three in the afternoon . . . 'Abbás Effendi came and I received him with joy and reverence. Advanced years have not affected his extraordinary sagacity. He stayed about an hour and talked of diverse subjects, exceedingly useful, which indicated the wide range of his knowledge and experience. He is indeed a man of learning and one of the great personalities of the East . . . After that we returned 'Abbás Effendi's visit . . . As to his addresses, they are immensely effective and have enjoyed wide circulation in America. Newspapers have reported and published them, and have appended the views of their ministers of religion. In short his powers attained such heights that the jealousy of the jealous was aroused. I stayed with him for a while. We talked together and his delectable speech greatly delighted me. Then I left, and I preserve for him in my heart affection and respect.[165]

CHAPTER 14

NEW ENGLAND
July 23rd–August 29th

'Abdu'l-Bahá left for Boston the next day, July 23rd. It was a short visit. The first night at the Hotel Victoria He spoke on the fundamentals of economic adjustment to a group of Bahá'ís and seekers. Newspaper reporters were also present and, as usual on these occasions, they asked 'Abdu'l-Bahá why He had come to the United States. He reiterated that He had come to participate in conferences on peace, and He uttered a warning that words were not sufficient to attain it. In the course of His talk 'Abdu'l-Bahá said:

> The fundamentals of the whole economic condition are divine in nature and are associated with the world of the heart and spirit . . . Strive therefore to create love in the hearts in order that they may become glowing and radiant. When that love is shining, it will permeate other hearts even as this electric light illumines its surroundings. When the love of God is established, everything else will be realized. This is the true foundation of all economics. Reflect upon it. Endeavour to become the cause of the attraction of souls rather than to enforce minds.[166]

The second night in Boston 'Abdu'l-Bahá spoke to the Theosophists in their hall at The Kensington, Exeter and Boylston Streets. During the day He had once again visited the headquarters of the Syrian society, the Golden Circle. When, on the following morning, He came out of

His hotel two Arabs ran forward and threw themselves at His feet, acclaiming Him as 'Yá Rasúlalláh' (O Messenger of God). 'Abdu'l-Bahá lifted them up and told them that He was not a 'Messenger of God', He was the 'servant of Bahá'. That same day He left for Dublin, New Hampshire, where He stayed until August 16th.

'Dublin is a beautiful mountain Summer resort,' writes Howard Colby Ives, 'where gathers each year a colony of wealthy intellectuals from Washington, D.C., and from various large centers. 'Abdu'l-Bahá's stay in that place for a period of three weeks offers another evidence of His unique power of adaptation to every environment; His dominant humility in every group, which, while seeming to follow He really led, and His manifest all-embracing knowledge.

'Picture, if you can, this Oriental, fresh from more than fifty years of exile and prison life, suddenly placed in an environment representing the proudest culture of the Western world. Nothing in His life, one would reasonably presume, had offered a preparation for such a contact.

'Not to His youth had been given years of academic and scholastic training. Not to His young manhood had been supplied those subtle associations during His formative years. Not upon His advancing age had been bestowed the comforts and leisure which invite the mind's expanse . . .

'How, then, can it be explained that in this environment He not only mingled with these highest products of wealth and culture with no slightest embarrassment to them or to Him, but He literally outshone them in their chosen field.

'No matter what subject was brought up He was perfectly at home in its discussion, yet always with an undercurrent of modesty and loving consideration for the opinions of others. I have before spoken of His unfailing courtesy . . . He "saw the Face of His Heavenly Father in every face" and reverenced the soul behind it. How could one be discourteous if such an attitude was held towards everyone!

'The husband of 'Abdu'l-Bahá's hostess in Dublin, who, while never becoming an avowed believer, had many opportunities of meeting and talking with the Master, when asked to sum up his impressions of Him, responded, after a little consideration: "I think He is the most perfect gentleman I have ever known."

'Consider. This was the verdict of a man of inherited wealth; of wide and profound culture; accustomed to judge men by delicate standards, and to whom the word "gentleman" connoted all which he held most admirable . . . '[167]

Howard Colby Ives was an eyewitness of the scene and the events he was describing. He was 'Abdu'l-Bahá's guest at the Dublin Inn, over the week-end of August 9th.

Mrs Parsons had a charming and extensive estate at Dublin. She put a large house on the estate at the disposal of 'Abdu'l-Bahá. He accepted her offer on the condition that He Himself should be responsible for all the expenses. However, while the members of His retinue and many of His guests stayed at that house, He chose to reside at the Inn, because it was lower down the mountainside and therefore warmer at night. When He was told that Mrs Parsons wished to withhold, for the time being, the news of His arrival, so that He could have a few days' rest, 'Abdu'l-Bahá replied: 'We have come here for work and service, not for enjoyment of air and scenery.' But, at the same time, He warned His attendants that since Dublin was a summer resort to which prominent people came, they ought to be on their guard, lest they give the impression that they had descended upon it to cast a net to catch the wealthy, the cultured, and the powerful. Only when asked, should they talk of the Cause.

It took the public only a day or two to become aware of the presence of 'Abdu'l-Bahá, and then Mr and Mrs Arthur Parsons invited their friends and acquaintances to meet Him. A luncheon party arranged for that purpose by Mrs

Parsons was described earlier in this book (p. 31). It was a shining illustration of the way 'Abdu'l-Bahá approached people and situations. Without sacrificing a principle or compromising the integrity of His station and stewardship He eschewed all manner of rigidity and uniformity. He was at ease with everyone and made everyone feel at ease. One day His attendants were remarking on the sweeping power of His speech: how encompassing it was, how incontestable were its arguments, how blissfully and perfectly phrased. 'Abdu'l-Bahá reminded them of the golden rule—that the nature and the requirements of the audience, the exigencies of the time and place must always be borne in mind, and that moderation was always essential.

The meetings at which He spoke in Dublin were many and various. The Unitarian Church was the milieu of one of those remarkable gatherings. 'Abdu'l-Bahá indeed had not gone to Dublin to rest, although the salubrious air of the mountain resort helped to restore some of His strength. Howard Colby Ives writes of that Sunday when 'Abdu'l-Bahá addressed the congregation of the Unitarian Church:

' . . . He had intimated that He would talk with me before the time for the service, so, about half-past-nine I was awaiting Him in one of the spacious private parlors of the Inn.

'The events of that day are among my clearest remembrances connected with the Master. At that time, about four months after my first meeting with Him . . . I was still, it seemed, almost as far away as ever from any true understanding . . .

' . . . He came into the room where I awaited Him and embraced me, asking if I were well and happy. We must always be happy, He said . . . God desires happiness for all His creatures . . .

'It was during this conversation that I asked Him again, as I often had, why I should believe in Bahá'u'lláh . . .

'He looked at me long and searchingly. His smile broadened . . . He seemed to be enjoying a heavenly situation which was not without its humorous side. Then He was lovingly grave again. After a somewhat lengthy silence He said that it was not given to everyone to speak often of . . . Christ to men. He said that I must thank God daily for this great bounty, for men have entirely forgotten the pure teachings of this "Essence of Severance". He remarked that . . . Bahá'u'lláh speaks of this in the *Book of Certitude* and that I should study it carefully. In that book is explained how these stars of the Heaven of Christ's Revelation have fallen to the earth of worldly desires . . . This condition is that to which Christ refers, He said, when He speaks of "the oppression or affliction of the Last Days." . . .

'Praise be to God that you are seeking Light. It behooves you to manifest Light; to express in word and deed the pure teachings of . . . Christ. To the proud we must be humble, He said; to the humble, compassionate; to the ignorant ones be as a student before his master; to the sinful ones be as the greatest sinner of all. To the poor be a benefactor; to the orphan, a father; to the aged, a son. Take guidance, not from leaders of sectarian theology but from the Sermon on the Mount. Seek no earthly reward, nay, rather, accept calamities in His service as His first disciples did.

'He smiled at me with such heavenly radiance that I sat enthralled and overcome with an emotion indescribable. Then he fell silent and His eyes closed. I thought He was weary, as doubtless He was for His constant activity gave Him little rest. But it was plain to me later that He must have been praying for me . . .

'He opened His eyes after a while, smiled again, and said that all who truly seek find; that the door to the World of Reality was never closed to those who patiently knock. This is the Day of attainment.

' . . . We sat in silence for some time and then a message

came that it was time to go to the church. He embraced me again and left me.

'For a little while I sat alone trying to adjust myself again to my surroundings, for I had truly been transported to another world.

'Then some friends came to ask me to accompany them to the church to hear the Master's talk.

'What His subject was I do not recall, nor does a single word of His address remain with me. My memory is all of the quiet New England church; the crowded pews, and 'Abdu'l-Bahá on the platform . . . His radiant smile and courteous demeanor. And His gestures! Never a dogmatic downward stroke of the hand; never an upraised warning finger; never the assumption of teacher to the taught. But always the encouraging upward swing of hands, as though He would actually lift us up with them. And His voice! Like a resonant bell of finest timbre; never loud but of such penetrating quality that the walls of the room seemed to vibrate with its music . . .

'That evening I felt that I must speak to 'Abdu'l-Bahá once more. My heart was too full of thankfulness to let me rest without the effort to express it to Him. So I watched for Him to come back to the Inn after His day was ended. It was quite late when at last I saw Him slowly ascending the stairs to His room.

'I can hardly believe now that I had the temerity to follow. He had entered the room when I reached it, and had closed the door. What gave me courage to knock I do not know; but knock I did, and He opened the door Himself. I did not know what to say. He beckoned me in and looked at me gravely. I stammered: "Will you please pray with me?"

'He motioned, and I knelt while He put His hands upon my head and chanted, in Persian, a brief prayer. It was all over within three minutes. But those moments brought to me a peace I had never known.'[168]

One afternoon 'Abdu'l-Bahá had spoken of the falsity of the premises of the materialist who only accepts as true and real what his senses can comprehend. Were it so, He had again said in jest, the cow should be reckoned to be the greatest of all the philosophers, because she had reached that conclusion without the pain of study. This reference to the cow had greatly amused His audience. When the meeting was over 'Abdu'l-Bahá was asked to make use of the motor car belonging to one of those present, for a drive in the country-side. As it happened they came upon a herd, and the cows ran away in all directions. Look Master, a lady said, philosophers are in flight. 'Abdu'l-Bahá was highly amused, and laughed most heartily.

Zarqání records that of the themes and topics which 'Abdu'l-Bahá touched upon in the course of His talks and conversations in Dublin, it was His unequivocal assertion of the divine origin of Islám and the station of its Founder which produced visible evidences of resentment, although there was no open dissent. Such a reaction was understandable in the Christian West.

Another day, 'Abdu'l-Bahá, again in a jestful mood, told His attendants that hard must be their plight, deserving sympathy, and sad their fate to have to enjoy such wonderful things of life in such pleasant surroundings, befriended and served by such very kind people. 'Come and partake,' He said, 'of these fruits and delicacies which Mrs Parsons has provided for you.' Then He told them gravely that they should consider how Bahá'u'lláh had raised them high in the esteem of the élite, how He had given them friends who loved them whole-heartedly, who served them with no ulterior motive, and not for the sake of any reward.

Another eyewitness has related the following story of 'Abdu'l-Bahá in Dublin. Early one morning, when He was in the grounds of the Inn dictating to a secretary, an old man, obviously a tramp, came shuffling along the street.

'Abdu'l-Bahá noticed him and told His secretary to go and call him in. He took the old man's dirt-crusted hands in His, and spoke to him with love and affection. It was as if He had known this weary, dejected tramp all His life. And then He saw how filthy and torn the old man's trousers were. At that hour of the day no one was about. 'Abdu'l-Bahá walked towards the porch of the Inn, wrapped His long-flowing 'abá round Himself, took off His own trousers, gave them to the old tramp, and told him: 'May God go with you.' (In the Holy Land, many a time did He invite a passing bedouin or a shepherd to come and sit beside Him and share His meal.)

'Abdu'l-Bahá's talk on August 14th was on the need for economic adjustment. Some misunderstanding must have arisen, because questions on this particular subject were put to Him after His departure from Dublin; and on the train to San Francisco, 'Abdu'l-Bahá addressed a Tablet to Mrs Parsons in which He outlined a pattern for a village community. He took the village as His starting point, because, in His own words, 'the farmer is the primary factor in the body politic'. In the *Tablet of the World*, Bahá'u'lláh had given primacy to agriculture in the organization of society.

Dr Henderson, a pioneer in organizing summer camps for high school boys, had a camp which had been functioning for some twenty years in the vicinity of Dublin. At his invitation 'Abdu'l-Bahá spent a day there, and highly commended the work to which Dr Henderson had devoted a lifetime. The boys, with the permission of 'Abdu'l-Bahá, took scores of photographs.

August 15th was the last day of His sojourn in Dublin. Mrs Parsons held a farewell meeting combined with musical recitations, and noted pianists played. Then 'Abdu'l-Bahá stood before the vast audience, many of whom had heard Him time and again, and He threw a challenge to them: 'I presented a variety of subjects to you. I gave you the

Message of God, expounded for you the mysteries of Scripture, proved for you the immortality of the soul. I explained at length the economic question and the Divine Teachings.' He shook hands with all of them. He called on others, who had not been present, and whom He had come to know. Mrs Parsons told Him that they all wished Him to prolong His stay. He would have liked to do so, He said, but He had to go to Green Acre and other localities, and raise the call of the Kingdom everywhere. Not much was left of His life, He added; therefore He must hasten to other climes, and carry the tidings of the Kingdom of Abhá.

On August 16th 'Abdu'l-Bahá journeyed to Green Acre in a car specially brought from there by Alfred Lunt. Green Acre, an estate of nearly two hundred acres, lies on the banks of the Piscataqua river in Eliot, Maine, four miles from the shores of the Atlantic; Portsmouth, New Hampshire, is close by. In 1894, in the wake of the Chicago Columbian Exposition of the previous year, Miss Sarah J. Farmer, a woman highly enlightened, had opened the estate as a conference centre for people of advanced and liberal views. Two years later she embraced the Bahá'í Faith. And when she went on pilgrimage to 'Akká, she offered the facilities of Green Acre to 'Abdu'l-Bahá. Such outstanding figures in America as John Greenleaf Whittier, Ralph Waldo Trine, John Fiske, Helen Campbell, Paul Carus and Booker T. Washington had, in the course of years, taken part in Green Acre conferences and substantially aided the development of the aims and purposes of Sarah Farmer. Mírzá Abu'l-Faḍl, too, had made notable contributions.

Some of 'Abdu'l-Bahá's efforts, during the week He stayed in the Inn at Green Acre, were inevitably directed towards countering the effects of the eccentric ideas being disseminated by various pseudo-mystics and cranks who were attracted to the free platform provided there. On one occasion He was seen distributing sweets to a group of people, telling them that they ought to eat and enjoy their food, in order to gain physical strength, that they should not allow themselves to be enfeebled by practising abstemiousness. Spirituality, He said, had nothing to do with abstaining from food, with the mortification of the flesh. On another occasion He spoke about the rigorous disciplines of the ascetics, and the harm ensuing from them. He cited superstitions to be found in India. He also had to face fortune-tellers and palmists whom He treated with great kindliness.

'Abdu'l-Bahá counselled the Bahá'ís not to intervene in the affairs of the Green Acre Fellowship. But eventually Sarah Farmer herself had to take steps to safeguard the future of the precious gift she had made to the people of America. To that end she called in the aid of Alfred Lunt who was a brilliant lawyer. The lawsuit which followed was carried to the Supreme Court of the State of Maine, and Alfred Lunt's labours were vindicated.[169] Today the Green Acre property (the home of a well-famed Summer School) is administered by the National Spiritual Assembly of the Bahá'ís of the United States. It includes the Inn, the Fellowship House, the Arts and Crafts Studio and a holding on Monsalvat where 'Abdu'l-Bahá stood and commended the wish of Sarah Farmer that a 'university of the higher sciences' should be built on that height.

Almost within minutes of His arrival at Green Acre, having taken only a short rest, 'Abdu'l-Bahá spoke briefly to the large group that had assembled to greet Him. Then He visited the sanatorium in Portsmouth where Sarah Farmer, an invalid, was a patient. Though ill and frail, she accompanied Him back to Green Acre. There in the evening He gave one of the longest talks of His entire tour. Thus He began:

Every subject presented to a thoughtful audience must be supported by rational proofs and logical arguments.

Proofs are of four kinds: first, through sense-perception; second, through the reasoning faculty; third, from traditional or scriptural authority; fourth, through the medium of inspiration. That is to say, there are four criteria or standards of judgment by which the human mind reaches its conclusions.

Then He proceeded to examine each of these criteria in detail, and having done so He declared:

Consequently it has become evident that the four criteria or standards of judgment by which the human mind reaches its conclusions are faulty and inaccurate. All of them are liable to mistake and error in conclusions. But a statement presented to the mind accompanied by proofs which the senses can perceive to be correct, which the faculty of reason can accept, which is in accord with traditional authority and sanctioned by the promptings of the heart, can be adjudged and relied upon as perfectly correct, for it has been proved and tested by all the standards of judgment and found to be complete. When we apply but one test there are possibilities of mistake . . .

We will now consider the subject of 'Love' which has been suggested, submitting it to the four standards of judgment . . .

We declare that love is the cause of the existence of all phenomena and that the absence of love is the cause of disintegration or non-existence. Love is . . . the bond of affiliation in all phenomena. We will first consider the proof of this through sense-perception.

He applied one criterion after another to the subject. He demonstrated how the power of attraction binds atoms and elements together—in the mineral kingdom, in the vegetable kingdom, and in the kingdom of man. 'As this is the superior kingdom,' He said, 'the light of love is more resplendent.'

There are various manifestations of this power of attraction in the human kingdom, but beyond them, He said:

> . . . we discover in the being of man the attraction of heart, the susceptibilities and affinities which bind men together, enabling them to live and associate in friendship and solidarity. It is therefore evident that in the world of humanity the greatest king and sovereign is love. If love were extinguished, the power of attraction dispelled, the affinity of human hearts destroyed, the phenomena of human life would disappear.

Next He proceeded to speak of the divine love:

> . . . consider and observe how the bestowals of God successively descend upon mankind; how the divine effulgences ever shine upon the human world. There can be no doubt that these bestowals, these bounties, these effulgences emanate from love . . . The phenomenal world through the resplendent effulgence of the sun is radiant and bright. In the same way the realm of hearts and spirits is illumined and resuscitated through the shining rays of the Sun of Reality and the bounties of the love of God . . .
>
> Consider to what extent the love of God makes itself manifest. Among the signs of His love which appear in the world are the dawning-points of His Manifestations. What an infinite degree of love is reflected by the Divine Manifestations toward mankind! For the sake of guiding the people They have willingly forfeited their lives to resuscitate human hearts. They have accepted the cross. To enable human souls to attain the supreme degree of advancement, They have suffered during their limited years extreme ordeals.
>
> . . . all the Divine Manifestations suffered, offered Their lives and blood, sacrificed Their existence, comfort and all They possessed for the sake of mankind. Therefore consider how much They love. Were it not for Their love

for humanity, spiritual love would be mere nomen-
clature. Were it not for Their illumination, human souls
would not be radiant. How effective is Their love! This is
a sign of the love of God . . .

. . . Were it not for the love of God all the spirits
would be inanimate. The meaning of this is not physical
death; nay, rather, it is that condition concerning which
Christ declared 'let the dead bury their dead,' for 'that
which is born of the flesh is flesh; and that which is born
of the Spirit is spirit'.* Were it not for the love of God
the pathway of the kingdom would not be opened . . .
Were it not for the love of God the Divine Prophets
would not have been sent to the world. The foundation
of all these bestowals is the love of God. Therefore in
the human world there is no greater power than the love
of God. It is the love of God which has brought us
together here tonight . . .

'We come to another aspect of our subject,' He said later
on. 'Are the workings and effects of love confined to this
world or do they extend on and on to another existence?
Will its influence affect our existence here only or will it
extend to the life everlasting?' Then following and applying
the criteria which He had laid down, 'Abdu'l-Bahá demonstrated that the human soul must be immortal. And with
these words He ended His talk:

. . . This is a subject of great importance. There are
innumerable proofs in support of it. I hope we may continue it at another time.

Before we leave I desire to offer a prayer in behalf of
Miss Farmer, for verily she has been the founder of this
organization, the source of this loving fellowship and
assemblage.

O Thou kind God! encircle these servants with the
glances of Thy providence. Set aglow the hearts of this

* Matt. viii: 22 and John iii: 6.

assemblage with the fire of Thy love. Illumine these faces with the light of heaven. Enlighten these hearts with the light of the most great guidance.

O God! the clouds of superstitions have covered the horizons of the hearts. O Lord! dispel these clouds so that the lights of the Sun of Reality may shine. O Lord! illumine our eyes so that we may behold Thy light. O Lord! attune our ears so that we may hear the call of the Supreme Concourse. O Lord! render our tongues eloquent so that we may become engaged in Thy commemoration. O Lord! sanctify and purify the hearts so that the effulgence of Thy love may shine therein.

O Thou kind Lord! bestow quick recovery through Thy power and bounty upon the founder of this Association. O Lord! this woman has served Thee, has turned her face towards Thy Kingdom and has established these conferences in order that reality might be investigated and the light of reality shine.

O Lord! be Thou ever her support. O Lord! be Thou ever her comforter. O Lord! bestow upon her quick healing. Verily, Thou art the Clement! Verily, Thou art the Merciful! Verily, Thou art the Generous.[170]

The next day (August 17th), 'Abdu'l-Bahá delivered several talks at Green Acre. On one occasion He said:

Although the body was weak and not fitted to undergo the vicissitudes of crossing the Atlantic, yet love assisted us and we came here. At certain times the spirit must assist the body. We cannot accomplish really great things through physical force alone; the spirit must fortify our bodily strength. For example, the body of man may be able to withstand the ordeal of imprisonment for ten or fifteen years under temperate conditions of climate and restful physical routine. During our imprisonment in 'Akká, means of comfort were lacking, troubles and persecutions of all kinds surrounded us, yet notwithstanding such distressful conditions we were able to endure these trials for forty years. The climate was very bad, necessities and conveniences of life were denied us, yet we endured this narrow prison forty years. What was the reason? The spirit was strengthening and resuscitating the body constantly. We lived through this long, difficult period in the utmost love and heavenly servitude. The spirit must assist the body under certain conditions which surround us, because the body of itself cannot endure the extreme pain of such hardships.

The human body is in reality very weak; there is no physical body more delicately constituted. One mosquito will distress it; the smallest quantity of poison will destroy it; if respiration ceases for a moment, it will die. What instrument could be weaker and more delicate? A blade of grass severed from the root may live an hour whereas a human body deprived of its forces may die in one minute. But in the proportion that the human body is weak, the spirit of man is strong. It can control natural phenomena; it is a supernatural power which transcends all contingent beings. It has immortal life which nothing can destroy or pervert. If all the kingdoms of life arise against the immortal spirit of man and seek its destruction, this immortal spirit singly and alone can withstand their attacks in fearless firmness and resolution because it is indestructible and empowered with supreme natural virtues. For this reason we say that the spirit of man can penetrate and discover the realities of all things, can solve the secrets and mysteries of all created objects. While living upon the earth it discovers the stars and their satellites; it travels underground, finds the metals in their hidden depths and unlocks the secrets of geological ages. It can cross the abysses of inter-stellar space and discover the motion of inconceivably distant suns. How wonderful it is! It can attain to the Kingdom of God. It can penetrate the mysteries of the Divine Kingdom and attain to life everlasting. It receives illumination from the light of God and reflects it to the whole universe. How wonderful it is! How powerful the spirit of man, while his body is so weak! If the susceptibilities of the spirit control him, there is no created being more heroic, more undaunted than man; but if physical forces dominate, you cannot find a more cowardly or fearful object because the body is so weak and incapable. Therefore it is divinely intended that the spiritual susceptibilities of man should gain precedence and overrule his physical forces. In this way he becomes fitted to dominate the human world by his nobility and stand forth fearless and free, endowed with the attributes of eternal life.[171]

On August 20th there arrived at Green Acre a young man, dishevelled, tremulous. His name was Fred Mortensen. Let him tell his story in his own words. He wrote it for the magazine, *The Star of the West*:

'In my youth my environment was not of the best and being around boys of hard character I guess I determined to be as tough as any, which I very easily did, though inwardly I always had a feeling to be above it all. Still I always felt that I should do in Rome as the Romans do. So I violated any law I saw fit, man's or God's. Strange as it seems to me at times, it was through coming into contact with these laws that I received the opportunity to be guided into this most wonderful Revelation.

'My dear mother had done everything in her power to make me a good boy. I have but the deepest love for her and my heart has often been sad when thinking how she must have worried for my safety as well as for my future well-being. Through it all and in a most wonderful way, with a god-like patience, she hoped and prayed that her boy would find the road which leadeth to righteousness and happiness. But environment proved a great barrier to her aspirations and every day in every way I became tougher and tougher. Fighting was a real pleasure, as welcome as a meal, and breaking a grocer's window to steal his fruit or what-not was, as I thought, a great joke.

'It happened that one night the "gang" was strolling along, just doing nothing in particular (looking for trouble I guess), when one of the gang said, "Oh look at the swell bunch of bananas." "Gee, I wisht I had some," another said. "Do you?" said I. About this time I heard a dog barking inside the store, and looking in, I saw a large bulldog. That seemed to aggravate me and, to show my contempt for the watch-dog, I guess, I broke the window, took the bananas, passed them around and we merrily strolled up the street . . . I plainly remember that it cost me sixteen dollars to pay for broken windows, to keep out of jail.

' . . . I was a fugitive for four years, having walked out of jail while awaiting trial. Then—a young fellow was being arrested and I, of course, tried to take him away from the policeman. While this was going on a couple of detectives happened along and in my haste to get away from them I leaped over a thirty-five foot wall, breaking my leg, to escape the bullets whizzing around about—and wound up in the "garden at the feet of the Beloved" as Bahá'u'lláh has so beautifully written it in the *Seven Valleys*.

'At this time I was defended by our departed, but illustrious Bahá'í brother, Albert Hall, to whom I owe many thanks and my everlasting good will for helping to free me from the prison of men and of self. It was he who brought me from out the dark prison house; it was he who told me, hour after hour, about the great love of 'Abdu'l-Bahá for all his children and that he was here to help us show that love for our fellowmen. Honestly, I often wondered then what Mr. Hall meant when he talked so much about love, God's love, Bahá'u'lláh's love, 'Abdu'l-Bahá's love, love for the Covenant . . . I was bewildered. Still, I returned, to become more bewildered, so I thought; and I wondered why . . . Thus the Word of God gave me a new birth . . .

'Again through the attraction of the Holy Spirit I was urged, so it seemed to me, to go to see 'Abdu'l-Bahá. He was at Green Acre, Maine, at this time, and when I heard the rumor that he might go back to his home (Palestine) and not come west, I immediately determined to go and see him. I wasn't going to miss meeting 'Abdu'l-Bahá after waiting so long to see him.

'So I left home, going to Cleveland, where I attended a convention of printers for a few days. But I became so restless I could not stay for adjournment. How often I have thought about that trip of mine from Cleveland to Green Acre! The night before leaving Cleveland I had a dream that I was 'Abdu'l-Bahá's guest, that I sat at a long table, and many others were there, too, and of how he walked up and down telling stories, emphasizing with his hand. This, later, was fulfilled and he looked just as I saw him in Cleveland.

'As my finances were low I of necessity must hobo my way to Green Acre. The Nickel Plate Railway was my choice, for conveyance to Buffalo, New York. From Buffalo I again rode the rods to Boston, a long ride from around midnight until nine next morning. The Boston and Maine Railway was the last link between 'Abdu'l-Bahá and the outside world so it seemed to me, and when I crawled off from the top of one of its passenger trains at Portsmouth, New Hampshire, I was exceedingly happy. A boat ride, a street car ride, and there I was, at the gate of Paradise. My heart beating double time, I stepped onto the soil of that to-be-famous center, tired, dirty, and wondering, but happy.

'I had a letter of introduction from Mr. Hall to Mr. Lunt, and in searching for him I met Mrs. Edward Kinney, who, dear soul, was kind enough to offer me a bed. She awakened me next morning about six o'clock, saying I'd have to hurry if I wished to see 'Abdu'l-Bahá.

'Arriving at the hotel I found quite a number of people there, on the same mission, to see 'Abdu'l-Bahá. Being one of the last arrivals, I was looking around, to make myself comfortable, when someone exclaimed, "Here he comes, now". Ahmad Sohrab did the introducing and interpreting. When Ahmad introduced me to him, to my astonishment he looked at me and only said, "Ugh! Ugh!" not offering to shake hands with me. Coming as I had, and feeling as I did, I was very much embarrassed. After greeting several others and when about to go to his room, he suddenly turned to me and said in a gruff voice (at least I thought so), "Sit down," and pointed to a chair—which I didn't care to do, as elderly ladies were standing. But what was I to do! I meekly obeyed, feeling rebellious over what had happened. Such a welcome, after making that difficult trip! My mind sure was in a whirl.

'The first man to receive an interview with 'Abdu'l-Bahá was a doctor; he had written a book on love. It seemed but a minute until Ahmad came down and said, " 'Abdu'l-Bahá wishes to see Mr. Mortensen." Why, I nearly wilted. I wasn't ready. I hadn't expected to be called until the very last thing. I had to go, and it was with a strange feeling in my heart and wondering, wondering what would happen next. He welcomed me with a smile and a warm hand-clasp, telling me to be seated, he sitting before me. His first words were, "Welcome! Welcome! You are very welcome,"— then, "Are you happy?"—which was repeated three times. I thought, why do you ask me that so many times? Of course I am happy; didn't I tell you so the first time?

'Then, "Where did you come from?"

'Answer: "From Minneapolis."

'Question: "Do you know Mr. Hall?"

'Answer: "Yes, he told me about the Cause."

'Question: "Did you have a pleasant journey?"

'Of all the questions I wished to avoid this was the one! I dropped my gaze to the floor—and again he put the question. I lifted my eyes to his and his were as two black, sparkling jewels, which seemed to look into my very depths. I knew he knew and I must tell, and as I answered I wondered what Ahmad thought—if I was a little unbalanced.

'I answered: "I did not come as people generally do, who come to see you."

'Question: "How did you come?"

'Answer: "Riding under and on top of the railway trains."

'Question: "Explain how."

'Now as I looked into the eyes of 'Abdu'l-Bahá I saw they had changed and a wondrous light seemed to pour out. It was the light of love and I felt relieved and very much happier. I explained to him how I rode on the trains, after which he kissed both my cheeks, gave me much fruit, and kissed the dirty hat I wore, which had become soiled on my trip to see him.

'When he was ready to leave Green Acre I stood nearby to say goodbye, and to my astonishment he ordered me to get into the automobile with him. After a week with him at Malden, Massachusetts, I left for home with never-to-be forgotten memories of a wonderful event—the meeting of God's Covenant, the Branch of that Pre-Existent Root, that wonderful Moon that shall shine as the Sun, as the light of seven days and to whom all shall bow and praise His Holy Name.

'A few weeks later I again had that wonderful privilege to be near the Covenant for a few moments.

'These events are engraved upon the tablet of my heart and I love every moment of them. The words of Bahá'u'lláh are my food, my drink and my life. I have no other aim than to be of service in his pathway and to be obedient to his Covenant . . . '[172]

On August 23rd 'Abdu'l-Bahá left for Malden. On the way there He once again called at the Portsmouth Sanatarium

to visit Sarah Farmer. In Malden He stayed at the home of
Miss Wilson. The Wilson house is today part of the endow-
ments of the American Bahá'í community. He told her that
in the United States He had stayed in two Bahá'í homes only,
Mrs Parsons' and hers. Malden is close to Boston, and
'Abdu'l-Bahá addressed three meetings in the latter city:
the New Thought Forum on August 25th, Franklin Square
House (a school for girls) on the 26th, and the Metaphysical
Club on the 27th. He told the audience at the Metaphysical
Club:

Upon the faces of those present I behold the expression
of thoughtfulness and wisdom, therefore I shall discourse upon a subject involving one of the divine
questions, a question of religious and metaphysical importance, namely the progressive and perpetual motion
of elemental atoms throughout the various degrees of
phenomena and the kingdoms of existence.

It will be demonstrated and become evident that the
origin and outcome of phenomena are identical and that
there is an essential oneness in all existing things . . .

The elemental atoms which constitute all phenomenal
existence and being in this illimitable universe are in
perpetual motion, undergoing continuous degrees of
progression. For instance, let us conceive of an atom in
the mineral kingdom progressing upward to the kingdom of the vegetable by entering into the composition
and fibre of a tree or plant. From thence it is assimilated
and transferred into the kingdom of the animal and finally
by the law and process of composition becomes a part of
the body of man . . . This motion or transference is progressive and perpetual . . .

In its ceaseless progression and journeyings the atom
becomes imbued with the virtues and powers of each
degree or kingdom it traverses. In the degree of the mineral
it possessed mineral affinities; in the kingdom of the

vegetable it manifested the virtue augmentative or power of growth; in the animal organism it reflected the intelligence of that degree, and in the kingdom of man it was qualified with human attributes or virtues.

Furthermore, the forms and organisms of phenomenal being and existence in each of the kingdoms of the universe are myriad and numberless. The vegetable plane or kingdom, for instance, has its infinite variety of types and material structures of plant life, each distinct and different within itself, no two exactly alike in composition and detail, for there are no repetitions in nature, and the virtue augmentative cannot be confined to any given image or shape. Each leaf has its own particular identity, so to speak, its own individuality as a leaf . . . As each of these forms has its individual and particular virtue, therefore each elemental atom of the universe has the opportunity of expressing an infinite variety of those individual virtues . . .

It is evident then that each elemental atom . . . is possessed of a capacity to express all the virtues of the universe. This is a subtle and abstract realization. Meditate upon it, for within it lies the true explanation of pantheism. From this point of view and perception, pantheism is a truth, for every atom . . . possesses or reflects all the virtues of life, the manifestation of which is effected through change and transformation. Therefore the origin and outcome of phenomena is verily the omnipresent God for the reality of all phenomenal existence is through Him. There is neither reality nor the manifestation of reality without the instrumentality of God. Existence is realized and possible through the bounty of God, just as the ray or flame emanating from this lamp is realized through the bounty of the lamp from which it originates. Even so all phenomena are realized through the divine bounty, and the explanation of true pantheistic statement and principle is that the phenomena of the universe find realization through the one Power animating and dominating all things; and all things are but manifestations of Its energy and bounty. The virtue of being and existence is through no other agency.

Then 'Abdu'l-Bahá spoke of the teachings of Bahá'u'lláh: the oneness of mankind, the oneness of revelation and religion, that ' . . . religion must be conducive to love and unity. If it proves to be the source of hatred and enmity its absence is preferable, for the will and law of God is love, and love is the bond between human hearts', that 'Religion must conform to science and reason, otherwise it is superstition. God has created man in order that he may perceive the verity of existence and endowed him with mind or reason to discover truth. Therefore scientific knowledge and religious belief must be conformable to the analysis of this divine faculty in man.' Furthermore, He said of the teachings of Bahá'u'lláh that 'Prejudices of all kinds, whether religious, racial, patriotic or political are destructive of divine foundations in man . . . ' 'Bahá'u'lláh,' He said, 'has proclaimed and promulgated the foundation of international peace . . . Bahá'u'lláh has announced that no matter how far the world of humanity may advance in material civilization, it is nevertheless in need of spiritual virtues and the bounties of God . . . '

And with these words He brought His talk at the Metaphysical Club of Boston to its end:

As the babe is born into the light of this physical world so must the physical and intellectual man be born into the light of the world of divinity. In the matrix of the mother the unborn child was deprived and unconscious of the world of material existence but after its birth it beheld the wonders and beauties of a new realm of life and being. In the world of the matrix it was utterly ignorant and unable to conceive of these new conditions but after its transformation it discovers the radiant sun,

trees, flowers and an infinite range of blessings and bounties awaiting it. In the human plane and kingdom man is a
captive of nature and ignorant of the divine world until
born of the breaths of the Holy Spirit out of physical
conditions of limitation and deprivation. Then he beholds
the reality of the spiritual realm and kingdom, realizes
the narrow restrictions of the mere human world of
existence and becomes conscious of the unlimited and
infinite glories of the world of God. Therefore, no matter
how man may advance upon the physical and intellectual
plane, he is ever in need of the boundless virtues of divinity,
the protection of the Holy Spirit and the face of God.[173]

CHAPTER 15

CANADA
August 30th–September 8th

Montreal, Canada, was the next destination of 'Abdu'l-Bahá. It was the only city in Canada that He visited. This was the city where May and William Sutherland Maxwell had established their home (see page 84). Their charming house, 716 Pine Avenue West, on the slope of Mount Royal, which Sutherland Maxwell had designed himself, and at which 'Abdu'l-Bahá arrived in the bright, moonlit evening of August 30th, is today the Bahá'í Shrine for Canada. The devoted and selfless services of May Maxwell in Paris and on the Canadian soil acted as a strong magnet to draw 'Abdu'l-Bahá to Montreal, but time was getting short, and the long journey to the Pacific coast still lay in front of Him. Of the members of His retinue He took only two with Him: Mírzá Maḥmúd-i-Zarqání and Aḥmad Sohráb.[174]

'Abdu'l-Bahá's visit to Montreal constituted a very remarkable episode in the whole of His American tour. To begin with, the newspaper coverage of His visit was particularly noteworthy. On the very evening of His arrival, John Lewis, editor of the *Montreal Daily Star*, was at the Maxwell home to meet Him. That newspaper and *The Gazette*, in reporting 'Abdu'l-Bahá's activities, provided such headlines as: 'Persian Teacher to Preach Peace'; 'Racialism Wrong, Says Eastern Sage, Strife and War Caused by Religious and National Prejudices'; 'Materialism No Philosophy, Says Oriental Seer'; 'Apostle of Peace

Meets Socialists, Abdul Baha's Novel Scheme for Distribution of Surplus Wealth'. These may well be compared with 'His Holiness Visits Us, Not Pius X but A. Baha' which appeared in a Chicago paper on September 14th. Furthermore the reportage in those Montreal papers was noticeably free of journalistic quirks and extravagances. In its issue of September 11th, the *Montreal Daily Star* carried an editorial under the heading: 'War Must Precede Universal Peace' which read as follows:

> Abdu'l Baha has preached Universal Peace for fifty years ... In a word, Abdu'l Baha is the great protagonist of Peace in the world today. To bring about its accomplishment is the practical corollary of the two tenets which are the foundation of his creed—the Fatherhood of God and the brotherhood of man. For forty years he was persecuted for preaching it, for twenty years imprisoned.
>
> Yet the universal peace for which he hopes and in which he believes has no resemblance to the fantastic chimera of slack-thinking sophists (with) the easy assumption that all things are as they ought to be ...
>
> For Abdu'l Baha, with all his hatred of war and horror at its moral and material results, has no delusions as to the conditions in Europe today or the trend of political events. 'It is futile to hope for any slackening of the present race of the nations to increase their armaments,' he says. 'A great war in Europe is a certainty before permanent peace can be established. International peace can only be reached by an international agreement entered into by all nations.'
>
> Strong words, those, from a teacher whose life has been spent in preaching peace on earth. There is no smug complacency about them nor any blinking the facts that one's fragile fabric of assertions may not be rudely destroyed. Abhorrent as war is to Abdu'l Baha and his followers, they have the moral courage to recognize and acknowledge the probability of its occurrence.

In an interview printed elsewhere in this issue Abdu'l
Baha elaborates more fully his views on the question.

Here are some extracts from that interview:

The venerable apostle of peace emphatically declared
that in the temper of the world today it was futile to hope
for any slackening of the present race of the nations to
increase their armaments. He reiterated his absolute
conviction that a great war in Europe was a certainty
before permanent peace would be established in the
world . . . 'As to the question of disarmament, all
nations must disarm at the same time. It will not do at
all, and it is not proposed, that some nations shall lay
down their arms while others, their neighbours, remain
armed. The peace of the world must be brought about by
international agreement. All nations must agree to disarm simultaneously . . . In the meantime, all people of
good-will must ever strive to make international peace
the great issue. They must work unceasingly to turn
public opinion in favour of this line of action . . . All
Europe is an armed camp . . . The very armaments themselves are productive of war . . . '175

'Abdu'l-Bahá said many a time, during His tour of Europe
and America, that Europe was like an arsenal, and it
needed just one spark to set it ablaze. And it happened as
He had foreseen. Subsequent to the carnage of that First
World War, sadly viewing the plight of mankind, He stated
categorically that 'another war, fiercer than the last, will
assuredly break out.' On November 28th 1931, the anniversary of the passing of 'Abdu'l-Bahá, His grandson,
Shoghi Effendi, the Guardian of the Faith, wrote:

Ten years ago, this very day, there flashed upon the world
the news of the passing of Him Who alone, through the
ennobling influence of His love, strength and wisdom,

could have proved its stay and solace in the many afflictions it was destined to suffer.

How well we, the little band of His avowed supporters who lay claim to have recognized the Light that shone within Him, can still remember His repeated allusions, in the evening of His earthly life, to the tribulation and turmoil with which an unregenerate humanity was to be increasingly afflicted. How poignantly some of us can recall His pregnant remarks, in the presence of the pilgrims and visitors who thronged His doors on the morrow of the jubilant celebrations that greeted the termination of the World War—a war which, by the horrors it evoked, the losses it entailed and the complications it engendered, was destined to exert so far-reaching an influence on the fortunes of mankind. How serenely, yet how powerfully, He stressed the cruel deception which a Pact, hailed by peoples and nations as the embodiment of triumphant justice and the unfailing instrument of an abiding peace, held in store for an unrepentant humanity. '*Peace, Peace,*' how often we heard Him remark, '*the lips of potentates and peoples unceasingly proclaim, whereas the fire of unquenched hatreds still smoulders in their hearts.*' How often we heard Him raise His voice, whilst the tumult of triumphant enthusiasm was still at its height and long before the faintest misgivings could have been felt or expressed, confidently declaring that the Document, extolled as the Charter of a liberated humanity, contained within itself seeds of such bitter deception as would further enslave the world. How abundant are now the evidences that attest the perspicacity of His unerring judgment![176]

It should not be assumed that the reportage in the newspapers of the United States was always unmitigated journalese. There were notable and outstanding exceptions; but the fact remains that in tone and range and substance the newspapers of Montreal excelled consistently. Walking one day into the room occupied by His attendants 'Abdu'l-Bahá was surprised to see a stack of newspapers laid in a corner. He was told that these were evidences of the power of His word and of the Cause, which they intended to dispatch to the East.

The day after His arrival in Montreal 'Abdu'l-Bahá went for a drive, and sighting the magnificent Roman Catholic Church of Notre Dame, He went in. When He came out, standing in the porch, He turned to those who were in His company and told them to take a lesson from that very church. It was the total self-abnegation of the apostles of Christ which had raised that splendorous edifice in a land far, far from the scene of their labours. Those disciples, said 'Abdu'l-Bahá, made a pact to go out into the wide world, preach the Gospel, and accept every tribulation for the sake of their Master. They stood by their pledge, and not a single one of them ever returned. And there beside them, He told that company, stood the concrete evidence of the selfless efforts of the disciples of Christ. Some years before, when perils surrounded Him on all sides, 'Abdu'l-Bahá had written in His Will and Testament:

> The disciples of Christ forgot themselves and all earthly things, forsook all their cares and belongings, purged themselves of self and passion and with absolute detachment scattered far and wide and engaged in calling the peoples of the world to the Divine Guidance, till at last they made the world another world, illumined the surface of the earth and even to their last hour proved self-sacrificing in the pathway of that Beloved One of God. Finally in various lands they suffered glorious martyrdom. Let them that are men of action follow in their footsteps!

Later that day, seated in the carriage, 'Abdu'l-Bahá recalled the time of Bahá'u'lláh's exile to Constantinople. An Ottoman soldier on horseback had come across their way, riding arrogantly along. Noticing the proud soldier, Mírzá Yaḥyá had bewailed their own plight. 'Where once were we, and what road are we taking now?' he had exclaimed, adding: 'They say that people will come to pay homage, but when will that be?' 'Abdu'l-Bahá had told Mírzá Yaḥyá that in future, when the bounties of God descend in their abundance, people far greater than that haughty soldier will come, under the shadow of the Word of God, to pay homage to the Faith. And now where is Mírzá Yaḥyá, 'Abdu'l-Bahá concluded, to witness what the power of Bahá'u'lláh has wrought; to see how Americans, in whose sight those Ottoman soldiers are of no consequence, pay homage to Him?

Across the road from the Maxwell home lived a rich family. In that family there was a nine-year-old girl, who was an invalid with little hope of recovery. Because of the urgent entreaty of the mother, who was also an invalid, 'Abdu'l-Bahá visited their home, on the morning following His arrival. He held the child in His arms and told the parents that their child would be restored to full health. And so it happened some months later, for the child completely recovered. From the home of that family 'Abdu'l-Bahá went to the shop which they owned and bought a number of valuable watches and rings. These He presented to various people. He also gave munificent tips to porters and waiters, maids and attendants. (But when, at the railway station at Buffalo, a cabman deliberately tried to overcharge Him, He firmly refused to pay the extra demanded and walked away. He said that giving in to such impertinence was open invitation to imposition.)

The first congregation which 'Abdu'l-Bahá addressed in Montreal was that of the Church of the Messiah, on September 1st. He said:

God the Almighty has created all mankind from the dust of earth. He has fashioned them all from the same elements; they are descended from the same race and live upon the same globe. He has created them to dwell beneath the one heaven. As members of the human family, and His children, He has endowed them with equal susceptibilities. He maintains, protects and is kind to all. He has made no distinction in mercies and graces among His children. With impartial love and wisdom He has sent forth His Prophets and divine teachings. His teachings are the means of establishing union and fellowship among mankind and awakening love and kindness in human hearts. He proclaims the oneness of the kingdom of humanity. He rebukes those things which create differences and destroy harmony; He commends and praises every means that will conduce to the solidarity of the human race. He encourages man in every step of advancement which leads to ultimate union. The Prophets of God have been inspired with the message of love and unity. The Books of God have been revealed for the upbuilding of fellowship and union. The Prophets of God have been the Servants of reality; Their teachings constitute the science of reality. Reality is one; it does not admit plurality. We conclude therefore that the foundation of the religions of God is one foundation. Notwithstanding this, certain forms and imitations have been persistently adhered to which have nothing to do with the foundation of the teachings of the Prophets of God. As these imitations are various and different, contention and strife prevail among the people of religious beliefs and the foundation of the religion of God has become obscured. Like beasts of prey, men are warring and killing each other, destroying cities and homes, devastating countries and kingdoms.

Having authoritatively and unequivocally, in a language clear, sublime and comprehensible by all, established and declared the basic verities of the Message of His Father, 'Abdu'l-Bahá proceeded to present and analyse the tragic plight of mankind, and the remedy demanded. He particu-

larly showed how blind prejudice can destroy all human
sensibility. He ended with a prayer:

> O Thou compassionate, Almighty One! This assemblage
> of souls have turned their faces unto Thee in supplication.
> With the utmost humility and submission they look to-
> ward Thy Kingdom and beg Thee for pardon and for-
> giveness. O God! endear this assembly to Thyself.
> Sanctify these souls and cast upon them the rays of Thy
> guidance. Illumine their hearts and gladden their spirits
> with Thy glad-tidings. Receive all of them in Thy holy
> Kingdom, confer upon them Thine inexhaustible bounty,
> make them happy in this world and in the world to come.
> O God! we are weak; give us strength. We are poor;
> bestow upon us Thine illimitable treasures. We are sick;
> grant us Thy divine healing. We are powerless; give us of
> Thy heavenly power. O Lord! make us useful in this
> world; free us from the condition of self and desire. O
> Lord! make us firm in Thy love and cause us to be loving
> toward the whole of mankind. Confirm us in service to
> the world of humanity, so that we may become the
> servants of Thy servants, that we may love all Thy
> creatures and become compassionate to all Thy people.
> O Lord! Thou art the Almighty! Thou art the Merciful!
> Thou art the Forgiver! Thou art the Omnipotent.[177]

That evening the fame of 'Abdu'l-Bahá's address at the
Church of the Messiah was spread abroad. There were constant telephone calls, and large numbers made their way to
the Maxwell home. 'Abdu'l-Bahá spoke to them. So forceful
was His speech, so emphatic His movement that His headgear fell off and He made no attempt to replace it. His head
bared, His locks scattered round His head, He went on
speaking for another half hour. Then He walked, through
the thronged assemblage, upstairs to His room. But people
could not tear themselves away, and 'Abdu'l-Bahá came back
and spoke once again. Even then, there were individuals

begging to be received by 'Abdu'l-Bahá in His room, and He received a good many. He decided that night to move to a hotel. The next day He went to the Hotel Windsor and took a suite of three rooms. But meetings at the Maxwell home continued to the end of 'Abdu'l-Bahá's stay in Montreal.

Apart from those gatherings at the Maxwell home and meetings at the hotel, 'Abdu'l-Bahá addressed two more audiences in places of public assemblage in Montreal, on September 3rd and 5th. Both occasions featured in the pages of *The Gazette*. The first one was thus reported the next day:

Passing from the inviting atmosphere of a drawing room meeting held in a Pine Avenue residence on Monday night to a socialistic and very cosmopolitan gathering held in Coronation Hall, associated with Jewish strikers, Abdu'l Baha the apostle of peace and concord exhibited his catholicity of spirit last night, and also developed in his address something more in the shape of practical politics as he unfolded a scheme for dealing with the superfluous wealth of a nation. How to obtain economic happiness was the theme of Abdu'l Baha's address.

The second audience, of 1200, heard 'Abdu'l-Bahá at St James Methodist Church. *The Gazette* wrote on September 6th:

... The eastern prophet proceeded to reiterate the teachings of Baha'u'llah under a number of headings. Investigate independently the realities, he said, for dissensions result from lack of that. The oneness of the race, the necessity of education, the folly of racial, national and patriotic strife, and the cultivation of the spiritual life were all briefly touched upon. Then the prophet came to the question of international peace, and depicted the growing armaments in Europe and their burden on the people. His remedy was the establishment of an international tribunal, which would apparently have greater powers than that of the Hague.

In concluding Abdu'l Baha expressed his appreciation of the justice and amity enjoyed on this continent and hoped the governments in America would play a leading part in establishing such a tribunal.

Mr. Recorder Weir, in moving a vote of thanks, said some people believed the race of prophets had become extinct, but it was a pleasure to listen to one who was in the lofty succession of the long line of prophets. He had brought a message that would not be speedily forgotten . . . [178]

'Abdu'l-Bahá was not well enough to keep to His schedule, and His departure from Montreal was delayed for several days. He would occasionally, when finding a moment of leisure, go out for a drive or a walk. One day He went all alone and boarded a tram car. The tram took Him some way out of the city. Alighting from that one He rode in another, which also had an outward route. He then took a taxi, but could not recall the name of the hotel. However, He could indicate the right direction to the cabman. With great mirth He related the story of His adventure to His attendants, which had brought to His mind an incident in the Holy Land. Áqá Faraj, a Bahá'í of 'Akká, had lost the way. 'Abdu'l-Bahá had told him to cast off the donkey's halter. The beast, finding itself free, had directed its steps to their destination. In the same manner, 'Abdu'l-Bahá said laughingly, He had rightly directed His cabman.

The journey to Buffalo, on September 9th, was very long and tiring. Trains had to be changed at Toronto. Taking a walk around the station there, 'Abdu'l-Bahá spoke of His great fatigue, wondering how He could go all the way to California; but go He must, for in the path of God troubles must rank as bounties, and toil as the greatest bestowal. Buffalo was reached at a late hour that night, and so the Bahá'ís of the town were not immediately informed of 'Abdu'l-Bahá's arrival.

CHAPTER 16

THE WESTWARD JOURNEY
September 9th–October 1st

Buffalo is in the State of New York, close to Niagara Falls.
When 'Abdu'l-Bahá viewed Niagara, He recollected the
much smaller waterfalls in Mázindarán, by the side of which,
He said, Bahá'u'lláh loved to pitch His tent. 'Abdu'l-Bahá's
attendants begged Him to take a few days' rest there. He
declined to entertain their plea: not even half a day, He said.
His stay in Buffalo lasted only two days. Early on September
12th He was on His way to Chicago, for a second visit,
though a short one. The previous evening in Buffalo He
had addressed the congregation of the Church of the Messiah,
North and Mariner Streets, and visitors had kept Him up till
two o'clock in the morning. One particular matter, which
displeased 'Abdu'l-Bahá in Buffalo, was the reference to Him,
in the *Buffalo Express* of September 11th, as 'The Persian
Prince'.

The railway station in Chicago was thronged with
Bahá'ís. They had come with bouquets of flowers. It must
have made a most impressive sight: 'Abdu'l-Bahá walking
through their ranks to an automobile which awaited Him,
greeting each one of them, talking to each. He drove to the
home of Mrs Corinne True,* whose services to the Institution of the Mashriqu'l-Adhkár in America were already
outstanding and were to become truly exemplary in the
years to come. Fujita, the young Japanese student who had

* Appointed a Hand of the Cause of God by the Guardian of
the Faith in February 1952.

first met 'Abdu'l-Bahá in Cleveland, was among the Bahá'ís forgathered in the home of Corinne True. 'Abdu'l-Bahá's face lighted up the moment He saw him; 'and how is our Japanese Effendi,' He said. Fujita accompanied Him to California to serve Him. At a later date, Fujita's unbounded, fervent devotion to 'Abdu'l-Bahá made him abandon all thought of a career and go to the Holy Land, where he served the pilgrims, and in other ways, both in the time of 'Abdu'l-Bahá and of Shoghi Effendi. Thousands have cherished the memory of meeting Fujita in the Holy Land.

Gatherings and meetings at 5338 Kenmore Avenue, the home of Corinne True, assumed larger and larger proportions. On one occasion three spacious rooms were full, and people had crowded the staircase as well. The only society or congregation which 'Abdu'l-Bahá addressed, on this second visit to Chicago, was the Theosophical Society. That was on September 14th, and the next day He was to speak in Kenosha, Wisconsin. It happened that when trains had to be changed, despite the efforts of His attendants and to their dismay, He missed the first connection. He told them not to be concerned; there must be a good reason. Travelling on the next train they came upon the wreckage of the previous one. There had been a collision. The Bahá'ís of Kenosha had prepared luncheon at their local centre. 'Abdu'l-Bahá spoke there and also later, at the home of a Bahá'í. That evening He addressed an audience at the Congregational Church and stayed overnight in Kenosha. Back in Chicago on the sixteenth, He bade farewell to the Bahá'ís of that city and promised to visit them a third time, on His return from California.

Here are extracts from that farewell talk:

I have spent a number of days among you, associating with you in love and fragrance . . . I pray in your behalf, seeking heavenly confirmations for you that each one may become a radiant candle shedding light in the world of humanity . . .

In the world of existence there are various bonds which unite human hearts but not one of these bonds is completely effective. The first and foremost is the bond of family relationship which is not an efficient unity, for how often it happens that disagreement and divergence rend asunder this close tie of association. The bond of patriotism may be a means of fellowship and agreement, but oneness of nativity will not completely cement human hearts; for if we review history we shall find that people of the same . . . nativity have frequently waged war against each other . . . Therefore this bond is not sufficient. Another means of seeming unity is the bond of political association where governments and rulers have been allied for reasons of intercourse and mutual protection, but which agreement and union afterward became subject to change and violent hatred even to the extreme of war and bloodshed. It is evident that political oneness is not permanently effective.

The source of perfect unity and love in the world of existence is the bond and oneness of reality. When the divine and fundamental reality enters human hearts and lives, it conserves and protects all states and conditions of mankind, establishing that intrinsic oneness of the world of humanity which can only come into being through the efficacy of the Holy Spirit. For the Holy Spirit is like unto the life in the human body, which blends all differences of parts and members in unity and agreement. Consider how numerous are these parts and members, but the oneness of the animating spirit of life unites them all in perfect combination. It establishes such a unity in the bodily organism that if any part is subjected to injury or becomes diseased, all the other parts and functions sympathetically respond and suffer owing to the perfect oneness existing. Just as the human spirit of life is the cause of coordination among the various parts of the human organism, the Holy Spirit is the controlling cause of the unity and coordination of mankind. That is to say, the bond or oneness of humanity cannot be effectively established save through the power of the Holy Spirit, for the world of humanity is a composite body and the Holy Spirit is the animating principle of its life.

. . . Today the greatest need of the world is the animating, unifying presence of the Holy Spirit. Until It becomes effective, penetrating and interpenetrating hearts and spirits, and until perfect, reasoning faith shall be implanted in the minds of men, it will be impossible for the social body to be inspired with security and confidence. Nay, on the contrary, enmity and strife will increase day by day and the differences and divergences of nations will be woefully augmented . . .

. . . For the betterment of the world Bahá'u'lláh endured all the hardships, ordeals and vicissitudes of life, sacrificing His very being and comfort, forfeiting His estates, possessions and honours—all that pertains to human existence—not for one year, nay, rather, for nearly fifty years. During this long period He was subjected to persecution and abuse, cast into prison, banished from His native land, underwent severities and humiliation and was exiled four times . . . He endured these ordeals and difficulties in order that this earthly human world might become heavenly, that the illumination of the Divine Kingdom should become a reality in human hearts, that . . . the happiness of the world of humanity be assured. He desired for all tranquillity and composure and exercised loving-kindness toward the nations regardless of conditions and differences. He addressed humanity, saying 'O humankind! Verily ye are all the leaves and fruits of one tree; ye are all one. Therefore associate in friendship; love one another; abandon prejudices of race; dispel forever this gloomy darkness of human ignorance, for the century of light, the Sun of Reality hath appeared . . . Lay aside all self-purposes and know for a certainty that all men are the servants of one God Who will bind them together in love and agreement.'

Inasmuch as great differences and divergences of denominational belief had arisen throughout the past, every man with a new idea attributing it to God, Bahá'u'lláh desired that there should not be any ground or reason for disagreement among the Bahá'ís. Therefore with His own pen He wrote the Book of His Covenant, addressing His relations and all people of the world, saying 'Verily, I have appointed One Who is the Centre of My Covenant. All must obey Him; all must turn to Him; He is the Expounder of My Book and He is informed of My purpose . . . Whatsoever He says is correct, for verily He knoweth the texts of My Book . . . ' The purpose of this statement is that there should never be discord and divergence among the Bahá'ís, but that they should always be unified and agreed . . . In all His Tablets, among which is the *Tablet of the Branch*, He has mentioned and explained the attributes and qualities of the personage to Whom He referred in the Book of His Covenant . . . He said 'Verily, He is the appointed one; other than He, there is none,' intending that no sects or prejudices should be formed, and preventing every man here and there with a new thought, from creating dissension and variance. It is as though a king should appoint a governor-general. Whosoever obeys him, obeys the king . . . Therefore whosoever obeys the Centre of the Covenant appointed by Bahá'u'lláh has obeyed Bahá'u'lláh, and whosoever disobeys Him has disobeyed Bahá'u'lláh . . .

. . . Beware! Beware! According to the explicit Covenant of Bahá'u'lláh you should care nothing at all for such a person . . . I have expounded these things for you, for the conservation and protection of the teachings of Bahá'u'lláh, in order that you may be informed, lest any souls shall deceive you and lest any souls shall cause suspicion among you. You must love all people, and yet if any souls put you in doubt, you must know that Bahá'u'lláh is severed from them. Whosoever works for unity and fellowship is a servant of Bahá'u'lláh, and Bahá'u'lláh is his assistant and helper. I ask God that He may cause you to be the very means of agreement and unity, that He may make you radiant, merciful, heavenly children of the Divine Kingdom; that you may advance day by day; that you may become as bright as these lamps, bestowing light upon all humanity. Salutations and farewell.[179]

'Abdu'l-Bahá had deemed it necessary to utter this grave warning in regard to the violation of the Covenant, because Dr Ibráhím Khayru'lláh resided in Chicago, and was attempting once again to cast doubts and stir discord. 'Abdu'l-Bahá spoke very sternly to a certain Dr Nutt, an associate of Khayru'lláh. He, Himself, 'Abdu'l-Bahá said, was a visitor to the United States, and many from all walks of life had come to meet Him, and He had received them all. If Khayru'lláh's intentions were pure, let him come in all sincerity, like everybody else; but Khayru'lláh expected 'Abdu'l-Bahá to send for him and seek his favours. This was on the day that 'Abdu'l-Bahá went to Kenosha, and He took that same Dr Nutt with Him, that he might witness all that happened. And this was the same Ibráhím Khayru'lláh who once could and did write a letter (in 1897) in such terms to 'Abdu'l-Bahá:

To the sacred court of my Master and the Master of the entire world . . . may my soul be a sacrifice unto the dust of His pathway: After offering obedience and servitude unto the sacred threshold of my Master, I beg to state that the believers in these regions and I greet the morn immersed in the sea of your bounties, and meet the night with the grace of your mercy which encompasses the East and the West of the earth, because you have turned unto them and unto me the glances of your favour. You have revealed of divine verses three Tablets: one for the believers in America, one for Antún Effendi Ḥaddád, and the last one for your servant, who forever and ever, lowly and poor, awaits the generous dispensations of his bountiful Lord . . . Enclosed with this petition are seventy-four petitions from those who have recently come into the Faith of God, and shall soon send other petitions. Seekers who wish to hear the Word of God and come into the knowledge of truth arrive in large numbers . . .

In the same letter Ibráhím Khayru'lláh informed 'Abdu'l-Bahá that he had established groups and centres in Chicago, Kenosha, Ithaca, Philadelphia, and New York; that the number of Bahá'ís in the last three was nearly three hundred; that he had insured the continuation of teaching work in those cities in his own absence; that Anṭún Ḥaddád* was confirmed in the Faith, and had the makings of a fine teacher to help him spread the Message of Bahá'u'lláh; that many of the American believers were desirous of reaching the 'sacred presence' of 'Abdu'l-Bahá, enquiring what 'Abdu'l-Bahá's 'commands were in that respect'; that he himself had begun writing his own book on the Faith; that he had sent to Professor Edward Browne 'incontrovertible proofs' from Biblical prophecies, indicating where commentators had gone wrong. And he had signed: 'Your obedient servant, Ibráhím Khayru'lláh.' It was the same man, who now in that autumn of 1912 more than a decade after his defection, was causing fresh anguish and sorrow.

Shu'áu'lláh, the son of Mírzá Muḥammad-'Alí, was also in the United States, striving to make mischief. Zarqání records that at that particular time 'Abdu'l-Bahá was often very sad and greatly concerned, and one day He remarked: 'Last night I did not sleep at all. Today the ship of the Cause of God is surrounded on all sides by severe storms, but the confirmations of the Ancient Beauty are with us.' On the

---

* Anṭún Ḥaddád, known in the West as Anton Haddad, also came from a Syrian Christian background and remained constant after Khayru'lláh's defection. He wrote *Divine Revelation, the Basis of Civilization* and *Message from 'Akká*.

train to Minneapolis, towards sunset, 'Abdu'l-Bahá's attendants heard His voice lamenting. They went nearer to hear
Him better. His eyes were open, looking at a fixed point.
Tristful and pensive He was intoning words in the manner of
a prayer, which His attendants could not distinguish. They
were also unable to verify whether He was asleep or awake.
Just then the train stopped at a station. One of His attendants asked if He wished to step out for a walk. In His
normal voice He answered in the negative.

It was on September 16th that 'Abdu'l-Bahá left for
Minneapolis, Minnesota. Prior to His leaving He was talking
to a newspaper proprietor in his hotel, and said:

A newspaper must in the first instance be the means of
harmony between the people. This is the prime duty of
the proprietors of newspapers to obliterate misunderstandings betwixt religions and races and nativities, and
promote the oneness of mankind.[180]

Again, the railway station in Chicago was thronged with
Bahá'ís, as 'Abdu'l-Bahá departed.

Minneapolis was reached late in the evening and 'Abdu'l-
Bahá was extremely fatigued. He went to the Plaza Hotel.
To the queries of newspaper reporters and the questions
of Bahá'ís He replied that He was very tired and would
meet them the next day. Many churches and congregations
had invited 'Abdu'l-Bahá to address them, but He had to
decline most of these invitations. He could not stay long in
Minneapolis.

The *Minneapolis Journal* of September 19th reported:

Long before the other guests at the Plaza Hotel were astir
today Abdul Baha Abbas, head of the Bahaists of the
world, who believes and teaches the eventual harmony
and unity of religious mankind, and who arrived last
night in Minneapolis for a two-day stay, was up and about

in parlor 603, pacing quietly across the room and back, and pausing occasionally to look meditatively out across Hennepin Avenue into Loring Park. At 7 a.m. the five members of his party called at his parlor to pay their respects. Dr. Clement Woolson of St. Paul called on behalf of the St. Paul Bahaists and Dr. H. S. Harper and Albert H. Hall of Minneapolis came next. Mrs. R. M. Passmore and Mrs. H. G. Harrison who had been in the country where Baha's influence is greatest . . . sent him messages of welcome . . . Dr. S. N. Deinard of the Jewish Reform Temple called to pay his respects and see if it would be possible to arrange for the Bahaist leader to address the Jewish people of Minneapolis. About a dozen men and women, who are local followers of Bahaism came into the room . . .

. . . It was finally arranged that Abdul Baha should speak at the Commercial Club at noon, call during an automobile trip today at the home of Dr. Woolson in St. Paul, and at the residence of Albert H. Hall . . . and speak tonight at the Jewish Reform Temple, Tenth Street and Fifth Avenue S. . . . There will be a short reception after the address . . . It was a program with physical effort enough in it to tax the abilities of a political campaigner, but Abdul Baha made light of that part of it . . .

Before going to the synagogue 'Abdu'l-Bahá said that it was His intention to prove and affirm there the truth of the mission of Jesus Christ, and added that were Bahá'u'lláh today in the Mansion of Bahjí, and were He to enter Bahá'u'lláh's presence and state that He was about to speak in a synagogue, Bahá'u'lláh would tell Him to speak of Jesus Christ. It was a remarkable occasion, for there was no dissent, but only profound gratitude and quick response.

The *Evening Tribune* of the same day wrote:

. . . Abdul Baha is one of the most picturesque religious figures in the Orient. He is 68 years old and was imprisoned for 50 years for his beliefs. The Baha has several hundred followers in the Twin Cities and thousands in the United States . . .

The Baha and his disciples, including some Twin City followers, took a half hour's constitutional in Loring Park . . .

The Baha walked slowly, contemplating the beauties of the park and watching the swans float on the mirror-like lake . . . He seemed to be absorbing the sunshine. The knot of followers were a few paces to the rear. They spoke in low voices and approached the Baha with deference . . .

'Newspapers', said the Baha, 'must be the first means of amity and understanding amongst men. All men must be the servants of one God, all must be united. Newspapers must be the heralds of the oneness of humanity . . .

'The time has come for the world of humanity to hoist the standard of the oneness of the human world, so that unity may connect all the nations of the world, so that dogmatic formulas and superstition may end, so that the essential reality underlying all the religions founded by all the prophets may be revealed . . . '

The next day 'Abdu'l-Bahá spoke both in Minneapolis and in St Paul. In the home of Albert Hall at Minneapolis (2030 Queen Avenue South) He said:

Philosophy is of two kinds; natural and divine. Natural philosophy seeks knowledge of physical verities and explains material phenomena whereas divine philosophy deals with ideal verities and phenomena of the spirit. The field and scope of natural philosophy have been greatly enlarged and its accomplishments are most praiseworthy, for it has served humanity; but according to the evidence of present world conditions, divine philosophy which has for its object . . . spiritual advancement, heavenly guidance for the development of the human race, attainment to the breaths of the Holy Spirit and know-ledge of the verities of God, has been outdistanced and neglected. Now is the time for us to make an effort and enable it to advance apace with the philosophy of material investigation so that awakening of the ideal virtues may progress equally with the unfoldment of the natural powers. In the same proportion that the body of man is developing, the spirit of man must be strengthened; and just as his outer perceptions have been quickened, his inner intellectual powers must be sensitized so that he need not rely wholly upon tradition and human pre-cedent. In divine questions we must not depend entirely upon the heritage of tradition and former human ex-perience; nay, rather, we must exercise reason, analyze and logically examine the facts presented so that con-fidence will be inspired and faith attained. Then and then only the reality of things will be revealed to us. The philosophers of Greece such as Aristotle, Socrates, Plato and others were devoted to the investigation of both natural and spiritual phenomena. In their schools of teaching they discoursed upon the world of nature as well as the world supernatural. Today the philosophy and logic of Aristotle are known throughout the world. Because they were interested in both natural and divine philosophy, furthering the development of the physical world of mankind as well as the intellectual, they ren-dered praiseworthy service to humanity . . . Man should continue both these lines of research and investigation so that all the human virtues, outer and inner, may be-come possible. The attainment of these virtues both material and ideal is conditioned upon intelligent investigation of the reality, by which investigation the sublimity of man and his intellectual progress is accom-plished. Forms must be set aside and renounced; reality must be sought. We must discover for ourselves where and what reality is. In religious beliefs nations and peoples today are imitators of ancestors and forefathers. If a man's father was a Christian, he himself is a Christian; a

Buddhist is the son of a Buddhist, a Zoroastrian of a Zoroastrian . . . The requirement in this day is that man must independently and impartially investigate every form of reality.[181]

At 870 Laurel Avenue, St Paul, the home of Dr and Mrs Clement Woolson, 'Abdu'l-Bahá told His audience:

The materialists hold to the opinion that the world of nature is complete. The divine philosophers declare that the world of nature is incomplete. There is a wide difference between the two. The materialists call attention to the perfection of nature, the sun, moon and stars, the trees in their adornment, the whole earth and the sea; even unimportant phenomena revealing the most perfect symmetry. The divine philosophers deny this seeming perfection and completeness in nature's kingdom, even though admitting the beauty of its scenes and aspects and acknowledging the irresistible cosmic forces which control the colossal sun-worlds and planets. They hold that while nature seems perfect, it is nevertheless imperfect because it has need of intelligence and education. In proof of this they say that man, though he be a very god in the realm of material creation is himself in need of an educator. Man undeveloped by education is savage, animalistic, brutal. Laws and regulations, schools, colleges and universities have for their purpose the training of man and his uplift from the dark border-land of the animal kingdom. What is the difference between the people of America and the inhabitants of Central Africa?

All are human beings . . . The difference and distinction between them is the degree of education . . . The people of Europe and America have been uplifted by education and training from the world of defects and have ascended toward the realm of perfection whereas the people of Africa, denied educational development, remain in a natural condition of illiteracy and deprivation; for nature is incomplete and defective . . . If a piece of ground be left in its natural and original state, it will either become a thorny waste or be covered by worthless weeds. When cleared and cultivated, this same unproductive field will yield plentiful harvests of food for human sustenance . . .

. . . But education is of various kinds. There is a training and development of the physical body which insures strength and growth. There is intellectual education or mental training for which schools and colleges are founded. The third kind of education is that of the spirit . . . For this reason the holy Manifestations of God appear in the human world. They come to educate and illuminate mankind, to bestow spiritual susceptibilities, to quicken inner perceptions and thereby adorn the reality of man—the human temple—with divine graces . . .

Consider the wonderful effect of spiritual education and training. By it the fisherman Peter was transformed into the greatest of teachers. Spiritual education made the disciples radiant lamps in the darkness of the world and caused the Christians of the first and second centuries to become renowned everywhere for their virtues. Even philosophers bore testimony to this. Among them was Galen the physician who wrote a book upon the subject of the progress of the nations. He was a celebrated philosopher of the Greeks; although not a Christian. In his book he has stated that religious beliefs exercise a tremendous influence upon civilization and that the world is in need of such belief. In proof of this, he says in substance 'In our time there is a certain people called Christians, who though neither philosophers nor scholastically trained, are superior to all others as regards their morality . . . ' This is evidence from the testimony of an intelligent outside observer that spiritual education is the light of the world of humanity and that its absence in the world is darkness itself . . .

. . . Man is first born from a world of darkness, the matrix of the mother, into this physical world of light.

In the dark world from whence he came he had no knowledge of the virtues of this existence. He has been liberated from a condition of darkness and brought into a new and spacious realm where there is sunlight, the stars are shining, the moon sheds its radiance, there are beautiful views, gardens of roses, fruits and all the blessings of the present world . . . Just as man has been physically born into this world, he may be reborn from the realm and matrix of nature; for the realm of nature is a condition of animalism, darkness and defect. In this second birth he attains the world of the Kingdom . . .

. . . May you all attain this second spiritual birth. 'That which is born of the flesh is flesh; that which is born of the spirit is spirit.'

I pray that the confirmation of God may descend upon you . . . [182]

William Jennings Bryan,[183] the future Secretary of State in the Wilson Administration, had his home in Lincoln, Nebraska. During his world tour (1905–6) Bryan had visited the Holy Land and had stayed in Haifa. He could not visit 'Abdu'l-Bahá in 'Akká because of the circumstances of the time. Now 'Abdu'l-Bahá decided to travel to Lincoln to meet him. Leaving Minneapolis on September 21st, He stopped at Omaha for the night. There He missed the train He intended to take to Lincoln by one minute, which delayed His departure until midnight. At the station a Bahá'í noticing some people with oriental headgear ran forward to enquire whether 'Abdu'l-Bahá was with them. Bahá'ís of Minneapolis had informed the Bahá'ís of Omaha, by telegram, that 'Abdu'l-Bahá would be passing through their city, but the latter had not been able to discover His plans. They were grateful for those few hours with Him.

At Lincoln 'Abdu'l-Bahá learned that Bryan was away, electioneering for Woodrow Wilson. He drove, however, to Bryan's residence, some distance out of the town, to meet Mrs Bryan and her daughter. The press was soon alerted to the arrival of 'Abdu'l-Bahá at Lincoln, and reporters came to interview Him. Arabs were among the people who sought to meet Him in the hotel. A sojourn of no more than twelve hours aroused considerable interest.

'Abdu'l-Bahá travelled again through the night, and reached Denver, Colorado, the next day in the afternoon. Mr and Mrs Ashton and other Bahá'ís of that city were at the station and accompanied Him to the Shirley Hotel. The long and tedious journey from Lincoln had left its mark, and yet, after only two hours' rest, 'Abdu'l-Bahá received the press, and then went to the home of Mrs Sidney Roberts, a Denver Bahá'í, where a vast number had gathered to meet Him. In the course of His talk, 'Abdu'l-Bahá said:

> ... God has chosen you for the worthy service of unifying mankind; God has chosen you for the purpose of investigating reality and promulgating international peace ... for the expression of love toward your fellow-creatures ... God has chosen you to blend together human hearts and give light to the human world. The doors of his generosity are wide, wide open to us but we must be attentive, alert and mindful, occupied with service to all mankind ... According to the teachings of Bahá'u'lláh you must love and cherish each individual member of humanity.
>
> The first sign of faith is love. The message of the holy Divine Manifestations is love; the phenomena of creation are based upon love; the radiance of the world is due to love; the well-being and happiness of the world depend upon it. Therefore I admonish you that you must strive throughout the human world to diffuse the light of love. The people of this world are thinking of warfare; you must be peacemakers. The nations are self-centred; you must be thoughtful of others rather than yourselves ... May each one of you be as a shining star in the horizon

of eternal glory. This is my wish for you and my highest hope. I have come long distances that you may attain these attributes and divine favours. Praise be to God! I have attended this meeting which has for its purpose the commemoration of God.[184]

The minister of the Second Divine Science Church (3929 West 38th Avenue) was at that meeting in the home of Mrs Roberts, and urgently invited 'Abdu'l-Bahá to address his congregation the following evening. The editor of the *Denver Post* sent an automobile to convey 'Abdu'l-Bahá and His entourage to the church. 'Abdu'l-Bahá remarked on this, attributing to the power and confirmations of Bahá'u'-lláh that a minister should ask with such eagerness for an address in his church, and that the editor of a newspaper should put a car at their disposal. 'Abdu'l-Bahá told that congregation:

God has desired for mankind the effulgence of love but through blindness and misapprehension man has enveloped himself in veils of discord, strife and hatred. The supreme need of humanity is cooperation and reciprocity. The stronger the ties of fellowship and solidarity amongst men the greater will be the power of constructiveness and accomplishment in all the planes of human activity. Without cooperation and reciprocal attitude, the individual member of human society remains self-centred, uninspired by altruistic purposes, limited and solitary in development like the animal and plant organisms of the lower kingdoms. The lower creatures are not in need of cooperation and reciprocity. A tree can live solitary and alone but this is impossible for man, without retrogression . . .

. . . God has destined and intended religion to be the cause and means of cooperative effort and accomplishment among mankind. To this end he has sent . . . the holy Manifestations of the Word in order that the

fundamental reality and religion of God may prove to be
the bond of human unity; for the divine religions revealed
by these holy Messengers have the one and same foundation . . .

Each one of the divine religions has established two
kinds of ordinances, the essential and the accidental. The
essential ordinances rest upon the firm, unchanging,
eternal foundations of the Word itself . . . The accidental
laws concern the administration of outer human actions
and relations . . . These are ever subject to change and
supersedure according to exigencies of time, place and
condition . . . Briefly, the foundation of the divine
religions is one eternal foundation but the laws for temporary conditions and exigencies are subject to change.
Therefore by adherence to these temporary laws, blindly
following and imitating ancestral forms, difference and
divergence have arisen among followers of the various
religions . . . Blind imitations and dogmatic observances
are conducive to alienation and disagreement . . . Therefore the religionists of the world must lay aside these
imitations and investigate the essential foundation or
reality itself which is not subject to change or transformation. This is the divine means of agreement and
unification . . .

After we have proved the validity of the Manifestations
of the Word of God by investigating the divine teachings,
we must discover for a certainty whether they have been
real educators of mankind . . .

The proof of the validity of a Manifestation of God is
the penetration and potency of His Word, the cultivation
of heavenly attributes in the hearts and lives of His followers and the bestowal of divine education upon the
world of humanity. This is absolute proof. The world is
a school in which there must be teachers of the Word of
God. The evidence of the ability of these teachers is
efficient education of the graduating classes . . .

My highest hope and desire is that the strongest and
most indissoluble bond shall be established between the

American nation and the people of the Orient . . . May the day come when through divine and spiritual activity in the human world, the religions shall be reconciled and all races of mankind come together in unity and love. Fifty years ago Bahá'u'lláh proclaimed the peace of the nations and oneness of the divine religions, addressing His words to all the kings and rulers of the world in specific Tablets. Therefore my supreme desire is the unity of the East and West, Universal Peace, and the oneness of the world of humanity.[185]

The minister of another church was present that evening, and he pleaded with 'Abdu'l-Bahá to address his congregation as well. But 'Abdu'l-Bahá had only one more day to give to Denver. That next day (September 26th) He received a number of the prominent people of the town at His hotel, spoke at another meeting in the home of Mrs Roberts in Sherman Street, and finally addressed a large meeting specially arranged at the Shirley Hotel by its proprietor and advertised by him. 'Abdu'l-Bahá commented to His attendants that man must himself be happy and attracted to attract others, that he must be moved, to move others. 'If you will do things to make me happy,' He said, 'then you will see the result.' Zarqání writes: 'Ladies and gentlemen staying at that hotel, who on the first day would not even look at us (the attendants of 'Abdu'l-Bahá), so overbearingly haughty were they, were striving that night to . . . be with us and would not be easily parted.'[186]

'Abdu'l-Bahá left Denver the next morning and, as the day lengthened and the night set in, the speed of the train and its jolting began to tell on Him. His attendants begged Him to have a short stop on the way; California was still distant. It was two o'clock past midnight when He alighted at Glenwood Springs and spent the day there. During the entire eight months of that year 1912 when 'Abdu'l-Bahá travelled and sojourned in America, this September 28th

was the only day He could be said to have rested and relaxed. He went to the mineral baths and had His lunch on the
spacious lawn of the Colorado Hotel. And even on that day,
as He stood by the cool stream and gazed at the verdant
mountain, sorrow surged within Him, because He could not
put aside the thought of the bleak prison-city and Bahá'u'-
lláh's incarceration inside its forbidding walls. He remembered that His Father once said: 'I have seen no
greenery for years.'

Several telegrams reached 'Abdu'l-Bahá at Glenwood
Springs, one of which was from Los Angeles informing Him
of deterioration in the condition of Thornton Chase, who
lay dangerously ill in hospital. This unexpected news
saddened Him greatly.

That midnight He continued His journey to California,
but at the end of another day's journey decided to stop at
Salt Lake City, Utah. He went to the Kenyon Hotel. Soon,
the following morning, the press was apprised of His arrival
and reporters came to visit Him. An Agricultural Conference
and Exhibition was in progress in Salt Lake City. There
'Abdu'l-Bahá ordered flower seeds for the gardens around
the Shrines in the Holy Land.

October 1st was the last day of the long journey to
California. 'Abdu'l-Bahá was now more refreshed for the
strenuous work that lay ahead of Him on the Pacific Coast.
On the train He spoke to His attendants of the supernal
powers of the Manifestations of God. St Peter, He said,
was a very simple man, unlettered, even unable to keep
count of the days of the week. He divided his bread into
seven portions and when he came to the seventh, he
knew it was the Sabbath. And yet what heights he attained,
what inner knowledge he gained, what glories he achieved
by the regenerative power of Jesus Christ. 'Abdu'l-Bahá
recalled a day in Ṭihrán when, as a small child, He was
seated by the side of the great, highly learned Siyyid Yaḥyay-

i-Dárabí, surnamed Vaḥíd. (This was the divine whom Muḥammad Sháh* commissioned and sent to investigate the
claims of the Báb, and who was enthralled and captivated
by the power and charm of the young Prophet of Shíráz.)
And there a wild-looking, unkempt dervish walked into the
room, his feet covered with mud. He was Mírzá 'Alíy-i-
Sayyáḥ,† who, more than once, went on foot to the fortress
of Máh-Kú where the Báb was imprisoned, bearing letters
and messages and coming back with messages and Tablets
from the Báb. Hearing that Sayyáḥ had just returned from
Máh-Kú, Vaḥíd kissed his mud-stained feet, for those feet
had trod the earth where the Báb had stood.

* Reigned 1834–48.
† Mírzá 'Alíy-i-Sayyáḥ was one of the four Bahá'ís exiled to
Cyprus in 1868. He passed away in that island. (It is uncertain
whether he had just arrived from Máh-Kú or Chihríq as the
accounts of several historians differ. Ed.)

CHAPTER 17

CALIFORNIA
October 1st–26th

It was about midnight of October 1st 1912, when 'Abdu'l-Bahá reached San Francisco. A house at 1815 California Street had been rented for Him. Because He had requested it, there were not many to greet Him at the terminus. But though the hour was late, many awaited His arrival at His San Francisco home, among them veterans of the Faith such as Mrs Helen S. Goodall, her daughter Mrs Cooper, and Mr and Mrs Ralston.

'Abdu'l-Bahá delivered His first public address in California at a Unitarian church in San Francisco on October 6th, and the following day He spoke at the Japanese Independent Church in Oakland (to the Japanese Young Men's Christian Association). He opened His talk with these words:

It is a great happiness to be here this evening, especially for the reason that the members of this Association have come from the region of the Orient. For a long time I have entertained a desire to meet some of the Japanese friends. That nation has achieved extraordinary progress in a short space of time; a progress and development which have astonished the world. Inasmuch as they have advanced in material civilization they must assuredly possess the capacity for spiritual development. For this reason I have an excessive longing to meet them. Praise be to God! this pleasure is now afforded me, for here in this city I am face to face with a revered group of the Japanese.

According to report the people of the Japanese nation are not prejudiced. They investigate reality. Wherever they find truth they prove to be its lovers. They are not attached tenaciously to blind imitations of ancient beliefs and dogmas. Therefore it is my great desire to discourse with them upon a subject in order that the unity and blending together of the nations of the East and the nations of the West may be furthered and accomplished. In this way religious, racial and political prejudice, partisan bias and sectarianism will be dispelled amongst men. Any kind of prejudice is destructive to the body-politic.

Then He spoke at length of the essential function of religion as the unifying power, of the advent of the great Educators of mankind, the Manifestations of God—Moses, Buddha, Zoroaster, Christ, Muḥammad, Bahá'u'lláh—of the oneness of Their purpose, and of Their solid achievements, and brought His discourse to its end in this fashion:

And ye who are the people of the Orient—the Orient which has ever been the dawning-point of lights—from whence the Sun of Reality has ever shone forth casting its effulgence upon the West—ye therefore must become the manifestations of lights. Ye must become brilliant lamps. Ye must shine as stars radiating the light of love toward all mankind. May you be the cause of love amongst the nations. Thus may the world become witness that the Orient has ever been the dawning-point of illumination, the source of love and reconciliation. Make peace with all the world. Love everybody; serve everybody. All are the servants of God. God has created all. He provideth for all. He is kind to all. Therefore must we be kind to all.

I am greatly pleased with this meeting. I am joyous and happy, for here in these western regions I find Orientals seeking education, and who are free from prejudice. May God assist you![187]

This talk was translated from Persian into English and from English into Japanese.

On the day after 'Abdu'l-Bahá's arrival at San Francisco, Dr David Starr Jordan, President of Leland Stanford Junior University near Palo Alto, called to invite Him to speak at his university. And on October 8th, an audience two thousand strong, comprising students, teaching staff, administrators, as well as leading men and women of the vicinity, gathered to hear 'Abdu'l-Bahá. It was a historic occasion for the Bahá'í Faith in California. Dr David Starr Jordan said: ' 'Abdu'l-Bahá will surely unite the East and the West: for He treads the mystic way with practical feet.' The discourse which 'Abdu'l-Bahá delivered that day was one of the greatest, most powerful of His ministry.

The greatest attainment in the world of humanity has ever been scientific in nature. It is the discovery of the realities of things. Inasmuch as I find myself in the home of science—for this is one of the great universities of the country, and well known abroad—I feel a keen sense of joy.

The highest praise is due to men who devote their energies to science; and the noblest centre is a centre wherein the sciences and arts are taught and studied. Science ever tends to the illumination of the world of humanity. It is the cause of eternal honour to man, and its sovereignty is far greater than the sovereignty of kings. The dominion of kings has an ending; the king himself may be dethroned; but the sovereignty of science is everlasting and without end. Consider the philosophers of former times. Their rule and dominion is still manifest in the world. The Greek and Roman kingdoms with all their grandeur passed away; the ancient sovereignties of the Orient are but memories, whereas the power and influence of Plato and Aristotle still continue . . . Kings have invaded countries and achieved conquest through the shedding of blood, but the scientist through his beneficent achievements invades the regions of ignorance conquering the realm of minds and hearts. Therefore his conquests are everlasting. May you attain extraordinary progress in this centre of education. May you become radiant lights flooding the dark regions and recesses of ignorance with illumination.

Inasmuch as the fundamental principle of the teaching of Bahá'u'lláh is the oneness of the world of humanity, I will speak to you upon the intrinsic oneness of all phenomena. This is one of the abstruse subjects of divine philosophy.

Fundamentally all existing things pass through the same degrees and phases of development, and any given phenomenon embodies all others. An ancient statement of the Arabian philosophers declares that 'All things are involved in all things.' It is evident that each material organism is an aggregate expression of single and simple elements, and a given cellular element or atom has its coursings or journeyings through various and myriad stages of life. For example we will say the cellular elements which have entered into the composition of a human organism were at one time a component part of the animal kingdom; at another time they entered into the composition of the vegetable and prior to that, existed in the kingdom of the mineral. They have been subject to transference from one condition of life to another, passing through various forms and phases, exercising in each existence special functions. Their journeyings through material phenomena are continuous. Therefore each phenomenon is the expression in degree of all other phenomena. The difference is one of successive transferences and the period of time involved in evolutionary process.

For example it has taken a certain length of time for this cellular element in my hand to pass through the various periods of metabolism . . .

Later on it will revert to its primordial elemental state in the mineral kingdom, being subject as it were to infinite journeyings from one degree of existence to another, passing through every stage of being and life. Whenever it appears in any distinct form or image it has its opportunities, virtues and functions. As each component atom or element in the physical organisms of existence is subject to transference through endless forms and stages, possessing virtues peculiar to those forms and stations, it is evident that all phenomena of material being are fundamentally one . . .

As this is true of material phenomena, how much more evident and essential it is that oneness should characterize man in the realm of idealism which finds its expression only in the human kingdom! Verily the origin of all material life is one and its termination likewise one. In view of this fundamental unity and agreement of all phenomenal life, why should man in his kingdom of existence wage war or indulge in hostility and destructive strife against his fellow-man? Man is the noblest of the creatures. In his physical organism he possesses the virtues of the mineral kingdom. Likewise he embodies the virtue augmentative or power of growth which characterizes the kingdom of the vegetable. Furthermore in his degree of physical existence he is qualified with functions and powers peculiar to the animal, beyond which lies the range of his distinctive human, mental and spiritual endowment. Considering this wonderful unity of the kingdoms of existence and their embodiment in the highest and noblest creature, why should man be at variance and in conflict with man? Is it fitting and justifiable that he should be at war, when harmony and interdependence characterize the kingdoms of phenomenal life below him? The elements and lower organisms are synchronized in the great plan of life. Shall man infinitely above them in degree be antagonistic and a destroyer of that perfection? . . .

From the fellowship and commingling of the elemental atoms life results. In their harmony and blending there is ever newness of existence . . . Just now the physical energies and natural forces which come under our immediate observation are all at peace. The sun is at peace with the earth upon which it shines. The soft breathing winds are at peace with the trees. All the elements are in harmony and equilibrium. A slight disturbance and discord among them might bring another San Francisco earthquake and fire.* A physical clash, a little quarrelling among the elements as it were, and a violent cataclysm of nature results. This happens in the mineral kingdom. Consider then the effect of discord and conflict in the kingdom of man, so superior to the realm of inanimate existence. How great the attendant catastrophe, especially when we realize that man is endowed by God with mind and intellect. Verily mind is the supreme gift of God. Verily intellect is the effulgence of God. This is manifest and self-evident.

For all created things except man are subjects or captives of nature; they cannot deviate in the slightest degree from nature's law and control. The colossal sun, centre of our planetary system, is nature's captive, incapable of the least variation from the law of command. All the orbs and luminaries in this illimitable universe are likewise obedient to nature's regulation. Our planet the earth acknowledges nature's omnipresent sovereignty. The kingdoms of the mineral, vegetable and animal respond to nature's will and fiat of control. The great bulky elephant with its massive strength has no power to disobey the restrictions nature has laid upon him, but man, weak and diminutive in comparison, empowered by mind which is an effulgence of divinity itself, can resist nature's control and apply natural laws to his own uses . . .

It [mind] has classified and adapted these laws to human needs and uses, this being contrary to the postulates of nature. For example electricity was once a hidden or latent natural force. It would have remained hidden if the human intellect had not discovered it. Man has broken

* 'Abdu'l-Bahá was referring to the earthquake and fire of 1906.

the law of its concealment, taken this energy out of the invisible treasury of the universe and brought it into visibility. Is it not an extraordinary accomplishment that this little creature man has imprisoned an irresistible cosmic force in an incandescent lamp? . . . All human discoveries were once secrets and mysteries sealed and stored up in the bosom of the material universe until the mind of man, which is the greatest of divine effulgences, penetrated them and made them subservient to his will and purpose . . . Notwithstanding this supreme bestowal of God which is the greatest power in the world of creation, man continues to war and fight, killing his fellow-man with the ferocity of a wild animal. Is this in keeping with his exalted station? . . .

If the animals are savage and ferocious it is simply a means for their subsistence and preservation. They are deprived of that degree of intellect which can reason and discriminate between right and wrong, justice and injustice; they are justified in their actions and not responsible. When man is ferocious and cruel toward his fellow-man it is not for subsistence or safety. His motive is selfish advantage and wilful wrong. It is neither seemly nor befitting that such a noble creature endowed with intellect and lofty thoughts, capable of wonderful achievements and discoveries in sciences and arts, potential with ever higher perceptions and the accomplishment of divine purposes in life should seek the blood of his fellowmen upon the field of battle . . .

God has created man lofty and noble; made him a dominant factor in creation. He has specialized man with supreme bestowals, conferred upon him mind, perception, memory, abstraction and the powers of the senses. These gifts of God to man were intended to make him the manifestation of divine virtues, a radiant light in the world of creation, a source of life and the agency of constructiveness in the infinite fields of existence . . .

In nature there is the law of the survival of the fittest. Even if man be not educated, then according to the natural institutes this natural law will demand of man supremacy. The purpose and object of schools, colleges and universities is to educate man and thereby rescue and redeem him from the exigencies and defects of nature and to awaken within him the capability of controlling and appropriating nature's bounties . . . It is not intended that the world of humanity should be left to its natural state. It is in need of the education divinely provided for it. The holy, heavenly Manifestations of God have been the teachers. They are the divine gardeners who transform the jungles of human nature into fruitful orchards and make the thorny places blossom as the rose. It is evident then that the intended and especial function of man is to rescue and redeem himself from the inherent defects of nature and become qualified with the ideal virtues of divinity. Shall he sacrifice these ideal virtues and destroy these possibilities of advancement? God has endowed him with a power whereby he can even overcome the laws and phenomena of nature, wrest the sword from nature's hand and use it against nature itself. Shall he then remain its captive, even failing to qualify under the natural law which commands the survival of the fittest? That is to say shall he continue to live upon the level of the animal kingdom without distinction between them and himself in natural impulses and ferocious instincts? . . .

Praise be to God! I find myself in an assemblage, the members of which are peace-loving and advocates of international unity. The thoughts of all present are centred upon the oneness of the world of mankind and every ambition is to render service in the cause of human uplift and betterment. I supplicate God that He may confirm and assist you, that each one of you may become a professor emeritus in the world of scientific knowledge, a faithful standard bearer of peace and bonds of agreement between the hearts of men.

Fifty years ago Bahá'u'lláh declared the necessity of peace among the nations and the reality of reconciliation between the religions of the world. He announced that the fundamental basis of all religion is one; that the essence of religion is human fellowship and that the differences in belief which exist are due to dogmatic interpretation and blind imitations which are at variance with the foundations established by the Prophets of God. He proclaimed that if the reality underlying religious teaching be investigated, all religions would be unified and the purpose of God which is love and the blending of human hearts would be accomplished. According to His teachings if religious belief proves to be the cause of discord and dissension, its absence would be preferable, for religion was intended to be the divine remedy and panacea for the ailments of humanity, the healing balm for the wounds of mankind. If its misapprehension and defilement have brought about warfare and bloodshed instead of remedy and cure, the world would be better under irreligious conditions.

Bahá'u'lláh especially emphasized International Peace . . . From every real standpoint there must and should be peace among all nations.

God created one earth and one mankind to people it. Man has no other habitation, but man himself has come forth and proclaimed imaginary boundary lines and territorial restrictions, naming them 'Germany,' 'France,' 'Russia,' etc. And torrents of precious blood are spilled in defence of these imaginary divisions of our one human habitation, under the delusion of a fancied and limited patriotism.

After all, a claim and title to territory or native land is but a claim and attachment to the dust of earth. We live upon this earth for a few days and then rest beneath it forever. So it is our graveyard eternally. Shall man fight for the tomb which devours him, for his eternal sepulchre? . . .

It is my hope that you who are students in this university may never be called upon to fight for the dust of earth which is the tomb and sepulchre of all mankind,

but that during the days of your life you may enjoy the
most perfect companionship one with another, even as
one family—as brothers, sisters, fathers, mothers—
associating together in peace and true fellowship.[188]

When 'Abdu'l-Bahá had finished speaking, Dr Jordan
asked the audience to stand to show its appreciation. The
applause and expressions of enthusiasm which followed
were truly striking. 'Abdu'l-Bahá had luncheon with the
President, spent the rest of the day in Palo Alto, and spoke
in the evening at its Unitarian Church.

His next major talk was delivered on October 10th to
the Open Forum in San Francisco. This was a gathering of
agnostics and freethinkers. 'Abdu'l-Bahá told them:

Although I was feeling indisposed this evening, yet owing
to the love I entertain for you I have attended this meeting.
For I have heard that this is an open forum, investigating
reality; that you are free from blind imitations, desiring to
arrive at the truth of things, and that your endeavours are
lofty. Therefore I have thought it expedient to discourse
upon the subject of 'Philosophy', which is alike interesting
to the East and the West, enabling us to consider the
analogies and differences between the philosophical
teachings of the Orient and Occident.

First, He demonstrated the unreliability of sense perception:

Among the senses, the most powerful and reliable is that
of sight. This sense views a mirage as a body of water and
is positive as to its character whereas a mirage is non-
existent. The sense of vision or sight sees reflected images
in a mirror as verities when reason declares them to be
non-existent. The eye sees the sun and planets revolving
around the earth whereas in reality the sun is stationary,
central, and the earth revolves upon its own axis. The

sense of sight sees the earth as a plane whereas the faculty
of reason discovers it to be spherical . . . The sense of
sight beholds a whirling spark of fire as a circle of light
and is without doubt as to it, whereas such a circle is non-
existent . . . Briefly, there are many instances and evidences which disprove the assertion that tangibilities and
sense impressions are certainties, for the senses are
misleading and often mistaken . . .

Next, He rejected the theory that man had his origin in
the animal kingdom:

Man is distinguished above the animals through his
reason. The perceptions of man are of two kinds—
tangible or sensible, and reasonable; whereas the animal
perceptions are limited to the senses, the tangible only.
The tangible perceptions may be likened to this candle,
the reasonable perceptions to the light. Calculations of
mathematical problems and determining the spherical
form of the earth are through the reasonable perceptions.
The centre of gravity is a hypothesis of reason. Reason
itself is not tangible, perceptible to the senses. Reason is an
intellectual verity or reality. All qualities are ideal realities,
not tangible realities. For instance we say this man is a
scholarly man. Knowledge is an ideal attainment not
perceptible to the senses . . .

As to the animal . . . it is minus the perception reasonable. It cannot apprehend ideal realities . . . The intelligence of an animal located in Europe could never have
planned the discovery of the continent of America . . .
The animal cannot penetrate the secrets of genesis and
creation. Beyond the tangibilities and impressions of the
senses it cannot accept anything . . .

Man, 'Abdu'l-Bahá asserted, was not descended from the
animal kingdom; man had always been potentially man, no

matter what forms he had assumed in his previous stages of existence.

> . . . This anatomical evolution or progression does not alter or affect the statement that the development of man was always human in type . . . The human embryo when examined microscopically is at first a mere germ or worm. Gradually as it develops it shows certain divisions; rudiments of hands and feet appear . . . Afterward it undergoes certain distinct changes until it reaches its actual human form and is born into this world. But at all times, even when the embryo resembled a worm, it was human in potentiality and character, not animal. The forms assumed by the human embryo in its successive changes do not prove that it is animal in its essential character . . . Realizing this we may acknowledge the fact that at one time man was an inmate of the sea, at another period an invertebrate, then a vertebrate and finally a human being standing erect. Though we admit these changes, we cannot say man is an animal . . .

The animal, 'Abdu'l-Bahá stressed, is a captive of nature and man is not; man can master nature, the animal cannot:

> Furthermore it is evident that in the world of nature conscious knowledge is absent. Nature is minus knowing, whereas man is conscious. Nature is devoid of memory; man possesses memory. Nature is minus perception and volition; man possesses both. It is evident that virtues are inherent in man which are not present in the world of nature. This is provable from every standpoint.
> If it be claimed that the intellectual reality of man belongs to the world of nature—that it is a part of the whole, we ask is it possible for the part to contain virtues which the whole does not possess? For instance is it possible for the drop to contain virtues of which the aggregate body of the sea is deprived? . . . Is it possible that the extraordinary faculty of reason in man is animal

in character and quality? On the other hand it is evident and true though most astounding that in man there is present this super-natural force or faculty which discovers the realities of things and which possesses the power of idealization or intellection. It is capable of discovering scientific laws, and science we know is not a tangible reality. Science exists in the mind of man as an ideal reality. The mind itself, reason itself is an ideal reality and not tangible.

Notwithstanding this, some of the sagacious men declare—we have attained to the superlative degree of knowledge; we have penetrated the laboratory of nature, studying sciences and arts; we have attained the highest station of knowledge in the human world; we have investigated the facts as they are and have arrived at the conclusion that nothing is rightly acceptable except the tangible which alone is a reality worthy of credence; all that is not tangible is imagination and nonsense.

Strange indeed that after twenty years' training in colleges and universities man should reach such a station wherein he will deny the existence of the ideal or that which is not perceptible to the senses. Have you ever stopped to think that the animal already has graduated from such a university? Have you ever realized that the cow is already a professor emeritus of that university? For the cow without hard labour and study is already a philosopher of the superlative degree in the school of nature. The cow denies everything that is not tangible, saying 'I can see! I can eat! therefore I believe only in that which is tangible!'

Then why should we go to the colleges? Let us go to the cow.[189]

Only two days after this remarkable meeting with freethinkers and agnostics, 'Abdu'l-Bahá delivered on October 12th, at Temple Emmanu-El,* to a Jewish congregation

* 450 Sutter Street, San Francisco.

of some two thousand people, many of whom were eminent in the Jewish community, the talk which was the towering climax to His matchless and strenuous work on the American continent. This is how He began:

The greatest bestowal of God in the world of humanity is religion; for assuredly the divine teachings of religion are above all other sources of instruction and development to man . . .

We will therefore investigate religion, seeking from an unprejudiced standpoint to discover whether it is the source of illumination, the cause of development and the animating impulse of all human advancement. We will investigate independently, free from the restrictions of dogmatic beliefs, blind imitations of ancestral forms, and the influence of mere human opinion; for as we enter this question we will find some who declare that religion is a cause of uplift and betterment in the world, while others assert just as positively that it is a detriment and a source of degradation to mankind. We must give these questions thorough and impartial consideration so that no doubt or uncertainty may linger in our minds regarding them.

How shall we determine whether religion has been the cause of human advancement or retrogression?

We will first consider the Founders of the religions—the Prophets—review the story of their lives, compare the conditions preceding their appearance with those subsequent to their departure, following historical records and irrefutable facts instead of relying upon traditionary statements which are open to both acceptance and denial.

After mention of Abraham and the Covenant that God made with Him, 'Abdu'l-Bahá turned to consider the achievements of Moses:

The children of Israel were in bondage and captivity in the land of Egypt four hundred years. They were in an extreme state of degradation and slavery under the tyranny and oppression of the Egyptians. While they were in the condition of abject poverty, in the lowest degree of abasement, ignorance and servility Moses suddenly appeared among them. Although He was but a shepherd, such majesty, grandeur and efficiency became manifest in Him through the power of religion, that His influence continues to this day. His prophethood was established throughout the land and the law of His Word became the foundation of the laws of the nations. This unique personage, single and alone, rescued the children of Israel from bondage through the power of religious training and discipline. He led them to the Holy Land and founded there a great civilization which has become permanent and renowned and under which these people attained the highest degree of honour and glory. He freed them from bondage and captivity. He imbued them with qualities of progressiveness and capability. They proved to be a civilizing people with instincts toward education and scholastic attainment. Their philosophy became renowned; their industries were celebrated throughout the nations. In all lines of advancement which characterize a progressive people they achieved distinction. In the splendour of the reign of Solomon their sciences and arts advanced to such a degree that even the Greek philosophers journeyed to Jerusalem to sit at the feet of the Hebrew sages and acquire the basis of Israelitish law. According to Eastern history this is an established fact. Even Socrates visited the Jewish doctors in the Holy Land, consorting with them and discussing the principles and basis of their religious belief. After his return to Greece he formulated his philosophical teaching of divine unity and advanced his belief in the immortality of the spirit beyond the dissolution of the body. Without doubt Socrates absorbed these verities from the wise men of the Jews with whom he came in contact. Hippocrates and other philosophers of the Greeks likewise visited Palestine and acquired wisdom from the Jewish

Prophets, studying the basis of ethics and morality, returning to their country with contributions which have made Greece famous.

When a movement fundamentally religious makes a weak nation strong, changes a nondescript tribal people into a mighty and powerful civilization, rescues them from captivity and elevates them to sovereignty, transforms their ignorance into knowledge and endows them with an impetus of advancement in all degrees of development —(this is not theory, but historical fact)—it becomes evident that religion is the cause of man's attainment to honour and sublimity.

But when we speak of religion we mean the essential foundation or reality of religion, not the dogmas and blind imitations which have gradually encrusted it and which are the cause of the decline and effacement of a nation. These are inevitably destructive and a menace and hindrance to a nation's life—even as it is recorded in the Torah and confirmed in history that when the Jews became fettered by empty forms and imitations the wrath of God became manifest . . .

Next 'Abdu'l-Bahá traced the history of the Babylonian captivity and, later, the Roman domination of the Jewish nation, and continued thus:

From this review of the history of the Jewish people we learn that the foundation of the religion of God laid by Moses was the cause of their eternal honour and national prestige, the animating impulse of their advancement and racial supremacy and the source of that excellence which will always command the respect and reverence of those who understand their peculiar destiny and outcome. The dogmas and blind imitations which gradually obscured the reality of the religion of God proved to be Israel's destructive influences causing the expulsion of these chosen people from the Holy Land of their Covenant and promise.

The divine mission and station of Moses stand unassailable, 'Abdu'l-Bahá asserted, and He went on to say:

> We should earnestly seek and thoroughly investigate realities, recognizing that the purpose of the religion of God is the education of humanity and the unity and fellowship of mankind. Furthermore we will establish the point that the foundations of the religions of God are one foundation. This foundation is not multiple for it is reality itself. Reality does not admit of multiplicity although each of the divine religions is separable into two divisions.

He developed this theme in detail, citing many instances of these divisions, of what is changeable and what is unchangeable in religion. The essential, fundamental teachings of the Manifestations of God, He explained, are related to Absolutes, and are thus immutable; the advancement of man is ever their purpose. But the secondary teachings, which are related to the conditions of the time, must be subject to change, since both man and his societies evolve.

'Abdu'l-Bahá had prepared the way for the central and challenging theme of His exposition, which He now unfolded to the congregation of Temple Emmanu-El:

> Christ ratified and proclaimed the foundation of the law of Moses. Muḥammad and all the Prophets have revoiced that same foundation of reality. Therefore the purposes and accomplishments of the divine Messengers have been one and the same. They were the source of advancement to the body-politic and the cause of the honour and divine civilization of humanity, the foundation of which is one and the same in every Dispensation. It is evident then that the proofs of the validity and inspiration of a Prophet of God are the deeds of beneficent accomplishment and greatness emanating from Him. If He proves to be instrumental in the elevation and betterment of mankind, He is undoubtedly a valid and heavenly Messenger.

I wish you to be reasonable and just in your consideration of the following statements:

At the time when the Israelites had been dispersed by the
power of the Roman Empire and the national life of the
Hebrew people had been effaced by their conquerors,
when the law of God had seemingly passed from them and
the foundation of the religion of God was apparently
destroyed, Jesus Christ appeared. When He arose among
the Jews, the first thing He did was to proclaim the validity
of the Manifestation of Moses. He declared that the Torah,
the Old Testament, was the Book of God and that all the
Prophets of Israel were valid and true. He extolled the
mission of Moses and through His proclamation the name
of Moses was spread throughout the world. Through
Christianity the greatness of Moses became known
among all nations . . .

Through the instrumentality of Christ—through the
translation of the New Testament, the little volume of the
Gospel—the Old Testament, the Torah, has been translated into six hundred languages and spread everywhere
in the world. The names of the Hebrew Prophets became
household words among the nations, who believed that
the children of Israel were verily the chosen people of
God, a holy nation under the especial blessing and protection of God, and that therefore the Prophets who had
arisen in Israel were the Day-springs of Revelation and
brilliant Stars in the heaven of the Will of God.

Therefore Christ really promulgated Judaism for He
was a Jew and not opposed to the Jews . . . That portion
of the ordinances of Moses which concerned transactions
and transient conditions underwent transformation, but
the essential teachings of Moses were revoiced and confirmed by Christ without change . . . Likewise through
the supreme efficacy and power of the Word of God He
united most of the nations of the East and the West . . .
He led them beneath the overshadowing tent of the oneness of humanity. He educated them until they became
united and agreed and through His spirit of conciliation

the Roman, Greek, Chaldean and Egyptian were blended in a composite civilization. This wonderful power and extraordinary efficacy of the Word prove conclusively the validity of Christ. Consider how His heavenly sovereignty is still permanent and lasting. Verily this is conclusive proof and manifest evidence.

From another horizon we see Muḥammad, the Prophet of Arabia, appearing. You may not know that the first address of Muḥammad to His tribe was the statement: 'Verily Moses was a Prophet of God and the Torah is a Book of God. Verily, O ye people, ye must believe in the Torah, in Moses and the Prophets. Ye must accept all the Prophets of Israel as valid.' In the Qur'án . . . there are seven statements or repetitions of the Mosaic narrative, and in all the historic accounts Moses is praised. Muḥammad announced that Moses was a great Prophet of God, that God guided Him in the wilderness of Sinai, that through the light of guidance Moses hearkened to the summons of God, that He was the Interlocutor of God, and the bearer of the Tablet of the Ten Commandments . . . Consider that Muḥammad was born among the savage and barbarous tribes of Arabia, lived among them, and was outwardly illiterate and uninformed of the Holy Books of God. The Arabian people were in the utmost ignorance and barbarism. They buried their infant daughters alive, considering this to be an evidence of a valorous and lofty nature. They lived in bondage and serfdom under the Persian and Roman governments and were scattered throughout the desert, engaged in continual strife and bloodshed. When the light of Muḥammad dawned, the darkness of ignorance was dispelled from the deserts of Arabia. In a short period of time those barbarous peoples attained a superlative degree of civilization which with Baghdád as its centre extended as far westward as Spain, and afterward influenced the greater part of Europe. What proof of prophethood could be greater than this, unless we close our eyes to justice and remain obstinately opposed to reason.

Today the Christians are believers in Moses, accept Him as a Prophet of God and praise Him most highly. The Muslims are likewise believers in Moses, accept the validity of His prophethood . . . Could it be said that the acceptance of Moses by the Christians and Muslims has been harmful and detrimental to those people? On the contrary it has been beneficial to them, proving that they have been fair-minded and just. What harm could result to the Jewish people then if they in return should accept Christ and acknowledge the validity of the prophethood of Muḥammad? By this acceptance and praiseworthy attitude the enmity and hatred which have afflicted mankind so many centuries would be dispelled, fanaticism and bloodshed pass away . . . Christians and Muslims believe and admit that Moses was the Interlocutor of God. What harm is there in this that the Jewish people should say that Christ was the Spirit of God, and Muḥammad the Messenger of God? Then there will be no more hatred and fanaticism, no more warfare and bloodshed.

Verily I now declare to you that Moses was the Interlocutor of God, a Manifestation of God; that Moses revealed the fundamental law of God; that He laid the basis for the civilization and progress of the world of man. What harm is there in this? Have I lost anything by saying this to you, and believing it as a Bahá'í? On the contrary it benefits me, and Bahá'u'lláh . . . confirms me, saying: 'You have been fair and just in your judgment; you have impartially investigated the truth and arrived at a true conclusion; you have announced your belief in Moses, a Prophet of God, and accepted the Torah, the Book of God' . . . Why not put an end to this religious strife and establish a bond of connection between the hearts of men? Why should not the followers of one religion praise the Founder or Teacher of another? . . . You would lose nothing by such action and statement. On the contrary you would contribute to the welfare of mankind. You would be instrumental in establishing the happiness of the world of humanity . . . Inasmuch as our

God is one God and the Creator of all mankind, He provides for and protects all. We acknowledge Him as a God of kindness, justice, and mercy. Why then should we His children and followers war and fight, bringing sorrow and grief into the hearts of each other? . . .

Praise be to God! . . . this century of radiance has dawned—this century wherein the reality of things is becoming evident, wherein science is penetrating the mysteries of the universe [and] the oneness of the world of humanity is being established . . . Shall we remain steeped in our fanaticisms and cling to our prejudices? Is it fitting that we should still be bound and restricted by ancient fables and superstitions of the past; be handicapped by superannuated beliefs and the ignorances of dark ages . . . shunning and anathematizing each other? Is this becoming? Is it not better for us to be loving and considerate toward each other? Is it not preferable to enjoy fellowship and unity; join in anthems of praise to the Most High God and extol all His Prophets in the spirit of acceptance and true vision? Then indeed this world will become a paradise and the promised Day of God will dawn. Then according to the prophecy of Isaiah the wolf and the lamb will drink from the same stream, . . . the lion and the calf pasture in the same meadow. What does this mean? It means that fierce and contending religions, hostile creeds and divergent beliefs will reconcile and associate, notwithstanding their former hatreds and antagonism . . . This is the spirit and meaning of Isaiah's words. There will never be a day when this prophecy will come to pass literally, for these animals by their natures cannot mingle and associate in kindness and love. Therefore this prophecy symbolizes the unity and agreement of races, nations and peoples who will come together in attitudes of intelligence, illumination and spirituality.

The age has dawned when human fellowship will become a reality.

The century has come when all religions shall be unified.

The Dispensation is at hand when all nations shall enjoy the blessings of International Peace.

The cycle has arrived when racial prejudice will be abandoned by tribes and peoples of the world.

The epoch has begun wherein all nativities will be conjoined in one great human family.

For all mankind shall dwell in peace and security beneath the shelter of the great tabernacle of the one living God.[190]

In the evening, at the meeting in the home of Mrs Goodall, 'Abdu'l-Bahá remarked that never before had anyone spoken in a synagogue to affirm that Christ was the Word of God and Muḥammad the Messenger of God. And noteworthy it was that no dissent was incurred. All that, He said, was only due to the confirmations of Bahá'u'lláh.

Mrs Hearst, who had led the first party of American pilgrims to the Holy Land, was estranged from the Faith. But she was still sufficiently attached to come in person and invite 'Abdu'l-Bahá and His attendants to spend a long weekend at her palatial home in the vicinity of Pleasanton. Because her invitation was sincere, 'Abdu'l-Bahá accepted it. As was customary for a woman of Mrs Hearst's standing, she had arranged a large house party that week-end, composed of the élite of Californian society. Mrs Hearst herself went to San Francisco on October 13th to escort 'Abdu'l-Bahá to her home. During the three days as her guest, He made no direct reference to the Faith, until she herself requested it while recalling her pilgrimage. Mrs Hearst recollected also the effect that the chanting of an Arabic prayer had had on her all those years ago in 'Akká, and expressed her ardent desire to hear such a prayer once again. 'Abdu'l-Bahá's voice rang out powerfully as He acceded to her wish and chanted a prayer in Arabic. The other guests sat spellbound, although they were not familiar with the language. The second day at the luncheon table, when asked to say a benediction, He uttered this prayer:

He is God! Behold us, O Lord, gathered at this board, thankful for Thy bounty, our gaze turned to Thy Kingdom. O Lord! Send down unto us Thy heavenly food and blessing from Thee. Verily, Thou art the Generous, and verily, Thou art the Beneficent, the Merciful.

And at dinner on the 15th He spoke this prayer:

He is God! O Lord! How shall we thank Thee! Thy bounties are limitless, and our gratitude but limited. How can the limited render thanks to the limitless? Incapable are we of offering thanks for Thy mercies. Utterly powerless, we turn unto Thy Kingdom, and beg Thee to increase Thy bestowal and bounty. Thou art the Giver, Thou art the Bestower, Thou art the Powerful.[191]

Before departing for San Francisco on the 16th, 'Abdu'l-Bahá asked to see all those who served in Mrs Hearst's household: maids, pages, groom, cook. He spoke to them affectionately. He stood as a father to them, He said, and wished them to have a memento of His visit. To each He gave two guineas. Then Mrs Hearst escorted 'Abdu'l-Bahá back to San Francisco. On the way, He warned her not to consider anyone a true Bahá'í who was covetous of the goods of others and who tried to extort money from them. Mrs Hearst's estrangement had, in fact, originated in such acts on the part of one or two individuals, she herself being the victim.

Bahá'ís of Seattle, Washington, and Portland, Oregon, felt dejected and deprived because 'Abdu'l-Bahá had not contemplated travelling northwards to their cities. 'Abdu'l-Bahá Himself was greatly saddened by this, and said that He could not bear to have anyone hurt or disappointed.

Nevertheless, these cities were too distant, time was getting short, and He had to go south to Los Angeles, to visit the grave of Thornton Chase. At this time Europe's peace was in jeopardy because of the partial attitudes of the Great Powers towards Turkey, which had been plunged into war and defeat by the action of the Balkan States. 'Abdu'l-Bahá explained that the plight of Turkey called for His early return to the Holy Land. So Bahá'ís of those northern cities came south and attained His presence in San Francisco.

'Abdu'l-Bahá visited Oakland on several occasions. On October 16th a Feast was held there at the home of Mrs Goodall and Mrs Cooper. Despite the journey from Mrs Hearst's home, and His attendance that afternoon at a San Francisco club to address its members, 'Abdu'l-Bahá travelled in the evening to Oakland to be with the Bahá'ís at the Feast. He spoke to them twice. That night He stayed in Oakland, returning to San Francisco the next day. It was then found that His signet ring was missing. Henceforth, He appended His signature to every Tablet He dictated or wrote.

'Abdu'l-Bahá's journey to Los Angeles on 18th October was for the specific purpose of visiting the grave of Thornton Chase. Although He spoke to groups of people in the hotel and met the press, He once again had to decline invitations to address societies and churches, as time would not allow it.

The cemetery was located outside the city. 'Abdu'l-Bahá took a tram car. Alighting, He walked very quietly into the cemetery until He approached the grave of Thornton Chase, when He remarked on the beauty of the surroundings. Then, leaning against a tree, He stood silently before that resting-place of the first Bahá'í of the Christian West. He asked for some flowers and, with great care and loving attention, He arranged them on the grave. Then, still facing the grave, He turned in the direction of 'Akká and chanted the Tablet of Visitation—the Tablet which is read in the Shrines of the Báb and Bahá'u'lláh. Following that, He chanted a prayer for Thornton Chase and spoke of the services which that dedicated man had rendered to the Faith. 'Abdu'l-Bahá had named him 'Thábit'—the Steadfast—in his lifetime. At the conclusion of His visit, 'Abdu'l-Bahá knelt on the ground and kissed the grave of Thornton Chase.*

When He arrived back at the hotel in Los Angeles a throng of people were awaiting Him. That night (October 18th) He was so exhausted that He could not eat. And yet the next day He had to meet a great number of Bahá'ís and others. A journalist, who had written about Mírzá Shu'áu'lláh, the son of Mírzá Muḥammad-'Alí, and had quoted him in his paper, insisted on questioning 'Abdu'l-Bahá about Shu'áu'lláh's relationship to Him. Mírzá Shu'áu'lláh was then living in California, and had given out that he was the grandson of Bahá'u'lláh and entitled to special consideration. To this persistent journalist 'Abdu'l-Bahá replied sternly that He would give him just one answer, after which the journalist should ask no more, and He would reply no more. That answer, 'Abdu'l-Bahá said, was exactly what Christ had uttered, when told that His brothers had come to see Him: 'my brethren are these which hear the word of God, and do it.'† Nevertheless, 'Abdu'l-Bahá added, His doors were open to anyone who wished to come.

Saying farewell to the Bahá'ís of Los Angeles, 'Abdu'l-Bahá told them that future years would reveal the stature of Thornton Chase, and that they should visit his grave every year on His behalf. The journey back to San Francisco on October 21st was by night. Although Mrs Goodall had reserved sleeping berths for all, 'Abdu'l-Bahá's mind was so

* See p. 66 for 'Abdu'l-Bahá's words on this occasion.
† A paraphrase of Mark iii. 35.

occupied that He could not sleep. On October 23rd He made a final visit to Oakland, and on the 25th, took leave of His friends in San Francisco.

That morning, as 'Abdu'l-Bahá came down the stairs, a great gathering of Bahá'ís, who were about to see the last of their Master, raised their voices in a crescendo of 'Alláh-u-Abhá'—God is the Most Glorious. 'Abdu'l-Bahá was deeply touched and His face reflected His emotion. He walked amidst them, greeted each one, gave each one attar of roses, and told them:

Here I want to bid you farewell. This meeting and assemblage are very moving. This is the last cup. How thankful we must be to the Blessed Perfection that He has brought the hearts so near to each other. This attar that I give you is but a token of the fragrance of the Abhá Paradise—the best of all fragrances. I am very sad to be separated from you and I do not know how to express it. It is not possible to give tongue to the feelings of the heart. I am greatly moved, because I saw the love of Bahá'u'lláh in you, I witnessed the light of Bahá'u'lláh in your beings. I am so moved that I cannot speak. I leave it to your hearts to feel what I feel. Although I am going away from you, you have your place in my heart. When I reach the Shrine of Bahá'u'lláh, I shall lay my head on the sacred threshold and beseech confirmation for every one of the friends. These days of our meeting were blissful days. They cannot be bettered. I met you every day, and I always found the hearts attracted, the eyes turned unto the Abhá Kingdom. There cannot be better days. Do you not forget them and I shall not. I beg of God that the results of this amity shall become evident, that it shall lead to spirituality in the world, to impart guidance to all who dwell on this earth. I hope for such results from this gathering that it will not be like other gatherings of people, who forget each other as soon as they disperse. It is certain that because this gathering has been a divine

assemblage, it will never be forgotten, and whenever recollected it will produce fresh delight. This is my wish.[192]

'Abdu'l-Bahá had yet one more city to visit in the West,
the capital of California. At the station in Sacramento an
automobile was waiting to take Him to luncheon. His hostess
desired Him to stay in her home, but He did not feel able to
accept, and went to the Hotel Sacramento, where a meeting
had been arranged for that night.

'Abdu'l-Bahá's talk that evening, in the Assembly Hall
of the hotel, was on the history and background of the Faith
and its basic principles. The interest shown was so intense
that another meeting in the same hall was announced for the
following morning. At this second meeting, 'Abdu'l-Bahá
said:

I have visited your capitol and its gardens. No other
capitol has such beautiful surroundings. Just as it is
imposing and distinguished above all others, so may the
people of California become the most exalted and perfect
altruists of the world. California is indeed a blessed country. The climate is temperate, the sun ever shining, the
fruits abundant and delicious. All outer blessings are
evident here. The Californians are a noble people; therefore I hope they may make extraordinary progress and
become renowned for their virtues.

The issue of paramount importance in the world today
is International Peace. The European continent is like an
arsenal, a storehouse of explosives ready for ignition, and
one spark will set the whole of Europe aflame, particularly
at this time when the Balkan question is before the world.
Even now war is raging furiously in some places . . .
Therefore the greatest need in the world today is International Peace . . . It is time for the abolition of warfare,
the unification of nations and governments . . . It is time
for cementing together the East and the West.

Inasmuch as the Californians seem peace-loving and

possessed of great worthiness and capacity, I hope that advocates of peace may daily increase among them until the whole population shall stand for that beneficent outcome. May the men of affairs in this democracy uphold the standard of international conciliation. Then may altruistic aims and thoughts radiate from this centre toward all other regions of the earth, and may the glory of this accomplishment forever halo the history of this country. May the first flag of International Peace be upraised in this State ...* May this centre and capitol become distinguished in all degrees of accomplishment; for the virtues of humanity and the possibilities of human advancement are boundless. There is no end to them and whatever be the degree to which humanity may attain, there are always degrees beyond. There is no attainment in the contingent realm of which it may be said 'Beyond this state of being and perfection there is no other,' or 'This has achieved the superlative degree.' No matter how perfect it may appear, there is always a greater degree of attainment to be reached. Therefore no matter how much humanity may advance there are ever higher stations to be attained because virtues are unlimited ...

Finally, to conclude His talk, 'Abdu'l-Bahá said:

Verily the century of radiance has dawned, minds are advancing, perceptions are broadening, realizations of human possibilities are becoming universal, susceptibilities are developing, the discovery of realities is progressing. Therefore it is necessary that we should cast aside all the prejudices of ignorance, discard superannuated beliefs in traditions of past ages and raise aloft the banner of international agreement. Let us co-operate in love, and through spiritual reciprocity enjoy eternal happiness and peace.[193]

* Thirty-three years later at San Francisco the Charter of the United Nations was drawn up and proclaimed.

After luncheon with the Bahá'ís of Sacramento, within a few hours 'Abdu'l-Bahá was on the train bound for Denver.

Before we close the account of 'Abdu'l-Bahá's visit to California, mention ought to be made of the newspaper, the *Palo Altan*, and H. W. Simkins, one of its editors. Mr Simkins devoted a whole issue of his paper (vol. x, no. 43) to the work and message of 'Abdu'l-Bahá. The facsimile of a Tablet dated October 17th, addressed to Mr Simkins, together with its translation, was printed in the same issue. It reads:

At the time I met you and felt the susceptibilities of your conscience my heart and soul became greatly attached to that dear friend and the utmost love was produced, and the spiritual emotions were obtained. Your visit gave me the utmost happiness. The address delivered in Stanford University and published completely in your paper was observed today—and on account of it I became both pleased and grateful. In order to express my pleasure and appreciation for this service of yours I am writing you this epistle. I shall never forget your cordiality, and as long as life lasts I shall remember you. I beg of God that that dear friend may become like unto a shining star in the horizon of reality, and become the cause of bestowing spiritual life upon the world of humanity.

The address delivered at the Jewish temple establishing the validity of Jesus Christ and inviting the Jews to believe in Him is enclosed herein. From its powerful contents you will realize that though there were many conservative Jews in the audience, yet in the most dauntless manner the validity of Christ was proven. After reading its contents should you think it best you may print it fully without abbreviation in the columns of your paper that others of the Jews may read it. Perchance this may prove an impetus for their respect for, and belief in Christ, that this strife and contention that has lasted between the two nations for two thousand years may disappear, and the oneness of the world of humanity be unveiled. Upon thee be greeting and praise.*

* This Tablet, translated by Mírzá Aḥmad Sohráb, is reproduced here exactly as it appeared in the pages of the *Palo Altan*, apart from omitting 'His Holiness' preceding 'Jesus Christ'. However, the present writer would have translated certain words and phrases differently: e.g. 'letter' instead of 'epistle', 'delicate' instead of 'dauntless'.

CHAPTER 18

FAREWELL TO AMERICA

'Abdu'l-Bahá left California on 26th October. His work in America was accomplished, He said, and now He would begin His journey back to the Holy Land, to the precincts of the Shrine of His Father.

On the train to Denver there were more than fifty Turks, who were going home to fight the battles of the Ottoman Empire against the Balkan confederates. A number of them sought to meet 'Abdu'l-Bahá. He arranged that they should be provided with all the necessities for making tea in their carriage as His guests. A dealer was going through the train, exhibiting and selling his merchandise. When 'Abdu'l-Bahá was examining some newly-mined stones which the dealer had, a number of children gathered around Him, eagerly eyeing the wares. 'Abdu'l-Bahá asked them what they wished to have, and bought a dollar's worth of goods for each. Then a few more children came by and for them, too, 'Abdu'l-Bahá purchased gifts. Passengers hearing of these happenings asked who the generous Easterner was and, when informed, expressed keen interest to hear of His teachings. Thus, much of 'Abdu'l-Bahá's time on the train was spent for the benefit and instruction of those enquirers, who were sitting or standing around Him.

Denver was reached at midnight of October 28th. This second stay in Denver lasted only twenty-four hours. Again He spoke at the home of Mrs Roberts, and also at the Church of the Messiah. The next midnight He took the train to Chicago. He was now hastening His return to the Eastern seaboard. 'Abdu'l-Bahá would not avail Himself of a sleeping-berth that night, but the second night on the train He told His attendants that they had had enough mortification and should engage sleepers. His attendants suggested that only the Master should have one, which 'Abdu'l-Bahá would not countenance on any account. 'No,' He said, 'we must be equal.'

Albert Windust, who was then editing the magazine, the *Star of the West*, and remained its editor for many years, joined the train before it arrived at Chicago, in order to welcome the Master. On that morning of October 31st, Bahá'ís of Chicago, jubilant and happy, had gathered in full force at the station. 'Abdu'l-Bahá told them that He had now been thrice to their city, and it was their turn to visit the Holy Land. He again stayed at the Hotel Plaza, and invitations began to come in abundance. Most of them He had to refuse because His sojourn could not be prolonged.

At two meetings 'Abdu'l-Bahá again warned the Bahá'ís of Chicago against the machinations of the violators:

> . . . Bahá'u'lláh has not left any possible room for dissension. Naturally there are some who are antagonistic, some who are followers of self-desire, others who hold to their own ideas and still others who wish to create dissension in the Cause. For example Judas Iscariot was one of the disciples yet he betrayed Christ. Such a thing has happened in the past, but in this day the Blessed Perfection has declared 'this person is the Expounder of My Book and all must turn to Him.' The purpose is to ward off dissension and differences among His followers . . . [194]

Speaking one day to a group of people on the true brotherhood which the Faith of Bahá'u'lláh promotes and inculcates, while it preserves, at the same time, degrees within the body-politic, 'Abdu'l-Bahá turned, with a smile, towards the ladies present and said that, in Europe and America, many men worked very hard so that their wives could have luxuries. He related, again with a smile, the story of a husband and wife who once visited Him. Some dust had settled on the wife's shoes, and she told her husband peremptorily to wipe it off, which he dutifully did. Did she do the same for her husband, 'Abdu'l-Bahá had queried. No, had been the reply, she cleaned his clothes. But that was not equality, 'Abdu'l-Bahá had remarked. 'Now, ladies,' 'Abdu'l-Bahá said, 'you must sometimes stand up for the rights of men.' It was all said with good humour, but the lesson was plain: moderation in all things.

November 3rd was the last day of 'Abdu'l-Bahá's third visit to Chicago. In the morning He spoke at a gathering in the hotel; next He gave a discourse at the Englewood Church; in the afternoon He spoke from the pulpit of the Congregational Church; in the evening He attended a Feast at the home of Mrs Davis, where He made His farewell.

On His way to Washington, 'Abdu'l-Bahá stopped for one night in Cincinnati, Ohio. At the Grand Hotel, where He stayed, a banquet had been arranged. 'Abdu'l-Bahá spoke particularly of Thornton Chase, his qualities and his great services to the Faith. Zarqání writes that some forty Bahá'ís could not tear themselves away, obtained rooms and spent the night at the Grand Hotel. The next morning, November 6th, 'Abdu'l-Bahá gave a second address in that hotel, and took the noon train to Washington.

In the capital 'Abdu'l-Bahá lived, as before, in a rented house. His first public engagement was the same evening at the Universalist Church. He told the congregation there:

The teachings of Bahá'u'lláh embody many principles; I am giving you a synopsis only. One of these principles concerns equality between men and women. He declared that as all are created in the image and likeness of the one

God, there is no distinction as to sex in the estimation of
God . . . In the lower kingdoms, the animal and vegetable, we find sex differentiation in function and organism.
All plants, trees and animals are subject to that differentiation by creation, but among themselves there is absolute
equality without further distinction as to sex. Why then
should mankind make a distinction which the lower
creatures do not regard? Especially so when we realize
that all are of the same kingdom and kindred; that all
are the leaves of one tree, the waves of one sea? The only
reasonable explanation is that woman has not been
afforded the same educational facilities as man. For if
she had received the same opportunities for training and
development as man has enjoyed, undoubtedly she would
have attained the same station and level . . . When Jesus
Christ died upon the cross the disciples who witnessed
His crucifixion were disturbed and shaken. Even Peter . . .
denied him thrice. Mary Magdalene brought them together and confirmed their faith, saying 'Why are ye
doubting? Why have ye feared? O thou Peter! Why didst
thou deny him? . . . The reality of Christ is ever-living,
everlasting, eternal. For that divine reality there is no
beginning, no ending, and therefore there can be no
death . . . ' In brief, this woman singly and alone was
instrumental in transforming the disciples and making
them steadfast. This is an evidence of extraordinary
power and supreme attributes, a proof that woman is the
equivalent and complement of man . . . [195]

In a talk, given the next day at the home of Mr and Mrs
Arthur Parsons, 'Abdu'l-Bahá spoke of the battles raging
in the Balkans, and of what Bahá'u'lláh had foretold
regarding the Ottoman Empire. He had in His hands a
copy of the *Kitáb-i-Mubín* (comprising Tablets of Bahá'u'lláh
and His Epistles to the rulers of the world) which had been
published in Bombay, twenty-two years before; and He
read from the Epistle to Sulṭán 'Abdu'l-'Azíz. 'Abdu'l-Bahá

mentioned, in that context, the writings of Professor Edward Browne, which had appeared in 1891 and subsequently, in which those warnings and prophecies of Bahá'u'lláh could be found. He also referred to the Epistle to Náṣiri'd-Dín Sháh, and thus concluded His talk:

> The purpose of these quotations is to show that Bahá'u'lláh's great endeavour in the East was to unify mankind, to cause them to agree and become reconciled, thereby manifesting the oneness of the world of humanity, preparing the way for International Peace and establishing the foundations of happiness and welfare. But the nations have not hearkened to His summons and message . . . Had they been attentive to His commands and received His admonitions they would have been protected. They would have enjoyed happiness and prosperity. They would have been bound together in ties of fellowship and brotherhood, availing themselves of the wonderful bounties of love and unity and dwelling in the delectable paradise of the Divine Kingdom. But alas! the commands and guidance of the Blessed One have been neglected and ignored. Day by day they have followed their own devices and imaginations, until now this fire of war is raging most furiously.[196]

The evening of November 8th was particularly memorable. 'Abdu'l-Bahá had been invited to speak at Eighth Street Temple, a Jewish synagogue. He said beforehand that He would speak exactly as He did in San Francisco, to proclaim and prove the divine origin of Christianity and Islám. And this is what He proceeded to do, in a manner both direct and fearless. He enunciated His theme at once:

> God is one; the effulgence of God is one; and humanity constitutes the servants of that one God. God is kind to all. He creates and provides for all; and all are under His care and protection. The Sun of Truth, the Word of God,

shines upon all mankind; the Divine cloud pours down its precious rain; the gentle zephyrs of His mercy blow, and all humanity is submerged in the ocean of His eternal justice and loving-kindness. God has created mankind from the same progeny in order that they may associate in good-fellowship, exercise love toward each other and live together in unity and brotherhood.

But we have acted contrary to the will and good-pleasure of God. We have been the cause of enmity and disunion . . .

Then 'Abdu'l-Bahá singled out 'religious belief' as a cause of 'alienation and estrangement', whereas

In reality the foundations of the divine religions are one and the same . . . Abraham was the Founder of reality. Moses, Christ, Muḥammad were the Manifestations of reality. Bahá'u'lláh was the Glory of reality. This is not simply an assertion; it will be proved.[197]

The body of 'Abdu'l-Bahá's talk was devoted to this proof, following to a degree, but with significant variations, the course of His propositions at Temple Emmanu-El in San Francisco (see pp. 298-9): the 'permanent and unchanging' foundation of all religion and the changing 'temporary laws'; the purpose of the appearance of Prophets of God; the missions of Moses, Christ and Muḥammad, and their effects. 'We see therefore,' He affirmed, 'that the proofs applicable to one Prophet are equally applicable to another.'

And He concluded with these eloquent and challenging words:

. . . since the Prophets themselves, the Founders, have loved, praised and testified of each other, why should we disagree and be alienated? God is one. He is the shepherd of all. We are His sheep and therefore should live together in love and unity. We should manifest the spirit

of justness and good-will toward each other. Shall we
do this, or shall we censure and pronounce anathema,
praising ourselves and condemning all others? What
possible good can come from such attitude and action?
On the contrary, nothing but enmity and hatred, injustice
and inhumanity can possibly result. Has not this been the
greatest cause of bloodshed, woe and tribulation in the
past?

Praise be to God! You are living in a land of freedom.
You are blessed with men of learning, men who are well
versed in the comparative study of religions. You realize
the need of unity and know the great harm which comes
from prejudice and superstition. I ask you, is not fellowship and brotherhood preferable to enmity and hatred in
society and community? . . . We must be united. We
must love each other. We must ever praise each other. We
must bestow commendation upon all people, thus remov-
ing the discord and hatred which have caused alienation
amongst men . . . This must be abandoned, and the way to
do it is to investigate the reality which underlies all the
religions. This underlying reality is the love of humanity.
For God is one and humanity is one, and the only creed
of the Prophets is love and unity.[198]

While 'Abdu'l-Bahá was speaking, some in the audience
became restless and showed their dissent. They signalled
to the interpreter that the time was late, that the talk had
broken the bounds of length, but 'Abdu'l-Bahá overlooked
their remonstrances and went on unperturbed. When He
sat down, the Rabbi, who presided, told the congregation
that whenever matters not to their liking were presented
to them they ought not to show open distress and displeasure, but should consider them serenely and dispas-
sionately to find where the truth lay.

The next day at the home of Mr and Mrs Parsons, 'Abdu'l-Bahá said: 'The address delivered last evening in the
Jewish synagogue evidently disturbed some of the people,

including the revered Rabbi who called upon me this afternoon. Together we went over the ground again, which I shall now review for your benefit. It was not possible to make the subject completely plain to the Rabbi last night, as he was very much pressed for time, but today the opportunity was sufficient for a reconsideration of the statements in detail . . . ' When 'Abdu'l-Bahá had gone over the whole ground again, the Rabbi had commented: 'I believe that what you have said is perfectly true, but I must ask one thing of you. Will you not tell the Christians to love us a little more?' And 'Abdu'l-Bahá had replied: 'We have advised them and will continue to do so.'

A banquet attended by about three hundred was held in the evening of November 9th at Rauscher's Hall. 'Abdu'l-Bahá rose from His seat to give flowers and sweets to those at each table. Then He addressed them:

I feel a keen sense of joy in being present at this banquet this evening, for—praise be to God!—before me are radiant faces, ears attuned to the melodies of the supreme concourse, hearts aglow with the fire of the love of God, spirits exhilarated through the glad-tidings of God, souls sheltered beneath the overshadowing power of the Kingdom of Abhá. I see before me an assemblage of souls who are of the 'chosen' and not of the 'many called'. And it is my hope that through the favours of Bahá'u'lláh He may continue to attract you to His Kingdom and render you victorious and triumphant in your service to the oneness and solidarity of mankind. May He assist all who are firm in establishing the unity of the inhabitants of this earth. May all of you thereby become my partners and coadjutors in servitude.

O Lord! Confirm and aid this assemblage. Confirm these souls through the breaths of Thy Holy Spirit. Enlighten the eyes by the vision of these radiant lights and make the ears joyful through the anthems of Thy call to service. O God! Verily we have gathered here in the fragrance of Thy love. We have turned to Thy Kingdom. We seek naught save Thee and desire nothing save Thy good-pleasure. O God! Let this food be Thy manna from heaven and grant this assemblage may be a concourse of Thy supreme ones. May they be the quickening cause of love to humanity and the source of illumination to the human race. May they be the instruments of Thy guidance upon earth. Verily Thou art Powerful, Thou art the Bestower, Thou art the Forgiver, and Thou art the Almighty!

And these were the concluding words of His address:

Therefore let us ever trust in God and seek confirmation and assistance from Him. Let us have perfect and absolute confidence in the bounty of the Kingdom. Review the events surrounding souls of bygone times in the beginning of their day; and again consider them when, through the aid and assistance of God, they proved to be the mighty ones of God. Remember that Peter was a fisherman, but through the bounty of the Kingdom he became the great apostle. Mary the Magdalene was a villager of lowly type, yet that selfsame Mary was transformed and became the means through which the confirmation of God descended upon the disciples. Verily she served the Kingdom of God with such efficiency that she became well-known and oft mentioned by the tongues of men. Even today she is shining from the horizon of eternal majesty. Consider how infinite is the bounty of God: that a woman such as Mary Magdalene should be selected by God to become the channel of confirmation to the disciples and a light of nearness in His Kingdom. Consequently trust ye in the bounty and grace of God and rest assured in the bestowals of His eternal outpouring. I hope that each one of you may become a shining light even as these electric lights are now brilliant in their intensity. Nay, may each one of you be a luminary like unto a sparkling star in the heaven of the Divine will. This is my supplication at the throne of God. This is my hope through the favours of Bahá'u'lláh. I offer this prayer in behalf of all of you and beg with a contrite heart that you may be assisted and glorified with an eternal bestowal.[199]

November 10th was the last day 'Abdu'l-Bahá spent in Washington, and two meetings were held. The first was at His residence: 1901 Eighteenth Street, N.W. 'Abdu'l-Bahá spoke of the opposition to the Faith that was bound to come: hostile comments would appear in the press, misrepresentations would be made. He told the Bahá'ís to remember the reception accorded to Christ and the early Christians, and to stand as firm and steadfast as they did.

. . . The philosophers of the times, Romans and Greeks, wrote against Christ. Even the kings wrote books of abuse, calumny and contempt. One of these kings was a Caesar.* He was also a philosopher. In his book he says concerning the people of Christ, 'The most degraded of people are the Christians . . . Jesus of Nazareth has led them astray . . .' There were many similar accounts. But remember that these statements did not affect the Cause of Christianity. On the contrary, Christianity advanced daily in power and potency.

Day by day the majesty of Christ grew in splendour and effulgence. Therefore my purpose is to warn and strengthen you against accusations, criticisms, revilings and derision in newspaper articles or other publications. Be not disturbed by them. They are the very confirmation of the Cause . . . May God confirm the day when a score of ministers of the churches may arise and with bared heads cry at the top of their voices that the Bahá'ís are misguided.[200] I would like to see that day, for that is the time when the Cause of God will spread. Bahá'u'lláh has

* Marcus Aurelius.

pronounced such as these the couriers of the Cause. They
will proclaim from pulpits that the Bahá'ís are fools;
that they are a wicked and unrighteous people; but be
ye steadfast and unwavering in the Cause of God. They
will spread the message of Bahá'u'lláh.

His Honour Mírzá Abu'l-Faḍl has written a treatise *
answering the criticisms of a London preacher. Each one
of you should have a copy. Read, memorize and reflect
upon it. Then when accusations and criticisms are
advanced by those unfavourable to the Cause, you will be
well armed.[201]

The second meeting was in the evening, held at the home
of Mr and Mrs Joseph H. Hannen, 1252 Eighth Street,
N.W. 'Abdu'l-Bahá was greatly fatigued, but also very
happy:

This is a beautiful assembly. I am very happy that the
whites and coloured are together. This is the cause of
my happiness, for you all are the servants of one God and
therefore brothers, sisters, mothers and fathers. In the
sight of God there is no distinction between white and
coloured; all are as one. Any one whose heart is pure is
dear to God whether white or coloured, red or yellow.
Among the animals, colours exist. The doves are white,
black, red, blue, but notwithstanding this diversity of
colour, they flock together in unity, happiness and fellowship, making no distinction among themselves, for they
are all doves. Man is intelligent and thoughtful, endowed
with powers of mind. Why then should he be influenced
by distinction of colour or race, since all belong to one
human family. There is no sheep which shuns another as if
saying 'I am white and you are black.' They graze together in complete unity, live together in fellowship and
happiness. How then can man be limited and influenced
by racial colours? . . .

* *The Brilliant Proof*, see p. 151.

I had a servant who was coloured; his name was
Isfandíyár. If a perfect man could be found in the world,
that man was Isfandíyár . . . Whenever I think of
Isfandíyár I am moved to tears although he passed away
fifty years ago. He was the faithful servant of Bahá'u'lláh
and was entrusted with His secrets. For this reason the
Sháh of Persia wanted him and inquired continually as
to his whereabouts. Bahá'u'lláh was in prison but the
Sháh had commanded many persons to find Isfandíyár.
Perhaps more than one hundred officers were appointed
to search for him. If they had succeeded in catching him
they would not have killed him at once. They would have
cut his flesh into pieces to force him to tell them the
secrets of Bahá'u'lláh. But Isfandíyár with the utmost
dignity used to walk in the streets and bazaars. One day
he came to us. My mother, my sister and myself lived in
a house near a corner. Because our enemies frequently
injured us, we were intending to go to a place where they
did not know us. I was a child at that time. At midnight
Isfandíyár came in. My mother said: 'O Isfandíyár, there
are a hundred policemen seeking for you. If they catch
you they will not kill you at once but will torture you with
fire. They will cut off your fingers. They will cut off your
ears. They will put out your eyes to force you to tell them
the secrets of Bahá'u'lláh. Go away! Do not stay here.'
He said 'I cannot go, because I owe money in the street
and in the stores. How can I go? They will say that the
servant of Bahá'u'lláh has bought and consumed the goods
and supplies of the storekeepers without paying for them.
Unless I pay all these obligations I cannot go. But if they
take me, never mind. If they punish me, there is no harm
in that. If they kill me, do not be grieved. But to go away
is impossible. I must remain until I pay all I owe. Then I
will go.' For one month Isfandíyár went about in the
streets and bazaars. He had things to sell and from his
earnings he gradually paid his creditors. In fact they were
not his debts but the debts of the court, for all our
properties had been confiscated. Everything we had was

taken away from us. The only things that remained were our debts. Isfandíyár paid them in full; not a single penny remained unpaid. Then he came to us, said 'goodbye' and went away. Afterward Bahá'u'lláh was released from prison. We went to Baghdád and Isfandíyár came there. He wanted to stay in the same home. Bahá'u'lláh, the Blessed Perfection, said to him: 'When you fled away there was a Persian minister who gave you shelter at a time when no one else could give you protection. Because he gave you shelter and protected you, you must be faithful to him. If he is satisfied to have you go, then come to us; but if he does not want you to go, do not leave him.' His master said: 'I do not want to be separated from Isfandíyár. Where can I find another like him, with such sincerity, such faithfulness, such character, such power? Where can I find one? O Isfandíyár! I am not willing that you should go, yet if you wish to go, let it be according to your own will.' But because the Blessed Perfection had said: 'You must be faithful,' Isfandíyár stayed with his master until he died. He was a point of light . . . his character was luminous, his mind was luminous, his face was luminous. Truly he was a point of light.

Then it is evident that excellence does not depend upon colour. Character is the true criterion of humanity . . . My hope is that the white and the coloured will be united in perfect love and fellowship, with complete unity and brotherhood. Associate with each other, think of each other and be like a rose-garden. Anyone who goes into a rose-garden will see various roses, white, pink, yellow, red, all growing together and replete with adornment. Each one accentuates the beauty of the other. Were all of one colour, the garden would be monotonous to the eye. If they were all white or yellow or red the garden would lack variety and attractiveness; but when the colours are varied . . . there will be the greatest beauty. Therefore I hope that you will be like a rose-garden. Although different in colours, yet—praise be to God!—

you receive rays from the same sun. From one cloud the rain is poured upon you. You are under the training of one gardener and this gardener is kind to all . . .

I hope you will continue in unity and fellowship. How beautiful to see coloured and white together! I hope, God willing, the day may come when I shall see the red men, the Indians with you, also Japanese and others. Then . . . a very wonderful rose-garden will appear in the world.[202]

Before 'Abdu'l-Bahá delivered that powerful and moving address, He was so exhausted that He had to recline on a couch, while He received individuals and groups and conversed with them. Yet, He delivered that address and had dinner in the company of those gathered at the home of Mr and Mrs Hannen; boarded the train the next morning (November 11th) for Baltimore, met a number of people at a hotel, addressed the congregation of a Unitarian church, and had luncheon (again in company) at the home of Mr and Mrs Struven; left for Philadelphia in the afternoon, met and talked with the Bahá'ís of that city in the station, boarded a train for the third time that day, and reached New York at one hour past midnight.

In New York, 'Abdu'l-Bahá stayed in the same house He had occupied before, which belonged to Mrs Champney. Again New Yorkers could see Him, morning and evening, pacing in the gardens by the riverside, relaxing for a few moments each day. Meetings of the Bahá'ís were regularly held at the home of Mrs Krug, 830 Park Avenue, in daytime, and at the home of Mr and Mrs Kinney, 780 West End Avenue, in the evenings, and there were others as well. 'Abdu'l-Bahá spoke at these gatherings and He also addressed audiences at public places, such as the Genealogical Hall (252 West Fifty-eighth Street), and the Theosophical Society (2228 Broadway). And His New York home was always open to visitors, and there were always visitors.

At the meeting in Genealogical Hall on November 17th, 'Abdu'l-Bahá said:

Bahá'u'lláh, the Sun of Truth, has dawned from the horizon of the Orient, flooding all regions with the light and life which will never pass away. His teachings which embody the divine spirit of the age and are applicable to this period of maturity in the life of the human world are:

The oneness of the world of humanity.
The protection and guidance of the Holy Spirit.
The foundation of all religion is one.
Religion must be the cause of unity.
Religion must accord with science and reason.
Independent investigation of truth.
Equality between men and women.
The abandoning of all prejudices among mankind.
Universal peace.
Universal education.
A universal language.
Solution of the economic problem.
An international tribunal.

Every one who truly seeks and justly reflects will admit that the teachings of the present day emanating from mere human sources and authority are the cause of difficulty and disagreement amongst mankind, the very destroyers of humanity, whereas the teachings of Bahá'u'lláh are the very healing of the sick world, the remedy for every need and condition. In them may be found the realization of every desire and aspiration, the cause of the happiness of the world of humanity, the stimulus and illumination of mentality, the impulse for advancement and uplift, the basis of unity for all nations, the fountain-source of love amongst mankind, the centre of agreement, the means of peace and harmony, the one bond which will unite the East and the West.[203]

News had, about this time, reached 'Abdu'l-Bahá that Áqá Riḍáy-i-Qannád, the stalwart Bahá'í of early days (see p. 220) had passed away. Speaking of him and his priceless services, 'Abdu'l-Bahá remarked that He must build Áqá Riḍá's grave with His own hands, and stand and pray before it.

A banquet was held in the evening of November 23rd at the Great Northern Hotel, 118 West Fifty-seventh Street. Speaking of that impressive gathering, 'Abdu'l-Bahá said in His talk:

. . . The effect of such an assembly as this is conducive to divine fellowship and strengthening of the bond which cements and unifies hearts. This is the indestructible bond of spirit which conjoins the East and West. By it the very foundations of race prejudice are uprooted and destroyed, the banner of spiritual democracy is hoisted aloft, the world of religion is purified from superannuated beliefs and hereditary imitations of forms, and the oneness of the reality underlying all religions is revealed and disclosed . . . Every limiting and restricting movement or meeting of mere personal interest is human in nature. Every universal movement unlimited in scope and purpose is divine. The Cause of God is advanced whenever and wherever a universal meeting is established among mankind.

Therefore endeavour that your attitudes and intentions here tonight be universal and altruistic in nature. Consecrate and devote yourselves to the betterment and service of all the human race. Let no barrier of ill-feeling or personal prejudice exist between these souls; for when your motives are universal and your intentions heavenly in character, when your aspirations are centred in the Kingdom, there is no doubt whatever that you will become the recipients of the bounty and good-pleasure of God.[204]

On November 26th, 'Abdu'l-Bahá told the Bahá'ís, at His home, that He was always greatly delighted to meet them all and would never forget their meetings; but if He could not meet every one of them every day, the real bond of love and affection between them would still remain strong, not affected at all. He said that He was much occupied; for a whole week letters from His sister, the Greatest Holy Leaf, and from His family had remained unopened. Just then He had been looking through some papers and had found the envelope from Haifa, but on being told that the Bahá'ís were awaiting Him He had come straight downstairs to the drawing-room to meet them together, because time did not permit meeting them individually; and yet, should anyone have any important matter to bring up, He would be happy to give the individual some minutes of His time. He wished, He said, that He could be with them all the time, because meeting them brought Him great happiness.

At the home of Mr and Mrs Kinney, on November 29th, 'Abdu'l-Bahá spoke about 'Sacrifice':

> . . . There are two kinds of sacrifice, the physical and the spiritual. The explanation made by the churches concerning this subject is in reality superstition. For instance it is recorded in the Gospel that Christ said: 'I am the living bread which came down from heaven: if any man eat of this bread, he shall live for ever.' He also said: 'This wine is my blood which is shed for the remission of sins.'* These verses have been interpreted by the churches in such a superstitious way that it is impossible for human reason to understand or accept the explanation.
>
> They say that Adam disobeyed the command of God and partook of the fruit of the forbidden tree, thereby committing a sin which was transmitted as a heritage to his posterity. They teach that because of Adam's sin all

* John vi. 51 and paraphrase of Matt. xxvi. 28.

his descendants have likewise committed transgression
and have become responsible through inheritance; consequently all mankind deserves punishment and must
make retribution; and that God sent forth His Son as a
sacrifice in order that man might be forgiven and the
human race delivered from the consequences of Adam's
transgression.

We wish to consider these statements from the standpoint of reason. Could we conceive of . . . the Divinity
Who is Justice itself, inflicting punishment upon the
posterity of Adam for Adam's own sin and disobedience?
Even if we should see a governor, an earthly ruler,
punishing a son for the wrong-doing of his father, we
would look upon that ruler as an unjust man . . .

There are other questions and evidences to be considered. Abraham was a Manifestation of God and a
descendant of Adam; likewise Ishmael, Isaac, Jeremiah
and the whole line of Prophets including David, Solomon
and Aaron were among his posterity . . . The explanation
is made that when Christ came and sacrificed Himself, all
the line of Holy Prophets who preceded Him became
free from sin and punishment . . . These interpretations
and statements are due to a misunderstanding of the
meanings of the Bible.

In order to understand the reality of sacrifice let us
consider the crucifixion and death of Jesus Christ. It is
true that He sacrificed Himself for our sake . . . When
Christ appeared, He knew that He must proclaim Himself
in opposition to all the nations and peoples of the earth.
He knew that mankind would arise against Him and
inflict upon Him all manner of tribulations. There is no
doubt that One who put forth such a claim as Christ
announced, would arouse the hostility of the world and
be subjected to personal abuse. He realized that His blood
would be shed and His body rent by violence. Notwithstanding His knowledge of what would befall Him, He
arose to proclaim His message, suffered all tribulation and
hardships from the people and finally offered His life as a

sacrifice in order to illumine humanity; gave His blood in order to guide the world of mankind. He accepted every calamity and suffering in order to guide men to the truth. Had He desired to save His own life and were He without wish to offer Himself in sacrifice He would not have been able to guide a single soul. There was no doubt that His blessed blood would be shed and His body broken. Nevertheless that Holy Soul accepted calamity and death in His love for mankind. This is one of the meanings of sacrifice.

As to the second meaning, He said: 'I am the bread which came down from heaven.'* It was not the body of Christ which came from heaven. His body came from the womb of Mary but the Christ perfections descended from heaven; the Reality of Christ came down from heaven. The Spirit of Christ and not the body descended from heaven. The body of Christ was but human. There could be no question that the physical body was born from the womb of Mary . . . Consequently by saying He was the bread which came from heaven He meant that the perfections which He showed forth were Divine perfections, that the blessings within Him were heavenly gifts and bestowals, that His Light was the Light of Reality. He said: 'If any man eat of this bread, he shall live forever.' That is to say whosoever assimilates these Divine perfections which are within Me will never die; whosoever has a share and partakes of these heavenly bounties I embody will find eternal life; he who takes unto himself these Divine lights shall find life everlasting. How manifest the meaning is! How evident! For the soul which acquires Divine perfections and seeks heavenly illumination from the teachings of Christ will undoubtedly live eternally. This is also one of the mysteries of sacrifice.

In reality Abraham sacrificed Himself, for He brought heavenly teachings to the world and conferred heavenly food upon mankind.

As to the third meaning of sacrifice, it is this: If you plant a seed in the ground a tree will become manifest

* John vi. 41.

from that seed. The seed sacrifices itself to the tree that will come from it. The seed is outwardly lost, destroyed, but the same seed which is sacrificed will be absorbed and embodied in the tree, its blossoms, fruit and branches. If the identity of that seed had not been sacrificed to the tree which became manifest from it, no branches, blossoms or fruits would have been forthcoming. Christ outwardly disappeared. His personal identity became hidden from the eyes even as the identity of the seed disappeared, but the bounties, Divine qualities and perfections of Christ became manifest in the Christian community which Christ founded through sacrificing Himself . . . Christ like unto the seed sacrificed Himself for the tree of Christianity . . .

As to the fourth significance of sacrifice, it is the principle that a reality sacrifices its own characteristics. Man must sever himself from the influences of the world of matter, from the world of nature . . . for the material world is the world of corruption and death . . .

That is to say man must sacrifice the qualities and attributes of the world of nature for the qualities and attributes of the world of God. For instance consider the substance we call iron. Observe its qualities; it is solid, black, cold. These are the characteristics of iron. When the same iron absorbs heat from the fire, it sacrifices its attribute of solidity for the attribute of fluidity. It sacrifices its attribute of darkness for the attribute of light which is a quality of the fire. It sacrifices its attribute of coldness to the quality of heat which the fire possesses; so that in the iron there remain no solidity, darkness or cold. It becomes illumined and transformed having sacrificed its qualities to the qualities and attributes of the fire.

Likewise man when separated and severed from the attributes of the world of nature sacrifices the qualities and exigencies of that mortal realm and manifests the perfections of the Kingdom, just as the qualities of the iron disappeared and the qualities of the fire appeared in their place.[205]

Before 'Abdu'l-Bahá reached the American shore, then during His eight months' tour of the continent, and also subsequent to His departure, Bahá'ís of North America tried time and again to offer Him money, to meet part or the whole of the expenses of His journey. They wrote or spoke to Him directly and sought the advice of the members of His retinue. 'Abdu'l-Bahá's response to all these appeals and approaches, while expressive of thankfulness, was totally in the negative. A large sum of money, sent earlier to Him in Egypt, was returned. To Mrs Parsons, Mrs Goodall, Mrs Cooper and others well endowed with riches, as well as to the less affluent, He said that they should give the money they were offering Him to the poor and the deprived. As His departure from the United States drew nigh, a number of Bahá'ís decided to go to 'Abdu'l-Bahá and plead with Him to accept their gifts. On November 30th they went to Him and made their supplication. 'Abdu'l-Bahá told them: 'I am very thankful for your services. Indeed you served me well, showed me great hospitality. Day and night you rose up to serve; you strove hard to disseminate the fragrances of God. I shall never forget your services because you have no purpose other than to seek the good-pleasure of God, and look for no station save entry into the Kingdom of God. Now you have brought gifts for the members of my family. These gifts are exquisite and most acceptable; but better than all these gifts are the gifts of the love of God to be preserved in the treasure-houses of the hearts. These gifts are evanescent, but those gifts are ever-lasting. These jewels should be kept in boxes and vaults, and in the end they perish. But those jewels remain in the treasure-houses of the hearts, and shall remain in the worlds of God forevermore. In my home they do not use diamond rings. They do not keep rubies. That home is free of such allurements. Now I have accepted these gifts, but I leave them in trust with you to sell them and send the money for the Ma<u>sh</u>riqu'l-A<u>dh</u>kár in Chicago.' The Bahá'ís renewed their plea, but 'Abdu'l-Bahá was adamant: 'I want to take on your behalf a gift which shall remain uncorrupted in the world of eternity: jewels that should belong to the treasuries of hearts; that is better.'[206]

'Abdu'l-Bahá sailed for Europe on December 5th. On board the S.S. *Celtic*, He bade farewell to the Bahá'ís of America:

This is my last meeting with you, for now I am on the ship ready to sail away. These are my final words of exhortation. I have repeatedly summoned you to the cause of the unity of the world of humanity, announcing that all mankind are the servants of the same God; that God is the Creator of all; He is the Provider and Life-giver; all are equally beloved by Him and are His servants upon whom His mercy and compassion descend. Therefore you must manifest the greatest kindness and love toward the nations of the world, setting aside fanaticism, abandoning religious, national and racial prejudice.

The earth is one nativity, one home, and all mankind are the children of one Father. God has created them and they are the recipients of His compassion. Therefore if any one offends another, he offends God. It is the wish of our heavenly Father that every heart should rejoice and be filled with happiness; that we should live together in felicity and joy. The obstacle to human happiness is racial or religious prejudice, the competitive struggle for existence and inhumanity toward each other . . .

Beware lest ye offend any heart, lest ye speak against any one in his absence, lest ye estrange yourselves from the servants of God. You must consider all His servants as your own family and relations. Direct your whole effort toward the happiness of those who are despondent, bestow food upon the hungry, clothe the needy and glorify the humble. Be a helper to every helpless one and manifest kindness to your fellow creatures in order that ye may attain the good-pleasure of God. This is conducive to the illumination of the world of humanity and eternal felicity for yourselves. I seek from God everlasting glory in your behalf; therefore this is my prayer and exhortation.

. . . your efforts must be lofty. Exert yourselves with heart and soul so that perchance through your efforts the light of Universal Peace may shine and this darkness of estrangement and enmity may be dispelled from amongst men; that all men may become as one family and consort together in love and kindness; that the East may assist the West and the West give help to the East— for all are the inhabitants of one planet, the people of one original nativity and the flocks of one shepherd.

. . . Consider the heedlessness of the world, for notwithstanding the efforts and sufferings of the Prophets of God, the nations and peoples are still engaged in hostility and fighting. Notwithstanding the heavenly commandments to love one another, they are still shedding each other's blood . . . Although they are the children of a compassionate God, they continue to live and act in opposition to His will and good-pleasure . . .

Your duty is of another kind, for you are informed of the mysteries of God. Your eyes are illumined, your ears are quickened with hearing. You must therefore look toward each other and then toward mankind with the utmost love and kindness. You have no excuse to bring before God if you fail to live according to His command, for you are informed of that which constitutes the good-pleasure of God. You have heard His commandments and precepts. You must therefore be kind to all men; you must even treat your enemies as your friends. You must consider your evil-wishers as your well-wishers. Those who are not agreeable toward you must be regarded as those who are congenial and pleasant; so that perchance this darkness of disagreement and conflict may disappear from amongst men and the light of the Divine may shine forth; so that the Orient may be illumined and the Occident filled with fragrance; nay, so that the East and

West may embrace each other in love and deal with one another in sympathy and affection. Until man reaches this high station, the world of humanity shall not find rest, and eternal felicity shall not be attained. But if man lives up to these Divine commandments, this world of earth shall be transformed into the world of heaven and this material sphere shall be converted into a paradise of glory. It is my hope that you may become successful in this high calling, so that like brilliant lamps you may cast light upon the world of humanity and quicken and stir the body of existence like unto a spirit of life. This is eternal glory. This is everlasting felicity. This is immortal life. This is heavenly attainment. This is being created in the image and likeness of God. And unto this I call you, praying to God to strengthen and bless you.[207]

Then 'Abdu'l-Bahá was gone.

PART III

EUROPE AND THE CLOSING YEARS

CHAPTER 19

THE SECOND VISIT TO BRITAIN

The White Star liner S.S. *Celtic* docked at Liverpool on Friday, December 13th 1912. Hippolyte Dreyfus-Barney from Paris, Elizabeth Herrick and Isabel Fraser of London, E. T. Hall and John Craven of Manchester, John Downs of Leeds, and 'Abdu'l-Bahá's son-in-law, Áqá Ahmad-i-Yazdí, were at the quayside. The members of His retinue, who had crossed the Atlantic with Him, were Mírzá Mahmúd-i-Zarqání, Siyyid Asadu'lláh-i-Qumí and Mírzá Ahmad Sohráb. In Liverpool, 'Abdu'l-Bahá stayed at the Adelphi Hotel. On December 14th, He addressed the Theosophical Society of that city, and on Sunday He spoke from the pulpit of the Pembroke Chapel. Sarah Ann Ridgeway,* the Bahá'í pioneer of the North of England, who had been unable to travel to Liverpool on Friday, came the next day to attain once more the presence of 'Abdu'l-Bahá. She had met Him first in London, in September of the previous year. Now, she had only a few more months to live; she died on May 11th 1913.

'Abdu'l-Bahá left for London on December 16th. Lady Blomfield with her daughters, as well as Ethel Rosenberg, Mrs Thornburgh-Cropper, Elsie Lee, Annie Gamble, Lutfu'lláh Hakím, Arthur Cuthbert and a number of other Bahá'ís were awaiting His arrival at the station. Lady Blomfield had moved out of her flat in Cadogan Gardens to put it once again at the disposal of 'Abdu'l-Bahá. The following day, Miriam Thornburgh-Cropper held a reception, where

* See n. 58.

'Abdu'l-Bahá spoke of His American tour. It seemed that 'Abdu'l-Bahá's first visit to the British metropolis was being re-enacted. There was, as before, a stream of visitors to 97 Cadogan Gardens: people from every walk of life came at all hours of the day and into the night. One day a lady arrived, who had not previously asked for an interview. There were others to meet 'Abdu'l-Bahá and she was told that it was not possible to see Him. She walked away, sad and forlorn; but before she had reached the street door someone, hurrying down the stairs, called her back: ' 'Abdu'l-Bahá will see you.' Leaving His visitors, He had walked to the door of the drawing-room and had told those who were in the hall: 'A heart has been hurt. Hasten, hasten, bring her to me.'

There was another occasion when a visitor came unexpectedly. Two ladies had arrived from Scotland to meet 'Abdu'l-Bahá, planning to take the night train back. Lady Blomfield had ensured that they would have an hour or two in the company of the Master, uninterrupted by anyone else. Then a journalist arrived. Breezy in manner, he crossed his legs, lighted a cigarette unasked, and kept up a barrage of questions. He was going to write an article and wanted a few telling points. Lady Blomfield and the ladies from Scotland were shocked, indeed scandalized. Shortly, 'Abdu'l-Bahá rose to His feet and beckoned the cheeky man to follow Him to another room.

'We looked at one another,' Lady Blomfield writes. 'The bore had gone, yes, but alas! so also had the Master.' (How well the present writer recalls Lady Blomfield relating this incident, and putting stress on the word 'bore'.)

Some time passed, and then Lady Blomfield sent a message by one of His attendants to 'Abdu'l-Bahá: 'Will you kindly say to 'Abdu'l-Bahá that the ladies with whom the appointment has been made are awaiting His pleasure.'

To their great delight, the ladies heard, very soon after,

the footsteps of 'Abdu'l-Bahá as He accompanied the 'bore' to the door of the flat. Then 'Abdu'l-Bahá came in, stopped in the doorway, looked at them gravely and said: 'You were making that poor man uncomfortable, so strongly desiring his absence; I took him away to make him feel happy.' 'Truly 'Abdu'l-Bahá's thoughts and ways were far removed from ours!' Lady Blomfield comments.[208]

Another day, a man, obviously battered by the world, came also without prior appointment. He had walked thirty miles to be there, and asked to see Lady Blomfield. He had a tragic tale to tell: 'I was not always as you see me now, a disreputable, hopeless object. My father is a country rector, and I had the advantage of being at a public school. Of the various causes which led to my arrival at the Thames embankment as my only home, I need not speak to you. Last evening I had decided to put an end to my futile, hateful life, useless to God and man. Whilst taking what I had intended should be my last walk, I saw "a Face" in the window of a newspaper shop. I stood looking at the face as if rooted to the spot. He seemed to speak to me, and call me to him. I read that he is here, in this house. I said to myself, "If there is in existence on earth that personage, I shall take up again the burden of my life" . . . Is he here? Will he see me? Even me?' Lady Blomfield said that of course He would.

'Abdu'l-Bahá Himself opened the door to the wretched tramp, His hand extended, His welcome warm and affectionate. Every word, every gesture indicated that 'Abdu'l-Bahá was indeed pleased and delighted to have this unexpected visitor. Other visitors, suitably dressed for a social call, looked surprised and astonished. The tramp, his head bowed, sat on a low chair next to 'Abdu'l-Bahá, Who took his hand and stroked his matted hair, and spoke to him: 'Be happy! Be happy! Do not be filled with grief when humiliation overtaketh thee. The bounty and power of God is without limit for each and every soul in the world. Seek for spiritual joy and knowledge, then, though thou walk upon this earth, thou wilt be dwelling within the divine realm. Though thou be poor, thou mayest be rich in the Kingdom of God.'

When the man rose to go, he was no longer a dejected tramp. To Lady Blomfield he said: 'Please write down for me His words. I have attained all I expected, and even more.'[209]

A visitor of a totally different category was the Prince Jalálu'd-Dawlih—the same prince during whose governorship the Bahá'ís of Yazd and its environs had suffered barbarous persecutions, in the year 1903 (see p. 103). He was now a broken man and an exile, seemingly contrite, asking for forgiveness. He threw himself at 'Abdu'l-Bahá's feet, but 'Abdu'l-Bahá would not permit him to humiliate himself.

Professor Edward Granville Browne visited 'Abdu'l-Bahá on December 18th.[210] It is certain that they had not met during 'Abdu'l-Bahá's previous visit to England. A letter from 'Abdu'l-Bahá to Edward Browne, preserved in Cambridge University Library, provides the definite evidence. Zarqání's Diary mentions only two meetings during 'Abdu'l-Bahá's second visit to London, whereas Lady Blomfield writes: 'Professor Edward Granville Browne, who had written much concerning the Bábís and the Bahá'ís, came from time to time, speaking in Persian with the Master, Who was delighted to see him, and talked over many things, especially the momentous occasion when that intrepid Cambridge Orientalist succeeded in obtaining permission to enter the presence of Bahá'u'lláh.'[211]

Ḥájí Abu'l-Ḥasan-i-Ardakání, better known as Ḥájí Amín (see p. 29) arrived from Paris on December 19th.[212] This well-tried veteran of the Faith had seen some of its darkest days. His visit to London was nearly miraculous and provided an incident which greatly amused 'Abdu'l-

Bahá. Hájí Amín's first attempt to reach London from Paris had ended when, in some inexplicable way, he found himself back in the French capital after crossing the Channel. Of course he could not speak either English or French, nor for that matter any other European language. He had names and addresses written out for him to show to officials and conductors, to help him on his journey. When, at last, Hájí Amín arrived in London, 'Abdu'l-Bahá laughingly told him that no doubt the Hájí could not forsake the delights of Paris and had to hurry back there.

The first public meeting which 'Abdu'l-Bahá addressed on this second visit to London was held at the Westminster Hotel, in the evening of December 20th. Sir Thomas Barclay was in the chair. Mrs Despard,* the famous suffragette leader, was present, and after 'Abdu'l-Bahá had given His address, both she and Alice Buckton spoke to express their gratitude and appreciation. When that most famous of all the suffragettes, Mrs Pankhurst, visited 'Abdu'l-Bahá and referred to Him as a 'prophet', He said with a broad smile: 'Oh, no! I am a man, like you.' A number of suffragettes, who called on Him on another occasion, were strongly advised to desist from violence, and to observe moderation. That was His counsel at all times.

Mushíru'l-Mulk,[213] the Persian Minister in London, visited 'Abdu'l-Bahá in the afternoon of December 20th. 'Abdu'l-Bahá told him of His work in America—'winning everlasting victories which will bring unfading glory to the peoples of the East'. Dúst-Muhammad Khán, the Mu'ayyiru'l-Mamálik, son-in-law of Násiri'd-Dín Sháh (reigned 1848–1896), and a prominent member of the Iranian aristocracy, had become so attached and devoted to the person of 'Abdu'l-Bahá that he was always seeking His presence, and could almost be counted a member of His retinue.

* Mrs Despard was the sister of Field-Marshal Sir John French, later the Earl of Ypres.

Alice Buckton's mystery play, *Eager Heart*, had its presentation at Church House, Westminster. 'Abdu'l-Bahá saw its performance on December 22nd. He had never before attended a theatre. In one of the scenes in which, despite all her longings and all the preparations she had made to receive the Messiah, Eager Heart failed to recognize the Infant Jesus and would not admit the Holy Family to her home, fatigued and hungry though they were, 'Abdu'l-Bahá was seen to be weeping. After the performance He joined the players on stage and spoke to them and the audience about the events which accompany the appearance of a Manifestation of God. That night after dinner, in the drawing-room of 97 Cadogan Gardens, He talked about Christ and His advent, about Christians of early days and particularly Mary Magdalene. Mary, He said, made her way to Rome, sought out the Emperor and interceded for the Jews whom Pontius Pilate was persecuting for having misled him to condemn Jesus to death. Christians, Mary told the Emperor, did not desire revenge. She begged him to send orders to Pilate to cease persecuting the Jews, and the Emperor complied with her wishes.

Nearly a month later, in the evening of January 17th, 'Abdu'l-Bahá told Gabrielle Enthoven: 'I will give you a play. It shall be called the Drama of the Kingdom.' The name that 'Abdu'l-Bahá had for Gabrielle Enthoven was 'Hamsáyih'—Neighbour—because she lived in the same block of flats. Mrs Enthoven did not write that play, but she allowed Mary Basil Hall* to do so.†

Reporters had a long interview with 'Abdu'l-Bahá on Christmas eve. As usual they wished to know where He had come from and why He was there in London. He told them

---

* Mary Blomfield, to whom 'Abdu'l-Bahá gave the name Parvine.

† See appendix I for 'Abdu'l-Bahá's outline of this drama, which was published in London in 1933.

of His journeys in the United States; of the conferences He had attended, the addresses He had delivered; of His aim and purpose to disseminate the Teachings of Bahá'u'lláh, to call upon the people to abandon their prejudices, realize their oneness, dwell in peace; for the greatest of all things in this epoch and era was the establishment of world peace, the uniting of religions and nations. He told them He was glad that London was the scene of a conference convened to terminate the war in the Balkans. Prior to His arrival in England, the London paper, the *Weekly Budget* of December 8th, had carried this item of news:

RETURN TO ENGLAND OF ABDUL BAHA

Persian Prophet Coming Back To London After Visit To U.S.

Abbas Effendi, or Abdul Baha (Servant of God), as he prefers to be called, is due to arrive in England on the *Celtic* on the 13th inst. By a strange coincidence he reaches London on the very day set for the peace negotiations.

Abdul Baha is known the world over as the Peace Prophet. With his father, the great Baha-u-llah, he suffered exile and willingly endured forty years in a Turkish prison rather than abjure his faith.

Baha-u-llah died in prison in 1892 and the universal religion which he revealed and which teaches how to attain to this 'most great peace', is being brought from the East to the West by the son Abdul Baha, who, through the advent of the Young Turks' supremacy, in 1908, gained his freedom. At that time the Young Turks' Committee of Union and Progress released all the political prisoners of the Ottoman Empire.

Since then he has travelled much. He was in London last year. It is said that there are upwards of 3,000,000 Bahais all over the world. Thousands have been thronging in America to hear his gentle message, which has constantly been alluded to by the Press as the most important

religious movement of the 'age'. He is returning to the
East, via London, and has been invited by wireless to
address the students at Oxford.

Tolstoy refers to Baha-u-llah in one of his books.
Speaking of the eternal enigma called life, and deploring
the fact that we spend our entire earth allotment of time
trying to solve the riddle, he goes on to add: 'But there
is a Persian prophet who holds the key.'

At the time of Tolstoy's death he was in communication
with Abdul Baha gathering material for a book on Baha-
u-llah.

Gertrude Atherton, in her new book on English life,
'Julia France and her Times', makes her heroine visit
Accre [sic] to see Abdul Baha and learn from him the
teachings which she epitomises as follows:

'The Bahai revelation makes its appeal to the brain, to
the advanced thinker, to those that feel the need of a
religion, but have long since outgrown all the silly old
dogmas, with their bathos and sentimentalities, primarily
intended only for the ignorant. Unity is right, freedom
of the political as well as the spiritual conscience, in other
words, the elimination of all that provokes war; which
means universal peace. Peace. Peace. Peace. That is the
keynote of the Bahai religion, as love was intended to be
of Christianity. All the best principles of the religions are
incorporated in this, all the barriers between them razed,
and all the nonsense and narrowmindedness left out.'

When 'Abdu'l-Bahá sat down to dinner on Christmas eve,
He said, playfully, that He was not hungry, but He had to
come to the dinner table because Lady Blomfield was very
insistent; two despotic monarchs of the East had not been
able to command Him and bend His will, but the ladies of
America and Europe, because they were free, gave Him
orders. Christmas day itself saw no diminution in the number
of visitors to 97 Cadogan Gardens. A lady who lived nearby
called early. She had come, she said, to be on Christmas day

in the presence of 'Abdu'l-Bahá, and in the company of the Bahá'ís of the East and the West. 'Abdu'l-Bahá told her that the Bahá'í Faith comprised all Faiths, and He quoted a line from Jalálu'd-Dín-i-Rúmí:*

Coming with a hundred, ninety is included therein.

Later, on Christmas day, He visited Lord Lamington (see p. 8). In the evening He went to a Salvation Army hostel, where some five hundred of society's wrecks were gathered. He spoke to them, and donated twenty guineas to the hostel to provide them with a good meal and another night, as His guests. He also inspected the sleeping accommodation of the hostel, and a children's home as well. When He reached Cadogan Gardens that night, it was apparent that the sight of the condition of the unfortunate had distressed Him. A good many of His talks, in His drawing-room during the Christmas week, were concerned with the Birth and the Advent of Christ and the significance of baptism. One day He walked for an hour or so in Hyde Park and Kensington Gardens. Afterwards He went to a Christmas party for the impoverished. Wherever He came across children He showed them such kindness and consideration that some of them thought He was Father Christmas, and sang a song in His praise. At His London home, that day, He related an incident of days long past in 'Akká:

'I encountered a number of the poor who were very hungry, and they came to me a-begging. I pointed out a grocer's shop to them that was well-provisioned, and told them to help themselves and eat all they could; I would be responsible. As soon as they heard me say that, those hungry ill-starred people made a rush and looted the shop. The shopkeeper was screaming that he was being robbed, but no one took any notice of him. They were eating even the

* The renowned mystic Persian poet, A.D. 1207–1273.

uncooked rice, and took provisions away with them.' Later, 'Abdu'l-Bahá compensated the grocer.

In the evening of that day, December 27th, Lady Blomfield held a reception and 'Abdu'l-Bahá spoke of the meeting of the East and the West.

One of 'Abdu'l-Bahá's visitors on December 29th was the Maharajah of Jhalawar. He was particularly devoted to the Master. In the afternoon Miss Annie Gamble* had a meeting at her home, and in the evening 'Abdu'l-Bahá spoke from a Methodist pulpit at King's Weigh House. The next day a Nineteen-Day Feast† was held at the home of Mrs Robinson. And on the last day of the year 'Abdu'l-Bahá visited Oxford to address a meeting at Manchester College.

The man who had taken the initiative to arrange that meeting was Thomas Kelly Cheyne, D. Litt., D.D. Lady Blomfield writes:

> The visit to Oxford was one of notable interest. The meeting between 'Abdu'l-Bahá and the dear, revered higher critic, Dr. T. K. Cheyne, was fraught with pathos. It seemed almost too intimate to describe, and our very hearts were touched, as we looked on, and realized something of the sacred emotions of that day.
>
> 'Abdu'l-Bahá embraced the Doctor with loving grace, and praised his courageous steadfastness in his life's work, always striving against increasing weakness, and lessening bodily health. Through those veiling clouds the light of the mind and spirit shone with a radiant persistence. The beautiful loving care of the devoted wife for her gifted, invalid husband touched the heart of 'Abdu'l-Bahá. With tears in His kind eyes He spoke of them to Mrs. Thornburgh-Cropper and myself on our way back to London.

* She was born in 1848, and lived to be ninety-nine.
† A gathering of Bahá'ís each Bahá'í month, for devotional, consultative, and social purposes.

'She is an angelic woman, an example to all in her unselfish love. Yes, she is a perfect woman. An angel.'

This lady was Elizabeth Gibson Cheyne, the very
specially gifted poetess.[214]

And Mírzá Maḥmúd-i-Zarqání writes:

On arriving at Oxford the Master first went to visit the
above-mentioned professor and conversed with him with
utmost kindness. And he showed the Master his writings
about the Faith, which he was continuing despite his
illness. In the condition he was in he was expressing his
faith and assurance with great fervour. His attitude of
belief and attentiveness so moved the Master that He,
several times, kissed him on the head and on the face, and
kept caressing his head. The Master had luncheon at the
home of Professor Cheyne.[215]

Cheyne, renowned as a higher critic, wrote an article on
the Faith which appeared in the *Christian Commonwealth*'s
issue of January 29th 1913. The next year, his book on the
Bábí and the Bahá'í Faiths, *The Reconciliation of Races and
Religions*, was published in London.* The chapter on 'Abdu'l-Bahá had the heading: 'Ambassador To Humanity'.
In the preface (pp. ix–x) he wrote:

Abdu'l Baha (when in Oxford) graciously gave me a
'new name'.† Evidently he thought that my work was
not entirely done, and would have me be ever looking
for help to the Spirit, whose 'strength is made perfect
in weakness'. Since then he has written me a Tablet
(letter), from which I quote the following lines:—

'*O thou my spiritual philosopher*,

'Thy letter was received. In reality its contents were
eloquent, for it was an evidence of thy literary fairness
and of thy investigation of Reality . . . There were

* See bibliography.   † Ruḥani (Spiritual).

many Doctors amongst the Jews, but they were all earthly, but St. Paul became heavenly because he could fly upwards. In his own time no one duly recognized him; nay, rather, he spent his days amidst difficulties and contempt. Afterwards it became known that he was not an earthly bird, he was a celestial one; he was not a natural philosopher, but a divine philosopher.

'It is likewise my hope that in the future the East and the West may become conscious that thou wert a divine philosopher and a herald to the Kingdom.'

Dr J. Estlin Carpenter,* Principal of Manchester College, presided at the meeting. He paid an eloquent tribute to 'Abdu'l-Bahá, to His work and the message which He had brought to the Western world. Although 'Abdu'l-Bahá's visit coincided with the Christmas vacation, a large audience gathered to hear Him speak. 'Abdu'l-Bahá spoke in particular of the place of science in the life of mankind, and of the supernatural which has dominion over nature. Afterwards, no one had any questions to put to Him. They were well content. Many of the academics met 'Abdu'l-Bahá later at the home of Dr and Mrs Cheyne. He returned to London in the evening.

Mrs Despard and a number of her colleagues in the Suffragette Movement arranged a meeting on January 2nd to hear 'Abdu'l-Bahá. Mrs Despard herself spoke first to present a brief history of the Faith. She mentioned Ṭáhirih as a pioneer. Lady Blomfield, too, spoke at that meeting. The Theosophical Society was the venue of 'Abdu'l-Bahá's public discourse the next day. On January 6th He travelled to

* Dr Carpenter in his book, *Comparative Religion* (London: Williams and Norgate, 1913), while referring to the Faith of the Báb and Bahá'u'lláh, writes: 'It, too, claims to be a universal teaching; it has already its noble army of martyrs and its holy books; has Persia, in the midst of her miseries, given birth to a religion which will go round the world?' (p. 71).

Edinburgh; for this journey Luṭfu'lláh Ḥakím joined His retinue.

'Abdu'l-Bahá was invited to Edinburgh by Dr and Mrs Alexander Whyte,* an invitation which had its origin in Mrs Whyte's visit to 'Akká in the year 1906. She wrote an account of it for the fourth volume of *The Bahá'í World* (1930–1932), which reflects so clearly her grasp of the universality of 'Abdu'l-Bahá's teaching that it seems pertinent to quote it here. There seems little doubt that Mrs Whyte's experience in 'Akká paved the way for the extraordinary reception accorded to 'Abdu'l-Bahá by leaders of thought in Edinburgh. This is her account:

> After retiring from his Chair in Edinburgh University Sir Alexander Simpson and my only sister Margo wintered in Egypt, 1905–6, and invited me and my friend, Mrs. Thornburgh-Cropper, to join them on their dahabeah. Mrs. Cropper had an invitation to visit 'Abbás Effendi, afterwards known as 'Abdu'l-Bahá, the leader of the Bahá'í Movement, then prisoner under the Turkish Government in the fort at 'Akká, and I was included in the invitation. Knowing of this possibility when in Cambridge some months before, I consulted Professor E. Granville Browne as to the proposed visit, and his answer was, 'Certainly, do not refuse so great an opportunity.'
>
> So it came that I spent two days in the prison-home of 'Abdu'l-Bahá . . .
>
> During the visit to the Tomb of Bahá'u'lláh, the figure of a boy was kneeling in rapt adoration, and the thought passed through my mind, 'What destiny lies before this

---

* The present writer met both Mrs Whyte and Alice Buckton sometime in the early thirties, at the home of Lady Blomfield, 8 Burgess Hill, London, N.W.2. Both were by then noticeably aged. Mrs Whyte had moved to London and lived very quietly at 22 Church Row, Hampstead. Alice Buckton was still active particularly for Chalice Well, Glastonbury.

boy (then 7 years old)?'* It was Shoghi Effendi, who, by his grandfather's will, has been, at the age of 24, made leader of the Movement.

Here let me include what I wrote of my visit in March 1906. High in a sea-girt fortress, overlooking the bay of 'Akká, is the prison-home of 'Abbás Effendi. The outlook at early dawn would awaken the dullest mind. From the tower sounds the Adhán, the call to prayer; from the fort the Turkish soldiers' reveille. Round the rocks which form the natural foundation of the house, break in unceasing roar the waves of the sea over which have come Crusaders and armies innumerable. As the mind's eye flashes back over history, it sees fleet after fleet, army after army led by all the chivalry of Europe, Dandolo, St. Louis, Richard Cœur de Lion, the very flower of Christendom, as it then understood itself. It recalls the passionate warfare of centuries, during which Cross and Crescent fought and the deadliest antagonism existed between Muslim and Christian.

Is it a small thing in the sight of the angels that a spirit is here which would shelter all nations, and inspires its followers to use every power and willingly shed their blood to reconcile these warring elements and spread the truth? That God, Who has spoken by all His prophets, has in these last times spoken among the Persians giving them a light which is leading them out into truth, freedom, love, so that they too, Muslims, use Christ's gospel as their own, and only long that all who name His Name be worthy of it?

The pilgrim to 'Akká is asked many questions on his return. Is this a prophet? A manifestation of divinity? In seeking an answer we must remember how easily, how constantly the East has ever used these names. And we must ask ourselves—what do we recognise as Divine? Is it enough of Divinity to see love made perfect through suffering a life-long patience, a faith which no exile or imprisonment can dim, a love which no treachery can

* In fact he was eleven years old.

alter, a hope which rises a pure clear flame after being drenched by the world's indifference through a lifetime? If that is not Divinity enough for this world, what is? There is no magic here; a material world today is too fond of seeking after magic, no magic but the old magic of Faith, Hope and Love. Or you ask, is this a progressive Movement, a step forward in the history of the world? Surely there can be no question as to the answer, for what do we find here? In the heart of a Turkish country, and at the centre of Muḥammadan power—that most conservative, cast-iron of systems conserved in a faith which is passionate, fierce, fanatical to the death—there to find preached freedom, education at all costs, absolute equality of men and women, the frank recognition of the value of Christian truth, the teaching that God has revealed Himself in all faiths, the love of God, and the brotherhood of all nations. What greater sign can you ask than the power to flood this old world with love and aspiration, with patience and courage? Where formerly after a foreigner had sat at table and used the cups, they must be broken, so great was the sense of contamination, now all are lovingly welcomed, everything is shared with love, warm, kindly, sympathetic love, and without money or price—ah! *that* the Western world will understand, if it understands nothing else. *Without money and without price, without bakhshish*, the curse of the East. Not the meanest servant would touch the Pilgrim's money. Is that Divine enough for our cold Western hearts who understand not the East, with its mystical longing, its patient age-long brooding over the mystery of life?

> '*The Roman legions thundered by*
> *She plunged in thought again.*'*
>
> .   .   .   .
>
> '*Oh, East is East, and West is West,*
> *And never the twain shall meet.*'

* A paraphrase from Matthew Arnold's *Obermann Once More.*

Not in Kipling's way will they meet, not in fleets and ironclads and armies, not in the 'Sergeant drilling Pharaoh's army'. No: but where the tides of faith rise, where love to God and service to man are flowing like a river,—there they meet and understand, and the deeper the understanding perhaps the more silent it is.

Let no one hearing of the teacher at 'Akká be disturbed and ask, how does this relate to my faith, my creed, my past experience? It disturbs nothing that is living or vital; it would only make Christians worthy of their great name.

But let everything that is dead, formal, Pharisaic, beware, for their day is over.

After the visit to the tombs the pilgrim will visit Bahjí, the garden where Bahá'u'lláh spent His days when the Turkish authorities gave him some relaxation of His prison rules. As he crosses the fields in Spring, the pilgrim's feet will be hidden by the red anemones and to the excited imagination of the devout their brilliant colour seems a symbol at once of the red page of martyrdom so keenly desired, so gladly secured by the martyrs of Shaykh Ṭabarsí, of Zanján and of Yazd, whose blood and passion has awakened to life thousands of sleeping hearts in Persia, and also of the glowing heart of love to God which shall yet unite East and West in one red flame.

However you look at this movement, or appraise its value—remember one thing—it is not centuries ago.

It is today. It is a living, growing vital force now, and may hold within itself the power to alter the destinies of millions of human beings. It has come at a time when conditions are entirely new, when conditions in interchange, communication, are universal, immediate, both on the material and probably also on the psychic plane. Him they gladly call Master has said that soon meetings will be held in Ṭihrán, in Washington, St. Petersburg, and London, all moved at one time by one spirit.

It has the vital force of the early Christian faith shown in glad martyrdom, in loving union, in happy service.

The blood of the martyrs of Shaykh Ṭabarsí, of Zanján, of Yazd, has not been shed in vain.

The early passion for the love of God, for truth and freedom, shown by the Báb and by Qurratu'l-'Ayn have kindled a fire which will not go out until many torches are lighted.

The wisdom and dignity of Him they call the Manifestation, and the laws given by Him have laid the foundations of a roadway, and now the Christ-like patience, love and tenderness of the Master and his illuminative interpretation of the Tablets and of current history shed light on the daily path of all who are privileged to know him. 'We may be separated in the body but we may all meet in the Spirit.'

Many of the laws cannot be acted upon at present under conditions of exile, imprisonment, persecution, daily hazard to life of all concerned. These relate in detail to education, condition of women, conditions of married life, women's property, and multitudes of other subjects, in which the East lingers behind the West, and many in which both West and East have much still to fulfil. The teaching is very clear as to the evil of begging or living on charity—everyone must work, or must have a profession or trade by which he can be independent.

The love of God is the way to all good.

All ways are acceptable to God and all have borne fruit.

Circumstances arose which obliged Mrs. Thornburgh-Cropper and myself to leave 'Akká suddenly.

His life, as the prisoner of the Sulṭán, was in continual danger by any sudden pressure from Constantinople and at that time it was not considered wise that visitors from the West should be too much in evidence. So it came that we could not have the farewell conversation we had promised ourselves. Instead I left a letter for him. In due time an answer came,* which has been translated into English by Munavvar <u>Kh</u>ánum. Here it is:

'May God illumine her face with the light of His love.

'Oh thou who art attracted by the love of God! I have read the letter which you wrote before leaving, and from its contents I became happy. I hope that your inner sight will be opened in such a manner that the realities of heavenly mysteries will become clear and apparent to you . . .

'Oh respected one! All prophets were sent and Christ manifested, and the Blessed Perfection also proclaimed the Word of God for this aim, that the world of humanity may become a heavenly world; the earthly, divine; the dark, enlightened; the satanic, angelic; and that unity, harmony and love may be produced between all the people of the world; that the essential union may appear, the foundation of disunion may be destroyed, and that everlasting life and grace may be the result.

'Oh esteemed one! Reflect upon the world of existence; union, harmony and intercourse is the cause of life, while dispersion and disunion is the cause of death.

'When you look at all the beings, you will see that each being found existence through the mingling of different elements, and when this combination of elements is dispersed, and unity is replaced by disunion, that existing being becomes non-existent and annihilated.

'Oh revered one! [Shoghi Effendi's translation begins here.] In cycles gone by, though harmony was established, yet, owing to the absence of means, the unity of all mankind could not have been achieved. Continents remained widely divided, nay even among the peoples of one and the same continent association and interchange of thought were well nigh impossible. Consequently intercourse,

* This Tablet of 'Abdu'l-Bahá is known as the Seven Lights or Candles of Unity. A section translated by Shoghi Effendi, and quoted in *The Goal of a New World Order*, is inserted in lieu of the original translation. (Cited *The World Order of Bahá'u'lláh*, pp. 38–9.)

understanding and unity amongst all the peoples and kindreds of the earth were unattainable. In this day, however, means of communication have multiplied, and the five continents of the earth have virtually merged into one. [The next sentence is from the original translation.] Individual travelling to all places and the exchange of ideas with all the people is facilitated and practicable to the greatest degree; it is such that each person through published news is able to be informed of the condition, religions and ideas of all nations. [Shoghi Effendi's translation is resumed here.] In like manner all the members of the human family, whether peoples or governments, cities or villages, have become increasingly interdependent. For none is self-sufficiency any longer possible, inasmuch as political ties unite all peoples and nations, and the bonds of trade and industry, of agriculture and education, are being strengthened every day. Hence the unity of all mankind can in this day be achieved. Verily this is none other but one of the wonders of this wondrous age, this glorious century. Of this past ages have been deprived, for this century—the century of light— has been endowed with unique and unprecedented glory, power and illumination. Hence the miraculous unfolding of a fresh marvel every day. Eventually it will be seen how bright its candles will burn in the assemblage of man.

'Behold how its light is now dawning upon the world's darkened horizon. The first candle is unity in the political realm, the early glimmerings of which can now be discerned. The second candle is unity of thought in world undertakings, the consummation of which will ere long be witnessed. The third candle is unity in freedom which will surely come to pass. The fourth candle is unity in religion which is the corner-stone of the foundation itself, and which, by the power of God, will be revealed in all its splendour. The fifth candle is the unity of nations—a unity which in this century will be securely established, causing all the peoples of the world to regard themselves as citizens of one common fatherland. The sixth candle is unity of races, making of all that dwell on earth peoples and kindreds of one race. The seventh candle is unity of language, i.e., the choice of a universal tongue in which all peoples will be instructed and converse. Each and every one of these will inevitably come to pass, inasmuch as the power of the Kingdom of God will aid and assist in their realization. [Shoghi Effendi's translation ends here.] Consider that in Persia, there were so many different classes, antagonistic sects and diverse ideas, that it was in a worse condition than the whole world; but now through the Holy Breath (of the Spirit) it has attained to such a degree of union and connection that these different people, antagonistic creeds, hostile classes, are as one soul. You will see them associating, conversing and communing with one another in perfect love, union, and fraternity. In large meetings, you see Christians, Jews, Zoroastrians and Muslims associating, and conversing with one another in perfect union, brotherhood, love, freedom, happiness and joy. There is no difference between them. Consider what the power of the Greatest Name has done . . .'

Dr Alexander Whyte was a prominent minister of the United Free Church of Scotland, well-known in academic circles. His son, Frederick Whyte, was a Member of Parliament at Westminster who, in later years, distinguished himself in the Colonial Service. The manse at 7 Charlotte Square, the home of Dr and Mrs Whyte, was attached to St George's United Free Church which is now known as St George's West.

On the train 'Abdu'l-Bahá told His attendants that they were going to a city where the work of teaching the Cause was just starting and that they should associate with the people with exemplary devotion. Then He told them the story of the Ṣúfí leader, Núr-'Alí Sháh, who had to flee his homeland because of the hostility of government and people, could not dwell in peace even in the neighbourhood of the holy Shrines of 'Iráq due to the opposition of the divines, and died an outcast in Baghdád. A few who had remained faithful to him in adversity, though heavily burdened with the cares of the world, pledged themselves not to allow the memory of their master to fade away. They arose with sincerity and determination and, although their work was not of high import, their success was great. How confirmed, said 'Abdu'l-Bahá to His attendants, *they* would be, whose task was to serve the Cause of Bahá'u'lláh, should they arise with equal devotion.

Dr and Mrs Whyte offered to 'Abdu'l-Bahá the hospitality of their home. He accepted their invitation, but took only one interpreter with Him. The rest of His attendants were housed in a nearby hotel. That same evening a number of the eminent citizens of Edinburgh came to Dr Whyte's home to meet 'Abdu'l-Bahá. The next day (January 7th) He drove in the morning to Castle Hill to visit the Outlook Tower museum. Professor Sir Patrick Geddes, a man renowned for his pioneering work in the field of education and social reform, the founder and president of the Outlook Tower Society, was there to receive 'Abdu'l-Bahá and show Him round that very interesting museum of history, sociology, and geography. Later in the day 'Abdu'l-Bahá drove down the Royal Mile and past Holyrood Palace, the ancient home of Scottish kings, and along the equally famous King's Drive.*

In the evening He addressed the Esperanto Society at the Freemasons' Hall in George Street. Their impressive programme, with 'Abdu'l-Bahá's photograph, announced the gathering as a 'Meeting of Edinburgh Citizens to Greet Abdul Baha (Abbas Effendi)'. The hall was packed. Many were standing and some three hundred had, perforce, to stay outside. Andrew Wilson, Special Councillor of the British Esperanto Association, greeted 'Abdu'l-Bahá on

* Now Queen's Drive.

behalf of the Esperantists, and the Reverend Dr John Kelman, who was in the chair, said:

> The spirit of God is working far beyond the limits of the Christian Church, or of the Christian nations. Christ's revelation, although final, is not yet closed, but is open to receive much interpretation and enrichment as centuries go on. In the West, we have built up a civilisation with much in it that is great and splendid, but its vitality has tended to grow feverish. Therefore, let us admire and welcome peace, love, and beauty, from whatever land or in whatever tongue they come.

'Abdu'l-Bahá's address was chiefly concerned with an auxiliary international language. Sir Patrick Geddes spoke afterwards to propose a vote of thanks.

The manse in Edinburgh's beautiful Charlotte Square now resembled 97 Cadogan Gardens in London. Visitors were constantly arriving. In the afternoon of January 8th a large body of Eastern students came—Egyptians, Indians, and Japanese—from the university. Early that evening 'Abdu'l-Bahá addressed a meeting at Rainy Hall, New College, The Mound, held under the auspices of the Outlook Tower Society. Sir Patrick Geddes presided. The *Scotsman* of January 9th carried a full report of 'Abdu'l-Bahá's discourse. He thus opened His address:

> I have pleasure in presenting myself to this gathering, so that I may explain to you certain of the principles of Bahá'u'lláh.
>
> Nearly sixty years ago, at a time when the Orient was engaged in warfare, when there was enmity between the different religions, . . . Bahá'u'lláh appeared. Darkness brooded over the horizon of the Orient; foul clouds of ignorance hid the sky; religious prejudice prevailed. The peoples of the Orient were as though submerged in a sea

of blind dogma and tradition. The votaries of the different religions hated each other; they never associated with each other in the same building. Had they done so, they would have considered themselves contaminated . . . Bahá'u'lláh, under such conditions, appeared, and boldly proclaimed the doctrine of the oneness of the whole of humanity.

Then He spoke of principles of the Faith concerning the 'Unity of Race', 'International Peace', 'Science and Religion', 'Religious and Racial Prejudice', the 'Equality of Men and Women', 'Universal Education', 'The Solution of the Economic Problem', and thus ended His talk: 'There are many other principles, but I have spoken [of] a few of them to you, and from these you will understand the *spirit* of the Bahá'í Revelation.'

Sir Patrick Geddes, in thanking 'Abdu'l-Bahá said:

This is a plant which has spread rapidly in the Persia of today. Yet one recognises in it a great similarity to plants that are growing near home. What struck me when 'Abdu'l-Bahá was speaking, was that He was giving expression to some wishes of our own hearts. We approve of the ideal He lays before us of education and the necessity of each one learning a trade, and His beautiful simile of the two wings on which society is to rise into a purer and clearer atmosphere, put into beautiful words what was in the minds of many of us. What impressed us most is that courage which enabled Him, during long years of imprisonment, and even in the face of death, to hold fast to His convictions.

The Reverend A. B. Robb, who followed, said:

We have been in the habit of sending missionaries from the West to the East to preach the Gospel. Today we have a missionary from the East to preach the old Gospel in a new and original way. After all, it is not the words which have impressed us so much as the life. He has a right to speak, for He has spent forty years of His life in prison for the sake of the truth which was revealed to Him. Dr. Kelman said last night that 'Abdu'l-Bahá was not here to proselytize. I am not so sure of that. I feel we are not preaching the Gospel we have heard to-day, though we are all longing to preach it, and perhaps 'Abdu'l-Bahá's address will give us some assistance to do so.

Dr Drummond spoke next to thank and praise 'Abdu'l-Bahá.

After 'Abdu'l-Bahá had left for London, a letter appeared in the Edinburgh *Evening News* of that city, on January 11th, over the signature: 'Old Paths'. Whoever 'Old Paths' was, he severely took to task the ministers of the church who had praised 'Abdu'l-Bahá. This one sentence is enough to show the stand of the writer: 'It is needless to say that the whole group of such phantasies utterly ignores the Fall and consequent depravity of the human race by nature, and, of course, repudiates the necessity of the New Birth, apart from which our Lord Himself declared it is impossible even to see the Kingdom of God.' Two days later, Miss E. H. C. Pagan made a spirited reply to 'Old Paths' in the pages of the same newspaper. She wrote:

In speaking of Bahaism, 'Old Paths' declares that there is not a fundamental doctrine in the word of God of which this so-called 'gospel' is not a negation. Now what are the fundamental doctrines of the word of God? If we go to the Fountainhead and ask 'Which is the greatest commandment of the Law?' we shall be told 'Thou shalt love the Lord thy God with all thy heart, and with all thy soul, and with all thy mind . . . And the second is like unto it. Thou shalt love thy neighbour as thyself. On these two commandments hang all the law and the prophets' (Matt. xxii. 36–40). Now in what sense is

Bahaism a negation of these two laws? The words of Bahá'u'lláh are 'O people of the world, the Creed of God is for love and union, make it not to be a cause of discord and dissension . . .'*

In the afternoon of January 9th, a number of well-known suffragettes and a number of prominent men opposed to them gathered at the manse to hear 'Abdu'l-Bahá. His tone and counsel of moderation subdued the audience. The evening of the same day, 'Abdu'l-Bahá spoke before the Theosophical Society of Edinburgh, at 28 Great King Street. Theosophists of neighbouring districts had come as well, and there was not room in that spacious hall for all who attended the meeting. David Graham Pole, the secretary of the Society, said in his opening remarks: ' 'Abdu'l-Bahá has tremendous spiritual powers. In my opinion, He is the focal point of the spiritual, intellectual, and theological forces of the present and future centuries.' At that very meeting the spiritual powers of 'Abdu'l-Bahá were particularly witnessed, even before He spoke, for He arrived very tired. Seated on the platform He looked exhausted. Lady Blomfield writes: 'Then, seeming to gather strength, He arose, and with voice and manner of joyous animation, and

---

* In the year 1947, when, as part of the Six Year Teaching Plan of the Bahá'ís of the British Isles, a fresh effort was being made in Edinburgh to bring the Teachings of Bahá'u'lláh to the notice of the public, at one of the meetings, held for that purpose, one or two men apparently of the ilk of 'Old Paths' vehemently attacked the Faith and its Founders. From the midst of the audience an old, shrivelled man, hitherto unnoticed, rose up to repudiate their arguments. He said that he counted it as the greatest boon of his life when, years before, in their city of Edinburgh, 'Abdu'l-Bahá had touched his head to give him His blessings. That old man, then retired, had been a noted physician and surgeon of Edinburgh. Dr Johnson, in the evening of his life, devoted his remaining days with vigour and youthful zest to the service of the Faith of Bahá'u'lláh.

eyes aglow, He paced the platform with a vigorous tread, and spoke with words of great power.'[216] He spoke of the renewal of religion from age to age. That night, He was the guest of the Theosophical Society for dinner, autographed a number of His own photographs which some of the members had, prayed for a young couple about to be married who, kneeling before Him, asked for His blessing, and wrote this prayer in the Society's book: 'He is God. O Lord! Cast a ray from the Sun of Truth upon this Society that it may be illumined'.

The next day 'Abdu'l-Bahá returned to London. Mrs Whyte wished to meet the hotel bill of 'Abdu'l-Bahá's attendants, but He would not accept her offer. Even more, He donated ten guineas to a charity sponsored by Mrs Whyte, and gave a guinea each to the household staff of the manse. They were overwhelmed by His kind words and attention to them. Tears welled in their eyes. Dr Whyte had expressed his own feelings, the day the Eastern students had come to the manse: 'Dear Master! In my time I have had many meetings in this house, but never have I seen a gathering like this. It reminds me of the words of St Paul that God "hath made of one blood all nations of men" (Acts xvii. 26), and of the words of Christ: ". . . they shall come from the east, and from the west, and from the north, and from the south, and shall sit down in the kingdom of God" ' (Luke xiii. 29).[217]

On January 11th, 'Abdu'l-Bahá addressed a large meeting at Caxton Hall, Westminster. Two eminent Persians were present. They marvelled at the powers which 'Abdu'l-Bahá had at His command, and at the appreciation and devotion displayed by the Westerners all around them. In the evening of the 14th, Mushíru'l-Mulk, the Persian Minister in London, gave a dinner party for 'Abdu'l-Bahá at the Legation. The Minister and his staff rejoiced over the news of 'Abdu'l-Bahá's visit to Scotland, the reception accorded

'ABDU'L-BAHÁ IN LONDON, 1911

'ABDU'L-BAHÁ IN CHICAGO, 1912

to Him in Edinburgh, the reports which had appeared in the press. That 'Abdu'l-Bahá had indeed brought glory to the people of the Orient was evident to them all, even as He had described it to the Minister, in their first meeting.

Another dinner party given for 'Abdu'l-Bahá was at the home of Sir Richard and Lady Stapley on January 12th. After dinner in the drawing-room, Sir Richard's distinguished guests were addressed by 'Abdu'l-Bahá. Following His address many questions were put to Him. He was asked whether unruly children should receive corporal punishment. His answer was very clear: not even the animal should be beaten. He was asked if, when a country was in a state of disorder and its people were oppressing one another, the people of another country should intervene to protect the weak. He said that mankind was one family, the earth was one homeland; there must be co-operation and mutual aid and protection, but intervention should be free of self-interest, and sound counsel should aim at reconciliation.

During the early part of January London skies had been very blue, but on the 13th thick fog descended. 'Abdu'l-Bahá spoke at Cadogan Gardens on the darkness of superstitions and imitations which cloud the Sun of Truth. The next day 'Abdu'l-Bahá visited the East End of London to speak at a Congregational church. Lady Blomfield writes: 'The congregation seemed spell-bound by the power which spread like an atmosphere from another, higher world.'[218]

'Abdu'l-Bahá travelled to Bristol on the 15th and stayed at the Clifton Guest House which belonged to Mr and Mrs Tudor-Pole. Dúst-Muḥammad Khán, the Mu'ayyiru'l-Mamálik, accompanied Him. In the evening He addressed a meeting in the Guest House, well-advertised in the newspapers and well-attended. Zarqání writes:

In the midst of it all [referring to the great reverence shown towards 'Abdu'l-Bahá by the members of the audience] I caught sight of Muʻayyiruʼl-Mamálik . . . I saw him standing awe-struck by the bows and curtseys of those outstanding people of the English nation . . . he was weeping, tears coursing down both cheeks, and that moved me so much that I was greatly affected, and wept and rejoiced too . . . In Britain, at large gatherings, I had noticed time and again the same reaction from men of his standing . . . who kept saying: ʻWhat great glory God conferred upon us . . . what a Sun of grandeur and felicity rose from the horizon of the East, but alas, alas, we did not heed it . . .ʼ[219]

ʻAbduʼl-Bahá returned to London the next day. Lady Blomfield presented Him with a statement regarding the Faith and ʻAbduʼl-Baháʼs presence in London which she wished to send to King George V, that perchance a meeting between the King and ʻAbduʼl-Bahá might be arranged. Lady Blomfield had connections with the Court, since her father-in-law, Dr Charles James Blomfield (1786–1857), Bishop of London for twenty-eight years, had been a tutor to Queen Victoria. ʻAbduʼl-Bahá expressed His admiration for the statement and its usefulness, but He advised against sending it to the King. He had come to the West, He said, to meet the poor, not monarchs and noblemen. However, He met any seeker with affection, but had no particular wish to meet the rulers. Moreover, He said, such moves could be misunderstood and misconstrued, and might create alarm.

On January 18th, ʻAbduʼl-Bahá went to the mosque at Woking, Surrey, to speak. Sir Richard and Lady Stapley escorted Him there in their automobile. First He had luncheon with a number of Muslim and Christian notables. The mosque itself could not hold the very large number of people gathered, comprising Turks, Indians, Egyptians, as well as British. He had to speak in the court outside. He was followed by Ameer Ali Syed, member of the Judicial

Committee of the Privy Council,* who paid Him high tribute. Lord Lamington had been unable to be present, and a deputy spoke on his behalf in terms of praise.

The next day, 'Abdu'l-Bahá was the guest of the Reverend Dr R. J. Campbell for luncheon. A number of divines had also been invited. 'Abdu'l-Bahá spoke to them of the meaning of the opening verses of the Gospel according to St John. In the evening of January 20th, a Rajput prince gave a dinner party for Him. 'Abdu'l-Bahá, in the course of His talk, spoke of the self-sacrifice of Kaykhusraw, a Bahá'í of Parsi origin. Sydney Sprague had fallen a victim to cholera in Punjab. When the Bahá'ís in Bombay heard of this, one of them named Kaykhusraw, with no thought of himself, rushed north to nurse him and was by his bedside day and night. Sprague recovered. Kaykhusraw contracted cholera and died.

In the afternoon of the 20th, Dr Felix Moscheles, who had spoken the praises of 'Abdu'l-Bahá at many a gathering, held a reception in his own home so that a number of notable people, who had hitherto not met 'Abdu'l-Bahá nor heard Him speak, would have this opportunity.

That evening He spoke at the Higher Thought Centre. It was His last engagement in London. On January 21st He left for Paris.

* And author of *The Spirit of Islam*, and other works.

CHAPTER 20

RETURN TO EUROPE

'Abdu'l-Bahá's second visit to Paris, which lasted several weeks, assumed certain characteristics of its own. He had few public engagements. But numbers of Bahá'ís had arrived from the East for the specific purpose of attaining His presence, such as the aforementioned Ḥájí Amín, Mírzá 'Azízu'lláh Khán-i-Varqá (the elder son of the martyr Varqá), Siyyid Aḥmad-i-Báqiroff, Mírzá Áqá Khán-i-Qá'im-Maqámí, and Mírzá 'Alí-Akbar-i-Rafsanjání. The last-named was sent by 'Abdu'l-Bahá to Switzerland, then to London and Stuttgart to teach the Faith. And so to them 'Abdu'l-Bahá gave much of His time. A photograph taken with Him under the arches of the Eiffel Tower shows that their number was not small.

Moreover, vicissitudes of fortune had brought to Paris a multitude of émigrés from Írán and the Ottoman Empire. These men were from the ranks both of reactionaries—supporters of the old régime—and of liberals and constitutionalists. Many of them sought 'Abdu'l-Bahá and requested to meet Him. To them, too, He gave of His time impartially. And there were some among the nobility of Írán, such as Mu'ayyiru'l-Mamálik, Intiẓámu's-Salṭanih and Mírzá Mihdí Khán-i-Ghaffárí,* who were unreservedly devoted to 'Abdu'l-Bahá and attended Him most of the time.

The Bahá'í community of Paris had fewer French than

* His titles were Vazír-Humáyún and Qá'im-Maqám; he had held ministerial posts under the old régime.

Americans, English and Persians. Hippolyte Dreyfus-Barney was in constant attendance upon 'Abdu'l-Bahá, as was M. Bernard who was killed in the first weeks of the Great War. Because of illness, 'Abdu'l-Bahá's movements were perforce restricted for a time, and He prolonged His stay in Paris. His drawing-room, however, was always thronged with visitors, as it had been in London, New York, Washington and San Francisco.

'Abdu'l-Bahá's Paris home was an apartment at 30 Rue St Didier which Hippolyte Dreyfus-Barney had rented for Him. In His drawing-room, during those weeks in Paris, 'Abdu'l-Bahá related many incidents and stories of earlier years in Írán, in Baghdád, in Adirnih, in 'Akká. He spoke on more than one occasion of the great Iranian statesman, Qá'im-Maqám-i-Faráhání,* Grand Vizier to Muḥammad Sháh. Had he not been put to death, 'Abdu'l-Bahá said, Írán would not have been ruined; moreover, had his country-men given ear, at a later time, to Divine counsel, ancient glory would not have departed.

On January 26th, 'Abdu'l-Bahá cabled to Áqá Muḥam-mad-Taqíy-i-Iṣfahání, a well-known Bahá'í of Cairo, to instruct that everything should be done for the comfort of Mírzá Abu'l-Faḍl, who, He said, was as His own self. News had reached Him of Mírzá Abu'l-Faḍl's failing health and powers. Ḥájí Amín, who was the trustee of the Huqúq,† had brought seven hundred pounds to present to 'Abdu'l-Bahá. In a humorous mood, 'Abdu'l-Bahá said that the Ḥájí had brought seven hundred pounds, but had already obtained a thousand pounds from Him for this and that. Zarqání comments that one indeed marvelled at the way

---

* Qá'im-Maqám-i-Faráhání was a close friend and associate of Mírzá Buzurg-i-Núrí, the father of Bahá'u'lláh. He was put to death in June 1835. Bahá'u'lláh extols him in one of His Tablets.

† An offering specified by Bahá'u'lláh.

'Abdu'l-Bahá administered His finances. He spent freely to uphold the dignity of the Faith, and gave generously to relieve distress and poverty, and to aid the sick. But He Himself did not possess a good winter coat. His attendants had to beg again and again to obtain His permission to order a new coat to be made for Him.

The Persian Minister in Paris, 'Abduṣ-Ṣamad Khán, the Mumtázu's-Salṭanih, called on 'Abdu'l-Bahá a week after His arrival. A number of noted Easterners were also present, who were united in saying that they felt very much at home in the presence of 'Abdu'l-Bahá. There was a samovar* in the drawing-room and tea was served in Persian fashion. 'Abdu'l-Bahá gave them an insight into the history of Islám and of Írán, telling them of events rarely recorded. That evening (January 27th) He returned the Minister's call.

'Abdu'l-Bahá was not sleeping well and occasionally fever troubled Him. But His engagements continued. Aḥmad Páshá and Munír Páshá,† prominent Ottomans of the old régime (together with their dependants) called on January 28th, as did a number of Persian notabilities. 'Abdu'l-Bahá told the latter that although the independence of Írán had been bartered away, there was no cause for despair. Írán would progress; her future was bright. He had spoken earlier of the dismal materialism overshadowing Paris, and He did so again the next day. In London He had felt happier because there was greater scope to disseminate the Faith.

'Abdu'l-Bahá wanted the Bahá'ís, who had come from

* A samovar, used by 'Abdu'l-Bahá in His travels, was given to Ziaullah Asgarzadeh (Díyá'u'lláh Aṣgharzádih), who left it to the Bahá'í Archives of the British Isles.

† Munír Páshá was Sulṭán 'Abdu'l-Hamíd's ambassador in Paris, who kept him constantly informed of the activities of exiled liberals, and warned him that the Young Turks and their Committee of Union and Progress were gaining ground. (See p. 123).

the East to visit Him, to have their meals daily in His Paris home. In the afternoon of January 29th, as 'Abdu'l-Bahá came from His room to the drawing-room and asked for tea, a visitor was announced whose presence there was most astonishing. This was Rashíd Páshá, an ex-válí of Beirut, whose overbearing attitude and hostility towards 'Abdu'l-Bahá, in the closing stages of His renewed incarceration within 'Akká, were notorious. 'Abdu'l-Bahá received him very kindly in His own room. Rashíd Páshá was now reverential and contrite. And the Bahá'ís present could not but look with great wonderment at what they were witnessing. With prompt courtesy, 'Abdu'l-Bahá returned Rashíd Páshá's call that very evening. When He came home that night, He related many incidents of the times when their afternoon visitor had held Syria in his grasp. In those days Rashíd Páshá had been after money from 'Abdu'l-Bahá and had sent his son to 'Akká, but 'Abdu'l-Bahá had paid scant attention to veiled hints. Then Rashíd Páshá himself came to Haifa and, although by official decree 'Abdu'l-Bahá was confined to the limits of the city walls, the Válí arranged with the Governor of 'Akká for 'Abdu'l-Bahá to see him in Haifa. Again 'Abdu'l-Bahá ignored all hints and allusions. As it happened, said 'Abdu'l-Bahá, the day we went to Haifa the Governor lost a valuable ring on the way. He told me of his loss on the return journey, and I assured him that he need not worry as it would be found. When we reached 'Akká I alighted by the goldsmith's shop, informed the goldsmith that a ring would be brought to him, and that he should bring it to me. Then I re-entered the carriage and went home with the Governor. The following morning the goldsmith brought me the very ring. I took it to the Governor who was amazed. He told Rashíd Páshá that 'Abbás Effendi knew Mawláná 'Alí's system of divination and had found his lost ring. Therefore, He should be left alone, for He was freely stating that should the whole world assemble and try to get Him out of prison, before the appointed time, they would find it an impossible task, but at the hour of liberation, if all the monarchs of the world should unite they would fail to deny Him His liberty. Since Rashíd Páshá had complete confidence in the Governor, he did, for some time, restrain his greed and halt his aggression.

A number of Iranian students visited 'Abdu'l-Bahá on January 31st. He spoke to them about agriculture and industry and commerce and told them that Írán needed iron-smelting plants, because industry and agriculture alike depended on foundries. In the evening of that day a meeting was held at the home of Monsieur and Mme Dreyfus-Barney. These weekly meetings of the Bahá'ís, to which seekers and enquirers came as well, were a regular feature of the life of the Paris community. Other homes, M. and Mme Scott's and Miss Edith Sanderson's, were also venues for these gatherings which 'Abdu'l-Bahá addressed from time to time.

One day 'Abdu'l-Bahá quoted a Persian verse that eating was for the purpose of living, and not the other way round. He also said that most Europeans were now acting as though man were made for work, and not work for man. Another day, after inspecting a children's home which was poorly supplied, He spoke of the many magnificent buildings kept solely for entertainment, while the poor were abandoned to such misery and wretchedness.

By the beginning of February Ríyáḍ Salím Effendi and Dr Ṣáliḥ, Bahá'ís of Egypt, had arrived, enlarging the ranks of visiting Bahá'ís. In the afternoon of February 6th, escorted by Hippolyte Dreyfus-Barney, 'Abdu'l-Bahá visited Versailles, and in the evening Professor 'Ináyatu'lláh Khán, an Indian who had called several times and asked to be permitted to present his art, sang and played his musical instrument. Afterwards 'Abdu'l-Bahá spoke about music and the celebrated Eastern musicians of bygone days. The strain on His health was now beginning to show. He was constantly seeing people and conversing with them. He said that His letters had been left unanswered; 'once I could get up at night and write, but I cannot do so now.'

On the evening of February 12th 'Abdu'l-Bahá was the guest of the Esperantists. Despite His increasing weakness He went to that banquet at Hôtel Moderne and delivered an address, and the next evening He addressed the Theosophists. On February 17th, He spoke at three meetings in the homes of Bahá'ís. That night He visited Pasteur Monnier's Theological Seminary and answered his questions. A statement He made, two days later, is of particular significance in the light of recent developments. He had been speaking of the great technological and scientific strides of the age; it would be meet, He said, if ways and means of reaching other planets were now devised.

Two Persians who detested each other came to call on Him on February 19th. As they arrived at the same time there was no turning back for either, but when they left they were happy and reconciled. A number of Persian students also called, some of whom were Bahá'ís; they were in Paris on government scholarships. As they were free, 'Abdu'l-Bahá asked them to spend the day there and expressed His hope that in the future they would contribute to the prosperity and well-being of Írán. Study those sciences, He said, that will benefit the nation. Some of them did rise to prominent positions in later years.

One of these Persian visitors, who had been several times to 30 Rue St Didier, told how he had been severely taken to task by a fanatical compatriot, and had written a long letter in reply. Zarqání quotes part of that letter:

... and thirdly, animals are tamed by kindness and affection; woe unto the man who would fall short of an animal. Fourthly, how can I fail to prize a person whom thousands have praised? Fifthly, if this revered being had no greatness in Him, then by what power has He established His authority among so many and captured the devotion of all these souls? Sixthly, the fact remains that, of all the fifteen million Persians, it is this high-minded man alone who, in an age such as this, has received such acclaim wherever He has gone. Even given that, as you say, He is not entitled to the rank and station attributed to Him, what doubt can there be about His other attainments? He brings glory to Írán and to the Orient.[220]

At the conclusion of the morning meeting on February 20th, Horace Holley's young child ran up to 'Abdu'l-Bahá. He picked the child up with great tenderness, and spoke of Ḥusayn, His own son, who had died in childhood. Ḥusayn used to creep into His bed, while He was asleep, and 'Abdu'l-Bahá said it was wonderful.

On February 21st, 'Abdu'l-Bahá gave a discourse at the Salle de Troyes. The meeting was arranged by *L'Alliance Spiritualiste*. Mme Jeanne Beauchamp recalled 'Abdu'l-Bahá's previous visit in 1911 and expressed their joy to welcome Him again. By the 26th 'Abdu'l-Bahá had succumbed to a severe cold, and the next day He could hardly speak. Yet He received visitors as He lay in bed.

In the meantime, the Bahá'ís of Germany had been pleading for 'Abdu'l-Bahá to visit their country, and on February 12th a letter had come from Budapest, from Mr and Mrs Stark, inviting Him to visit Hungary. During the first week of March, a number of Bahá'ís arrived from Germany, among them Miss Alma Knobloch, their pioneer teacher. They once again begged for the bounty of receiving Him. But 'Abdu'l-Bahá's health was still precarious, and His physical weakness precluded a long journey for the time being.

Whenever He could He would go out to return the visits of notables, such as the Iranian Minister in Paris and Munír Páshá. But His speaking at meetings, either in His own drawing-room or at the homes of the Bahá'ís of Paris, had to be halted. Professor and Mrs Edward Browne called on March 9th. 'Abdu'l-Bahá talked with Edward Browne for more than an hour. He was very tired that evening and spoke of hastening to the Holy Land.

'Abdu'l-Bahá moved from His apartment to a hotel in Rue Lauriston, near Place de l'Étoile, on March 19th; and there He celebrated the Festival of Naw-Rúz on the 21st. He had a number of guests for luncheon that day. Many of the Eastern notabilities, who called on Naw-Rúz, were much surprised to find themselves in His presence in each other's company. Only a few years earlier they would never have thought it possible. Later in the day 'Abdu'l-Bahá, accompanied by Hippolyte Dreyfus-Barney, went to the Iranian Legation, where He gave an address. And He spoke again that evening in the home of the Dreyfus-Barneys.

At last 'Abdu'l-Bahá was well enough to travel, on March 30th, to Stuttgart. His attendants were Siyyid Aḥmad-i-Báqiroff, Mírzá Maḥmúd-i-Zarqání, Siyyid Asadu'lláh and Mírzá Aḥmad Sohráb. 'Abdu'l-Bahá told them to change completely from Eastern garb to European dress, and to discard their oriental headgear. Bahá'ís of Stuttgart had not been informed of His departure from Paris, because He wished to arrive unannounced. German Bahá'ís had been told previously not to attempt to obtain any newspaper publicity for His visit to their country. He reached Stuttgart early in the evening of April 1st and took rooms in Hotel Marquardt, near-by the station, which was the best in the town. Then He let His attendants telephone to some of the Bahá'ís and inform them of His arrival. Much surprised, these Bahá'ís hurried to His hotel. 'Abdu'l-Bahá explained that He had wanted His arrival to be a complete surprise. He loved the Bahá'ís of Stuttgart, He said, and had spoken often of the sterling qualities of German Bahá'ís, of their sincerity and steadfastness; therefore the Faith would gain great strength in their midst.

Bahá'ís streamed into the hotel the next morning. It was planned that 'Abdu'l-Bahá would meet them at His hotel in the mornings, and at other times He would go out to meetings at their homes or elsewhere. That evening, as 'Abdu'l-Bahá's car drew up before the house where a meeting had been arranged, the cry of 'Yá Bahá'u'l-Abhá' went up from a large number gathered outside. The next day, 'Abdu'l-Bahá remarked that the hotelier might leave his hotel and seek refuge elsewhere, because of such numbers pouring in. Indeed the staff of the hotel were shaken and astonished to see so many of their countrymen pay such attention and respect to an Easterner who, as it seemed, had come from nowhere. One of the Bahá'ís asked 'Abdu'l-Bahá what to say when people enquired who He was. Tell them, He said, that He was a person calling men to the Kingdom of God, a promoter of the Faith of Bahá'u'lláh, a herald of peace and reconciliation, and an advocate of the oneness of humanity.

A clergyman of Stuttgart had been greatly impressed by *Some Answered Questions*,* and requested 'Abdu'l-Bahá's permission to translate the book into German. This permission was given to him; but to his next request to be permitted to communicate these teachings to the Kaiser, 'Abdu'l-Bahá replied that it was not advisable, because the Emperor was proud and would not deign to listen.

In the evening of April 3rd, 'Abdu'l-Bahá addressed a large audience in the upper hall of the City (Burger) Museum. Sohráb's English translation of 'Abdu'l-Bahá's talk was, in

* See pp. 82–3.

turn, rendered into German by Herr Eckstein. 'Abdu'l-Bahá
said:

I came from a distant land. I have travelled twenty
thousand miles until I came to you in Stuttgart. Forty
years I was a prisoner. I was young when I was put into
prison and my hair was white when the prison doors
opened. After all these long years of the sufferings of
prison life I willingly took upon myself all the hardships
of a long journey. Now I am here in order to be united
with you, in order to meet you. My purpose is that perchance you may illumine the world of humanity; that
all men may unite in perfect love and friendship; that
religious prejudices, national prejudices, race distinctions,
all may be completely abandoned. The religions of today
consist of dogmas. Because these dogmas differ from each
other, discord and even hatred is manifest. Religion must
be the basis of all good fellowship. Think of the turmoil
that today exists in the Balkans;* how much blood is
shed; how many thousands of mothers have lost their
sons, how many children have become orphans, and how
many buildings, villages, and cities have been destroyed!
The Balkan states have become a volcano. All this ruin
originates from the prejudices created by the different
dogmas, called forth by superstitions and race prejudices.

The essence of the religion of God is love, and the Holy
Books bear testimony to that, for the essence of the
religion of God is the light of the world of humanity; but
mankind today has forgotten what constitutes true religion. Each nation and each people today hold to some
definite dogma.

. . . These traditions and these dogmas are like the
husks surrounding the kernel. We must release the kernel
from the husk. The world of humanity is in the dark.
Our aim is to illumine mankind . . . It is our hope that

* War flared up again in the Balkans between February 3rd
1913, and April 23rd. It was followed by the third Balkan War
(May 19th–August 10th).

this darkness may be dispelled and that the rays of the Sun of Reality will shine again . . . This century is the century of light. This period is the period of science. This cycle is the cycle of reality. This age is the age of progress and freedom of thought. This day is the greatest day of the Lord . . . This time is the time in which all is resurrected into new life. Therefore, I desire that all may be united in harmony. Strive and work so that the standard of the world of human Oneness may be raised among men, so that the lights of universal peace may shine and the East and the West embrace, and the material world become a mirror of the Kingdom of God, that eternal light may shine forth and that the day [may] break which will not be followed by night . . .[221]

'Abdu'l-Bahá's visit to Esslingen was particularly moving and impressive. Anna Koestlin had organized a meeting (which was more like a festival) on behalf of the children whom she taught. Alma Knobloch wrote to her sister Pauline (Mrs Joseph Hannen) in America:

We have had some wonderful meetings; the one in Esslingen surpassed them all. It was the children's meeting, last Friday, April 4th, 1913, in the afternoon. They had secured a very pretty hall, which was most beautifully decorated with greens, plants and flowers, with large and small tables near the walls and round tables in the center. About fifty children and eighty adults were present. In a smaller room adjoining the hall the children had been assembled holding flowers in their hands, forming two lines for Abdul-Baha to pass through. It looked most beautiful as Abdul-Baha came upstairs. He passed through a short hall and looked so pleased and delighted to see the dear children.[222]

The children presented their flowers to 'Abdu'l-Bahá and He gave them boxes of chocolates and sweets. Later He spoke to them all—children and adults, young and old—and a photograph was taken outside the hall, 'Abdu'l-Bahá seated in their midst. The following day at His hotel He spoke with great joy of the previous day's gathering at Esslingen.

On April 5th, 'Abdu'l-Bahá spoke at a number of meetings. In the evening He addressed the Esperanto Society, whose president, Professor Christaller, offered Him a warm welcome. The day ended with dinner at the home of Herr Eckstein. Other Bahá'ís whose homes 'Abdu'l-Bahá visited, where meetings were held, included Consul and Frau Schwarz, Herr and Frau Schweizer, and Herr and Frau Herrigel. The Schweizers lived in the town of Zuffenhausen.

The first meeting of the day on Sunday, April 6th, was at the Hotel Marquardt. So many were there and so many tarried behind, once the meeting was over, that 'Abdu'l-Bahá teased them, saying that they would be forcing the owner of the hotel to run away. In the afternoon, 'Abdu'l-Bahá was driven in the Black Forest. Bahá'ís had gathered at the park in Wagenburg. As there were too many to photograph together, several group photographs were taken with 'Abdu'l-Bahá in the centre of each. In the evening, there was a public meeting at the Obere Museum, and once more the attendance was high. 'Abdu'l-Bahá and His attendants had dinner that night at the home which Miss Knobloch shared with Fräulein Döring.

'Abdu'l-Bahá intended to leave for Budapest on April 7th, but was persuaded by Consul Schwarz to visit Bad Mergentheim, approximately sixty miles distant from Stuttgart, where the Consul owned the hotel and the mineral bath. 'Abdu'l-Bahá said at Bad Mergentheim that since He had left Persia He had never until then heard so many nightingales singing in such beautiful surroundings. However, He would not stay more than one night. For years a monument to commemorate 'Abdu'l-Bahá's visit, consisting of a metal plaque of His profile mounted on stone, stood in parkland in Bad Mergentheim. It was removed when the Nazis came to power. As far as can be ascertained, it was melted down.

'Abdu'l-Bahá returned to Stuttgart the next day and had luncheon at the home of Consul and Frau Schwarz. All day the Bahá'ís streamed in to visit Him until His train left for Budapest at 8 p.m. Wilhelm Herrigel joined His retinue for this journey to act as translator.

Next morning (April 9th) trains had to be changed in Vienna. A number of Iranian Bahá'ís awaited 'Abdu'l-Bahá's arrival at the station. Since trains for Budapest set out from another station, they had some minutes with Him.

Prior to 'Abdu'l-Bahá's visit to Budapest no one had taught the Faith of Bahá'u'lláh in the capital of Hungary. So there were no Bahá'ís in Budapest to meet Him at the station. Mr and Mrs Stark and a few others, who had invited 'Abdu'l-Bahá to visit their city, had mistakenly gone to the wrong station to greet Him. But they knew that He was to stay at the Hotel Ritz. There they offered Him their welcome and 'Abdu'l-Bahá made reply:

I hope that we shall all be confirmed to serve the world of humanity, because no service is greater today than promoting the oneness of mankind and international peace, so that people may be freed from the bonds of ancient prejudices and harmful imitations, cleansed of religious, national, racial, political and patriotic prejudices. As long as these prejudices remain, felicity and ease will not be fully revealed in the world of man. At a time when the East was enveloped and thickly beset by the gloom and darkness of such prejudices, Bahá'u'lláh appeared like the sun upon the horizon. He declared the oneness of the world of humanity. He said that all peoples constitute one mankind, are servants of one God, descended from the same ancestry; they are the flock of one God and He is their real shepherd; He loves His flock and all are dear to Him. While He is kind to all, loves all and feeds and protects all, why should we be unkind, one to the other; why should we engage in warfare? . . .[223]

Reporters, apprised of 'Abdu'l-Bahá's arrival, hurried to interview Him. Photographs of Him outside the hotel appeared in their papers. A man, who saw 'Abdu'l-Bahá walking by the riverside, recognized Him by His photograph and approached to ask the favour of His autograph on the margin of the newspaper. In the morning of April 10th a number of well-known academics, among whom were Arabs and Turks, called on Him. They included Dr Agnas Goosen, the Rector of the University, Professor Julius Germanus, and Dr Alexander Giesswein, a Member of Parliament. Sirdar Omrah Singh of Punjab was another visitor. The Sirdar spoke of Professor Arminius Vambéry, who greatly desired to meet 'Abdu'l-Bahá but was too ill to leave his house. 'Abdu'l-Bahá promised to go Himself to visit him. That evening 'Abdu'l-Bahá addressed the Theosophical Society. The next day He received a deputation from the Turkish Association. These were young men come to present Him with an address of welcome. Inviting them to be seated, 'Abdu'l-Bahá spoke to them: His great hope, He said, was to see the East and the West reconciled; to bring that about would be a great service to mankind. But, in truth, there was no east nor west; the whole earth was one. Any point on it was east of another and west of yet another; all these points constituted one globe, one homeland, and mankind was one family. He was very glad to see an association that worked for the progress of Easterners and their friendship with the people of the West, and He wished them all success, all confirmation.

During the afternoon of April 11th, 'Abdu'l-Bahá

returned the visits of Professor Ignaz Goldziher* and other notabilities, and engaged in long conversations with them. When He arrived at the hall of the Old Building of Parliament for the public meeting, He was very fatigued, barely able to speak. Yet He delivered a powerful discourse, and the audience, which had in it a number of the prominent men and academics of Budapest, showed that it had greatly appreciated the talk. The next morning (April 12th), 'Abdu'l-Bahá's visitors included the president of the Túránian Society. 'Abdu'l-Bahá spoke of the need for that supernatural power which, transcending all human limitations of racialism and nationalism, and overcoming all forces of materialism, could and would bring and bind together men all over the world.

In the afternoon He went, as He had promised, to visit Arminius Vambéry. This learned orientalist was one of the most colourful figures of the nineteenth century, of the same mould as Sir Richard Burton (1821–1890). As Burton had daringly made the pilgrimage to Mecca and Medina, under the name of Mírzá 'Abdu'lláh-i-Shírází, a devout Persian, and passed unnoticed, so Arminius Vambéry had travelled to Bukhárá as Rashíd Effendi, a genuine Osmanli (Ottoman). It was no less risky and perilous an undertaking, since the Emirs (Amírs) of Bukhárá had no hesitation in beheading indiscreet infidels, to which the fate of two brave British officers, Colonel C. Stoddart and Captain Arthur Conolly, amply testified. Vambéry had changed national garbs as well as religious affiliations several times. Born in 1832, he was now in his eighty-second year and had only a few more months to live. He died on September 15th. That very first

* Ignaz Goldziher (1850–1921) was the first person of the Jewish Faith to occupy a professional chair in the University of Budapest. His fame as an orientalist was world-wide and he represented Hungary and her Academy of Sciences at many international gatherings of savants.

encounter with 'Abdu'l-Bahá completely captivated him, as the letter he wrote (see p. 8) bears out. The next day, despite his illness and infirmity and the bitterly cold weather, he betook himself to 'Abdu'l-Bahá's hotel to meet Him once again. But 'Abdu'l-Bahá had gone to the studio of Professor Robert A. Nadler, a well-known portrait painter, for a sitting. Vambéry waited for a long while, until his weak condition forced him to return home. Before he departed he told 'Abdu'l-Bahá's attendants of the intense devotion evoked in him. That same afternoon 'Abdu'l-Bahá visited Sirdar Omrah Singh. The Sirdar, too, was greatly devoted to the person of 'Abdu'l-Bahá.

Though a blizzard was raging, a good many people came to 'Abdu'l-Bahá's hotel that evening of April 13th and stayed till late, listening to His address. Indeed the weather was proving very inclement and snowfalls were frequent.

The next morning 'Abdu'l-Bahá was preparing to leave for Vienna, when the president of the Túránian Society was announced. He requested 'Abdu'l-Bahá to delay His departure because they had planned another meeting for Him, and had widely advertised it. 'Abdu'l-Bahá acceded to this request. He then returned the call of the Ottoman Consul-General, and visited Arminius Vambéry, who was overjoyed. In the evening He addressed the meeting organized by the Túránian Society, at the hall of the Old Building of Parliament, then a museum. The gathering was large and truly appreciative.

'Alí 'Abbás Áqá, a Tabrízí carpet merchant, had during that week become so attached to 'Abdu'l-Bahá that he gave a dinner party for Him at his own home, on the same evening of April 14th. The Ottoman Consul-General was among the guests.

On April 15th 'Abdu'l-Bahá had symptoms of a severe cold, and He could not travel to Vienna until the 19th. Mr and Mrs Stark and Sirdar Omrah Singh attended Him most of the time. He assured them of success in days to come, should they be firm and steadfast.

'Abdu'l-Bahá reached Vienna in the evening of April 19th and took residence in the Grand Hotel. The aftermath of His severe cold and the vagaries of the weather still troubled Him. The Turkish Ambassador in Vienna had asked his Consul-General in Budapest to inform him of the date of 'Abdu'l-Bahá's arrival. 'Abdu'l-Bahá decided to pay him the first visit. The Ambassador, although a man exceedingly fanatical, was so impressed by this visit that he insisted on keeping 'Abdu'l-Bahá for luncheon. When 'Abdu'l-Bahá returned to His hotel, Frau Tyler and Herr Kreuz, two Theosophists who had been at the station the previous night to greet Him, called to convey the greetings of other Theosophists and to express their eager desire to hear His discourse that evening. After they had gone, 'Abdu'l-Bahá went out for a walk. As it happened, a collection was being made for charity. Whenever 'Abdu'l-Bahá met the collectors He gave them money. In the park children were playing, and to them, too, He gave money. Whatever He and His attendants had in their pockets was given away, and He said, laughing, that the people had made them penniless that day. When He went to the Theosophical Hall He had to walk up one hundred and twenty steps, because the building was new and no lift had yet been installed.

The next day (April 20th) a number of Theosophists called on Him at the hotel. In the afternoon and evening, 'Abdu'l-Bahá was the guest of the Persian Minister and the Turkish Ambassador, respectively. On April 21st, the Persian Minister called in the morning. Later in the day 'Abdu'l-Bahá went for a drive, and in the evening He, once again, addressed the members of the Theosophical Society. Some Iranian residents of Vienna visited Him on the 23rd. To them He spoke at length of the sad conditions in their country. The Theosophists heard Him for a third time that evening. Before 'Abdu'l-Bahá left Vienna Frau Tyler called to express her newly-found devotion, and He also received among others Baroness von Suttner, a well-known worker for the cause of peace. On April 24th He travelled back to Stuttgart, where He arrived in the early hours of the following morning.

'Abdu'l-Bahá stayed, once again, in the Hotel Marquardt. During this second visit to Stuttgart, which also lasted a week, He was mostly unwell. The cold contracted in Budapest had persisted and was now affecting His chest. The Bahá'ís of Stuttgart had arranged and advertised a meeting for the evening of the 25th at the Burger Museum. In the afternoon the condition of His chest worsened, causing great concern. Physicians told Him that He should not go out, and should use His voice as little as possible. His attendants, whom He had sent on to the meeting, felt that the large and eager assemblage there would be disappointed and dismayed should they be deprived of meeting 'Abdu'l-Bahá. They returned to the hotel with a plan which they thought would both safeguard 'Abdu'l-Bahá's health and make it possible for the people to meet Him. A saloon car, well-protected from the elements, would take 'Abdu'l-Bahá to the Museum where, in a room apart from the main hall, people could be allowed into His presence. As soon as they presented this plan to 'Abdu'l-Bahá and told Him of the eagerness and disappointment of the audience, He arose. Physicians had made Him stay indoors, He said; but His health was for the purpose of serving the Faith. While Wilhelm Herrigel was giving a talk in His stead, He walked into the hall, to the utmost delight and surprise of the audience, and using His full voice delivered a discourse on the need of world peace and the power that can guarantee it. The talk over, 'Abdu'l-Bahá was about to leave and return quickly to His hotel, when a voice was heard, wailing. He stopped and asked His attendants to make enquiries. It was found that a lady who had tried to reach 'Abdu'l-Bahá, and had been kept back by the press of the crowd, was weeping. 'Abdu'l-Bahá stayed to speak to her words of great kindness. The next day, to questions about His health, He answered that the previous night's venture, although considered very risky, had proved the right medicine for Him.

The war in the Balkans was mentioned in conversation that day. 'Abdu'l-Bahá advised the Bahá'ís to talk of their own war against materialism and ignorance; the Balkan war led to death, their war to life; that war led to disaster, their war always to glory and victory. Christ waged this war on the Cross and triumphed over all. A man from Switzerland was among His visitors. To him He said that His stay in Switzerland had been too short and He had not met many people there, but He could feel that they were people of great capabilities, and when the Cause reached them, it would find devoted advocates.*

On April 27th a number of children were brought to the hotel. The sight of children always gave 'Abdu'l-Bahá great joy. He said that He particularly loved children because they were nearer to the Kingdom of God. Later, the parents of one child told Him how, when asked to pray for the Master's health, the child had replied that He would go away if He recovered; 'we don't want him to go away'. 'Abdu'l-Bahá was greatly touched.

Although He had felt better, and had gone out of doors and to meetings as well, physicians warned Him, on April 29th, not to attend meetings or tax His voice. Should He follow their advice, He would be able to travel to Paris within three days.

On the morning of May 1st 'Abdu'l-Bahá met the Bahá'ís

* 'Abdu'l-Bahá had stayed in Geneva at the G^d Hôtel de la Paix on September 2nd–3rd 1911, before proceeding to London.

of Stuttgart in groups. He spoke very tenderly to them. To one group He said that He wished to converse with them, but His chest was not helpful; He would always anticipate their good news. To another, He spoke of the two ways in which people say farewell; for some, memories gradually fade away (out of sight, out of mind), but others keep their memories ever fresh. There were Bahá'ís whom He had not seen for years; He was in Europe, they were in Persia, but they were always in His mind and close to Him. To a third group He said that, although His time in Stuttgart was limited, He hoped that the harvest would prove limitless.

Then He left for Paris. That morning He had been speaking to Bahá'ís at His hotel all the while, assuring them of His love and admiration.

On this third visit to Paris 'Abdu'l-Bahá resided at Hôtel Baltimore, in Avenue Kléber, Arrondissement (Borough) XVI. His physical strength had suffered greatly and He was unable, on several occasions, to go to the meetings held in the homes of the Bahá'ís. But He was always receiving visitors at the hotel, giving a talk whenever they gathered in numbers. He also kept, as far as possible, His daily habit of a walk out of doors. One day, although He had guests for luncheon, He found it impossible to sit much longer at the table and had to go to His room to rest. Another day He was heard calling Siyyid Asadu'lláh and telling that faithful attendant, in jest, to fear God and bring Him a cup of coffee, for He was feeling weak and the hotel food did not suit Him. On May 8th, at the conclusion of the morning meeting in the hotel, He said: 'The Blessed Perfection has trained me to shoulder the burdens of others, not to put mine on others' shoulders'.[224] Two days later He spoke of the Covenant, that its purpose was to safeguard the strength and the power of the Cause; without it the circle of Bahá'ís would have broken up completely. 'Some people have imagined,' He said, 'that the Blessed Perfection has taken relations between father and son into account. They do not know that He has instituted the power of the Covenant for the propagation of the Cause of God and for the victory of His Word.'[225] A lady offered Him five hundred francs which He declined to accept, but because she pleaded very hard He advised: Let it be sent to Dr Moody for the Tarbíyat School in Ṭihrán.

Letters came pouring in. 'Abdu'l-Bahá said that He read them, but could not answer them all, as there was no time. Some people seemed to think that He corresponded only with them and so kept writing, whereas He had to correspond with people all over the world. (One day in Egypt, suffering from high fever, He was handed a long letter which He read to the end. He then commented that a long sheet had been covered with very small handwriting and, ill as He was, He had read every word of it, only to find that the letter had nothing noteworthy to convey; writing must be for expressing a purpose, and not to the end of stringing words together and uttering banal formalities.)

Ra<u>sh</u>íd Pá<u>sh</u>á and the Persian Minister called on 'Abdu'l-Bahá again, and He spoke to them at length about His travels in America. Some evenings His meal consisted only of a cup of milk and a piece of bread. He described it as a healthy meal, and recalled that Bahá'u'lláh had said that during His sojourn in Sulaymáníyyih His food was just milk most of the time, and sometimes milk and rice cooked together. One day He came across an excellent brand of China tea in a shop, bought some, brewed it Himself in the hotel and poured out cups for His attendants. Despite His preoccupations (which never left Him free) and the indifferent state of His health, His sense of humour was always showing itself in diverse ways. One morning He called to His attendants to be good and behave themselves, to bring in the samovar, and lay the tea things on the table; tea beside the samovar is particularly delicious, He said.

On one occasion He spoke, with great feeling, of the services rendered by Mírzá Ḥasan, the 'King of the Martyrs', his brother, Mírzá Ḥusayn, the 'Beloved of the Martyrs', and Mírzá Fatḥ-'Alí-i-Ardistání,* to whom Bahá'u'lláh gave the surname: Fatḥ-i-'Aẓam (Greatest Victory). Bahá'u'lláh had said that on His journey from Baghdád to Constantinople Fatḥ-i-'Aẓám had been with Him in spirit. 'Abdu'l-Bahá also spoke, on that occasion, of how Mullá Ḥusayn-i-Bushrú'í, the Bábu'l-Báb (Gate to the Gate)— the first believer in the Báb—had come to realize the superior qualities of Mullá Muḥammad-'Alíy-i-Barfurúshí, the Quddús, just by sitting and listening to him one evening in Mázindarán; and of how amazed the Bábís were, the next morning, to see Mullá Ḥusayn, their leader and guide, standing in humble devotion in the presence of Quddús.

A Bahá'í came to 'Abdu'l-Bahá to speak on behalf of a young Persian, who was trying to attach himself to the Faith. 'Abdu'l-Bahá explained that should anyone commit a hundred wrongs against His own person He would overlook them all and treat the offender with kindness; should anyone act treasonably towards His own person, He would act towards the offender as if he were someone most trusted, but He ('Abdu'l-Bahá) could never countenance nor aid any deed which would injure the Faith. To murder Him, 'Abdu'l-Bahá said, would be preferable to defrauding others; murdering Him would not harm the Faith, defrauding people would. Another Persian came to ask for financial help. 'Abdu'l-Bahá gave him the money, but advised him not to be a wastrel. He, Himself, had to bear certain expenses for the sole purpose of maintaining the dignity of the Faith.

Some of the Iranian notables invited 'Abdu'l-Bahá to take an automobile ride one afternoon. They went to the famous racecourse at Longchamps. But 'Abdu'l-Bahá

* Great-grandfather of Hushmand Fatheazam, member of the Universal House of Justice.

returned soon. He preferred walking to riding, and went out for a long walk with Dr Muḥammad Khán, one of the Iranian Bahá'ís then in Paris. That night (May 18th) He sat up with M. and Mme Richard until midnight, talking about mysticism and Ṣúfí tenets and practices, in answer to their questions.

'Abdu'l-Bahá visited an eminent member of the Persian aristocracy on May 22nd. The nobleman was overwhelmed and bowed to kiss His hands. He described to 'Abdu'l-Bahá an occasion in London, where he had found himself seated near a lady who wore a simple, inexpensive ring set with cornelian. His curiosity had led him to ask why, to be told: 'You are a Persian and should know that the Name of Bahá'u'lláh is inscribed on this ringstone.' Feeling both shame at his ignorance, and elation at this evidence of Persia's influence in high circles in London, he realized that his hostility to the Faith of Bahá'u'lláh had vanished then and there. Later, 'Abdu'l-Bahá visited Mme Jackson, who was ill and confined to her home, and that evening, He received Albert Dawson, editor of the *Christian Commonwealth*.

On May 23rd, Bahá'ís came with bouquets of flowers throughout the day, as it was the anniversary of the birth of 'Abdu'l-Bahá, but He told them that the day should be considered and celebrated only as the anniversary of the Declaration of the Báb. That was why it was a blessed Day. It was incidental that He had been born on the same date. The Feast was celebrated in the evening at the home of Laura and Hippolyte Dreyfus-Barney.

'Abdu'l-Bahá moved, on the 27th, to the hotel in Rue Lauriston where He had stayed before. He was very tired, and needed a few days' rest before people learned where He resided. Aḥmad Páshá and the Dreyfus-Barneys, who knew that hotel meals did not suit 'Abdu'l-Bahá, had food specially cooked for Him in their homes, but He asked them not to do so.

May 30th witnessed a noteworthy gathering at the home of the Dreyfus-Barneys, when diverse nationalities were represented. Consul Schwarz had come from Germany and spoke at the meeting. In His talk, 'Abdu'l-Bahá underlined the true import of that harmonious and loving association of people of so many origins, brought about by the power of Bahá'u'lláh.

'Abdu'l-Bahá's historic visit to the Western world was now approaching its end. Mírzá 'Alí-Akbar-i-Nakhjavání arrived back from the Holy Land on June 1st, with the news of a considerable number of pilgrims awaiting 'Abdu'l-Bahá's return. A Persian, who had not hitherto visited 'Abdu'l-Bahá, called on June 2nd and was amazed to find so many of his prominent compatriots there. No better proof of the powers of 'Abdu'l-Bahá was needed, he said. Many of these notable men had once been bitter opponents of the Faith of Bahá'u'lláh, assailing it and its followers, wherever and whenever they could; and now in the French capital, they were rendering homage to the Head of that Faith.

In the evening of June 6th, Aḥmad 'Izzat Páshá—who had been the right-hand man of Sulṭán 'Abdu'l-Ḥamíd, fleeing Turkey when his master's fall was imminent—gave a dinner party for 'Abdu'l-Bahá. Two days later a Persian prince, who was both young and haughty, called at 'Abdu'l-Bahá's hotel. Soon after him Aḥmad 'Izzat Páshá arrived. 'Izzat's attitude of reverence taught the young prince a lesson which he took to heart.

On June 12th at 8 a.m. 'Abdu'l-Bahá left His hotel for the station. There he spoke with the Bahá'ís who had come to say farewell, urging them to be united at all times. At noon His train left for Marseilles, which it reached twelve hours later. He stayed the night at a hotel next to the station, and boarded the P. & O. steamer, *Himalaya*, at 9 a.m. the next morning.

'Abdu'l-Bahá's historic tour of the West was over.

His retinue now consisted of Siyyid Asadu'lláh-i-Qumí, Mírzá 'Alí-Akbar-i-Na<u>kh</u>javání, Mírzá Maḥmúd-i-Zarqání and Mírzá Aḥmad Sohráb.

An Indian passenger, a resident of Allahabad, had his cabin next to 'Abdu'l-Bahá's. He and a number of other Indians spent some hours in His presence. A British consular official and his daughter also sought to meet Him and presented Him with an English magazine which carried His photograph and an account of His visit to the mosque at Woking.

In the afternoon of June 17th 1913, 'Abdu'l-Bahá landed at Port Said.

CHAPTER 21

TO EGYPT AND THE HOLY LAND

'Abdu'l-Bahá had decided not to travel to the Holy Land immediately. Pilgrims assembled in Haifa were called by cable to come to Egypt. As the hotel in which they were to be housed proved too small for their numbers and activities, a huge tent of the type which Egyptians used for public functions was pitched on the roof of the hotel. There were constant gatherings under the shade of that tent. Meetings were held there at which 'Abdu'l-Bahá oftentimes spoke. Soon after His arrival at Port Said He remarked that, at a time when the heat of the summer drove people to Paris, He had come away from Paris to Egypt. He recalled that in the days of Bahá'u'lláh cholera broke out four times in the Holy Land. It touched the environs of 'Akká and reached the Lebanon, but within 'Akká there was no cholera. Immediately after the ascension of Bahá'u'lláh there was another outbreak of the epidemic, this time inside the city walls. 'Abdu'l-Bahá, feeling that He could not stay at Bahjí and leave the Bahá'ís of 'Akká to themselves, returned to the city, only to find that other people had fled 'Akká and put their homes in the care of the Bahá'ís. He appointed watchmen to guard these houses. All the Bahá'ís escaped the ravages of the epidemic. Then cholera died down in the city, but appeared in the neighbourhood, at which the people who had abandoned their homes rushed back to 'Akká.

Another day, under that tent, 'Abdu'l-Bahá, looking at the ranks assembled, said it was truly remarkable that such a gathering had been made possible. The issue of the *Egyptian Gazette* for Friday, June 27th, carried an article under the headlines: 'Abdul Baha in Egypt. Wonderful Scenes in Port Said. Eastern Bahais Assembled in Force.' 'Abdu'l-Bahá was now kept more occupied than ever. There were so many pilgrims, so many Bahá'ís of Egypt to meet and converse with, and a great many letters to answer. Letters, petitions and cables came pouring in from the East and the West. All the Tablets belonging to this period are in His own handwriting.

And there were not only Bahá'ís to meet. On June 24th, He had written and spoken much. At the end of the day, greatly fatigued, He was on the point of leaving the house for His daily walk, when a group of Christian missionaries, men and women, appeared at His door and asked to meet Him. 'Abdu'l-Bahá received them with His usual courtesy and kindness. Before long, they were harshly criticising the Muslims and Islám. 'Abdu'l-Bahá told them that what they were talking about was not the true Islám, but imitations and trivialities; and He reminded them of a verse in the Qur'án about Christ: 'Those who have believed, the Jews, the Christians, and the Sabeans, who believe in God and the Day of Judgment and do righteously, have their reward with their Lord. Neither is there fear for them, nor are they to grieve (II.59).' One of the missionaries said that in the Gospels Christ is extolled as the Son of God—the highest possible station—whereas in the Qur'án no such reference is made to Jesus. To this 'Abdu'l-Bahá replied that the term 'Son of God' was current in the days of Moses and Jesus, and was applied to the whole of Israel; He referred them to Exodus (iv. 22–3)—'And thou shalt say unto Pharaoh, Thus saith the Lord, Israel is my son, even my firstborn: And I say unto thee, Let my son go, that he may serve me: and if thou refuse to let him go, behold, I will slay thy son, even thy firstborn.'

Cares of many kinds occupied the mind of 'Abdu'l-Bahá at this period, and His fever kept recurring. But His sense of humour never deserted Him. One day He asked Ḥusayn Rúḥí how many pupils there were in his school. 'One hundred and sixty,' he replied. 'Abdu'l-Bahá commented that Rúḥí must certainly be both busy and rich, for he had one hundred and sixty students, but 'Abdu'l-Bahá had not a single one. Could Ḥusayn Rúḥí find Him some?

Mírzá Ja'far-i-Raḥmáníy-i-Shírází (Hádíoff) invited all the Bahá'ís in Port Said to dinner. There were more than seventy of them. They ate under the tent and 'Abdu'l-Bahá served the food, and then gave them all sweets. The next day (June 28th) most of the pilgrims, who had come over from Haifa, departed.

At this time 'Abdu'l-Bahá was disturbed by the news of Mírzá Abu'l-Faḍl's continued illness. He sent Mírzá Muḥsin-i-Afnán (His son-in-law), and then Siyyid Jalál (the son of the Bahá'í poet, Síná), to Alexandria to see that Mírzá Abu'l-Faḍl lacked nothing.

Among 'Abdu'l-Bahá's ever-increasing mail, a number of letters arrived one day from Istanbul. They were from some of the notables, written in Turkish, and they brought joy to 'Abdu'l-Bahá. He said He would go to Istanbul and raise the call of Bahá'u'lláh but for the dire consequences which would ensue in the Holy Land. Many would turn to the Faith, the wrath of the fanatics would be aroused, and they would assail the Shrines.

Siyyid Asadu'lláh, who had served 'Abdu'l-Bahá in America and Europe and was now seventy-six years old, set out on July 10th for the Caucasus, after asking 'Abdu'l-Bahá to be allowed to go and teach the Faith there. The next day, because of adverse weather in Port Said, 'Abdu'l-Bahá left for Ismá'ílíyyah. He took Mírzá Munír and Áqá Khusraw with Him. A few Bahá'ís, whom 'Abdu'l-Bahá summoned to Ismá'ílíyyah a week later, found Him sitting up in bed in the hotel of J. Bosta, with high fever and weaker than He had been. In that state He was attending to His mail.

Ismá'ílíyyah was less humid, but 'Abdu'l-Bahá's feverish condition became worse. It was thought that Ramlih, a suburb of Alexandria, might prove more salubrious. So on July 17th 'Abdu'l-Bahá travelled to Alexandria. After a stay of two weeks in the Hotel Victoria at Ramlih, He moved to a house which He rented in the vicinity of Maẓlúm Páshá Station. He also rented a second house for His secretaries and others who would be coming to visit Him. A third house was secured nearby for Mírzá Abu'l-Faḍl.

Lua Getsinger arrived at Port Said on July 23rd, and Edward Getsinger soon after. Lua was not to see her native land again. Isabel Fraser* came at a later date, summoned by 'Abdu'l-Bahá for a mission He wished to entrust to her. There were other Western Bahá'ís in Egypt, such as Mrs Stannard, an English lady who, in future years, established the Bahá'í Bureau in Geneva; and Dr Joseph de Bons, a French dental surgeon who practised in Cairo, and Mme de Bons (Edith MacKaye), first to accept the Faith from May Maxwell in Paris.†

One morning, around six o'clock, 'Abdu'l-Bahá went to the house where His secretaries lived, to find most of the residents still asleep. He Himself had already attended to His correspondence and other matters, and had written several Tablets. The air of Ramlih suited Him and His health improved.

* Later, Isabel Chamberlain (d. 1939). She compiled the book, *Abdul-Baha on Divine Philosophy*, consisting of talks delivered in Paris.

† Dr and Mme de Bons were early pioneers of the Bahá'í Faith in Switzerland; their daughter, Mme Haenni de Bons, continues this service.

'ABDU'L-BAHÁ ON HIS RETURN TO THE HOLY LAND, DECEMBER 1913

Third from the right, front row: Shoghi Effendi

SIGNING A TABLET OUTSIDE HIS HOUSE IN HAIFA

Individual Bahá'ís, and particularly the Bahá'ís of the East, wrote to Him on every conceivable subject; one would ask His advice about purchasing a piece of land, another would request a name for a child newly-born; one would ask Him whether to marry, another whether to make a certain journey. He always had misunderstandings to resolve, feelings to soothe. Bahá'í groups, communities, and spiritual assemblies, as more of them came into being, also took more and more of His time, for counsel, advice and guidance. His correspondence was not limited to the Bahá'ís. Many were the people, not His adherents, who wrote to Him and had replies. Societies and congresses and conferences in the West were, by now, also writing to Him. Soon after He reached Egypt, He received a letter, through its secretary, from the Sixth International Congress of Free and Progressive Christians and other Religious Liberals, meeting in Paris.

'Abdu'l-Bahá's eldest grandson, Shoghi Effendi; His sister, the Greatest Holy Leaf; and His eldest daughter arrived from Haifa on August 1st. A Bahá'í going to 'Abdu'l-Bahá's house, early one morning, heard Shoghi Effendi chanting a prayer and 'Abdu'l-Bahá instructing him.

'Abbás Ḥilmí Páshá, the Khedive of Egypt, met 'Abdu'l-Bahá for the third time on August 17th, and Prince Muḥammad-'Alí the brother of the Khedive (see p. 230) called on 'Abdu'l-Bahá a month later. 'Uthmán Páshá Murtaḍá, the Khedive's chamberlain, was devoted to 'Abdu'l-Bahá, and was the intermediary arranging meetings between Him and 'Abbás Ḥilmí Páshá ('Abbás II). A Tablet which 'Abdu'l-Bahá addressed to 'Uthmán Páshá in October 1919 (five years after 'Abbás Ḥilmí was deposed) is indicative of the stature of the man: he is called 'Amír-al-wafa'—the Prince of Fidelity.

Among the visitors who sought to meet 'Abdu'l-Bahá in Ramlih were deputies of the Turkish Parliament and members of the academic staff of the Syrian Protestant College (American University of Beirut). Bahá'í students of the college, who were spending their summer holidays on Mount Carmel, also went to Ramlih, in two groups, to attain the presence of 'Abdu'l-Bahá.

In the course of the summer months and early autumn, 'Abdu'l-Bahá's health greatly improved, but as the year advanced, old symptoms returned. Fever and insomnia began, once again, to drain His physical strength. The attempts instigated by Tamaddun'ul-Mulk (who had been in London during 'Abdu'l-Bahá's first visit), to divide the Bahá'ís in Ṭihrán, and the increasingly erratic behaviour of Dr Amínu'lláh Faríd (Fareed), brought Him much suffering and sorrow. He went for a few days to Abúqír (Aboukir), but the change of scenery gave Him no relief and He decided to leave Egypt, especially since His family and the Bahá'ís of the Holy Land were begging Him to return. He boarded a Lloyd Triestino boat on December 2nd. There were two stops at Port Said and Jaffa, and the Bahá'ís of these towns had the opportunity of being with 'Abdu'l-Bahá for a short while. Early in the afternoon of December 5th, the boat cast anchor in the harbour of Haifa. 'Abdu'l-Bahá sent His attendants ashore and told them not to let the Bahá'ís assemble at the landing-stage. He Himself disembarked at nightfall.

Emogene Hoagg, who was in Haifa awaiting His arrival, wrote:

> ... In Abdul-Baha's house, there is a very large central room around which are the other rooms, and in it Persian rugs were spread and tables placed upon which were fruits and sweets.
> ... When Abdul-Baha's voice was heard as he entered, the moment was intense—and as he passed through to his room, all heads were bowed. In a few moments he

returned to welcome all. He sat in a chair at one end of the room, and most of the believers sat on the floor. Abdul-Baha was tired so remained but a short time, and after a prayer chanted by his daughter Zia Khanum [Ḍíá'íyyih Khánum, the eldest daughter of 'Abdu'l-Bahá], went to his room.

Then the ladies vacated so that the men might enter. To see the faces of those sturdy, earnest men—faces that spoke the fervour of their faith, the earnestness and resoluteness of their purpose—was something to remember. I am sure not an eye was dry; old and young, with happiness filling their hearts, could not refrain from exhibiting their emotion. He welcomed them, and seating himself on the floor, spoke to them a short time, after which he retired . . .[226]

The next morning 'Abdu'l-Bahá went up the mountain to the Shrine of the Báb—the mausoleum which His indefatigable labours had raised with untold heartache. The Bahá'ís of the Holy Land and the pilgrims had already gathered there and lined the pathway which led to the Shrine. 'Abdu'l-Bahá beckoned to them to enter the eastern foreroom of the inner shrine; He, all alone, entered the western foreroom.

The next day they were His guests for luncheon at 'Akká, after which they went to Bahjí and to the Shrine of Bahá'u'-lláh. But 'Abdu'l-Bahá, Himself, was not there. He had to be alone to put His forehead on the threshold of the room where the human temple of His Father rested, and unburden His heart.

In the late afternoon Bahá'ís had forgathered in the railway station. Large numbers of the inhabitants of 'Akká had also come. 'Abdu'l-Bahá was on the train from Haifa. By a vast assemblage, among them many of the notables of 'Akká and Haifa, He was escorted to the city which had held Him captive for long, long years.

The death of Mírzá Abu'l-Faḍl, which occurred in Cairo on January 21st 1914, brought deep sorrow to 'Abdu'l-Bahá. Speaking at His home, the next day, He said:

> . . . No matter how much we want to console ourselves, we cannot be consoled. How good for man to be like this, so that the hearts of all the friends are attracted to him in every way. While in Alexandria, every time my heart was depressed, I used to go and meet him and at once my depression vanished. He was very truthful. He never harbored deceit and revenge.[227]

Bahá'í history has so far not recorded anyone equal to Mírzá Abu'l-Faḍl in learning. Combined with that vast learning were rare detachment and humility. Isabel Fraser, who had seen him frequently at Ramlih, wrote after his death:

> . . . With all his book learning he was not at all 'bookish' . . . the same dignity and impressiveness with which he discussed a verse of the Koran [Qur'án] with the learned sheiks [Shaykhs], he put into the meeting of some sojourning American; often finishing with a personal pleasantry, for he was a ready humorist and made his guests instantly at ease. He had the placidness of a child and the air of one who was never in a hurry and had plenty of time to make radiantly happy the place where God had placed him . . .
>
> One day when I was at his house, there were about twenty sheiks who had come over from Alexandria to visit him. One who seemed to be the leader was a very learned and gorgeously attired young sheik, who said with some pride that he had been educated in the oldest university in the world. He was the editor of a magazine in Alexandria and had come to interview Mirza Abul-Fazl, who for more than an hour had been listened to with absorbed attention. His talk was interspersed with

an occasional jest and his sharp eye would glance from one face to another to see if his point was understood . . .

Suddenly Abdul-Baha appeared. Mirza Abul-Fazl faced the door, the rest of us had our backs to it and did not see him; there was a moment of silence and Mirza Abul-Fazl stood with his head bowed, his whole attitude changed. He immediately became the most humble and respectful of servitors. Then quickly arranging a chair for Abdul-Baha, he told him in a low voice, in answer to his questions, the subject under discussion . . .[228]

In the first half of the year 1914 pilgrims were continuously arriving at 'Abdu'l-Bahá's door, from both the East and the West. And He was also constantly receiving all manner of men. Dr Howard Bliss, President of the Syrian Protestant College, visited Him on February 15th. A group of tourists from England called on Him on the 22nd. Another day, as He was dictating Tablets, two Arabs who hated the sight of each other were announced at short intervals. 'Abdu'l-Bahá told them stories to make them laugh. Then He said that His home was the home of peace and joy, laughter and exultation; they should not go out of it with the feeling of enmity in their hearts. Leaving them for a while, He returned with sweets and two Persian silk handkerchiefs, one for each. These were to be the token of their pledge of friendship. They recognized that God had directed their steps to 'Abdu'l-Bahá's home that morning, and went away from His presence joyous and full of laughter.

But 'Abdu'l-Bahá was fatigued and weighed down with the cares of His stewardship, almost beyond endurance. It was in those months that He wrote this Tablet:

Friends! The time is coming when I shall be no longer with you. I have done all that could be done. I have served the Cause of Baha'u'llah to the utmost of my ability. I have laboured night and day, all the years of my life. O how I long to see the loved ones taking upon themselves the responsibilities of the Cause! Now is the time to proclaim the Kingdom of Baha! Now is the hour of love and union! This is the day of the spiritual harmony of the loved ones of God! All the resources of my physical strength I have exhausted, and the spirit of my life is the welcome tidings of the unity of the people of Baha. I am straining my ears toward the East and toward the West, toward the North and toward the South that haply I may hear the songs of love and fellowship chanted in the meetings of the faithful. My days are numbered, and, but for this, there is no joy left unto me. O how I yearn to see the friends united even as a string of gleaming pearls, as the brilliant Pleiades, as the rays of the sun, as the gazelles of one meadow!

The mystic Nightingale is warbling for them all; will they not listen? The Bird of Paradise is singing; will they not heed? The Angel of Abha is calling to them; will they not hearken? The Herald of the Covenant is pleading; will they not obey?

Ah me I am waiting, waiting, to hear the joyful tidings that the believers are the very embodiment of sincerity and truthfulness, the incarnation of love and amity, the living symbols of unity and concord. Will they not gladden my heart? Will they not satisfy my yearning? Will they not manifest my wish? Will they not fulfil my heart's desire? Will they not give ear to my call?

I am waiting, I am patiently waiting.[229]

Then came a time when 'Abdu'l-Bahá would no longer permit pilgrims to come, and on June 29th pilgrims present in the Holy Land were instructed to leave. 'This is the day of farewell,' 'Abdu'l-Bahá said, 'and the time of leave-taking is very hard. The Arabian poet says, "The days of my union with the beloved were so few that the greeting was the farewell." Indeed, I am deeply grieved, but I do not say good-bye to you because there is a complete connection among the hearts, and among the souls there is unity and agreement. We never have a separation from one another. This nearness and remoteness concerns the world of bodies. In the world of spirits and souls there is union, never separation. The heart feels the union. The eye sees and carries the sight to the heart which becomes affected. When the heart is engaged with the friends there is no separation, especially if you go in service to the Cause of God . . .'[230]

Mírzá 'Alí-Akbar-i-Nakhjavání and Mírzá Maḥmúd-i-Zarqání, the faithful attendants and companions of His tour of America and Europe, 'Abdu'l-Bahá directed to the Caucasus and India, respectively.* Mrs Emogene Hoagg was directed to Italy.

'Abdu'l-Bahá knew that the storm which He had predicted was about to break over Europe and over the world.

By the middle of the year the defection of Dr Faríd had come into the open, and the Bahá'ís of the West had to be protected. Faríd was travelling in Europe in defiance of 'Abdu'l-Bahá, announcing his arrival beforehand so that meetings would be organized for him. In London, the King's Weigh Hall had been booked and the meeting was advertised. It was summer-time and Lady Blomfield was not in London. However, the timely intervention of Dr Luṭfu'lláh Ḥakím prevented Faríd from speaking. Some of the Bahá'ís were badly shaken by the incident and a few fell away. Annie Gamble, at whose home the issue was decided and the community was saved, proved a rock of strength. George Latimer and Charles Mason Remey were also present at this time, having come from the United States to tour Europe, at the bidding of 'Abdu'l-Bahá. After a stay of three months in Paris, they had arrived in London, and would later proceed to Holland and Germany.

* The present writer has clear memories of meeting Mírzá Maḥmúd-i-Zarqání, in Poona, during the years of the First World War.

As late as the middle of July, 'Abdu'l-Bahá instructed Dr Ḥabíbu'lláh Khudábakhsh (now Dr Mu'ayyad), who had just completed his medical studies in the Syrian Protestant College, and 'Azízu'lláh Bahádur, who was still a student (and both of whom were in Haifa), to go immediately to Europe to counter Faríd's activities. They were in Stuttgart when the war broke out. Then 'Abdu'l-Bahá recalled them to Haifa, and specified that George Latimer and Charles Mason Remey should accompany them. They reached Alexandria on September 28th, and Haifa on October 5th.

Laura and Hippolyte Dreyfus-Barney set out for the United States. Mrs Chevalier was active there as Dr Faríd's emissary.

But Faríd's efforts came to naught, as the efforts of all who violated the Covenant had come to naught. The prime cause of his downfall was his insatiable greed for money. At various times, and under a variety of pretexts, he had tried to get money from Bahá'ís, particularly wealthy individuals in the United States, such as Mrs Hearst and Mrs Parsons. To some he had whispered that 'Abdu'l-Bahá needed money although, as they had noticed, He would not openly accept it from them; but if they would let him have it, he would see that 'Abdu'l-Bahá received it in due course. From others he had asked for money to have a hospital constructed on Mount Carmel. All this had caused grave disquiet in the United States. 'Abdu'l-Bahá had suffered silently, but did not include him in His retinue when He left for Europe. Faríd's insinuations and accusations, levelled against the person of 'Abdu'l-Bahá, at this period in 1914, were nothing new in the history of violation. But his ingratitude was particularly obnoxious, because it was 'Abdu'l-Bahá Who had seen to his education from childhood and had kept him at universities in the United States.

Faríd's father, Mírzá Asadu'lláh, who travelled from the Holy Land to London to try to make him desist from his activities, not only failed in his mission, but eventually went over to his side. Sydney Sprague, the husband of his sister, also joined him; and it was not until 1937 that Sprague realized how grievously he had erred. Back once more in the circle of the Faith, he made a trip to South America to teach, and died soon after his return to the United States. But Dr Faríd trod the wilderness to the bitter end.*

War had come to Europe, and Turkey was about to commit herself to the cause of the Central Powers: Germany and Austria-Hungary. Although she had had successive and decisive defeats in Tripolitania and in the Balkans within the previous three years, her rulers, the Young Turks, and particularly the triumvirate of Enver (Anvar) Páshá, Tal‘at Páshá and Jamál Páshá, forced her into another trial of strength, the outcome of which must have seemed hazardous and uncertain. By the end of October 1914 the die had been cast, and in the first week of November Russia, Great Britain, and France found themselves obliged to declare war on Turkey, which was followed on November 14th by Turkey's declaration of holy war. That declaration was wrested from the Caliph, Sultán Muḥammad V, by the reckless directors of the destinies of the Ottoman Empire.

With Turkey in the war, the Near East was thrown into new turmoil, and ‘Abdu'l-Bahá was beset by fresh perils.

* He died in 1953.

CHAPTER 22

THE WAR YEARS

The Ottoman Empire had always had subjects who sought to destroy it. In return for their unruliness they had received condign punishment. As far back as the sixteenth century, under Sulṭán Selim I, 'The Grim' (reigned 1512–1520), the Shí‘ahs of Anatolia, who favoured Selim's rival, Sháh Ismá‘íl I, the Safavid ruler of Írán, were massacred in their thousands. Greeks and Slavs, Macedonians and Albanians had, in the course of years, rebelled, met with harsh suppression and finally obtained their freedom. With the overthrow of despotism new hopes had arisen, but were soon dashed by the Young Turks.

Within a few weeks of Turkey's entry into the war, the British occupied the port of Baṣrah, deposed the Khedive of Egypt, proclaimed a protectorate over the country, and set policies in motion which would affect profoundly the future of the Ottoman realms. Arabs, the largest minority in the Ottoman Empire, had already shown signs of restiveness and were to pay for it dearly in Damascus at the hands of Jamál Páshá. Uprisings among them, particularly the revolt of the Sharíf of Mecca, were still far off, but signs were discernible and the Turks were suspicious. It was also apparent that the call for a holy war (Jihád), coming from Istanbul, would go unheeded. Except for a tiny number, the Muslims of the Indian sub-continent ignored it and, even more, did not hesitate to fight the Turks.

Spies were everywhere in the Holy Land and authorities were becoming increasingly repressive. Fear was abroad, a fear which could sweep over the population like an epidemic, a fear such as was felt in Great Britain and France at the outbreak of the Second World War, when the opening of hostilities brought the prospect that whole towns and cities might be razed to the ground. An enemy warship did bombard the railway bridges between 'Akká and Haifa. On that occasion a shell came down in the garden of Riḍván but did not explode. One day, when the sea was calm with hardly a ripple on it, and rocks, far from the shore, were clearly visible under a sunny sky, the people of 'Akká took them for warships and fled *en masse*.

It was against such a background that 'Abdu'l-Bahá decided to move the Bahá'ís of Haifa and 'Akká away from the hysteria of the officials and the people around them. As a temporary home for them He chose the Druze village of Abú-Sinán, situated to the east of 'Akká. 'Abdu'l-Bahá Himself stayed in 'Akká with one attendant, and occasionally spent a night or two in Abú-Sinán. Shaykh Ṣáliḥ, the Druze chief, had put his own house at the disposal of 'Abdu'l-Bahá, and that was where His family lived. Quarters were found for the other Bahá'ís in the homes of villagers. Bahá'u'lláh had once lived for three months among these friendly people in the foothills of Galilee. The room in the house of Shaykh Mazrúq, which He had occupied, was always left untenanted.

Dr Ḥabíbu'lláh Khudábakhsh (Dr Mu'ayyad) ran a dispensary at Abú-Sinán, to which people who were not members of the Bahá'í community soon came for treatment. They received equal attention but paid according to their means. For most of them the treatment was free. Dr Mu'ayyad performed operations as well and was assisted by Lua Getsinger. Badí' Bushrú'í, another graduate of the Syrian Protestant College, ran a school, side by side with the dispensary, for the children of the Bahá'ís. Life was naturally rather primitive in this isolated village in the hills. On

Mount Carmel, the sole occupant of the pilgrim house was the veteran, Ḥájí Mírzá Ḥaydar-'Alí.

Mírzá Faḍlu'lláh Khán Banán reached Haifa from Shíráz with the offerings of the Bahá'ís of that city, on January 19th 1915. His arrival was the last link with the outside world for a long time. Banán's* journey was fraught with considerable difficulty, for he had to make his way from India to Haifa. To have succeeded was indeed an achievement.

However, sometime during the war years an Arab Bahá'í, advanced in years, named Ḥájí Ramaḍán, braving all hazards, managed to reach Ṭihrán. His perilous journey included walking for forty-five days. He delivered to the Bahá'ís a Tablet entrusted to him by 'Abdu'l-Bahá, and returned bearing gold and letters. A second time he attempted that heroic feat, but he did not reach his destination, and no trace of him was ever found.

Early in 1915, Jamál Páshá appeared on the scene, Commander of the 4th Army Corps, whose mission was to overrun the Suez Canal and drive the British out of Egypt. With him came a reign of terror. The whole of Syria (including the Holy Land) was under his martial control. Throughout 1915 and into the following year, Jamál Páshá was bringing Arab nationalists to trial in his military courts. Thirty-four of them were executed, and many more were deported. Mírzá Muḥammad-'Alí and his associates, long discredited and cowed into silence, now found fresh opportunities to plot against 'Abdu'l-Bahá. They went to Jamál Páshá with various tales. Majdi'd-Dín told him that 'Abdu'l-Bahá was hostile to the Committee of Union and Progress. The tent which Bahá'u'lláh had used, the violators gave to Jamál Páshá. It was a tent under which, 'Abdu'l-Bahá is reported to have said, 'representatives of the Most Great Peace' should have met.[231] Then in order to create

* Banán passed away only recently. As far as the present writer knows he has not left a full record of that remarkable journey.

confusion, the violators set rumours afoot that the military government had banished 'Abdu'l-Bahá to Damascus.

When Jamál Páshá encamped in the vicinity of 'Akká, he told the Governor that he must see 'Abdu'l-Bahá at once. Riding His donkey 'Abdu'l-Bahá went to the military cantonment. Jamál Páshá received Him courteously, but told Him that He was a religious mischief-maker, which was the reason He had been put under restraint in the past. It happened that, in the days of 'Abdu'l-Ḥamíd, Jamál Páshá himself had been known as a political mischief-maker. So 'Abdu'l-Bahá now replied that mischief-making was of two kinds: political and religious; and then, pointing at the arrogant Páshá, He said that so far the political mischief-maker had not caused any damage, and it was to be hoped that the religious mischief-maker would not do so either.

Lady Blomfield has recorded another encounter between 'Abdu'l-Bahá and Jamál Páshá, the story being related by Mírzá Jalál, a son-in-law of 'Abdu'l-Bahá:

At the beginning of the year 1916, at about seven o'clock one morning, 'Abdu'l-Bahá sent me for His faithful coachman. 'Tell Isfandíyár to have my carriage brought, and you and Khusraw be ready to accompany me to Nazareth in half an hour.' We did as He commanded, and at the appointed time 'Abdu'l-Bahá left His home in Haifa, accompanied by Khusraw and me. That day the health of 'Abdu'l-Bahá was not very satisfactory, as one could see by the signs of weariness on His blessed face. However, the Commander-in-chief of the Syrian and Palestine fronts was in Nazareth. He was Jamál Páshá, and 'Abdu'l-Bahá was determined to meet him there, so in spite of His great fatigue and physical weakness, the Beloved started on His journey . . .

'Abdu'l-Bahá . . . arrived at Nazareth in the evening at seven o'clock, and took up His residence at the German Hotel.

The next day the Master was invited to lunch at the home of one of the notables of the town of Nazareth. He was one of the Fahúm family. On that day Jamál Páshá, and nearly two hundred of the war leaders, were present at the lunch where the Master sat down at one o'clock and arose from the table at four.

During all those hours 'Abdu'l-Bahá was speaking in Turkish on philosophical and scientific subjects, and on heavenly teachings. So intense was His utterance that all stopped eating while they listened to His blessed words.

. . . Jamál Páshá, who had been His great enemy because of false accusations, had not paid the proper respect to 'Abdu'l-Bahá when He had first arrived. Now, however, having heard the Master speak so learnedly and wisely, he was most deferential and full of all kinds of politeness. When the time came for the Master to rise, Jamál Páshá most courteously held the Beloved's arm to assist Him to leave the table, and himself led the way to the reception room, and seated the Master comfortably.

Finally, after answering more questions, and giving wondrous light on many subjects, the Master arose to bid farewell to His host. Jamál Páshá accompanied Him out of the house, and to the bottom of the steps, and would have gone further with the Master, but was thanked with great kindness and urged by 'Abdu'l-Bahá to return. This was that Jamál Páshá who was not accustomed to rise from his seat to pay respect to any one . . . 'Abdu'l-Bahá was excessively fatigued, and remained that night at the German Hotel at Nazareth . . .[232]

But in time the constant insinuations of the violators had their effect. Jamál Páshá stated that he would crucify 'Abdu'l-Bahá, when he returned victorious from his campaigns. When he did come back, however, he was in full flight, defeated and humiliated, and could not stop to carry out his threat.

In the early months of the war, 'Abdu'l-Bahá said one

day that, if it had not been for the intrigues of the violators, He would have gathered together some of the leading men among the Muslims and the Christians of the Holy Land and would have counselled them to concert their efforts to prevent disorder. But the actions of the violators prevented this.

Relative inactivity and increasing isolation, in the opening months of 1915, made 'Abdu'l-Bahá remark, on another occasion, that He wished He had gone to India, where His presence had been fervently requested. Not having work to do, He said, had an adverse effect on His physical condition. But although pilgrims could no longer come and correspondence was almost halted, 'Abdu'l-Bahá was kept occupied with local affairs, and soon the task of raising and providing food for the Bahá'í community and many others in need faced Him. The mismanagement and the impositions of the Ottoman overlord were gradually leading to a state of near famine.

No matter how relaxed or arduous life might be, 'Abdu'l-Bahá always found or recalled a humorous situation. A cat purring beside His chair would amuse Him: this cat, He remarked, is indeed joyous, so carefree, so free of fear. A donkey standing in the street made Him remember that He saw no donkeys anywhere in the United States, and reminded Him of a polar bear in the Paris Zoo. People were staring at the bear, He said, and the animal was staring back, as if wanting to say: how did I get entangled with these folk? A man passing by the gates of 'Abdu'l-Bahá's house in Haifa, carrying a basket, put it down as soon as he saw Him, saying that he could not find a porter and had to carry the basket himself. 'Abdu'l-Bahá remarked afterwards that a man should not feel ashamed of doing useful work. Someone had written to ask where 'Abdu'l-Bahá was. Tell him, 'Abdu'l-Bahá replied with a smile: in front of a cannon.

The war fever slowly abated and life in 'Akká and Haifa, although not back to normal, became calmer and more sedate as the year advanced. 'Abdu'l-Bahá felt then that the Bahá'ís could return to their homes. Edith Sanderson, who had remained behind when other Western Bahá'ís had gone, and had moved to Abú-Sinán, left as early as January 1915. Well before Italy's entry into the war on the side of the Allies in May 1915, she had obtained a passage on an Italian boat. On May 5th the sojourn of the Bahá'ís at Abú-Sinán came to an end. On that day, the box that contained the portraits of the Báb and Bahá'u'lláh, which was always kept in the room of the Greatest Holy Leaf, was brought back to Haifa by Badí' Bushrú'í and Dr Mu'ayyad. Ten days later the doctor himself, who had rendered sterling services, set out for Persia by the Baghdád route. From Persia, where the Bahá'ís were still being persecuted, news had come of a fresh martyrdom. Shaykh 'Alí-Akbar-i-Qúchaní, a highly learned and respected Bahá'í teacher, who had served the Faith with distinction in the Caucasus and India, was shot while making purchases in the bazar of his native town. 'Abdu'l-Bahá sent this cable to a Bahá'í of Mashhad: '[May] My life be a sacrifice unto 'Alí-Akbar. I am well. 'Abbás'.

Írán fared very badly during the war. None of the belligerents respected her declared neutrality. Her own people adopted active partisan attitudes, the majority favouring Turkey and Germany. German and Turkish, Russian and British agents were everywhere. Russia and Turkey fought their battles in the north and the north-west of the country, each side receiving substantial aid from the Iranians. The British occupied the port of Bushire (Búshihr) in August 1915, and landed a small force at Bandar 'Abbás in March 1916, under Brigadier-General Sir Percy Sykes who, driving inland to Kirmán, Yazd and Isfahán, reached Shíráz in November. The central government was powerless. Bandits and highwaymen, as long as they did not get in the way of the belligerents, had the freedom of the roads and caravan routes. 'Abdu'l-Bahá had foreseen these lamentable events and had spoken of them to His countrymen in Paris. Bahá'ís had their share of tribulation. For them tragedy was never far off, and it was easy to make them suffer in order to appease others. The martyrdom of Mírzá Faḍlu'lláh, the Mu'ávinu't-Tujjár, a well-known merchant of Naráq (near Káshán), was a case in point. In Sulṭánábád (now Arák) a family of seven were slain in their home, in the dead of night.

With the Bahá'ís back in Haifa, weekly gatherings were resumed in the house of 'Abdu'l-Bahá, and it was in that latter half of the year 1915 that *The Memorials of the Faithful* took shape. These short biographies of early Bahá'ís, so eloquent and pellucid, animated and moving, were spoken by 'Abdu'l-Bahá in these meetings. Each one, a sparkling gem, will remain unmatched. Seventy-nine people are mentioned, and most of them are those who were exiled with Bahá'u'lláh to 'Akká. But others are included such as Ḥájí Mírzá Muḥammad-Taqí, the Vakílu'd-Dawlih (the builder of the Mashriqu'l-Adhkár of 'Ishqábád) and his brother, Ḥájí Mírzá Muḥammad-'Alí. Ṭáhirih, although a luminary of the Bábí Dispensation, also features in that galaxy. These talks of 'Abdu'l-Bahá were compiled into a book which was published in Haifa in 1924, with the title: *Tadhkiratu'l-Vafá*—The Memorials of the Faithful.

To this period (and a little beyond) also belongs a slim volume: *Risáliy-i-Tis'a-'Asharíyyih*—Nineteen Discourses on the lives of the Báb and His two heralds: Shaykh Aḥmad-i-Aḥsá'í and Siyyid Kázim-i-Rashtí. These discourses were written by Aḥmad Sohráb, at the instruction of 'Abdu'l-Bahá, for the use of the Bahá'í youth at meetings in the pilgrim house on Mount Carmel. 'Abdu'l-Bahá Himself corrected and amended them. *Nineteen Discourses*, together with a short autobiographical monograph by Áqá Muḥammad

Muṣṭafáy-i-Baghdádí* (who in his childhood went to Persia with his father, Shaykh Muḥammad-i-Shibl, in the company of Ṭáhirih), was published in Cairo in 1919, by Shaykh Muḥíyyi'd-Dín-i-Kurdí, an outstanding pupil of Mírzá Abu'l-Faḍl.

As the war years followed their weary course, the depredations and misgovernment of Ottoman authorities, to which was added devastation caused by locusts, led to increasing scarcities and hardships. 'Abdu'l-Bahá now arose to alleviate suffering. There were properties and lands in the Jordan Valley and beyond, at Samrah and 'Adasíyyih, and by the shores of the Sea of Galilee (Lake Tiberias), which 'Abdu'l-Bahá could cultivate for food. Some of these were part of the endowments of the Shrines of Bahá'u'lláh and the Báb. Sons of Mírzá Muḥammad-Qulí, the faithful half-brother of Bahá'u'lláh, owned land at Nuqayb, on the northern shore of the Sea of Galilee, where Mírzá Muḥammad-Qulí was buried.

In the past, 'Abdu'l-Bahá had stayed at Tiberias from time to time, whenever He needed a respite from the humidity of the coast. But in summer time the heat in Tiberias, and in the lands that lie below it, is intense and onerous. Until the return of normal conditions, 'Abdu'l-Bahá had to spend days and weeks in and around Tiberias. The wheat He sent to 'Akká was given into the care of a lady named Sakínih Sulṭán,[233] in whom He had great confidence. In a Tablet addressed to her, dated Shavvál 15th 1336 A.H. (July 26th 1918) ,'Abdu'l-Bahá says that because it has been very hot, so hot as to affect His breathing, perforce He has had to return to Tiberias. If He obtains relief in Tiberias, He will stay until all the wheat is secured; otherwise He will have to return to 'Akká and Haifa. He has sent some wheat

* Dr Zia (Ḍíyá) Baghdádí, son of Áqá Muḥammad-Muṣṭafá, was a well-known and much-loved figure in the American Bahá'í community for three decades. He died in 1937.

for the time being, to be distributed according to the list enclosed. He also states that prices have gone up considerably, more than threefold, in comparison with the previous year; the cost of transport is also doubled and trebled. It is indicated that there was a shortage of camels for transport, because 'Abdu'l-Bahá states that much more wheat will be dispatched when camels are available. In another Tablet, in which Sakínih Sulṭán is told to give two kayls* of wheat to Áqá Jamshíd, 'Abdu'l-Bahá says that He yearns to visit the Shrine of Bahá'u'lláh; He has been so heavily occupied that He has been prevented from going there.

Most of the communications to Sakínih Sulṭán, regarding the distribution of wheat, consist of a list of names and quantities. The brevity of the following may be indicative of how pressing time was:

	Ratls†
Neighbours' daughters	25
'Abdu'r-Raḥmán the son of Aḥmad Effendi	30
Ḥanná's wife	15
The fat woman	25
Rafí'ih	25
	120

Although at 'Abdu'l-Bahá's table, both before and after the war, His guests were provided with choice dishes, and there were times when He Himself cooked for them, His own food was often a very simple fare. He took little meat, and hardly any fruit. His preference was for milk, cheese and herbs such as mint, tarragon and basil.

The ravages of war were mounting. The British-Indian army was pushing forward in Mesopotamia, and in spite of

* Kayl was a measure for grain.
† Raṭl in Syria was equivalent to 5 lbs.

its grave set-back in April 1916, at Kút-al-'Amárah, it retrieved its position and captured Baghdád in March 1917. A month later the United States declared war on Germany. The isolation of the Holy Land was almost complete.

Shoghi Effendi said of 'Abdu'l-Bahá in those days:

> Agony filled His soul at the spectacle of human slaughter precipitated through humanity's failure to respond to the summons He had issued, or to heed the warnings He had given. Surely sorrow upon sorrow was added to the burden of trials and vicissitudes which He, since His boyhood, had borne so heroically for the sake, and in the service, of His Father's Cause.
>
> And yet during these somber days, the darkness of which was reminiscent of the tribulations endured during the most dangerous period of His incarceration in the prison-fortress of 'Akká, 'Abdu'l-Bahá, whilst in the precincts of His Father's Shrine, or when dwelling in the House He occupied in 'Akká, or under the shadow of the Báb's sepulcher on Mt. Carmel, was moved to confer once again, and for the last time in His life, on the community of His American followers a signal mark of His special favor by investing them, on the eve of the termination of His earthly ministry, through the revelation of the Tablets of the Divine Plan, with a world mission, whose full implications even now, after the lapse of a quarter of a century, still remain undisclosed, and whose unfoldment thus far, though as yet in its initial stages, has so greatly enriched the spiritual as well as the administrative annals of the first Bahá'í century.[234]

The Tablets of the Divine Plan are fourteen in number and were revealed at two separate times: eight of them in 1916, and six in 1917.[235] They can be thus tabulated:

1. Revealed on Sunday morning, March 26th 1916, in 'Abdu'l-Bahá's room at the house in Bahjí, addressed to the Bahá'ís of nine North-Eastern States of the United States:

Maine, New Hampshire, Rhode Island, Connecticut, Vermont, Pennsylvania, Massachusetts, New Jersey, and New York.

2. Revealed on Monday morning, March 27th 1916, in the garden adjacent to the Shrine of Bahá'u'lláh, addressed to the Bahá'ís of sixteen Southern States of the United States: Delaware, Maryland, Virginia, West Virginia, North Carolina, South Carolina, Georgia, Florida, Alabama, Mississippi, Tennessee, Kentucky, Louisiana, Arkansas, Oklahoma, and Texas.

3. Revealed on Wednesday morning, March 29th 1916, outside the house in Bahjí, and addressed to the Bahá'ís of twelve Central States of the United States: Michigan, Wisconsin, Illinois, Indiana, Ohio, Minnesota, Iowa, Missouri, North Dakota, South Dakota, Nebraska, and Kansas.

4. Revealed on Saturday morning, April 1st 1916, in 'Abdu'l-Bahá's room at the house in Bahjí, addressed to the Bahá'ís of eleven Western States of the United States: New Mexico, Colorado, Arizona, Nevada, Utah, California, Wyoming, Montana, Idaho, Oregon, and Washington.

5. Revealed on Wednesday morning, April 5th 1916, in the garden adjacent to the Shrine of Bahá'u'lláh, and addressed to the Bahá'ís of Canada, Newfoundland, Prince Edward Island, Nova Scotia, New Brunswick, Quebec, Manitoba, Alberta, Ontario, Saskatchewan, British Columbia, Yukon, Mackenzie, Ungava, Keewatin, Franklin Islands, and Greenland.

6. Revealed on Saturday morning, April 8th 1916, in the garden outside the Shrine of Bahá'u'lláh, and addressed to the Bahá'ís of the United States and Canada.

7. Revealed on Tuesday morning, April 11th 1916, in 'Abdu'l-Bahá's room at the house in Bahjí, and addressed to the Bahá'ís of the United States and Canada.

8. Revealed on Wednesday morning, April 19th 1916, in 'Abdu'l-Bahá's room at the house in Bahjí; on Thursday

morning, April 20th, in the pilgrims' quarters of the house in Bahjí; on Saturday morning, April 22nd, in the garden adjacent to the Shrine of Bahá'u'lláh, and addressed to the Bahá'ís of the United States and Canada.

9. Revealed on Friday morning, February 2nd 1917, in Ismá'íl Áqá's room at the house of 'Abdu'l-Bahá in Haifa, and addressed to the Bahá'ís of the nine North-Eastern States of the United States.

10. Revealed on Saturday morning, February 3rd 1917, in the same room in Haifa, and addressed to the Bahá'ís of the sixteen Southern States of the United States.

11. Revealed in the forenoon of Thursday, February 8th 1917, in Bahá'u'lláh's room at the house of 'Abbúd in 'Akká, and addressed to the Bahá'ís of the twelve Central States of the United States.

12. Revealed in the evening of Thursday, February 15th 1917, in Bahá'u'lláh's room at the house of 'Abbúd in 'Akká, and addressed to the Bahá'ís of the eleven Western States of the United States.

13. Revealed on Wednesday morning, February 21st 1917, in Bahá'u'lláh's room at the house of 'Abbúd in 'Akká, and addressed to the Bahá'ís of Canada.

14. Revealed in the afternoon of Thursday, March 8th 1917, in the summer-house (Ismá'íl Áqá's room) at 'Abdu'l-Bahá's house in Haifa, and addressed to the Bahá'ís of the United States and Canada.

The eight Tablets of 1916, revealed between March 26th and April 22nd—a time of special bounty for Bahá'ís, between Naw-Rúz (New Year) and Riḍván (the anniversary of the Declaration of Bahá'u'lláh)—include 'Abdu'l-Bahá's first messages to each of the five regions of the United States and Canada, where, although the Faith of Bahá'u'lláh had been known for 'about twenty-three years . . . no adequate and befitting motion' had 'been realized'; and include also three general Tablets embodying His 'mandate' to 'carry the fame of the Cause of God to the East and to the West and spread the Glad Tidings of the appearance of the Kingdom of the Lord of Hosts throughout the five continents of the world.'

Of these general Tablets, the first ('O ye blessed souls,' it began) directed attention, by name, to the territories, republics and islands of the Western Hemisphere (not including those in Canada and the United States). The second general Tablet ('O ye real Bahá'ís of America') was a call to look to the 'other continents of the globe'—'to Europe, Asia, Africa, Australia and the Islands of the Pacific'. Poignantly reminding them of His own longing 'to travel through these parts, even if necessary on foot and with the utmost poverty'—but 'now . . . not feasible' to his 'great regret'—He urged the believers to 'add a thousand times' to their efforts, for the more 'the circle of your exertion . . . is broadened and extended, the greater will be your confirmation'. The third general Tablet, ('O ye apostles of Bahá'u'lláh—May my life be a ransom to you!'), is a soul-stirring summons to 'the heavenly armies' of the Lord of Hosts, Bahá'u'lláh, imparting to them the three conditions on which their attainment to 'this supreme station' depends. So significant and potent is this Tablet, that it is quoted in full in Appendix II.

The six Tablets of 1917 expanded and reinforced 'Abdu'l-Bahá's guidance to the five regions of the United States and Canada, and concluded with a final general Tablet ('O ye heavenly souls, sons and daughters of the Kingdom'), which contained a remarkable exposition of the nature of collective centres—national, patriotic, political, cultural, and intellectual, which are but 'child's play' compared to the eternal Collective Centre of the 'sacred religions'—and renewed His appeal to travel throughout the Western Hemisphere.

For each of the five regions, and at the conclusion of the

four general Tablets, 'Abdu'l-Bahá revealed prayers of great beauty and power which continue to inspire, guide, and solace the Bahá'ís wherever they may be. In these Tablets He described in matchless words the qualities which must characterize the Bahá'í teacher, who 'must be heavenly, lordly and radiant', with his 'intention . . . pure, his heart independent, his spirit attracted, his thought at peace, his resolution firm, his magnanimity exalted and in the love of God a shining torch'. Wondrous promises He made, for various regions such as Panama, Greenland, and Canada, for the American Indians and the Eskimos, and most especially for the American believers and all who would arise in this Day to serve the Cause of Bahá'u'lláh:

'The earth will become illumined with the light of God. That light is the light of unity.'

'This is the most great work! Should you become confirmed therein, this world will become another world, the surface of the earth will become the delectable Paradise, and eternal Institutions be founded.'

'At present your confirmation is not known and understood . . . I hope that ere long it may throw a mighty reverberation through the pillars of the earth.'

In all, 'Abdu'l-Bahá mentioned by name in these Tablets some 120 territories and islands, to which the message of Bahá'u'lláh should be carried. When He did so, there were Bahá'ís in only 35 countries. Immediate response came from loving and devoted hearts, but before 'the proclamation of the oneness of humanity' could be raised to all the world 'systematically and enthusiastically', the Administrative Order had first to be developed as an instrument of collective teaching—a tremendous labour of sixteen years initiated by the Guardian of the Faith after 'Abdu'l-Bahá's passing—so that by 1937 the first stage in fulfilling the Tablets of the Divine Plan could be inaugurated in the First

Seven Year Plan of the American Bahá'í community. Since then, the launching of a number of teaching plans of limited scope in all continents, and the undertaking of two successive world-encompassing projects in which the Bahá'ís of the whole world have participated, have revealed the potentialities of the master-plan which the mind of 'Abdu'l-Bahá conceived in those years of sorrow and stress. But much still lies in the lap of the future, for the Tablets of the Divine Plan are no less than 'Abdu'l-Bahá's charter for the teaching of the Faith of Bahá'u'lláh throughout His Dispensation.*

On December 9th 1917, General Allenby entered Jerusalem. It now seemed certain that the days of the Ottoman rule in the Holy Land were numbered. But the life of 'Abdu'l-Bahá was still in danger. Let those who helped to avert that danger speak. First, Lady Blomfield:

In the spring of 1918, I was much startled and deeply disturbed by a telephone message: ' 'Abdu'l-Bahá in serious danger. Take immediate action.' It came from an authoritative source. There was not a moment to be lost. Every available power must be brought to bear to save the Master.

I went at once to Lord Lamington. His sympathetic regard for 'Abdu'l-Bahá, his understanding of the ramifications and 'red tape' necessary for 'immediate action' were of priceless value.

A letter was immediately written to the Foreign Office explaining the importance of 'Abdu'l-Bahá's position, His work for true peace, and for the spiritual welfare of many thousands of people. Through the influence of Lord Lamington, and his prompt help, the letter, with its

* All quotations in the paragraphs on the Tablets of the Divine Plan come from these Tablets. (See bibliography.)

alarming news, was at once put into the hands of Lord Balfour.*

That very evening a cable was sent to General Allenby with these instructions, 'Extend every protection and consideration to 'Abdu'l-Bahá, His family and His friends, when the British march on Haifa.'

So a terrible tragedy was averted, by the promptness and understanding of Lord Lamington and the power of Lord Balfour, his colleagues in the Cabinet here in London, and by the devotion, efficiency, and promptitude of Major Tudor-Pole at the Turkish end, for Haifa was still in the hands of the Turks.

The Turks had been so aroused by the enemies of the Master that they had threatened to crucify Him, and all His family, on Mount Carmel.

When General Allenby took Haifa, several days before it was believed possible for him to do so, he sent a cablegram to London which caused everybody to wonder, and especially filled the hearts of the Bahá'ís in all the world with deep gratitude to the Almighty Protector.

The cable of General Allenby was as follows: 'Have to-day taken Palestine. Notify the world that 'Abdu'l-Bahá is safe.'[236]

Major Tudor-Pole writes:

It must have been in the early spring of 1918 that I began to feel acute anxiety for 'Abdu'l-Bahá's safety at Haifa, and that of His family and followers there. I came out of the line in December 1917 during the attack on Jerusalem, and being temporarily incapacitated for active service, was transferred to Intelligence, first at Cairo and later at Ludd, Jaffa, and Jerusalem . . .

With an advance base at and around Jaffa, we were beginning to prepare for a move towards Haifa and the

* Then, the Right Honourable Arthur Balfour, Secretary of State for Foreign Affairs.

north at that time. For several reasons, including shortage of men and munitions, the British advance was delayed well into the summer of 1918.

Meanwhile, the news reaching me concerning 'Abdu'l-Bahá's imminent danger became more and more alarming. I tried to arouse interest in the matter among those who were responsible for Intelligence Service activities . . . I also brought the matter before my own chief, General Sir Arthur Money (Chief Administrator of Occupied Enemy Territory) . . .

At this time chance brought me into touch with an officer whose social and political connexions in London were strong. Through his courtesy and interest I was enabled to get an urgent message through to the British Foreign Office.

Through friends associated with the Bahá'í Cause in England, an independent avenue of approach to the ruling powers in London was discovered.

By these means Lord Balfour, Lord Curzon, and others in the Cabinet were advised as to the critical situation at Haifa. Lord Lamington's influence proved of special help at this time. The upshot of these various activities bore fruit, and the Foreign Office sent a despatch to General Allenby instructing him to ensure the safety of 'Abdu'l-Bahá and His family and entourage so soon as the British Army captured Haifa.

This despatch passed through my hands in Cairo *en route* for Army Headquarters at Ludd, . . . and Intelligence was requested to make urgent enquiry. In due course this demand for information reached the Headquarters of Intelligence at the Savoy Hotel, Cairo, and ultimately (when enquiries elsewhere had proved fruitless) was passed to me for action. As a result, General Allenby was provided with full particulars in regard to 'Abdu'l-Bahá . . . and the history of the Movement of which He was the Master.

Allenby at once issued orders to the General Commanding Officer in command of the Haifa operations to the effect that immediately the town was entered, a British guard was to be posted at once around 'Abdu'l-Bahá's house, and a further guard was to be placed at the disposal of His family and followers. Means were found for making it known within the enemy lines that stern retribution would follow any attempt to cause death or injury to the great Persian Master or to any of His household . . .

When Haifa was ultimately taken, these instructions for posting a guard were duly carried out, and all dangers of death or accident were thereby averted . . .

It was a wonderful experience in the midst of the chaos of war conditions to visit the Master at His Mount Carmel home, which even at that time was a haven of peace and refreshment.

I can remember Him, majestic yet gentle, pacing up and down His garden whilst He spoke to me about eternal realities, at a time when the whole material world was rocking on its foundations. The divine power of the spirit shone through His presence, giving one the feeling that a great prophet from Old Testament days had risen up in a war-stricken world, as an inspirer and spiritual guide for the human race.

One or two incidents which happened shortly afterwards, connected with the capture of Haifa, are worthy of record.

During the British advance from the south, field batteries were placed in position on high ground immediately to the south-east of Mount Carmel, the intention being to shell Haifa at long range over Mount Carmel itself. Some of the Eastern Bahá'ís living on the northern slopes of Mount Carmel becoming agitated, went to 'Abdu'l-Bahá's residence and expressed fear as to the tragic course of possible events. According to an eye-witness of this scene (from whom I obtained the story when I reached Haifa), 'Abdu'l-Bahá calmed His excited followers and called them to prayer. Then He told them that all would be well, and that no British shells would cause death or damage to the population or to Haifa and its environs. As a matter of historical fact, the range of the field batteries in question was inaccurate, the shells passing harmlessly over the town and falling into the Bay of 'Akká beyond.

Another incident of those stirring times is worthy of record, although I am not able to vouch for its complete accuracy at first hand. Before the fall of Haifa, 'Abdu'l-Bahá was discussing the British campaign with a few of His followers in His garden one day. He then predicted that, contrary to the general expectation, the taking of Haifa and the walled town of 'Akká would come about almost without bloodshed. This prediction was verified by the facts. He also stated that the Turks would surrender 'Akká (supposed to be impregnable) to two unarmed British soldiers. The resultant facts so far as I was able to gather them were as follows:—

Subsequent to the entry of our troops into Haifa, the front line was pushed forward half-way across the Bay of 'Akká, and outposts were placed in position on the sands of the Bay some four miles from 'Akká itself. 'Akká, as a fortified and walled town, was believed to be filled with Turkish troops at this time. Very early one morning two British Army Service soldiers, who had lost their bearings in the night, found themselves at the gates of 'Akká, believing erroneously that the town was already in British hands. However, the Turkish rearguard troops had been secretly evacuated only eight hours earlier, and the Mayor of the town, seeing British soldiers outside the gates, came down and presented them with the keys of the town in token of surrender! It is credibly stated that the dismayed Tommies, being unarmed, dropped the keys and made post haste for the British lines![237]

On September 23rd, British forces coming along the coastal road, rounded the promontory of Mount Carmel and appeared before Haifa. The Mayor and the notables went out to offer their submission. The first question that the British commanding officer put to the Mayor of Haifa was: 'Is 'Abdu'l-Bahá in this city? Is He safe?' 'Abdu'l-Bahá was sitting calm and unperturbed in the forecourt of His house. Bahá'ís were there around Him, tense and awaiting news. Indian army outriders arrived post-haste at the gates of the house. The next evening, the Governor of Jerusalem came in person to pay his respects. Lt-Colonel (later Sir) Ronald Storrs was not a stranger. He had known 'Abdu'l-Bahá as far back as the days of His incarceration within the city walls of 'Akká. He came again, the following morning—September 25th—before returning to Jerusalem.

CHAPTER 23

THE LAST YEARS OF HIS MINISTRY

The course of the war still had a few more weeks to run, but the isolation of the Holy Land was over. The first post-war contact with Bahá'í circles outside the Holy Land was provided with the arrival of Major Tudor-Pole at Haifa. He attained the presence of 'Abdu'l-Bahá, in the house of 'Abbúd in 'Akká, on November 19th 1918. He wrote:

> . . . The Master was standing at the top [of the stairway] waiting to greet me with that sweet smile and cheery welcome for which he is famous. For seventy-four long years Abdul-Baha has lived in the midst of tragedy and hardship, yet nothing has robbed or can rob him of his cheery optimism, spiritual insight and keen sense of humour.
>
> He was looking little older than when I saw him seven years ago, and certainly more vigorous than when in England after the exhausting American trip. His voice is as strong as ever, his step virile, his hair and beard are (if possible) more silver-white than before . . .
>
> . . . He still . . . spends a few weeks now and again in the Acca prison house, that has now become his property . . .
>
> After lunch Abdul-Baha drove me out to the Garden Tomb of Baha'o'llah about two miles from the city . . . He approached the Tomb in complete silence, praying with bent head—a wonderfully venerable figure in his white turban and flowing grey robe.
>
> On reaching the portal to the Tomb itself, the Master prostrated himself at length, and kissed the steps leading

to the inner chamber. There was a majestic humility about the action that baffles description . . .

. . . Then I went to pay my respects to the Military Governor . . .

. . . I returned to the prison house and spent the evening with the Master, supping with him and answering his questions about the new administration.

Then I slept in the room next Abdul-Baha's (which was Baha'o'llah's before him)—simple attics with stone floors and practically no furniture. Abdul-Baha still gives away all money, and lives the life of poverty himself.

Before breakfast the house was filled with believers who had come to receive the morning blessing.

I had brought Abdul-Baha letters from all parts of the world, and he spent the morning dictating replies for me to take away. I gave him the Persian camel-hair cloak, and it greatly pleased him, for the winter is here, and he had given away the only cloak he possessed. I made him promise to keep this one through the winter anyway, and I trust he does.

At lunch we had another long talk; then came the leave-taking and the Master's blessing. He sent greetings by me to all his friends in Egypt, Europe, England and America!

As I drove off on my return to Haifa, I caught a glimpse of the Master, staff in hand, wending his way through the awful Acca slums, on his way to attend the local Peace celebrations . . . He stands out a majestic figure . . .[238]

Shoghi Effendi wrote at the same time to Dr Luṭfu'lláh Ḥakím in London:

Captain [later Major] Tudor-Pole surprised and gladdened us with his unexpected arrival from Egypt . . . The Beloved has been sojourning for a month and a half at Acca, visiting almost daily the Tomb of his father and offering his thanksgivings for the bounty, care and protection of the Blessed Perfection . . .

I am so glad and privileged to be able to attend to my

IN THE GARDEN OF THE SHRINE OF BAHÁ'U'LLÁH

INVESTITURE AT HAIFA

Seated: 'Abdu'l-Bahá *Left to right:* Colonel E. A. Stanton, C.M.G., Military Governor of Haifa;
W. F. Bustání, Local Adviser to the Governor; Badí' Bushrú'í, M.A., District Officer Haifa
Behind left: the Head of the Druze Community; S̱h̲ay̲k̲h̲ Muḥammad Murád, Muftí of Haifa

Beloved's services after having completed my course of Arts and Sciences in the American University of Beirut. I am so anxious . . . to hear from you and of your services to the Cause for by transmitting them to the Beloved I shall make him happy, glad and strong . . .[239]

Until he left for England in the spring of 1920, to continue his studies at Balliol College, Oxford, Shoghi Effendi acted as 'Abdu'l-Bahá's secretary and translated His Tablets addressed to the Bahá'ís of the West.

Laura and Hippolyte Dreyfus-Barney were the first pilgrims who arrived from the West, at the conclusion of the war. Major Tudor-Pole facilitated their journey through the official channels in Cairo. Soon after this they went to the United States.

As soon as the Holy Land had passed out of the hands of its Ottoman rulers, Mrs Parsons had written to 'Abdu'l-Bahá to request Him to revisit America. A few days before, a Feast was being held in Chicago (on October 16th) at the home of Mr and Mrs Leo Perron. The suggestion was made there to supplicate 'Abdu'l-Bahá to come again. The House of Spirituality (the Local Spiritual Assembly) of Chicago decided that such a supplication should go out from all the Bahá'ís of the land. When it was finally drawn up with the agreement of other local communities, it bore more than a thousand signatures. It read:

To our Beloved Abdul-Baha:

We, thy humble servants in America, rejoice that the door of communication is at last open and we beg of God that it may ever remain so.

Unworthy are we, yet we supplicate thee, we beseech thee, if it be God's will, to turn thy blessed countenance toward us, that all the regions of the West, even as the East, may be quickened by thy glorious presence.

In the past thou didst promise us, in words creative of

fulfillment, that, when the hearts of the friends were united, then again thou wouldst visit America.

Our hearts are united in incessant longing for thee, in complete dependence upon thy love and thy veriest command. May our overwhelming need of thee draw thee speedily to the West and to us, who greet thee in the sacred, wondrous name of El-Abha.[240]

'Abdu'l-Bahá replied in May 1919 that their unity and constancy would be the magnet to draw Him to America. Previously, He had cabled that the Convention about to be held at Hotel McAlpin, New York City, should be the 'Convention of the Covenant', because it was to be the occasion for the unveiling of the Tablets of the Divine Plan. These Tablets had lain for a while, during the war, in the vaults under the mausoleum on Mount Carmel. On December 23rd 1918, Aḥmad Sohráb left the Holy Land to take them to America. During that memorable Convention, April 26th–30th (the annual meeting of Bahá'í Temple Unity), the Tablets were presented and read to the American Bahá'ís.*

With the war at an end, letters and supplications were pouring in. On January 29th 1919, Shoghi Effendi informed Dr Baghdádí, in the United States, that nearly a hundred Tablets had been revealed for the Bahá'ís in America; some had been sent and others would follow. The Bahá'ís of the East and of Europe were also having their share of this bounty.† Pilgrims, too, were now arriving from both the East and the West. And the officials of the newly-established

* The first five Tablets had been published in *Star of the West*, Vol. VII, in the issue of September 8th 1916.

† Between 1909 and 1916, a collection in three volumes of 'Abdu'l-Bahá's Tablets was published in New York. Preponderantly addressed to American Bahá'ís, they also contained Tablets written to communities and individuals in other parts of the world.

British administration were calling more and more on 'Abdu'l-Bahá.

The military administration opened a relief fund in Haifa to which 'Abdu'l-Bahá contributed fifty Egyptian pounds.* His name stood at the head of the list. Later He made a further contribution; the following letter of February 10th 1919 speaks for itself:

Your Eminence:

I have today received from your grandson [Shoghi Effendi] the sum of £50 as a further donation from yourself to the Haifa Relief Fund. Please accept on behalf of the committee of management, my very sincerest and most grateful thanks for this further proof of your well-known generosity and care of the poor, who will forever bless you for your liberality on their behalf. Please accept the sincerest assurance of my deepest regards and respect.

(Signed) G. A. Stanton, Colonel, Military Governor.[241]

Another relief project which 'Abdu'l-Bahá greatly encouraged was the Save the Children Fund, which functions today all over the world. Eglantyne Jebb was the founder of the organization which was set up to do exactly what its name indicated. She and her sister were moved to action, in the first instance, particularly by the pitiful condition of children in Central and Eastern Europe. Lady Blomfield, who was a friend of Eglantyne Jebb, had become associated with her in this humanitarian work and, since she was living a good part of the year in Geneva, she had established a special 'Blomfield Fund' at 4 Rue Massot in that city, which was the headquarters of the International Union of Save the Children (Union Internationale de Secours aux Enfants). The purpose of the Blomfield Fund (sponsored in London

* At that time the Egyptian pound was worth slightly more than the pound sterling.

by Lord Weardale) was to finance 'workrooms for children or for other relief work of a constructive character, which will increasingly constitute a more and more important part of the activities of the Save the Children Fund movement.' The foregoing lines are quoted from a pamphlet which Lady Blomfield wrote under the title, *The First Obligation*. This is the Foreword to that pamphlet:

Extract from a Tablet written to Lady Blomfield by Sir Abdul Baha Abbas, K.B.E., and dated Mount Carmel, Palestine, 23rd July 1921.

The Pamphlet thou didst compile, appealing to the World of Humanity to help these desolate children is very much approved of, and at its beginning, write these words:

To contribute towards the cause of these pitiful children, and to protect and care for them is the highest expression of altruism and worship, and is well-pleasing to the Most High the Almighty, the Divine Provider. For these little ones have no protecting father and mother, no kind nurse, no home, no clothing, no food, no comfort, no place of rest.

In all these things they call for our kindness, they merit our help, they are deserving of mercy and of our utmost pity.

The eyes of all who love Justice are filled with tears, and every understanding heart burneth with pity!

Oh ye peoples of the World, show Compassion!

Oh ye Concourse of the Wise, hold out your hands to help!

Oh ye Nobles, show Loving Kindness. Be Bountiful!

Oh ye Wealthy of the Earth, shower Contributions!

Oh ye Men, strong and brave of heart, manifest your Benevolence!

'Abdu'l-Bahá's commendation of those who worked for the Save the Children Fund is also contained within that pamphlet.* The following is an extract from a Tablet (of June 1920) written to one such worker:

My hope is that, through the especial Grace of God, this Association (Save the Children Fund) will be confirmed (assisted and strengthened by Divine Power); that it may day by day progress both spiritually and materially; . . . that it may be protected from every danger; and that the Oneness of Humanity may, through the work of this Society (Save the Children Fund) raise its banner at the zenith of the world.

In the evening of July 21st 1919 a banquet was held at Bahjí, offered by a pilgrim. Some forty sat at the richly laden table. 'Abdu'l-Bahá walked round serving the guests. Bedouins had encamped nearby, and they too received a generous share. Then their children came, and to each child 'Abdu'l-Bahá gave a coin. The next morning, when the pilgrims and guests had gone back to Haifa and 'Akká, and 'Abdu'l-Bahá was sitting in the garden adjacent to the Shrine of Bahá'u'lláh, revealing Tablets addressed to the Bahá'ís of the West, fathers of those children came to offer Him their gratitude for His generosity to their children, and to ask for His blessing.

Meanwhile the Peace Conference in Paris was dragging on amidst fresh controversies and mounting misery in Eastern and Central Europe. In a Tablet addressed to David Buchanan of Portland, Oregon, 'Abdu'l-Bahá wrote:

Thy letter dated December 2nd, 1918, was received. Although the representatives of various governments are assembled in Paris in order to lay the foundations of Universal Peace and thus bestow rest and comfort upon the world of humanity, yet misunderstanding among

* See Appendix III.

some individuals is still predominant and self-interest still prevails. In such an atmosphere, Universal Peace will not be practicable, nay rather, fresh difficulties will arise. This is because interests are conflicting and aims are at variance . . .[242]

On December 17th of that year, 1919, 'Abdu'l-Bahá revealed one of His most remarkable Tablets, addressed to the Central Organization For A Durable Peace at The Hague. This organization was not an official body. The president of its Executive Committee was Dr H. C. Dresselhuys of Holland. Great Britain was represented by G. Lowes Dickinson and Austria by Professor Dr H. Lammasch, well-known progressive thinkers in their respective countries. 'Abdu'l-Bahá wrote:

> O ye esteemed ones who are pioneers among the well-wishers of the world of humanity!
> The letters which ye sent during the war were not received, but a letter dated February 11th, 1916, has just come to hand, and immediately an answer is being written. Your intention deserves a thousand praises, because you are serving the world of humanity, and this is conducive to the happiness and welfare of all. This recent war has proved to the world and the people that war is destruction while Universal Peace is construction . . .

'Abdu'l-Bahá explained what the basic principles of the Faith were, warned the Committee that others might come from the East presenting these teachings as their own, and on the question of peace He wrote:

> . . . although the League of Nations has been brought into existence, yet it is incapable of establishing Universal Peace. But the Supreme Tribunal which . . . Bahá'u'lláh has described will fulfil this sacred task with the utmost might and power. And his plan is this: that the national

assemblies of each country and nation—that is to say parliaments—should elect two or three persons who are the choicest men of that nation, and are well informed concerning international laws and the relations between governments and aware of the essential needs of the world of humanity in this day. The number of these representatives should be in proportion to the number of inhabitants of that country. The election of these souls who are chosen by the national assembly, that is, the parliament, must be confirmed by the upper house, the congress and the cabinet and also by the president or monarch so these persons may be the elected ones of all the nation and the government. From among these people the members of the Supreme Tribunal will be elected, and all mankind will thus have a share therein, for every one of these delegates is fully representative of his nation. When the Supreme Tribunal gives a ruling on any international question, either unanimously or by majority-rule, there will no longer be any pretext for the plaintiff or ground of objection for the defendant. In case any of the governments or nations, in the execution of the irrefutable decision of the Supreme Tribunal, be negligent or dilatory, the rest of the nations will rise up against it, because all the governments and nations of the world are the supporters of this Supreme Tribunal. Consider what a firm foundation this is! But by a limited and restricted *League* the purpose will not be realized as it ought and should . . .[243]

'Abdu'l-Bahá addressed a second and shorter Tablet to the Hague Committee, in July 1920. He wrote:

Your kind answer to my letter, dated 12th of June 1920, has arrived and greatly pleased me. Praise be unto God, that it was indicative of the fact that your motive and purpose is identical with that of ours. Its contents also consisted of spiritual susceptibilities which are expressive of sincere love.

We, Baha'is, feel great affection towards that honorable Assembly. Therefore have we sent two honored persons* to that highly esteemed Assembly as a sign of strong relationship.

Today the most important problem in the affairs of the world of humanity is that of the Universal Peace, which is the greatest means contributing to the very life and happiness of mankind. Without this most luminous reality it is impossible for humanity to attain to actual comfort and proficiency. Nay rather, shall it have, day by day, some actual misfortune and tragedy . . .[244]

Lord Lamington was, in the early part of 1919, directing the Syrian Relief work, with his headquarters at Damascus. He called on 'Abdu'l-Bahá on July 15th to receive in his own words 'the blessings' of the Master. To 'Abdu'l-Bahá's expressed purpose to return the visit Lord Lamington said: 'No, my duty and my privilege is to call on you personally and I do not wish you to take the trouble to come over to me.' Lord Lamington came again on the 17th to bid farewell. He was returning to Britain. On this occasion 'Abdu'l-Bahá gave him His ring (see page 522). To Lord Lamington's query, 'Abdu'l-Bahá said that if circumstances permitted, He would go to visit 'Ishqábád, then Japan and India.

Major-General Watson, the Chief Administrator of the Southern Section of occupied territory, met 'Abdu'l-Bahá in Haifa, on August 23rd, at the home of Colonel Stanton, the Military Governor. On October 4th, 'Abdu'l-Bahá, at the invitation of Major Williamson, the acting Military Governor of Haifa, went aboard a warship, H.M.S. *Marlborough*, which had taken part in the Battle of Jutland. He was shown round the ship, and when He was having tea with the Commander of the ship, Major Williamson, and Captain Lowick (deputy Military Governor of 'Akká), He said that this was the first time in His life that He had

* The Hand of the Cause Ibn-i-Asdaq and Ahmad Yazdaní.

been on board a man-of-war, and He hoped and trusted that all the implements and means of warfare would be turned one day into means to promote peace and industrial prosperity, and that all the men-of-war would eventually become merchant ships, thereby stimulating trade and industry.

In the afternoon of October 20th, two Indian soldiers, devout Muslims, arrived at the door of 'Abdu'l-Bahá's house and asked to meet Him. Their camp was some distance from Haifa and they had walked all the way. They had first heard of Him in India, had been to Mecca, where they performed the rites of pilgrimage, and now, at the first opportunity, had come to meet Him; it was their duty they felt. Kneeling before Him they wept with joy. 'Abdu'l-Bahá was most kind to them and greeted them as a father. Later, they followed 'Abdu'l-Bahá to the Shrine of the Báb.

There were many such incidents in the life of 'Abdu'l-Bahá.

And many were the pilgrims who were now arriving from the West, among them Dr and Mrs Baghdádí (who stayed for a year), George Latimer, Mr and Mrs William Randall with their daughter Margaret, Mrs Corinne True and her daughter, Edna True. Dr John Ebenezer Esslemont arrived on November 4th. He wrote in his immortal work, *Bahá'u'-lláh and the New Era*:

During the winter of 1919–20 the writer had the great privilege of spending two and a half months as the guest of 'Abdu'l-Bahá at Haifa and intimately observing his daily life. At that time, although nearly seventy-six years of age, he was still remarkably vigorous, and accomplished daily an almost incredible amount of work. Although often very weary he showed wonderful powers of recuperation, and his services were always at the disposal of those who needed them most. His unfailing patience, gentleness, kindliness and tact made his presence like a benediction. It was his custom to spend a large part of each night in prayer and meditation*. From early morning until evening, except for a short siesta after lunch, he was busily engaged in reading and answering letters from many lands and in attending to the multitudinous affairs of the household and of the Cause. In the afternoon he usually had a little relaxation in the form of a walk or a drive, but even then he was usually accompanied by one or two, or a party of, pilgrims with whom he would converse on spiritual matters, or he would find opportunity by the way of seeing and ministering to some of the poor. After his return he would call the friends to the usual evening meeting in his salon. Both at lunch and supper he used to entertain a number of pilgrims and friends, and charm his guests with happy and humorous stories as well as precious talks on a great variety of subjects. 'My home is the home of laughter and mirth,' he declared, and indeed it was so. He delighted in gathering together people of various races, colours, nations and religions in unity and cordial friendship around his hospitable board. He was indeed a loving father not only to the little community at Haifa, but to the Bahá'í community throughout the world.[245]

Dr Esslemont tells us in the Introduction to his book that he had brought the manuscript with him to Haifa, at the invitation of 'Abdu'l-Bahá, Who discussed it with him on several occasions, and made some 'valuable suggestions for its improvement'. 'Abdu'l-Bahá's intention was to have it translated into Persian so that he could read and amend it where necessary; but He was able to correct only three and a half chapters before His passing. In 1924 Dr Esslemont

* 'Abdu'l-Bahá oftentimes woke up at midnight to pray and meditate and reveal Tablets, having gone to bed two or three hours earlier. (H.M.B.)

left England for Haifa at Shoghi Effendi's invitation, where he died in November 1925, and was posthumously named a Hand of the Cause of God by the Guardian of the Faith.

Mírzá Asadu'lláh, Fáḍil-i-Mázindarání—a learned Bahá'í of Írán—was one of the pilgrims who came at the close of 1919. 'Abdu'l-Bahá directed him to the United States. Fáḍil reached New York in time for the Twelfth Annual Convention (1920) of Bahá'í Temple Unity which was being held, once again, at Hotel McAlpin. He stayed for a year in America, travelling around the country to assist and stimulate the Bahá'í communities.*

On Tuesday, April 27th, in the afternoon session of the Convention, the design for the Mashriqu'l-Adhkár at Wilmette, Illinois, was finally chosen by the forty-nine delegates present. Designs were submitted by three architects—Louis Bourgeois, William Sutherland Maxwell, and Charles Mason Remey—and Louis Bourgeois' design was chosen by a majority vote of the delegates. Upon Remey's proposal the decision to adopt Bourgeois' plan was made unanimous. The work of boring the ground for the foundation of the building was started on September 24th 1920.

On that same April 27th of 1920, in the garden of the Military Governor of Haifa, 'Abdu'l-Bahá was invested with the insignia of the Knighthood of the British Empire. That knighthood was conferred on Him in recognition of His humanitarian work during the war for the relief of distress and famine. He accepted the honour as the gift of a 'just king' but never used the title. Lady Blomfield writes:

The dignitaries of the British crown from Jerusalem were gathered in Haifa, eager to do honour to the Master, Whom every one had come to love and reverence for His life of unselfish service. An imposing motor-car

* Fáḍil left the United States on July 9th 1921, bound for the Holy Land.

had been sent to bring 'Abdu'l-Bahá to the ceremony. The Master, however, could not be found. People were sent in every direction to look for Him, when suddenly from an unexpected side he appeared, alone, walking His kingly walk, with that simplicity of greatness which always enfolded Him.

The faithful servant, Isfandíyár, whose joy it had been for many years to drive the Master on errands of mercy, stood sadly looking on at the elegant motor-car which awaited the honoured guest.

'No longer am I needed.'

At a sign from Him, Who knew the sorrow, old Isfandíyár rushed off to harness the horse, and brought the carriage out at the lower gate, whence 'Abdu'l-Bahá was driven to a side entrance of the garden of the Governorate of Phoenicia.

So Isfandíyár was needed and happy.[246]

French forces occupied Damascus on July 24th 1920, and King Fayṣal (Faisal) lost his throne. The following year he gained another throne, in 'Iráq. In between, he journeyed here and there. His journeyings took him to Haifa and into the presence of 'Abdu'l-Bahá. General Allenby was another distinguished visitor. He and his wife had luncheon with 'Abdu'l-Bahá at Bahjí, and 'Abdu'l-Bahá, Himself, conducted them to the Shrine of Bahá'u'lláh. Sir Herbert (later Viscount) Samuel was appointed High Commissioner for Palestine in 1920, once the Mandate had been established. He called several times on 'Abdu'l-Bahá at His home in Haifa.

Dr Ba<u>gh</u>dádí, after a year's absence, arrived back in the United States in October 1920; he had much to tell the American Bahá'ís. 'Abdu'l-Bahá had told him the story of the widow of a martyr in Persia. She had two children to bring up and earned a livelihood by knitting socks. One pair she knitted to provide her children with the necessities of life, and one pair she knitted to earn money to give to the funds for the Mashriqu'l-Adhkár in America. On the question of racial harmony, 'Abdu'l-Bahá had reminded Dr Baghdádí of His statement, when in America, that blood would flow if nothing were done to establish harmony between the black and the white.

The first responses to the Tablets of the Divine Plan (see p. 420) brought particular joy to 'Abdu'l-Bahá. Clara and Hyde Dunn set out from California to settle in Australia, where they arrived in April 1920. Father Dunn, as Hyde Dunn came to be called, was then sixty-two years old. He lived to see the establishment of a National Spiritual Assembly in Australia and New Zealand in 1934, and on his death in February 1941 the Guardian of the Faith accorded him the honour of being Australia's 'spiritual conqueror' and, some years later, also a Hand of the Cause. Mother Dunn, in her turn, was raised to the rank of a Hand of the Cause by the Guardian, in February 1952, and continued her valiant and inspiring services into her ninety-second year. She died in November 1960.

Martha Root, who was a journalist by profession, embarked for South America in July 1920. This was the start of her travels to every part of the globe—of visits to kings and queens, presidents and statesmen, to universities and colleges and the eminent figures of the academic world, as well as to many others outstanding among men, and of attendance at diverse gatherings and conferences—with the sole object of making known the name of Bahá'u'lláh, and of acquainting those directing the affairs of mankind with His Teachings. That heroic woman left this world in Honolulu, in 1939, just when the Second World War had broken out and fresh miseries were to come. By the Guardian of the Faith, whom she had served with such love and fidelity, she was honoured with this promise after her death: 'Posterity will establish her as foremost Hand of Cause which 'Abdu'l-Bahá's Will has raised up in first Bahá'í century.'

The last month of 1920 witnessed the death of two Bahá'ís, one still young and one very, very old, whose services enriched the annals of the Apostolic Age of the Faith of Bahá'u'lláh. Lillian Kappes, the distinguished teacher of the Tarbíyat School, whose services 'Abdu'l-Bahá had so much valued, died on December 1st in Ṭihrán and Ḥájí Mírzá Ḥaydar-'Alí, the veteran of so many battles, died in Haifa on December 27th.

The first All-India Bahá'í Convention was held in Bombay at the close of the year, December 27th to 29th. It sent a supplication to 'Abdu'l-Bahá to visit India. The *Times of India* copiously reported the proceedings of the Convention. An eminent visitor was Sir Patrick Geddes, who then held the Chair of Botany at the Bombay University, and he wrote for the *Bahá'í News* of Bombay:

My first acquaintance with the illustrious and saintly leader of the Bahai Movement was as one of his chairmen in course of his lectures in Edinburgh on his tour through the West some years ago before the war. After this meeting he became interested in the practical methods of my 'Outlook Tower' at Edinburgh, and found in these something of that incorporation of science into life, and, therefore, into religion, which is one of the tenets in which the Bahai organization, guided by his teaching, takes so eminent a lead among the religious bodies of the present. He indeed then asked me to deliver a public lecture on those lines to those attending his teachings, which I did under his chairmanship.

During each of the past two years I have been town-planning in Palestine and not only for Jerusalem, but also for his own home city of Haifa, and have thus had more than one opportunity of meeting him again.

On the last occasion of calling on him, I had the

pleasant duty of conveying to him a unanimous request
from 'Pro-Carmel', a new society of citizens, founded on
the lines of the better-known 'Pro-Jerusalem', and with
the same purpose of advancing all the common interests
of the city, without distinction of race, party or creed, and
thus embracing all. Their desire was that he should
become the President of this new Society, which unites
Moslems, Jews, Christians and Bahais in the work of
social service and of civic and regional improvements in
all respects, moral and educational, as well as material,
hygienic, architectural and artistic, etc.

This office and leadership he cordially accepted to the
great satisfaction of all concerned, since all Haifa looks
up to and is proud of him as the foremost of their fellow-
citizens.

He also approved and authorized the proposed town-
planning scheme, as arranged between the City Engineer,
Dr. Ciffrin, and myself so far as his fairly extensive
property (on the slope of Carmel above Haifa) is concerned. He granted the land for the two new public
roads which are required, without accepting compensation
on the land taken, and he also presented a substantial
piece of ground for the public school which is required in
that vicinity, some 4,000 square metres.

Dr. Ciffrin, in his architectural capacity has produced
a fine scheme for a monumental stairway and cypress
avenue leading uphill from the Templar Boulevard upon
the level plain, to the central meeting place of the Bahai
community in Haifa, which as all Bahais doubtless know,
contains the Tomb of the Bab.

For this scheme (of which the design is a gift by Dr.
Ciffrin), between £2,000 and £3,000 will be required; but
he and I and other friends and sympathizers are confident
that this sum will readily be subscribed within a reasonable
time by the many members and friends of the Bahai
Cause throughout the world. Sir Abbas at once expressed
himself as approving the design, and gratified by it, as at
once a useful and needed access, and a beautiful and

dignified memorial. He granted the land, and promised also to compensate from his own ground, the small portion of a Moslem neighbor's ground which is also required to complete the scheme. He further gave a subscription of £100 to begin the list; but while authorizing us to open a subscription list, and send it to friends and sympathizers, he charged us to be careful to explain this as a purely voluntary matter, and not to represent him as in any way pressing his followers or friends to subscribe, and this we of course promised to do . . .[247]

The construction of the Mashriqu'l-Adhkár in the United States was raising many problems, and the advice of the Master was sought. 'Abdu'l-Bahá told the American Bahá'ís to take these matters to the coming Convention.

In the Holy Land, Fujita had arrived from the United States and Luṭfu'lláh Ḥakím from London, to serve 'Abdu'l-Bahá. They helped chiefly with the reception of pilgrims. A house close to 'Abdu'l-Bahá's house had been prepared for pilgrims from the West. Mrs Emogene Hoagg looked after the pilgrims there during the summer of 1921. A little above 'Abdu'l-Bahá's house, land was purchased on the other side of the road for the building of a Western pilgrim house in the future.

'Abdu'l-Bahá was particularly unwell in the early part of 1921. In March He went to stay for a while in Tiberias. Back in Haifa, He would spend some nights on Mount Carmel in the vicinity of the Shrine of the Báb.

That summer 'Abdu'l-Bahá received a letter from Dr Auguste (August-Henri) Forel, the celebrated Swiss psychiatrist and entomologist. Later Forel wrote in his testament:

In the year 1920, at Karlsruhe, I first made acquaintance with the supraconfessional world-religion of the Baha'i, founded in the East seventy years ago by the Persian

Baha'u'llah. It is the true religion of the welfare of human society, it has neither priests nor dogmas, and it binds together all the human beings who inhabit this little globe. I have become a Baha'i. May this religion continue and be crowned with success; this is my most ardent wish.[248]

The Tablet which 'Abdu'l-Bahá addressed to him, in answer to his letter, is described by Shoghi Effendi as 'one of the most weighty the Master ever wrote'.[249] These are the opening words of the Tablet:

O revered personage, lover of truth! Thy letter dated July 28th 1921, hath been received. The contents thereof were most pleasing and indicated that, praised be the Lord, thou art as yet young and searchest after truth, that thy power of thought is strong and the discoveries of thy mind manifest.

And these the concluding words:

In conclusion, these few words are written, and unto everyone they will be a clear and conclusive evidence of the truth. Ponder them in thine heart. The will of every sovereign prevaileth during his reign, the will of every philosopher findeth expression in a handful of disciples during his lifetime, but the Power of the Holy Spirit shineth radiantly in the realities of the Messengers of God, and strengtheneth their will in such wise as to influence a great nation for thousands of years and to regenerate the human soul and revive mankind. Consider how great is this power! It is an extraordinary Power, an all-sufficient proof of the truth of the mission of the Prophets of God, and a conclusive evidence of the power of a Divine Inspiration.

The Glory of Glories rest upon thee.[250]

The isolation from the Holy Land, imposed by the war, had given an opportunity to the violators in the United States (to whose band Dr Faríd was added) to agitate afresh. They had tried very hard to split the American Bahá'í community, and 'Abdu'l-Bahá's last years became even more burdened, because of their activities, but in the end they failed miserably.

In His last Tablet addressed to the Bahá'ís of America, only a fortnight before His passing, 'Abdu'l-Bahá wrote:

O ye friends of God! 'Abdu'l-Bahá is day and night thinking of you and mentioning you, for the friends of God are dear to Him. Every morning at dawn I supplicate the Kingdom of God and ask that you may be filled with the breath of the Holy Spirit, so that you may become brilliant candles, shine with the light of guidance and dispel the darkness of error. Rest assured that the confirmations of the Abhá Kingdom will continuously reach you.

Through the power of the divine springtime, the downpour of the celestial clouds and the heat of the Sun of Reality, the tree of life is just beginning to grow. Before long, it will produce buds, bring forth leaves and fruits, and cast its shade over the East and the West. This Tree of Life is the Book of the Covenant.

In America, in these days, severe winds have surrounded the Lamp of the Covenant, hoping that this brilliant Light may be extinguished, and this Tree of Life may be uprooted. Certain weak, capricious, malicious and ignorant souls have been shaken by the earthquake of hatred, of animosity, have striven to efface the Divine Covenant and Testament, and render the clear water muddy so that in it they might fish. They have arisen against the Centre of the Covenant like the people of the Bayán who attacked the Blessed Beauty and every moment uttered a calumny. Every day they seek a pretext and secretly arouse doubts, so that the Covenant of Bahá'u'lláh may be completely annihilated in America.

O friends of God! Be awake, be awake; be vigilant, be vigilant . . .

Yá Bahá'u'l-Abhá! 'Abdu'l-Bahá did not rest a moment until He had raised Thy Cause and the Standard of the Kingdom of Abhá waved over the world. Now some people have arisen with intrigues and evil aspirations to trample this flag in America, but My hope is in Thy confirmations . . .[251]

On November 12th, just sixteen days before His ascension, 'Abdu'l-Bahá sent a cable to Roy Wilhelm in New York, which showed the depth of His concern for that community of the West whose creation, training, and protection had constituted one of the major aspects of His ministry. This cable is the expression of His heart-felt longing for their spiritual safety:

I implore health from divine bounty, Abbas.

The American Bahá'í community remained firm and undivided.

CHAPTER 24

THE PASSING OF 'ABDU'L-BAHÁ

The night of July 10th 1921 'Abdu'l-Bahá was on Mount Carmel by the Shrine of the Báb. There, He revealed a Tablet and a prayer in honour of a 'kinsman of the Bab',* who had died recently. 'Abdu'l-Bahá beseeched God, in that prayer, for His own release from this world. He spoke of His 'loneliness', of being 'broken-winged', 'submerged in seas of sorrows': 'O Lord! My bones are weakened, and the hoar hairs glisten on My head . . . and I have now reached old age, failing in My powers . . . No strength is there left in Me wherewith to arise and serve Thy loved ones . . . O Lord, My Lord! Hasten My ascension unto Thy sublime Threshold . . . and My arrival at the Door of Thy grace beneath the shadow of Thy most great mercy . . .'

That prayer was answered less than five months later. He passed away in the early hours of November 28th.

The physician, who was summoned to His bedside at that hour, and closed His eyes, was Dr Florian Krug of New York, the same man who once bitterly resented the Faith of Bahá'u'lláh, and wanted alienists to examine his wife because of her intense devotion to it. He had now come, a pilgrim, with his wife, and 'Abdu'l-Bahá had allocated them a room in the compound of His own house.

A special announcement, issued in the morning, by the family of 'Abdu'l-Bahá and the Bahá'ís of Haifa, gave the

* That 'kinsman of the Báb' was the father of the present writer, who had died in Ṭihrán, on May 6th.

public the news of His passing and of the funeral arrangements for the following day. However,

Early on Monday morning . . . the news of this sudden
calamity had spread over the city, causing an unprecedented stir and tumult, and filling all hearts with un-
utterable grief.[252]

In the afternoon this statement appeared:

We all belong unto God and unto Him do we all return.
The Islamic Association announces with much regret the
passing of the highly-learned, greatly-erudite, generous
benefactor, His Eminence 'Abdu'l-Bahá 'Abbás. His bier
will be carried from His home, to-morrow, Tuesday, at
9 o'clock in the morning. You are requested to accept
this announcement as a special invitation to assemble for
His funeral procession. May God immerse Him in His
boundless mercy, and grant solace unto His family and
His people.

In the land that we know as the Holy Land, in all its
turbulent history of the last two thousand years, there had
never been an event which could unite all its inhabitants of
diverse faiths and origins and purposes, in a single expression
of thought and feeling, as did the passing of 'Abdu'l-Bahá.
Jews and Christians and Muslims and Druzes, of all per-
suasions and denominations; Arabs and Turks and Kurds
and Armenians and other ethnic groups were united in
mourning His passing, in being aware of a great loss they
had suffered.

In a 'Private Memorandum' sent from 61, St James's
Street, London, S.W.1, Major Tudor-Pole wrote:

On Tuesday 29th of November, 1921, at 9.30 a.m., a
cablegram addressed 'Cyclometry London' reached this

office. It had been despatched from Haifa at 3 p.m. on
28th November, 1921, and contained the following
momentous news:

'His Holiness Abdul Baha ascended to the Kingdom
of Abha. Please inform friends.' (signed) 'Greatest Holy
Leaf'. Friends in London were notified immediately by
wire, telephone and letter, and a cablegram was despatched
to the Holy Family at Haifa expressing the sorrowing
loving sympathy of all the Friends in this country.

Cables were sent to the High Commissioner and Sir
Wyndham Deedes at Jerusalem, and every step was taken
by the British Authorities in Palestine to show respect
for the memory of the Beloved Departed, and to render
any services required by the Family and the Bahai
Community at Haifa and Acre.

At the suggestion of Ziaoullah Asgarzade, a cable was
despatched to the Bahai community at Askarabad [ob-
viously refers to 'Ishqábád] in Central S. Asia (near the
Persian Frontier) notifying the Friends of the Master's
ascension and conveying the love and sympathy of Friends
in every part of the world.

In order to ensure the delivery of this cable, arrangements were made with the American Red Cross Authorities and the British Trade Mission at Moscow, to
persuade the Soviet Foreign Minister to allow this
important message to be telegraphed on to Askarabad.

Lord Lamington, when wiring his condolences, advised this office that he had asked the Colonial Office to
arrange for British representation at the Master's funeral.

General Sir Arthur Money, K.C.B., K.B.E., C.S.I.,
formerly Chief Administrator of Palestine, writing on
2/12/21, said:

'I am grieved to learn of the death of Abdul Baha. I
had a strong regard and admiration for him and always
valued his advice. He exercised all his influence in
Palestine for good, and was always ready to assist the
Administration toward the establishment of law and
order.

In New York, Roy Wilhelm received this cable from Haifa, on November 28th:

Wilhelmite N.Y. His Holiness Abdul Baha ascended to Abha Kingdom. Inform friends, Greatest Holy Leaf.

And from the United States this message went out to the Holy Land, on behalf of the Executive Board of the Bahá'í Temple Unity:

He doeth whatsoever He willeth. Hearts weep at most great tribulation. American friends send through Unity Board radiant love, boundless sympathy, devotion. Standing steadfast, conscious of his unceasing presence and nearness.

The Bahá'ís of Ṭihrán sent the following message through their Spiritual Assembly to the Bahá'ís of America and Britain:

Light of Covenant transferred from eye to heart. Day of teaching, unity, self-sacrifice.

The valiant Bahá'ís of Germany sent this cable to the Greatest Holy Leaf:

All believers deeply moved by irrevocable loss of our Master's precious life. We pray for heavenly protection of Holy Cause and promise faithfulness and obedience to Centre of Covenant.

Winston Churchill, the Secretary of State for the Colonies, cabled the High Commissioner for Palestine

. . . to convey to the Bahai Community, on behalf of His Majesty's Government, their sympathy and condolence on the death of Sir 'Abdu'l-Baha Abbas K.B.E.

Viscount Allenby, the High Commissioner for Egypt, wired the following message, on November 29th, also through the intermediary of Sir Herbert Samuel, the High Commissioner for Palestine:

Please convey to the relatives of the late Sir 'Abdu'l-Baha 'Abbas Effendi and to the Bahai community my sincere sympathy in the loss of their revered leader.

Another message which came through the office of the High Commissioner for Palestine was from the Commander-in-Chief of the Egyptian Expeditionary Force:

General Congreve begs that you will convey his deepest sympathy to the family of the late Sir 'Abbas al-Bahai.

The Council of Ministers in Baghdád forwarded this message, dated December 8th:

His Highness Sayed Abdurrahman, the Prime Minister, desires to extend his sympathy to the family of His Holiness 'Abdu'l-Baha in their bereavement.

'For the Holy Family Theosophical Society send affectionate thoughts' was another message which came from London.

A leading figure of the town of Nazareth wired:

With the profoundest sorrow and regret we condole with you on the occasion of the setting of the Day-Star of the East. We are of God, and to Him we shall return.

Many more were the messages of condolence that reached the family of 'Abdu'l-Bahá.

Shoghi Effendi and Lady Blomfield wrote, in *The Passing of 'Abdu'l-Baha*:

We have now come to realize that the Master knew the day and hour when, his mission on earth being finished, he would return to the shelter of heaven. He was, however, careful that his family should not have any premonition of the coming sorrow. It seemed as though their eyes were veiled by him, with his ever-loving consideration for his dear ones, that they should not see the significance of certain dreams and other signs of the culminating event. This they now realize was his thought for them, in order that their strength might be preserved to face the great ordeal when it should arrive, that they should not be devitalized by anguish of mind in its anticipation.

Out of the many signs of the approach of the hour when he could say of his work on earth: 'It is finished', the following two dreams seem remarkable. Less than eight weeks before his passing the Master related this to his family:

'I seemed to be standing within a great Mosque . . . in the place of the Imam himself. I became aware that a large number of people were flocking into the Mosque; more and yet more crowded in, taking their places in rows behind me, until there was a vast multitude. As I stood I raised loudly the "Call to Prayer". Suddenly the thought came to me to go forth from the Mosque.

'When I found myself outside I said within myself, "For what reason came I forth, not having led the prayer? But it matters not; now that I have uttered the Call to Prayer, the vast multitude will of themselves chant the prayer . . ."'

A few weeks after the preceding dream the Master came in from the solitary room in the garden, which he had occupied of late, and said:

'I dreamed a dream and behold the Blessed Beauty . . . came and said unto me, "Destroy this room!"'

The family, who had been wishing that he would come and sleep in the house, not being happy that he should be alone at night, exclaimed, 'Yes Master, we think your dream means that you should leave that room and come into the house.' When he heard this from us, he smiled meaningly as though not agreeing with our interpretation. Afterwards we understood that by the 'room' was meant the temple of his body.

A month before his last hour, Doctor Sulaymán Rafat Bey, a Turkish friend, who was a guest in the house, received a telegram telling him of the sudden death of his brother. 'Abdu'l-Bahá speaking words of comfort to him, whispered, 'Sorrow not, for he is only transferred from this plane to a higher one; I too shall soon be transferred, for my days are numbered.' Then patting him gently on the shoulder, he looked him in the face and said, 'And it will be in the days that are shortly to come.'

In the same week he revealed a Tablet* to America, in which is the following prayer:

'Yá Bahá'i'l-Abhá! (O Thou the Glory of Glories) I have renounced the world and the people thereof, and am heart-broken and sorely afflicted because of the unfaithful. In the cage of this world, I flutter even as a frightened bird, and yearn every day to take my flight unto Thy Kingdom.

'Yá Bahá'i'l-Abhá! Make me to drink of the cup of sacrifice and set me free. Relieve me from these woes and trials, from these afflictions and troubles. Thou art He that aideth, that succoureth, that protecteth, that stretcheth forth the hand of help.'

On the last Friday morning of his stay on earth (November 25th) he said to his daughters: 'The wedding of Khusraw must take place today. If you are too much occupied, I myself will make the necessary preparations, for it must take place this day.' . . .

'Abdu'l-Bahá attended the noonday prayer at the

* The last Tablet to America. See p. 450.

Mosque. When he came out he found the poor waiting for the alms, which it was his custom to give every Friday. This day, as usual, he stood, in spite of very great fatigue, whilst he gave a coin to every one with his own hands.

After lunch he dictated some Tablets, his last ones, to Ruhi Effendi. When he had rested he walked in the garden. He seemed to be in a deep reverie.

His good and faithful servant, Isma'il Aqa, relates the following:

'Some time, about twenty days before my Master passed away I was near the garden when I heard him summon an old believer saying:

' "Come with me that we may admire together the beauty of the garden. Behold, what the spirit of devotion is able to achieve! This flourishing place was, a few years ago, but a heap of stones, and now it is verdant with foliage and flowers. My desire is that after I am gone the loved ones may all arise to serve the Divine Cause and, please God, so it shall be. Ere long men will arise who shall bring life to the world."

'A few days after this he said: "I am so fatigued! The hour is come when I must leave everything and take my flight. I am too weary to walk." Then he said: "It was during the closing days of the Blessed Beauty, when I was engaged in gathering together His papers, which were strewn over the sofa in His writing chamber at Bahji that He turned to me and said, 'It is of no use to gather them, I must leave them and flee away.'

' "I also have finished my work, I can do nothing more, therefore must I leave it and take my departure."

'Three days before his ascension whilst seated in the garden, he called me and said, "I am sick with fatigue. Bring two of your oranges for me that I may eat them for your sake." This I did, and he having eaten them turned to me, saying "Have you any of your sweet lemons?" He bade me fetch a few . . . Whilst I was plucking them, he came over to the tree, saying, "Nay, but I must gather them with my own hands." Having eaten of the fruit he turned to me and asked "Do you desire anything more?" Then with a pathetic gesture of his hands, he touchingly, emphatically and deliberately said:

' "Now it is finished, it is finished!"

'These significant words penetrated my very soul. I felt each time he uttered them as if a knife were struck into my heart. I understood his meaning but never dreamed his end was so nigh.'

It was Ismaʿil-Aqa who had been the Master's gardener for well nigh thirty years who, in the first week after his bereavement, driven by hopeless grief, quietly disposed of all his belongings, made his will, went to the Master's sister and craved her pardon for any misdeeds he had committed. He then delivered the key of the garden to a trusted servant of the Household and, taking with him means whereby to end his life at his beloved Master's Tomb, walked up the Mountain to that sacred place, three times circled round it and would have succeeded in taking his life had it not been for the opportune arrival of a friend, who reached him in time to prevent the accomplishment of his tragic intention.

Later in the evening of Friday he ['Abdu'l-Bahá] blessed the bride and bridegroom who had just been married. He spoke impressively to them. 'Khusraw,' he said, 'you have spent your childhood and youth in the service of this house: it is my hope that you will grow old under the same roof, ever and always serving God.'

During the evening he attended the usual meeting of the friends in his own audience chamber.

In the morning of Saturday, November 26th, he arose early, came to the tea room and had some tea. He asked for the fur-lined coat which had belonged to Baha'u'llah. He often put on this coat when he was cold or did not feel well, he so loved it. He then withdrew to his room, lay down on his bed and said, 'Cover me up. I am very cold. Last night I did not sleep well, I felt cold. This is serious, it is the beginning.'

After more blankets had been put on, he asked for the fur coat he had taken off to be placed over him. That day he was rather feverish. In the evening his temperature rose still higher [it reached 104° F.], but during the night the fever left him. After midnight he asked for some tea.

On Sunday morning (November 27th) he said: 'I am quite well and will get up as usual and have tea with you in the tea room.' After he had dressed he was persuaded to remain on the sofa in his room.

In the afternoon he sent all the friends up to the Tomb of the Bab, where on the occasion of the anniversary of the declaration of the Covenant a feast was being held, offered by a Parsi pilgrim* who had lately arrived from India.

At four in the afternoon being on the sofa in his room he said: 'Ask my sister and all the family to come and have tea with me.'

After tea the Mufti of Haifa and the head of the Municipality, with another visitor, were received by him. They remained about an hour. He spoke to them about Baha'u'llah, related to them his second dream, showed them extraordinary kindness and even more than his usual courtesy. He then bade them farewell, walking with them to the outer door in spite of their pleading that he should remain resting on his sofa. He then received a visit from the head of the police, an Englishman, who, too, had his share of the Master's gracious kindness. To him he gave some silk hand-woven Persian handkerchiefs, which he very greatly appreciated.

His four sons-in-law and Ruhi Effendi came to him after returning from the gathering on the mountain. They said to him: 'The giver of the feast was unhappy because you were not there.' He said unto them:

'But I was there, though my body was absent, my spirit

* Áqá Rustam Ardashír.

was there in your midst. I was present with the friends at the Tomb. The friends must not attach any importance to the absence of my body. In spirit I am, and shall always be, with the friends, even though I be far away.'

The same evening he asked after the health of every member of the Household, of the pilgrims and of the friends in Haifa. 'Very good, very good' he said when told that none were ill. This was his very last utterance concerning his friends.

At eight in the evening he retired to bed after taking a little nourishment, saying: 'I am quite well.'

He told all the family to go to bed and rest. Two of his daughters however stayed with him. That night the Master had gone to sleep very calmly, quite free from fever. He awoke about 1.15 a.m., got up and walked across to a table where he drank some water. He took off an outer night garment, saying: 'I am too warm.' He went back to bed and when his daughter Ruha Khanum, later on, approached, she found him lying peacefully and, as he looked into her face, he asked her to lift up the net curtains, saying:

'I have difficulty in breathing, give me more air.' Some rose water was brought of which he drank, sitting up in bed to do so, without any help. He again lay down, and as some food was offered him, he remarked in a clear and distinct voice:

'You wish me to take some food, and I am going?' He gave them a beautiful look. His face was so calm, his expression so serene, they thought him asleep . . .

His long martyrdom was ended![253]

When Dr Florian Krug was summoned quickly and arrived hastily, 'Abdu'l-Bahá 'had gone from the gaze of his loved ones'.

Grace and Florian Krug, Louise and John Bosch from California, Ethel Rosenberg from London, and Fräulein

Johanna Hauff from Stuttgart were the Western pilgrims present in Haifa at that poignant hour, as well as Curtis Kelsey from the United States, who was in Haifa to attend to electrical installations in the Shrine of the Báb.

Soon after 'Abdu'l-Bahá had passed out of this world, Western pilgrims were allowed into the room where His body lay. Louise Bosch wrote on December 5th to Ella Cooper:

At first we were as dumb and speechless, bewildered. We stood or kneeled before the bed. We gazed upon his face and could not trust our eyes. At last the bewilderment subsided and the trust asserted itself. Was it true that his eyes would open no more? Would he not open his eyes to look upon us again? Would he not open his lips to say that he was not dead? We asked the doctors [by then other physicians had been sent for] if he was dead. They said yes, the heart had ceased to beat; they said it was useless to try to revive him—it could not be done. Then, after awhile, the mosquito netting over the bed was let down, and this covered from our eyes the earthly remains of our Lord. We got up and went into the adjacent room, and the door of the room out of which we came was closed.

But before this, the blood of the wounds of this blow had begun to flow, and the hurt and the pain and the moans increased with every minute. We five European pilgrims* were in the room together with the holy family, and the holy mother† held my husband's hand and the Greatest Holy Leaf held mine. After a time we went back to the Pilgrim House, leaving the holy family alone. It was still night—no moon at all. Not long afterward the dawn broke, and at last the sun rose with great effulgence over the scene of this memorable night . . .[254]

* Mr and Mrs Bosch were Swiss, though living in California.
† Munírih Khánum, the wife of 'Abdu'l-Bahá.

In the words of Shoghi Effendi and Lady Blomfield:

> The eyes that had always looked out with loving-kindness upon humanity, whether friends or foes, were now closed. The hands that had ever been stretched forth to give alms to the poor and the needy, the halt and the maimed, the blind, the orphan and the widow, had now finished their labour. The feet that, with untiring zeal, had gone upon the ceaseless errands of the Lord of Compassion were now at rest. The lips that had so eloquently championed the cause of the suffering sons of men, were now hushed in silence. The heart that had so powerfully throbbed with wondrous love for the children of God was now stilled. His glorious spirit had passed from the life of earth, from the persecutions of the enemies of righteousness, from the storm and stress of well nigh eighty years of indefatigable toil for the good of others.[255]

Sorrow and anguish were most intense. But decisions had to be taken, preparations had to be made. First of all, where was to be the resting-place of the earthly remains of 'Abdu'l-Bahá? It was remembered that there was another vault next to the vault where the remains of the Báb lay. The Greatest Holy Leaf decided that 'Abdu'l-Bahá's tomb should be there. A coffin was expeditiously obtained and John Bosch assisted the sons-in-law of 'Abdu'l-Bahá to place His body in the coffin. But so hurriedly had the coffin been made that its lid could not be properly secured. The night following the interment, Luṭfu'lláh Ḥakím sat in the vault and kept watch until the deficiency could be righted.

The funeral of 'Abdu'l-Bahá was indeed a funeral the like of which the Holy Land had never witnessed:

> The High Commissioner of Palestine, Sir Herbert Samuel, the Governor of Jerusalem, the Governor of Phoenicia, the Chief Officials of the Government, the Consuls of

WALKING UP THE MOUNTAIN

Close to the Shrine of the Báb

'ABDU'L-BAHÁ'S ROOM IN HIS HOUSE
IN HAIFA

And the bed in which He passed away

CABLE TO THE GREATEST HOLY LEAF

From Díyá'u'lláh Aṣgharzádih

Both the Persian and the English are in the handwriting of Shoghi Effendi

the various countries, resident in Haifa, the heads of the various religious communities, the notables of Palestine, Jews, Christians, Moslems, Druses, Egyptians, Greeks, Turks, Kurds, and a host of his American, European and native friends, men, women and children, both of high and low degree, all, about ten thousand in number, mourning the loss of their Beloved One.

This impressive, triumphal procession was headed by a guard of honour, consisting of the City Constabulary Force, followed by the Boy Scouts of the Moslem and Christian communities holding aloft their banners, a company of Moslem choristers chanting their verses from the Quran, the chiefs of the Moslem community headed by the Mufti, a number of Christian priests, Latin, Greek and Anglican, all preceding the sacred coffin, upraised on the shoulders of his loved ones. Immediately behind it came the members of his family, next to them walked the British High Commissioner, the Governor* of Jerusalem and the Governor of Phoenicia. After them came the Consuls and the notables of the land, followed by the vast multitude of those who reverenced and loved him.

On this day there was no cloud in the sky, nor any sound in all the town and surrounding country through which they went, save only the soft, slow, rhythmic chanting of Islam in the Call to Prayer, or the convulsed sobbing moan of those helpless ones, bewailing the loss of their one friend, who had protected them in all their difficulties and sorrows, whose generous bounty had saved them and their little ones from starvation through the terrible years of the 'Great Woe'.

'O God, my God!' the people wailed with one accord, 'Our father has left us, our father has left us!'

O the wonder of that great throng! Peoples of every religion and race and colour, united in heart through the Manifestation of Servitude in the life-long work of 'Abdu'l-Baha!

As they slowly wended their way up Mount Carmel,

* Sir Ronald Storrs.

the Vineyard of God, the casket appeared in the distance to be borne aloft by invisible hands, so high above the heads of the people was it carried. After two hours walking, they reached the garden of the Tomb of the Bab. Tenderly was the sacred coffin placed upon a plain table covered with a fair white linen cloth. As the vast concourse pressed round the Tabernacle of his body, waiting to be laid in its resting place, within the vault, next to that of the Bab, representatives of the various denominations, Moslems, Christians and Jews, all hearts being ablaze with fervent love of 'Abdu'l-Baha, some on the impulse of the moment, others prepared, raised their voices in eulogy and regret, paying their last homage of farewell to their loved one. So united were they in their acclamation of him, as the wise educator and reconciler of the human race in this perplexed and sorrowful age, that there seemed to be nothing left for the Bahais to say.

The following are extracts from some of the speeches delivered on that memorable occasion.[256]

The first speaker was Yúsuf al-Khaṭíb, a well-known Muslim orator. He said:

O concourse of Arabians and Persians! Whom are ye bewailing? Is it he who but yesterday was great in his life and is today in his death greater still? Shed no tears for the one that hath departed to the world of Eternity, but weep over the passing of Virtue and Wisdom, of Knowledge and Generosity. Lament for yourselves, for yours is the loss, whilst he, your lost one, is but a revered Wayfarer, stepping from your mortal world into the everlasting Home. Weep one hour for the sake of him who, for well nigh eighty years, hath wept for you! Look to your right, look to your left, look East and look West and behold, what glory and greatness have vanished! What a pillar of peace hath crumbled! What eloquent lips are hushed! Alas! In this tribulation there is no heart but aches with anguish, no eye but is filled with tears. Woe unto the poor, for lo! goodness hath departed from them, woe unto the orphans, for their loving father is no more with them! Could the life of Sir 'Abdu'l-Baha Abbas have been redeemed by the sacrifices of many a precious soul, they of a certainty would gladly have offered up their lives for his life. But Fate hath otherwise ordained. Every destiny is predetermined and none can change the Divine Decree. What am I to set forth the achievements of this leader of mankind? They are too glorious to be praised, too many to recount. Suffice it to say, that he has left in every heart the most profound impression, on every tongue most wondrous praise. And he that leaveth a memory so lovely, so imperishable, he, indeed, is not dead. Be solaced then, O ye people of Baha! Endure and be patient; for no man, be he of the East or of the West, can ever comfort you, nay he himself is even in greater need of consolation.[257]

Indeed, the poor lamenting their plight were saying, one to the other: 'What will happen to us now? Who will look after us now? We are orphaned. What can we do now but go away and die.'

The next speaker was Ibráhím Naṣṣár, a celebrated Christian writer, and he said:

I weep for the world, in that my Lord hath died; others there are who, like unto me, weep the death of their Lord . . . O bitter is the anguish caused by this heart-rending calamity! It is not only our country's loss but a world affliction . . . He hath lived for well-nigh eighty years the life of the Messengers and Apostles of God. He hath educated the souls of men, hath been benevolent unto them, hath led them to the Way of Truth. Thus he raised his people to the pinnacle of glory, and great shall be his reward from God, the reward of the righteous! Hear me O people! 'Abbas is not dead, neither hath the light of

Baha been extinguished! Nay, nay! this light shall shine with everlasting splendour. The Lamp of Baha, 'Abbas, hath lived a goodly life, hath manifested in himself the true life of the Spirit. And now he is gathered to glory, a pure angel, richly robed in benevolent deeds, noble in his precious virtues. Fellow Christians! Truly ye are bearing the mortal remains of this ever lamented one to his last resting place, yet know of a certainty that your 'Abbas will live forever in spirit amongst you, through his deeds, his words, his virtues and all the essence of his life. We say farewell to the material body of our 'Abbas, and his material body vanisheth from our gaze, but his reality, our spiritual 'Abbas, will never leave our minds, our thoughts, our hearts, our tongues.

O great revered Sleeper! Thou hast been good to us, thou hast guided us, thou hast taught us, thou hast lived amongst us greatly, with the full meaning of greatness, thou hast made us proud of thy deeds and of thy words. Thou hast raised the Orient to the summit of glory, hast shown loving kindness to the people, trained them in righteousness, and hast striven to the end, till thou hast won the crown of glory. Rest thou happily under the shadow of the mercy of the Lord thy God, and He verily, shall well reward thee. [258]

The Christian writer was followed by the Muftí of Haifa, Muḥammad Murád, who said:

I do not wish to exaggerate in my eulogy of this great one, for his ready and helping hand in the service of mankind and the beautiful and wondrous story of his life, spent in doing that which is right and good, none can deny, save him whose heart is blinded . . .

O thou revered voyager! Thou hast lived greatly and hast died greatly! This great funeral procession is but a glorious proof of thy greatness in thy life and in thy death. But O, thou whom we have lost! Thou leader of men, generous and benevolent! To whom shall the poor

now look? Who shall care for the hungry? and the desolate, the widow and the orphan?

May the Lord inspire all thy household and thy kindred with patience in this grievous calamity, and immerse thee in the ocean of His grace and mercy! He verily,
is the prayer-hearing, prayer-answering God.[259]

Another distinguished Muslim, 'Abdu'lláh Mukhliṣ,
followed the Muftí of Haifa:

. . . the sun of knowledge has set; the moon of virtues
has disappeared; the throne of glory has crumbled, and
the mountain of kindness is levelled by the departure of
this benevolent one from the mortal world to the immortal
realm. I do not need to explain the sublimity of the great
one whom we have lost or to enumerate his great qualities, for all of you who are just are witnesses and can
testify to what has been given him of personal beauty,
beauty of his character, greatness of his heart, vastness
of the sea of his knowledge and generosity . . . I beg your
pardon if I fail in doing my duty as far as faithfulness is
concerned or if I am unable to pay the generous one who
has departed what he deserves of the best and highest
praise, because what my tongue utters has emanated from
a tender memory and broken heart. Indeed, they are
wounds and not words; they are tears and not phrases . . .
'This calamity has made all previous calamities to be
forgotten. But this calamity will never be forgotten.'[260]

Next, Shaykh Yúnus al-Khaṭíb, a Muslim poet of note,
recited a poem he had composed; and he was followed by
Bishop Bassilious, the head of the Greek Catholic Church
of Haifa, who dwelt particularly on 'Abdu'l-Bahá's humanitarian deeds, His generosity to the poor, His charm and
majesty of mien. Then came the turn of the youth to pay

homage and tribute. Wadí' Bustání, a young Christian, had a poem to offer. Here are some lines from it:

> In the souls and in the minds thou art immortal. One like thee, who has all perfections, virtues and honors, is eternal . . . O Abdul-Baha, O son of Baha'ullah! May my life be a sacrifice to one like thee. Thou art the all-wise, and all else beside thee are only learned. What can the poets say in thy day? O Abdul-Baha, O son of Baha'ullah! Thou wert just as God wanted thee to be and not as others wished. Thou hast departed in the Holy Land wherein Christ and the Virgin Mary lived. The land that received Mohammed; the land the dust of which is blessing and wealth . . . We shall be sustained by this Tomb and the One it contains. The covenant of love and devotion will remain forever between us.[261]

The eighth speaker was Salomon Bouzaglo, one of the leading figures of the Jewish population of Haifa, who spoke most eloquently in French:

> 'Dans un siècle de positivisme exagéré et de matérialisme effréné, il est étonnant et rare de trouver un philosophe de grande envergure tel que le regretté 'Abdu'l-Baha 'Abbas parler à notre coeur, à nos sentiments et surtout chercher à éduquer notre âme en nous inculquant les principes les plus beaux, reconnus comme étant la base de toute religion et de toute morale pure. Par ses écrits, par sa parole, par ses entretiens familiers comme par ses colloques célèbres avec les plus cultivés et les fervents adeptes des théories sectaires, il a su persuader, il a pu toujours convaincre. Les exemples vivants sont d'un autre pouvoir. Sa vie privée et publique était un exemple de dévouement et d'oubli de soi pour le bonheur des autres . . .
> 'Sa philosophie est simple, direz vous, mais elle est grande par cette même simplicité, étant conforme au

caractère humain qui perd de sa beauté lorsqu'il se trouve faussé par les préjugés et les superstitions . . . 'Abbas est mort à Haïffa, en Palestine, la Terre Sacrée qui a produit les prophètes. Devenue stérile et abandonnée depuis tant de siècles elle ressucite de nouveau et commence à reprendre son rang, et sa renommée primitive. Nous ne sommes pas les seuls à pleurer ce prophète, nous ne sommes pas les seuls à le glorifier. En Europe, en Amérique, que dis-je, dans tout pays habité par des hommes conscients de leur mission dans ce bas monde assoiffé de justice sociale, de fraternité, on le pleurera aussi. Il est mort après avoir souffert du despotisme, du fanatisme et de l'intolérance. Acre, la Bastille turque, lui a servi de prison pendant des dizaines d'années. Bagdad la capitale Abbasside a été aussi sa prison et celle de son père. La Perse, ancien berceau de la Philosophie douce et divine, a chassé ses enfants qui ont conçu leurs idées chez elle. Ne voit-on pas là une volonté divine et une préférence marquée pour la Terre Promise qui était et sera le berceau de toutes les idées généreuses et nobles? Celui qui laisse après lui un passé aussi glorieux n'est pas mort. Celui qui a écrit d'aussi beaux principes a agrandi sa famille parmi tous ses lecteurs et a passé à la postérité, couronné par l'immortalité.'[262]

Here is a resumé of this speech:

It is indeed strange that in an age of gross materialism and lack of faith a great philosopher such as He whom we mourn—'Abdu'l-Bahá 'Abbás—should appear. He speaks to our hearts, our consciences. He satisfies our thirsty souls with teachings and principles that are the basis of all religion and morality. In His writings and public talks, and in His intimate conversations He could always convince the most learned and the most orthodox. His life was the living example of self-sacrifice, of preferring the good of others to one's own.

The philosophy of 'Abdu'l-Bahá is simple and plain,

yet sublime. It accords with human character. Its virtues overcome prejudice and superstition . . . 'Abbás has passed away in Haifa, in Palestine, in the Holy Land wherein prophets have always appeared. The ancient glory of this land is restored. We are not the only ones who weep for Him, in Whom we take pride. In Europe, in America, in every country, people athirst for social justice and brotherhood also weep for Him. He suffered from despotism, fanaticism and intolerance. For decades, 'Akká—the Bastille of the Ottomans—held Him a prisoner. Baghdád—the 'Abbasid capital—also served as a prison for Him and for His Father. Persia—the ancient cradle of divine philosophy—threw out her children, whose ideas were conceived in her land. Cannot we witness the manifestation of Divine Will to exalt the Holy Land that it become, once again, the cradle of noble and generous ideals? He, Who has left such a glorious heritage, is not dead. He, Who has promulgated such great principles, is immortal in the memory of posterity.

Shaykh As'ad Shuqayr, a prominent Muslim citizen of 'Akká, admired for his scholarship and eloquence, was the next speaker, after whom Muḥammad Ṣafadí, a well-known Muslim poet, read his threnody. Shaykh As'ad spoke of 'Abdu'l-Bahá as

. . . one of the inhabitants of Acca because these inhabitants lived with him for more than forty years. His meetings were meetings of learning wherein he explained all the heavenly books and traditions . . . His philanthropies to the widows and orphans were never interrupted . . . He had so great a station; yet he never failed to help the distressed! In the winter season he met with the learned and notables of Acca at the home of Sheikh Ali Meeri, and in the summer the meetings were held in a court in the Fakhoreh* . . . In both of those meetings

* The district in which the house of 'Abbúd is situated.

the attendants found him a book of history, a commentary on all the heavenly Scriptures, a philosophy of the pages of contemporary events that pertain to scientific or artistic topics. Then he moved to Haifa, and then went to Europe and America where he gave comprehensive and eloquent addresses and exhortations. His intention was to bring about unity among religions and sects and to remove the severe strife from their hearts and from their tongues, to urge them to take hold of the essence and let go the non-essential. He did that by presenting his message in a scientific manner. A group of Persians and others criticized him and found fault with his ideals in pamphlets they published and spread. Nevertheless, without paying any attention to their criticism and opposition, nor being hurt by their hatred and enmity, he went forward and proclaimed his teachings. It is the law of God among His creatures—a law which will not be changed—that the originator and declarer of principles must inevitably have those who agree and praise and those who disagree and reject.[263]

And here are a few lines from Muḥammad Ṣafadí's poem:

*On Sunday night heaven was opened and the spirit of
   Abdul-Baha flew with its glory.*

It was received and entertained by the prophets . . .

*O Mount Carmel, thou art now more proud than the heaven,
   for thou hast become the holiest mountain . . .*

*I shall weep with tears for thee as long as I am living;
   how often thou didst wipe them with thy hands . . .*[264]

Funeral orations delivered, the High Commissioner stepped forth to perform his act of homage and other officials followed him.

> . . . then came the moment when the casket which held the pearl of loving servitude passed slowly and triumphantly into its simple, hallowed resting place.
>
> O the infinite pathos! that the beloved feet should no longer tread this earth! That the presence which inspired such devotion and reverence should be withdrawn![265]

Shoghi Effendi and Lady Blomfield tell us:

Of the many and diverse journals that throughout the East and West have given in their columns accounts of this momentous event, the following stand as foremost among them:

Le Temps, the leading French paper, in its issue of December 19, 1921, under the title 'Un Conciliateur' (a peacemaker), portrays graphically the life of Abdu'l-Baha, the following being some of its extracts:

'Un prophète vient de mourir en Palestine. Il se nommait Abdoul Baha, et il était fils de Bahaou'llah, qui créa le bahaisme, religion "unifiée" qui n'est autre que le babisme qu'avait observé le Comte de Gobineau. Le Bab, Messie du Babisme, se proposait modestement de régénerer la Perse, ce qui lui couta la vie, en 1850. Bahaou'llah et son fils Abdoul Baha, "l'esclave de son père", n'ambitionnaient pas moins que la régéneration du monde. Paris a connu Abdoul Baha. Ce viellard magnifique et débonnaire répandit parmi nous la parole sainte il y a quelque dix ans. Il était vêtu d'une simple robe vert olive et coiffé d'un turban blanc . . . Sa parole était douce et berceuse, comme une litanie. On l'écoutait avec un plaisir recueilli, encore qu'on ne le comprit point; car il parlait en persan . . . Le bahaisme, c'est en somme la religion de la charité et de la simplicité. C'est en même temps, amalgamés le judaisme, le christianisme, le protestantisme, et la libre pensée. Abdoul Baha se réclamait de Zoroastre, de Moise, de Mahomet et de Jésus. Peut-être jugerez vous que cette unification est à la fois trop nombreuse et confuse. C'est qu'on ne comprend rien aux choses sacrées si l'on n'est inspiré par la foi . . . Sous le turban blanc ses yeux reflétaient l'intelligence et la bonté. Il était paternel, affectueux et simple. Son pouvoir, semblait-il, lui venait de ce qu'il savait aimer les hommes et savait se faire aimer d'eux. Appelé à témoigner de l'excellence de cette religion naïve et pure, nous pûmes honnêtement confesser notre foi par cette formule: "Que les religions sont belles quand elles ne sont pas encore." '

The *Morning Post*,* two days after his passing, among other highly favourable comments, concluded its report of the Movement in the following words:

'The venerated Baha'u'llah died in 1892 and the mantle of his religious insight fell on his son Abdul'Baha, when, after forty years of prison life, Turkish constitutional changes permitted him to visit England, France and America. His persistent messages as to the divine origin and unity of mankind were as impressive as the Messenger himself. He possessed singular courtesy. At his table Buddhist and Mohammedan, Hindu and Zoroastrian, Jew and Christian, sat in amity. "Creatures," he said, "were created through love; let them live in peace and amity." '

The *New York World* of December 1921 publishes the following:

'Never before 'Abdu'l Baha did the leader of an Oriental religious movement visit the United States . . . As recently as June of this year a special correspondent of "The World" who visited this seer thus described him: "Having once looked upon 'Abdu'l Baha, his personality

* This British daily paper was incorporated with the *Daily Telegraph* in 1937.

is indelibly impressed upon the mind: the majestic venerable figure clad in the flowing aba, his head crowned with a turban white as his head and hair; the piercing deep set eyes whose glances shake the heart; the smile that pours its sweetness over all." . . .

'Even in the twilight of his life 'Abdu'l Baha took the liveliest interest in world affairs. When General Allenby swept up the coast from Egypt he went for counsel first to 'Abdu'l Baha. When Zionists arrived in their Promised Land they sought 'Abdu'l Baha for advice. For Palestine he had the brightest hopes. 'Abdu'l Baha believed that Bolshevism would prove an admonition to the irreligious world. He taught the equality of man and woman, saying: "The world of humanity has two wings, man and woman. If one wing is weak, then the bird cannot fly" . . .'

The *Times of India* in its issue of January 1922, opens one of its editorial articles as follows:

'In more normal times than the present the death of 'Abdu'l Baha, which was sorrowfully referred to at the Bahai Conference in Bombay, would have stirred the feelings of many who, without belonging to the Bahai brotherhood, sympathize with its tenets and admire the life-work of those who founded it. As it is we have learned almost by chance of this great religious leader's death, but that fact need not prevent our turning aside from politics and the turmoil of current events to consider what this man did and what he aimed at.'

Sketching then in brief an account of the History of the Movement it concludes as follows:

'It is not for us now to judge whether the purity, the mysticism and the exalted ideas of Bahaism will continue unchanged after the loss of the great leader, or to speculate on whether Bahaism will some day become a force in the world as great or greater than Christianity or Islam; but we would pay a tribute to the memory of a man who wielded a vast influence for good, and who, if he was destined to see many of his ideas seemingly shattered in the world war, remained true to his convictions and to his belief in the possibility of a reign of peace and love, and who, far more effectively than Tolstoi, showed the West that religion is a vital force that can never be disregarded.'[266]

To return to Major Tudor-Pole's memorandum:*

The *London Times* printed an obituary notice on 30/11/21 in the course of which it said: 'Abdul Baha was a man of great spiritual power and commanding presence and his name was held in reverence throughout the Middle East and elsewhere.'. . .

Light, dated 3/12/21, appreciatively refers to Abdul Baha as 'the head of the great Bahai Movement which numbers several millions of followers throughout the world all working for Peace and Human Brotherhood.'

The *Daily Mirror* published a good photograph of the Master on 2/12/21, with a short notice, and the *Daily Mail* writing on 1/12/21, says: 'The journeying forth of one of the very few missionaries of an Asiatic faith is recalled by news of the death of Sir Abdul Baha Abbas al Bahai. The Bahai claimed that his faith expressed the essential truth of all the Religions of the world.'

In the same article reference was made to the Master's visit to London in 1911 and this called forth the following reply, dated 5/12/21:

'Editor of *Daily Mail*. Dear Sir, In your appreciative notice concerning Sir Abdul Baha Abbas al Bahai, you refer to his visit to London in 1911 in a manner which suggests that this venerable Eastern seer preached rather than practised the simple life.

'It was the privilege of Abdul Baha's London friends to ensure his comfort while he was in our midst, but it would be untrue to say that he did not live the simple life himself.

'The present writer was the guest of Abdul Baha on

* Cited p. 453.

several occasions in the East and was an eye-witness of the Spartan simplicity in which he lived. The Bahai leader never possessed more than one coat, he lived on frugal diet and was ever ready to share what little he possessed with the poor. During the war many hundreds of people in Palestine would have died of starvation had it not been for the noble way in which Abdul Baha cared for them. The memory of a life so completely dedicated to the service of humanity will remain an inspiration with many millions of people throughout the world. Yours truly, W. Tudor-Pole.'

. . . .

Shogi Rabbani, the Master's grandson, reached London from Oxford, midday on 29/11/21, and has been lovingly cared for at the home of Miss Grand* by Lady Blomfield, Miss Grand and Dr. J. E. Esslemont. He and his sister, together with Lady Blomfield, sailed for Haifa on December 16th., 1921.

. . . .

It is perhaps not out of place to record that the British High Commissioner for Palestine, Sir Herbert Samuel, greatly revered Abdul Baha, and often consulted him concerning Palestine affairs. The news of the Master's death caused him much sorrow.

. . . .

The London Editor of the *New York World* called on the present writer on 1/12/21, and sent a special cable to his paper in New York on the same evening.

. . . .

A short Memoir of the Master's life is being prepared for the January *Theosophist* at the special request of the

* Miss Grand was from Toronto, Canada. She lived for some years in London, and her generosity helped to maintain a Bahá'í Centre in Upper Regent Street.

General Secretary of the Theosophical Society in London.

.   .   .   .

As I write certain memories come back to me with a strange insistence. I remember standing beside the Master in the pulpit of the City Temple, London, watching over five thousand (5000) people breathlessly absorbed in listening to Abdul-Baha's living spiritual words, and in watching his every smile and movement.

I remember walking with him through the woods at Clifton, 1911, when he spoke of the coming of a spiritual renaissance within the Christian churches; or wandering along the Banks of the Seine at sunset, 1913, when the Master spoke of the Great War that was to come, and the Most Great Peace that would ultimately follow it.

I have sat beside him at Ramleh, Alexandria, beneath the palms, and while he spoke of the essential unity of all mankind. There were Christians, Jews, Moslems, Parsis, Hindoos and Freethinkers sitting around him on that occasion, one and all united with the same faith and aspiration.

I remember walking alone with the Master on Mount Carmel's slopes, sharing his frugal meals in his Haifa house, listening to his melodious chanting within the Garden Tomb, living as one of the family within Bahaullah's house at Acre.

The Friends who read these words will bring to memory many similar scenes within their own experience and will remain ever thankful for such memories.

There is no Death. The Master lives in our midst, and the great spiritual work of human redemption goes forward unceasingly.

Despite the apparent world tribulations of the present hour, the Dawn of a new Day approaches, and it is the privilege of every man and woman alive to-day to work serenely and faithfully for the Coming of the World Peace and true human brotherhood.

May the blessing of the Bab, Baha'u'llah and Abdul Baha, and all the Supreme Concourse rest upon us now and always.*

The narrative of Shoghi Effendi and Lady Blomfield continues:

On the seventh day after the passing of the Master, corn was distributed in his name to about a thousand poor of Haifa, irrespective of race or religion, to whom he had always been a friend and a protector. Their grief at losing the 'Father of the Poor' was extremely pathetic. In the first seven days also from fifty to a hundred poor were daily fed at the Master's house, in the very place where it had been his custom to give alms to them.

On the fortieth day there was a memorial feast, given to over six hundred of the people of Haifa, Acre and the surrounding parts of Palestine and Syria, people of various religions, races and colour. More than a hundred of the poor were also fed on this day. The Governor of Phoenicia, many other officials and some Europeans were present.

The feast was entirely arranged by the members of the Master's household. The long tables were decorated with trailing branches of Bougainvilliers [sic]. Its lovely purple blooms mingled with the white narcissus, and with the large dishes of golden oranges out of the beloved Master's garden made a picture of loveliness in those spacious lofty rooms, whose only other decoration was the gorgeous yet subdued colouring of rare Persian rugs. No useless trivial ornaments marred the extreme dignity of simplicity.

The guests received, each and all, the same welcome. There were no 'chief places'. Here as always in the Master's home, there was no respecting of persons.

* This Memorandum was never published, so far as the present writer knows.

After the luncheon the guests came into the large central hall, this also bare of ornament, save only for the portrait of him they had assembled to honour and some antique Persian tapestries hung upon one wall. Before this was placed a platform from which the speeches were made to the wrapt and silent throng, whose very hearts were listening.

The Governor of Phoenicia, in the course of his address, spoke the following: . . . 'Most of us here have, I think, a clear picture of Sir 'Abdu'l Baha 'Abbas, of his dignified figure walking thoughtfully in our streets, of his courteous and gracious manner, of his kindness, of his love for little children and flowers, of his generosity and care for the poor and suffering. So gentle was he, and so simple that, in his presence, one almost forgot that he was also a great teacher and that his writings and his conversations have been a solace and an inspiration to hundreds and thousands of people in the East and in the West.' . . .

Others who followed spoke in appreciation of the work and life of 'Abdu'l Baha. The following are only a few extracts from their addresses:

'A voice calling aloud from Teheran, echoed from 'Iraq, sounding in Turkish lands, swaying the Holy Land which hearkened to its melody, and wherein it rose, developed and deepened, till at last its reverberations resounded throughout Egypt, stretched across the seas to the West and thence to the New World.

'A voice summoning mankind to love, to unity and to peace; a voice the source whereof, had it been anything but purity of motive, could in no wise have succeeded in sending its waves with the swiftness of lightning throughout the world.

'Hail to 'Abbas, the pride and glory of the East, in an age that has witnessed the rise of knowledge and the fall of prejudice; he who has attained the glorious summit of greatness; he whom the Standards of triumph have hastened to welcome; he whose star arose in Persia, shedding its light upon the minds of men, the signs of which have multiplied in the heaven of glory till it set in full radiance on this our horizon; he whose principles have humbled the peoples and kindreds of the world even as Baha himself had done before him . . .

'I believe and firmly believe, that he whose loss we now lament, having lived eighty years in this world below counselling the peoples of the world with his tongue, guiding them by his pen, setting before them a goodly example by his glorious deeds, has now chosen to lead and guide them by his silence.

'Let us then in our thoughts and meditations pay our tribute to him. And though the other day at his door I made you weep, yet now it is my duty to appeal and ask you to forget your sorrow and refrain from lamentation and cease from shedding tears. Truly, Sir 'Abbas departed from us in body, but he ever lives with us in his abiding spirit, in his wondrous deeds. Though he has passed away, yet he has left for us a glorious heritage in the wisdom of his counsels, the rectitude of his teachings, the benevolence of his deeds, the example of his precious life, the sublimity of his effort, the power of his will, his patience and fortitude, his steadfastness to the end.' 267

The Will and Testament of 'Abdu'l-Bahá, entrusted to the care of the Greatest Holy Leaf, was in a sealed envelope, addressed to Shoghi Effendi. Its contents could not be made known until Shoghi Effendi reached Haifa. And it was the Greatest Holy Leaf who sent out a cable on January 16th 1922, informing the Bahá'ís of the world:

In Will Shoghi Effendi appointed Guardian of Cause and Head of House of Justice.

Some years before His passing, a prayer was written by 'Abdu'l-Bahá, which carried this preface:

Whoso reciteth this prayer with lowliness and fervour will bring gladness and joy to the heart of this servant; it will be even as meeting him face to face.

That prayer is recited at His Shrine, and it is fitting that this chapter should close with it, even as did *The Passing of 'Abdu'l-Baha* by Shoghi Effendi and Lady Blomfield:

HE IS THE ALL-GLORIOUS

O God, my God! Lowly and tearful, I raise my suppliant hands to Thee and cover my face in the dust of that Threshold of Thine, exalted above the knowledge of the learned, and the praise of all that glorify Thee. Graciously look upon Thy servant, humble and lowly at Thy Door, with the glances of the Eye of Thy Mercy, and immerse him in the Ocean of Thy Eternal Grace.

Lord! He is a poor and lowly servant of Thine, enthralled and imploring Thee, captive in Thy hand, praying fervently to Thee, trusting in Thee, in tears before Thy Face, calling to Thee and beseeching Thee, saying:

O Lord, my God! Give me Thy Grace to serve Thy loved ones, strengthen me in my servitude to Thee, illumine my brow with the Light of adoration in Thy Court of Holiness, and of prayer to Thy Kingdom of Grandeur. Help me to be selfless at the heavenly entrance of Thy Gate, and aid me to be detached from all things within Thy Holy Precincts. Lord! Give me to drink from the chalice of selflessness; with its robe clothe me, and in its ocean immerse me. Make me as dust in the pathway of Thy loved ones, and grant that I may offer up my soul for the earth ennobled by the footsteps of Thy chosen ones in Thy Path, O Lord of Glory in the Highest!

With this prayer doth Thy servant call Thee, at dawntide and in the night-season. Fulfil his heart's desire. O Lord! Illumine his heart, gladden his bosom, kindle his light, that he may serve Thy Cause and Thy servants.

Thou art the Bestower, the Pitiful, the Most Bountiful, the Gracious, the Merciful, the Compassionate!

CHAPTER 25

THE WILL AND TESTAMENT

'Abdu'l-Bahá wrote His Will and Testament, which is in three parts, at different times during the seven-year period (1901–1908) of His incarceration within the city walls of 'Akká. Characterized by the Guardian of the Faith as 'this supreme, this infallible Organ for the accomplishment of a Divine Purpose,' and as 'an Instrument which may be viewed as the Charter of the New World Order which is at once the glory and the promise of this most great Dispensation,' the Will and Testament of 'Abdu'l-Bahá is manifestly a document of momentous and incalculable significance.

It is not proposed here to scrutinize it closely. Much has been, much will be written in an effort to elucidate its far-reaching implications, for it is the founding Charter of the Administrative Order of Bahá'u'lláh—the 'nucleus' and 'very pattern' of the Order 'destined to embrace in the fullness of time the whole of mankind'. In this document 'Abdu'l-Bahá 'unveiled' the character of the Administrative Order of the Faith, 'reaffirmed its basis, supplemented its principles, asserted its indispensability, and enumerated its chief institutions'. [268]

But there are three provisions of the Will which must be mentioned here, for through them 'Abdu'l-Bahá created infallible protection for the Cause of Bahá'u'lláh after His passing. Briefly, He appointed His successor, defended him from any possible challenge, and defined the means by which the Universal House of Justice, the supreme body instituted by Bahá'u'lláh, should come into being.

The Will opens with this majestic passage:

All praise to Him Who, by the Shield of His Covenant, hath guarded the Temple of His Cause from the darts of doubtfulness, Who by the Hosts of His Testament hath preserved the Sanctuary of His Most Beneficent Law and protected His Straight and Luminous Path, staying thereby the onslaught of the company of Covenant-breakers, that have threatened to subvert His Divine Edifice; Who hath watched over His Mighty Stronghold and All-glorious Faith, through the aid of men whom the slander of the slanderer affect not, whom no earthly calling, glory, and power can turn aside from the Covenant of God and His Testament, established firmly by His clear and manifest words, writ and revealed by His All-Glorious Pen and recorded in the Preserved Tablet.

Salutation and praise, blessing and glory rest upon that primal branch of the Divine and Sacred Lote-Tree, grown out, blest, tender, verdant, and flourishing from the Twin Holy Trees; the most wondrous, unique, and priceless pearl that doth gleam from out the Twin surging seas; upon the offshoots of the Tree of Holiness, the twigs of the Celestial Tree, they that in the Day of the Great Dividing have stood fast and firm in the Covenant; upon the Hands (pillars) of the Cause of God that have diffused widely the Divine Fragrances, declared His Proofs, proclaimed His Faith, published abroad His Law, detached themselves from all things but Him, stood for righteousness in this world, and kindled the Fire of the Love of God in the very hearts and souls of His servants; upon them that have believed, rested assured, stood steadfast in His Covenant, and followed the Light that after my passing shineth from the Dayspring of Divine Guidance—for behold! he is the blest and sacred bough that hath branched out from the Twin Holy Trees.* Well

* A reference to Bahá'u'lláh and the Báb, from both of Whom Shoghi Effendi was descended.

is it with him that seeketh the shelter of his shade that shadoweth all mankind.

Thus, at the very outset a succession was established and Bahá'ís knew to whom they had to turn. Later, in the first section of the Will and Testament, the successor was specifically named and his authority was elevated above that of all others:

O my loving friends! After the passing away of this wronged one, it is incumbent upon the Aghsán (Branches),* the Afnán (Twigs)† of the Sacred Lote-Tree, the Hands (pillars) of the Cause of God, and the loved ones of the Abhá Beauty to turn unto Shoghi Effendi—the youthful branch branched from the Two hallowed and sacred Lote-Trees and the fruit grown from the union of the Two offshoots of the Tree of Holiness— as he is the sign of God, the chosen branch, the guardian of the Cause of God, he unto whom all the Aghsán, the Afnán, the Hands of the Cause of God, and His loved ones must turn . . .

The sacred and youthful branch, the guardian of the Cause of God as well as the Universal House of Justice, to be universally elected and established, are both under the care and protection of the Abhá Beauty, under the shelter and unerring guidance of His Holiness, the Exalted One (may my life be offered up for them both).‡ Whatsoever they decide is of God. Whoso obeyeth him not, neither obeyeth them, hath not obeyed God . . . It is incumbent upon the House of Justice, upon all the members of the Aghsán, the Afnán, the Hands of the Cause of God to show their obedience, submissiveness, and subordination unto the guardian of the Cause of God, to turn unto him and be lowly before him . . .

* Relatives of Bahá'u'lláh.
† Relatives of the Báb.
‡ These terms refer to Bahá'u'lláh and the Báb, respectively.

It should be pondered that if the despotic ruler of the Ottoman Empire or any other adversary had terminated the life of 'Abdu'l-Bahá during the period in which the Will was written, the Head of the Faith would have been a child of about ten years of age. Shoghi Effendi was born in 1897.

Before specifically naming Shoghi Effendi the Guardian of the Cause of God, 'Abdu'l-Bahá related the story of Mírzá Yaḥyá's rebellion against Bahá'u'lláh,* and then showed how and why His own half-brother Mírzá Muḥammad-'Alí, designated by Bahá'u'lláh in His Book of Testament as the Greater Branch, had forfeited his station and could not be the Head of the Faith:

> O ye that stand fast and firm in the Covenant! The Centre of Sedition, the Prime Mover of mischief, Mírzá Muḥammad-'Alí, hath passed out from under the shadow of the Cause, hath broken the Covenant, hath falsified the Holy Text, hath inflicted a grievous loss upon the true Faith of God, hath scattered His people, hath with bitter rancour endeavoured to hurt 'Abdu'l-Bahá, and hath assailed with the utmost enmity this servant of the Sacred Threshold. Every dart he seized and hurled to pierce the breast of this wronged servant, no wound did he neglect to grievously inflict upon me, no venom did he spare but he poisoned therewith the life of this hapless one. I swear by the most holy Abhá Beauty and by the Light shining from His Holiness, the Exalted One (may my soul be a sacrifice for their lowly servants), that because of this iniquity the dwellers in the Pavilion of the Abhá Kingdom have bewailed, the Celestial Concourse is lamenting . . . So grievous the deeds of this iniquitous person became that he struck with his axe at the root of

* See H. M. Balyuzi, *Edward Granville Browne and The Bahá' Faith*, for a full account.

the Blessed Tree, dealt a heavy blow at the Temple of the Cause of God, deluged with tears of blood the eyes of the loved ones of the Blessed Beauty, cheered and encouraged the enemies of the One True God, by his repudiation of the Covenant turned many a seeker after Truth aside from the Cause of God, revived the blighted hopes of Yaḥyá's following, made himself detested, caused the enemies of the Greatest Name to become audacious and arrogant, put aside the firm and conclusive verses, and sowed the seeds of doubt. Had not the promised aid of the Ancient Beauty been graciously vouchsafed at every moment to this one, unworthy though he be, he surely would have destroyed, nay exterminated, the Cause of God and utterly subverted the Divine Edifice. But, praised be the Lord, the triumphant assistance of the Abhá Kingdom was received, the hosts of the Realm above hastened to bestow victory . . . Now, that the true Faith of God may be shielded and protected, His Law guarded and preserved, and His Cause remain safe and secure, it is incumbent upon everyone to hold fast unto the Text of the clear and firmly established blessed verse, revealed about him . . . He (Bahá'u'lláh) sayeth, glorious and holy is His Word: 'My foolish loved ones have regarded him even as my partner, have kindled sedition in the land and they verily are of the mischief-makers.' Consider, how foolish are the people! They that have been in His (Bahá'u'lláh's) Presence and beheld His Countenance, have nevertheless noised abroad such idle talk, until, exalted be His explicit words, He said: 'Should he for a moment pass out from under the shadow of the Cause, he surely shall be brought to naught.' Reflect! What stress He layeth upon one moment's deviation: that is, were he to incline a hair's breadth to the right or to the left, his deviation would be clearly established and his utter nothingness made manifest . . .

What deviation can be greater than breaking the Covenant of God! What deviation can be greater than interpolating and falsifying the words and verses of the

Sacred Text, even as testified and declared by Mírzá Badí'u'lláh! What deviation can be greater than calumniating the Centre of the Covenant himself! What deviation can be more glaring than spreading broadcast false and foolish reports touching the Temple of God's Testament! What deviation can be more grievous than decreeing the death of the Centre of the Covenant . . .

'Abdu'l-Bahá mentioned next the details of the intrigues of Mírzá Muḥammad-'Alí and his associates, intrigues which had led to the dispatch of a Commission of Enquiry from Istanbul (see pp. 112 and 118), and concluded:

The Committee of Investigation hath approved and confirmed these calumnies of my brother and ill-wishers and submitted them to the presence of His Majesty the Sovereign. Now at this moment a fierce storm is raging around this prisoner who awaiteth, be it favourable or unfavourable, the gracious will of His Majesty, may the Lord aid him by His grace to be just. In whatsoever condition he may be, with absolute calm and quietness, 'Abdu'l-Bahá is ready for self sacrifice and is wholly resigned and submitted to His Will. What transgression can be more abominable, more odious, more wicked than this!

In like manner, the focal Centre of hate, hath purposed to put 'Abdu'l-Bahá to death and this is supported by the testimony written by Mírzá Shu'áu'lláh himself and is here enclosed . . .

In short, O ye beloved of the Lord! The Centre of Sedition, Mírzá Muḥammad-'Alí, in accordance with the decisive words of God and by reason of his boundless transgression, hath grievously fallen and been cut off from the Holy Tree. Verily, we wronged them not, but they have wronged themselves!

Despite a thorough exposition of the evil deeds of the violators of the Covenant, in the second part of the Will and

Testament, 'Abdu'l-Bahá offered a prayer for them. 'The breakers of the Covenant are consigned to the wrath of God, but for these same people, the contemptible enemies of 'Abdu'l-Bahá, there is only this':[269]

I call upon Thee, O Lord my God! with my tongue and with all my heart, not to requite them for their cruelty and their wrong-doings, their craft and their mischief, for they are foolish and ignoble and know not what they do. They discern not good from evil, neither do they distinguish right from wrong, nor justice from injustice. They follow their own desires and walk in the footsteps of the most imperfect and foolish amongst them. O my Lord! Have mercy upon them, shield them from all afflictions in these troubled times and grant that all trials and hardships may be the lot of this Thy servant that hath fallen into this darksome pit. Single me out for every woe and make me a sacrifice for all Thy loved ones. O Lord, Most High! May my soul, my life, my being, my spirit, my all be offered up for them. O God, my God! Lowly, suppliant, and fallen upon my face, I beseech Thee with all the ardour of my invocation to pardon whosoever hath hurt me, forgive him that hath conspired against me and offended me, and wash away the misdeeds of them that have wrought injustice upon me. Vouchsafe unto them Thy goodly gifts, give them joy, relieve them from sorrow, grant them peace and prosperity, give them Thy bliss and pour upon them Thy bounty.

Thou art the Powerful, the Gracious, the Help in Peril, the Self-Subsisting!

And that prayer is immediately followed by these words:

O dearly beloved friends! I am now in very great danger and the hope of even an hour's life is lost to me. I am thus constrained to write these lines for the protection of the Cause of God, the preservation of His Law, the safe-guarding of His Word and the safety of His Teachings.

By the Ancient Beauty! This wronged one hath in no wise borne nor doth he bear a grudge against any one; towards none doth he entertain any ill-feeling and uttereth no word save for the good of the world. My supreme obligation, however, of necessity, prompteth me to guard and preserve the Cause of God . . .

And this is the conclusion of the second part of 'Abdu'l-Bahá's Will, written, as the above words testify, at the height of crisis both for Himself and for the Cause of God:

O God, my God! I call Thee, Thy Prophets and Thy Messengers, Thy Saints and Thy Holy Ones, to witness that I have declared conclusively Thy Proofs unto Thy loved ones and set forth clearly all things unto them, that they may watch over Thy Faith, guard Thy Straight Path, and protect Thy Resplendent Law. Thou art, verily, the All-Knowing, the All-Wise!

It should be noted that the authority of the Universal House of Justice is not derived from the Will and Testament of 'Abdu'l-Bahá. That authority was conferred by Bahá'u'-lláh. But the Will of 'Abdu'l-Bahá clarified its station and instituted the electorate which would choose its members.

And now, concerning the House of Justice which God hath ordained as the source of all good and freed from all error, it must be elected by universal suffrage, that is, by the believers. Its members must be manifestations of the fear of God and day-springs of knowledge and understanding, must be steadfast in God's faith and the well-wishers of all mankind. By this House is meant the Universal House of Justice, that is, in all countries, a secondary House of Justice must be instituted, and these secondary Houses of Justice must elect the members of the Universal one. Unto this body all things must be referred. It enacteth all ordinances and regulations

that are not to be found in the explicit Holy Text. By this
body all the difficult problems are to be resolved . . .

Just as provisions concerning the Guardian of the Faith
are included in the three sections of the Will, so, too, the
authority of the Universal House of Justice is, in each part,
asserted and underlined. The extract just quoted comes
from the first part; here are extracts from parts two and
three:

> . . . Unto the Most Holy Book every one must turn and
> all that is not expressly recorded therein must be referred
> to the Universal House of Justice. That which this body,
> whether unanimously or by a majority doth carry, that
> is verily the Truth and the Purpose of God himself . . .
> . . . All must seek guidance and turn unto the Centre
> of the Cause and the House of Justice. And he that turneth
> unto whatsoever else is indeed in grievous error.

The Will and Testament of 'Abdu'l-Bahá constitutes the
'indissoluble link' between the Revelation of Bahá'u'lláh
and the universal Order which it is the purpose of that
Revelation to promote. It is the very Charter of that Order
and compels the most persistent and earnest study of all
who seek to understand the destiny of mankind in this age.
In the words of the Guardian of the Faith, the Will and
Testament of 'Abdu'l-Bahá is 'His greatest legacy to posterity' and 'the brightest emanation of His mind'.*

The counsel contained in these lines, from the first part
of 'Abdu'l-Bahá's Testament, illumines the way through
centuries unborn:

> O ye beloved of the Lord! In this sacred Dispensation,
> conflict and contention are in no wise permitted. Every

* The Will and Testament is published in full in *The Covenant
of Bahá'u'lláh* (see bibliography), together with extracts from the
Guardian's words concerning it.

aggressor deprives himself of God's grace. It is incumbent upon everyone to show the utmost love, rectitude of conduct, straightforwardness, and sincere kindliness unto all the peoples and kindreds of the world, be they friends or strangers. So intense must be the spirit of love and loving kindness, that the stranger may find himself a friend, the enemy a true brother, no difference whatsoever existing between them. For universality is of God and all limitations earthly. Thus man must strive that his reality may manifest virtues and perfections, the light whereof may shine upon everyone. The light of the sun shineth upon all the world and the merciful showers of Divine Providence fall upon all peoples. The vivifying breeze reviveth every living creature and all beings endued with life obtain their share and portion at His heavenly board. In like manner, the affections and loving kindness of the servants of the One True God must be bountifully and universally extended to all mankind. Regarding this, restrictions and limitations are in no wise permitted.

Wherefore, O my loving friends! Consort with all the peoples, kindreds, and religions of the world with the utmost truthfulness, uprightness, faithfulness, kindliness, goodwill, and friendliness; that all the world of being may be filled with the holy ecstasy of the grace of Bahá, that ignorance, enmity, hate, and rancour may vanish from the world and the darkness of estrangement amidst the peoples and kindreds of the world may give way to the Light of Unity. Should other peoples and nations be unfaithful to you show your fidelity unto them, should they be unjust toward you show justice towards them, should they keep aloof from you attract them to yourself, should they show their enmity be friendly towards them, should they poison your lives sweeten their souls, should they inflict a wound upon you be a salve to their sores. Such are the attributes of the sincere! Such are the attributes of the truthful!

A WORD IN CONCLUSION

This book has attempted to tell the story of 'Abdu'l-Bahá. But now we must go back to what was said in the opening chapter:

No description can measure up to the theme of a life which transcended every barrier to its total fulfilment. It lies beyond the range of assessment because every event in the life of the Son of Bahá'u'lláh carries a major accent.

And we must read once again these words of Shoghi Effendi with which the book commenced:

He is, and should for all time be regarded, first and foremost, as the Centre and Pivot of Bahá'u'lláh's peerless and all-enfolding Covenant, His most exalted handiwork, the stainless Mirror of His light, the perfect Exemplar of His teachings, the unerring Interpreter of His Word, the embodiment of every Bahá'í ideal, the incarnation of every Bahá'í virtue, the Most Mighty Branch sprung from the Ancient Root, the Limb of the Law of God, the Being *'round Whom all names revolve,'* the Mainspring of the Oneness of Humanity, the Ensign of the Most Great Peace, the Moon of the Central Orb of this most holy Dispensation—styles and titles that are implicit and find their truest, their highest and fairest expression in the magic name 'Abdu'l-Bahá.

To those words Shoghi Effendi added:

He is, above and beyond these appellations, the 'Mystery of God'—an expression by which Bahá'u'lláh Himself has chosen to designate Him, and which, while it does not by any means justify us to assign to Him the station of Prophethood, indicates how in the person of 'Abdu'l-Bahá the incompatible characteristics of a human nature and superhuman knowledge and perfection have been blended and are completely harmonized.

'Abdu'l-Bahá was the Mystery of God. Who, then, can portray Him?

THE DRAMA OF THE KINGDOM

This is the outline for *The Drama of the Kingdom*, which
'Abdu'l-Bahá gave to Gabrielle Enthoven (see p. 348).
The outline was used later by Parvine (Mary Basil Hall)
as the basis of the play which she wrote, under this title.
(London: The Weardale Press Limited, 1933.) 'Abdu'l-Bahá
had no notes and spoke without pause, except for translation.

The Herald of the Kingdom stands before the people.
Wonderful music swells from an unseen orchestra,
moving and soul-inspiring. The music becomes soft,
while the Herald proclaims the coming of the Kingdom.
He holds a trumpet to his mouth.

The curtain rises. The stage is crowded with men and
women. All are asleep. At the sound of the trumpet they
begin to awake.

Suddenly the music breaks forth. The people hear and
wonder. They rise and question one another, saying:
'What is this? Whence comes this music?' Some return
to their occupations, unheeding. First a few talk together,
then one ceases his work, and proceeds to make enquiries.
A merchant, leaving his stall, comes to ask the meaning
of the eager group. A soldier, who is practising arms,
withdraws from his comrades and joins those who are
wondering.

Here, a banker is seen counting his money; his attention
is attracted. He pauses in his calculation, and asks: 'What
is the news?'

There are seen dancers and others holding revelry.

Some of them come forth and ask the news, questioning the Herald.

Now those who come to ask are more or less divided into the following groups. First those who, having heard of the Coming of the Promised One, frown and shrug their shoulders, returning to their work, scoffing and disbelieving. The second type are those who hear the music, strain their ears to catch the meaning of the Message, and their eyes to discern the Mystery.

The blind receive their sight, the deaf their hearing, and those who were dead arise and walk, still wrapped in the garments of death.

Then there are those who will not believe until they have had signs revealed to them, who crave for proof, saying: 'But we want to see the earthquake. If the Promised One is indeed come, the sun should not give his light, the moon should be darkened, and the stars should fall. We await our Promised One till these signs be fulfilled. We expect to see him descend from heaven in clouds of great glory.'

Those who believe shout: 'The Promised One has come!'

Those who doubt cry: 'What proof is there? Show us a proof!'

They who understand explain: 'Whence did Christ come? He came from heaven, though they who scoffed at Him said: "We know this man, he comes from Nazareth." This is the real meaning: His spirit came from heaven, while His body was born of an earthly mother. As it was then, so is it with the Second Coming.'

'But we await the signs,' say the doubting ones. 'How, otherwise, shall we know? The earth must shake, the mountains be rent asunder. The Promised One shall conquer the East and the West.'

One arises and tells the people that these signs did not come outwardly, nor will they again. Those who look with the eyes of Truth shall see that these portents are of the Spirit.

The Eternal Sovereignty descends from heaven, the body is of the earth. The mountains are men of high renown, whose famous names sink into insignificance, when the dawn of the Manifestation fills the world with light. The pomp of Annas and Caiaphas is outshone by the simple glory of the Christ. The earthquake is the wave of spiritual life, that moves through all living things and makes creation quiver.

The prophecies of the Coming of Christ were mystical. The prophecies concerning the Second Coming are also mystical. The earthquakes and unrest, the darkening of the sun and moon, the falling of the stars—all these foretell the humiliation of those whom the world considers great. Theologians wrapped in blind traditions, the bigots and the hypocrites: such will fall.

Now these sayings will be divided between different people, altogether forming a conversation, questions, answers, exclamations of wonder, and so forth.

Now a procession passes. The Pageant of the World. Grand nobles and kings, high priests and dignitaries of the Churches, jewelled and gorgeously dressed. They look with scorn on those who believe, saying: 'Why should we leave our ancient religions?' They look like devils of malice and oppression. Yet each is miserable. One falls, the others pass on. One is dying, the others take no heed. Another breathes his last. They do not stop by the way.

The poor who have believed look on sadly.

The scene changes. A banquet hall. The table is spread with all delicious foods. The orchestra is playing heavenly music. The lights become gradually more brilliant, until the whole hall is shining. Round the table sit the very poor in torn garments. An Oracle arises and cries: 'The Kingdom of God is like a feast! Remember what Christ said! Here we see the Kingdom! The greatest and the worldly wise are not here, but the poor are here!'

Each sings from the joy of his heart, and there is great rejoicing. Some dance, one plays the flute, everyone is radiantly happy. Someone addresses the people. While this man is speaking they say: 'Hear him! Hear his eloquence! We know him. He was poor and ignorant, and now he is wise!' And so they wonder and question one another. A woman rises and speaks, laughing and happy. The people are surprised, saying: 'But what has happened? Yesterday this woman was sad, and angry. Her heart was full of sorrow and disappointment. Why is she so joyous?'

A man enters with a sack of gold and begins to offer it to the people, but they refuse, one saying: 'I am rich, I do not need your gold.' 'Nor I.' 'Nor I.' The man with the gold is surprised and says: 'We know you are poor and starving. Why do you not accept my gold?'

Then a teacher comes and speaks on a high plane of philosophy and science. All those who listen wonder, for he had been ignorant and accounted of no importance. How is he now so learned?

Another comes with shining eyes, gazing with joy on the beautiful surroundings. The people wonder and say: 'How is this? Yesterday he was blind.'

Another hears beautiful music and he tells the people that a few hours ago he was deaf to all sound.

'A miracle! A miracle! Here is one who was dead, and now he is walking before us!'

One arises and says: 'You know the cause of these miracles? It is the Heavenly food! Everlasting life is for him who partakes of it.'

When the people hear this they shout with one will: 'Glad tidings! Glad tidings! Glad tidings!'

Each one is supremely happy. They sing an Alleluia.

'O God, we were poor, Thou hast made us rich!
We were hungry, Thou hast made us satisfied!
Athirst were we, and Thou hast given us the Water of Life!
Our eyes were blinded, Thou hast given us sight!
We were dead, Thou hast given unto us Life Eternal!

We were of the earth, Thou hast made us the children
of Heaven!
We were outcasts, Thou hast made us beloved!
We were helpless, Thou hast made us powerful!
We praise Thee, O Lord!'

After this song, glorious diadems descend from Heaven
and rest on each head. They shine with the radiance of
Heavenly jewels. All wonder and ask questions. One
arises and says: 'These are the crowns of the Kingdom!
Ye are all Heavenly rulers! Ye shall have eternal dominion!
Ye shall have everlasting glory! The illumination of the
Spirit is yours. God hath chosen you for His service!'
They take their crowns and kiss them, and again place
them on their heads.

Then they begin to pray and supplicate:

'O God! O Almighty!
'We give Thee thanks for these proofs of Thy bounty!
Thou hast given us Life! Make us faithful, so that the
fire of Thy Love may fill our hearts, that Thy Light
may illumine our faces! Suffer us to be firm unto Christ,
Who gave up His life for us!'

The curtain falls.

In the last scene one of those who believe is taken by
the persecutors. 'We mean to kill you,' they say. 'I am
ready. I am happy,' he answers. With hands raised to
Heaven, he cries: 'O God, make me ready!' Then he
gives himself up to death. Another is taken, and dies
praising God and His mercy to mankind.

The third is a beautiful girl in a white garment, wearing
a heavenly crown upon her head. Everyone gazes at her
in wonder. She is seated, apart. A messenger comes from
the king with an offer of great riches if she will but give
up the Cause which she has embraced. She answers: 'I
have not accepted this Cause blindly through tradition.
I have seen Reality with mine own eyes. The Truth is
in my heart. How should I renounce my faith thus lightly?'

Her father comes and entreats her to give up her faith.

She answers: 'Can you say there is no sun, when you have seen the light? I have seen the sun. You are blind. Awake! The sun is shining! Awake!'

Another messenger comes. This time from a great prince who wishes to wed her on condition that she gives up her Faith.

'I know no prince save God. I will not close mine eyes to the glory of the King of Kings!'

They bring her jewels and an earthly crown. 'Take these!' they say.

'These to me are so many pebbles. The jewels I treasure are the jewels of the Knowledge of God. Those earthly stones may be broken or lost. Behold my crown! These are eternal gems! For those earthly stones that are doomed to perish, shall I give up this everlasting diadem?'

They say: 'We shall imprison you.'

'I am ready.'

'We shall beat you.'

'I am ready.'

'You shall be killed.'

'Is that true? Do you mean it? Good news! Good news! For then I shall be free. My soul will escape like a bird at liberty from this earthly cage of my body. Then shall I be free. Now am I in chains. These bonds shall be broken. Kill me! Kill me!'

They slay her. One after another is martyred. Their bodies are covered with shrouds, and after a great silence, people enter and lift the coverings in awe and reverence. They stand wondering, as lights appear and shine upwards from the prostrate forms. Some question as to the meaning of this. 'These are the spirits of those martyred ones, freed from their bodies. Now they enjoy eternal liberty. See, they ascend to the Kingdom!'

Realising this, the people are wonderstruck and amazed. They cry: 'What bounty God has bestowed on them! They are so free and joyful! Now can they wing their way to the Sun of Reality! Their souls return to the Sun from which they came!'

FROM *THE TABLETS OF THE DIVINE PLAN* *

To the believers of God and the maid-servants of the Merciful of the Bahá'í Assemblies in the United States of America and Canada.

Upon them be Bahá'u'lláh El-Abhá!

He is God!

O ye apostles of Bahá'u'lláh—May my life be a ransom to you!

The blessed Person of the Promised One is interpreted in the Holy Book as the Lord of Hosts—the heavenly armies. By heavenly armies those souls are intended who are entirely freed from the human world, transformed into celestial spirits and have become divine angels. Such souls are the rays of the Sun of Reality who will illumine all the continents. Each one is holding in his hand a trumpet, blowing the breath of life over all the regions. They are delivered from human qualities and the defects of the world of nature, are characterized with the characteristics of God, and are attracted with the fragrances of the Merciful. Like unto the apostles of Christ, who were filled with Him, these souls also have become filled with His Holiness Bahá'u'lláh; that is, the love of Bahá'u'lláh has so mastered every organ, part and limb of their bodies, as to leave no effect from the promptings of the human world.

* Bahá'í Publishing Trust (Wilmette, Illinois, 1962).

These souls are the armies of God and the conquerors of the East and the West. Should one of them turn his face toward some direction and summon the people to the Kingdom of God, all the ideal forces and lordly confirmations will rush to his support and reinforcement. He will behold all the doors open and all the strong fortifications and impregnable castles razed to the ground. Singly and alone he will attack the armies of the world, defeat the right and left wings of the hosts of all the countries, break through the lines of the legions of all the nations and carry his attack to the very center of the powers of the earth. This is the meaning of the Hosts of God.

Any soul from among the believers of Bahá'u'lláh who attains to this station, will become known as the Apostle of Bahá'u'lláh. Therefore strive ye with heart and soul so that ye may reach this lofty and exalted position, be established on the throne of everlasting glory, and crown your heads with the shining diadem of the Kingdom, whose brilliant jewels may irradiate upon centuries and cycles.

O ye kind friends! Uplift your magnanimity and soar high toward the apex of heaven so that your blessed hearts may become illumined more and more, day by day, through the Rays of the Sun of Reality, that is, His Holiness Bahá'u'lláh; at every moment the spirits may obtain a new life, and the darkness of the world of nature may be entirely dispelled; thus you may become incarnate light and personified spirit, become entirely unaware of the sordid matters of this world and in touch with the affairs of the divine world.

Consider you what doors His Holiness Bahá'u'lláh has opened before you, and what a high and exalted station He has destined for you, and what bounties He has prepared for you! Should we become intoxicated with this cup, the sovereignty of this globe of earth will become lower in our estimation than the children's plays. Should they place in the arena the crown of the government of the whole world, and invite each one of us to accept it, undoubtedly we shall not condescend, and shall refuse to accept it.

To attain to this supreme station is, however, dependent on the realization of certain conditions:

The first condition is firmness in the Covenant of God. For the power of the Covenant will protect the Cause of Bahá'u'lláh from the doubts of the people of error. It is the fortified fortress of the Cause of God and the firm pillar of the religion of God. Today no power can conserve the oneness of the Bahá'í world save the Covenant of God; otherwise differences like unto a most great tempest will encompass the Bahá'í world. It is evident that the axis of the oneness of the world of humanity is the power of the Covenant and nothing else. Had the Covenant not come to pass, had it not been revealed from the Supreme Pen and had not the Book of the Covenant, like unto the ray of the Sun of Reality, illuminated the world, the forces of the Cause of God would have been utterly scattered and certain souls who were the prisoners of their own passions and lusts would have taken into their hands an axe, cutting the root of this Blessed Tree. Every person would have pushed forward his own desire and every individual aired his own opinion! Notwithstanding this great Covenant, a few negligent souls galloped with their chargers into the battlefield, thinking perchance they might be able to weaken the foundation of the Cause of God: but praise be to God all of them were afflicted with regret and loss, and ere long they shall see themselves in poignant despair. Therefore, in the beginning one must make his steps firm in the Covenant so that the confirmations of Bahá'u'lláh may encircle from all sides, the cohorts of the Supreme Concourse may become the supporters and the helpers, and the exhortations and advices of 'Abdu'l-Bahá, like unto the pictures engraved on stone, may remain permanent and ineffaceable in the tablets of the hearts.

The second condition: Fellowship and love amongst the believers. The divine friends must be attracted to and enamored of each other and ever be ready and willing to sacrifice their own lives for each other. Should one soul from amongst the believers meet another, it must be as though a thirsty one with parched lips has reached to the fountain of the water of life, or a lover has met his true beloved. For one of the greatest divine wisdoms regarding the appearance of the Holy Manifestations is this: The souls may come to know each other and become intimate with each other; the power of the love of God may make all of them the waves of one sea, the flowers of one rose garden, and the stars of one heaven. This is the wisdom for the appearance of the Holy Manifestations! When the most great bestowal reveals itself in the hearts of the believers, the world of nature will be transformed, the darkness of the contingent being will vanish, and heavenly illumination will be obtained. Then the whole world will become the Paradise of Abhá, every one of the believers of God will become a blessed tree, producing wonderful fruits.

O ye friends! Fellowship, fellowship! Love, love! Unity, unity!—So that the power of the Bahá'í Cause may appear and become manifest in the world of existence. Just at this moment I am engaged in your commemoration and this heart is in the utmost glow and excitement! Were you to realize how this consciousness is attracted with the love of the friends, unquestionably you would obtain such a degree of joy and fragrance that you would all become enamored with each other!

The third condition: Teachers must continually travel to all parts of the continent, nay, rather, to all parts of the world, but they must travel like 'Abdu'l-Bahá, who journeyed throughout the cities of America. He was sanctified and free from every attachment and in the utmost severance. Just as His Holiness Christ says, 'Shake off the very dust from your feet.'

You have observed that while in America many souls in the utmost of supplication and entreaty desired to offer some gifts, but this servant, in accord with the exhortations and behests of the Blessed Perfection, never accepted a thing, although on certain occasions we were in most straitened circumstances. But on the other hand, if a soul for the sake of God, voluntarily and out of his pure desire, wishes to offer a contribution (toward the expenses of a teacher) in order to make the contributor happy, the teacher may accept a small sum, but must live with the utmost contentment.

The aim is this: The intention of the teacher must be pure, his heart independent, his spirit attracted, his thought at peace, his resolution firm, his magnanimity exalted and in the love of God a shining torch. Should he become as such, his sanctified breath will even affect the rock; otherwise there will be no result whatsoever. As long as a soul is not perfected, how can he efface the defects of others. Unless he is detached from aught else save God, how can he teach severance to others!

In short, O ye believers of God! Endeavor ye, so that you may take hold of every means in the promulgation of the religion of God and the diffusion of the fragrances of God.

Amongst other things is the holding of the meetings for teaching so that blessed souls and the old ones from amongst the believers may gather together the youths of the love of God in schools of instruction and teach them all the divine proofs and irrefragable arguments, explain and elucidate the history of the Cause, and interpret also the prophecies and proofs which are recorded and are extant in the divine Books and Epistles regarding the Manifestation of the Promised One, so that the young ones may go in perfect knowledge in all these degrees.

Likewise, whenever it is possible a committee must be organized for the translation of the Tablets. Wise souls who have mastered and studied perfectly the Persian, Arabic, and other foreign languages, or know one of the foreign languages, must commence translating Tablets and books containing the proofs of this Revelation, and publishing those books, circulate them throughout the five continents of the globe.

Similarly, the Magazine, the *Star of the West*, must be edited with the utmost regularity, but its contents must be the promulgation of the Cause of God that both East and West may become informed of the most important events.

In short, in all the meetings, whether public or private, nothing should be discussed save that which is under consideration, and all the articles be centered around the Cause of God. Promiscuous talk must not be dragged in and contention is absolutely forbidden.

The teachers traveling in different directions must know the language of the country in which they will enter. For example, a person being proficient in the Japanese language may travel to Japan, or a person knowing the Chinese language may hasten to China, and so forth.

In short, after this universal war, the people have obtained extraordinary capacity to hearken to the divine teachings, for the wisdom of this war is this: That it may become proven to all that the fire of war is world-consuming, whereas the rays of peace are world-enlightening. One is death, the other is life; this is extinction, that is immortality; one is the most great calamity, the other is the most great bounty; this is darkness, that is light; this is eternal humiliation and that is everlasting glory; one is the destroyer of the foundation of man, the other is the founder of the prosperity of the human race.

Consequently, a number of souls may arise and act in accordance with the aforesaid conditions, and hasten to all parts of the world, especially from America to Europe, Africa, Asia and Australia, and travel through Japan and

China. Likewise, from Germany teachers and believers may travel to the continents of America, Africa, Japan and China; in brief, they may travel through all the continents and islands of the globe. Thus in a short space of time, most wonderful results will be produced, the banner of Universal Peace will be waving on the apex of the world and the lights of the oneness of the world of humanity may illumine the universe.

In brief, O ye believers of God! The text of the Divine Book is this: If two souls quarrel and contend about a question of the Divine questions, differing and disputing, *both are wrong*. The wisdom of this incontrovertible law of God is this: That between two souls from amongst the believers of God, no contention and dispute may arise; that they may speak with each other with infinite amity and love. Should there appear the least trace of controversy, they must remain silent, and both parties must continue their discussions no longer, but ask the reality of the question from the Interpreter. This is the irrefutable command!

Upon you be Bahá El-Abhá!

Supplication

O God! O God! Thou seest that black darkness hath encompassed all the regions, all the countries are burning with the conflagration of dissension and the fire of war and carnage is ignited in the Easts of the earth and the Wests thereof. The blood is being shed, the corpses are outstretched and the heads are decapitated and thrown on the ground in the battlefield.

Lord! Lord! Have pity on these ignorant ones, look upon them with the eye of forgiveness and pardon. Extinguish this fire so that these gloomy clouds covering the horizon may be scattered; the Sun of Reality may shine forth with the rays of conciliation; this darkness be rent asunder and all the countries be illumined with the lights of peace.

Lord! Awaken them from the depths of the sea of animosity, deliver them from these impenetrable darknesses, establish affinity between their hearts and enlighten their eyes with the light of peace and reconciliation.

Lord! Rescue them from the fathomless depths of war and bloodshed! Arouse them out of the gloom of error, rend asunder the veil from their eyes, brighten their hearts with the light of guidance, deal with them through Thy favor and mercy and do not treat them according to Thy justice and wrath through which the backs of the mighty ones are shaken!

Lord! Verily the wars have prolonged, the calamities have increased, and every building hath turned into ruin.

Lord! Verily the breasts are agitated and the souls are convulsed. Have mercy on these poor ones and do not leave them to do with themselves that which they desire!

Lord! Send forth throughout Thy countries humble and submissive souls, their faces illumined with the rays of guidance, severed from the world, speaking Thy remembrance and praise and diffusing Thy holy fragrances amongst mankind!

Lord! Strengthen their backs, reinforce their loins and dilate their breasts with the signs of Thy most great love.

Lord! Verily they are weak and Thou art the Powerful and the Mighty; and they are impotent and Thou art the Helper and the Merciful!

Lord! Verily the sea of transgression is waving high and these hurricanes will not be calmed down save through Thy boundless grace which hath embraced all the regions!

Lord! Verily the souls are in the deep valleys of lust and nothing will awaken them save Thy most wonderful bounties.

Lord! Dispel these darknesses of temptations and illumine

the hearts with the lamp of Thy love, through which all the countries will be enlightened. Confirm those believers who, leaving their countries, their families and their children, travel throughout the regions for the sake of the love of Thy beauty, the diffusion of Thy fragrances and the promulgation of Thy teachings. Be Thou their companion in their loneliness, their helper in a strange land, the remover of their sorrow, the comforter in their calamity, their deliverer in their hardship, the satisfier of their thirst, the healer of their malady and the allayer of the fire of their longing.

Verily, Thou art the Clement, the Possessor of Mercy, and Verily, Thou art the Compassionate and the Merciful.

Haifa, Palestine,
April 19, 20, and 22, 1917.

TABLETS FROM 'ABDU'L-BAHÁ REGARDING THE SAVE THE CHILDREN FUND*

To one worker He wrote:

My hope is that thou mayest be confirmed in the great cause (of saving children), which is the greatest service to the world of mankind. For the poor children are perishing from hunger and their condition is indeed pitiable. This is one of the evils of the war.

The English Lady who has established this Committee (Save the Children Fund) is assuredly confirmed by the favours of the Kingdom of God.

This lady and her sister (her co-worker in starting the movement) are really serving according to the principles of Baha-Ullah. I enclose two pictures of mine, which thou wilt deliver to them. To these two esteemed ladies convey on my behalf greeting and say: 'Ye are serving the world of mankind, and the Divine Sacred Threshold; ye are glorified by His Holiness Baha-Ullah for ye are acting in accordance with his commands.

'My hope is that ye may become two resplendent torches of the world of mankind, may serve Divine Civilisation, may attain everlasting Life, and may be favoured in the Divine Immortal Kingdom.'

In another tablet (June 1920) to a worker, He wrote:

Upon her be the Light of God the Most Luminous:
Oh, thou who art attracted to the Kingdom of God! The

* These Tablets appear in a pamphlet entitled 'The First Obligation' by Lady Blomfield, printed in London by Caledonian Press, Ltd. No date is shown.

letter written at Easter has been received. Its contents gave (me) the greatest joy—that praise be unto God, such an Association has been formed (for the relief of destitute children and orphans) in which almost every nation and every religion is represented.

My hope is that, through the especial Grace of God, this Association (Save the Children Fund) will be confirmed (assisted and strengthened by Divine Power); that it may day by day progress both spiritually and materially; that it may at last enter into the Heavenly Pavilion of Unity; that it may embark in the ship of real, Eternal Life; that it may be protected from every danger; and that the Oneness of Humanity may, through the work of this Society (Save the Children Fund) raise its banner at the zenith of the world.

'A GREAT PRINCE SPEAKS OF 'ABDU'L-BAHÁ'

Extracts from Martha Root's account of her interview with Prince Muḥammad-'Alí Pá<u>sh</u>á, the brother of the Khedive of Egypt, which was published in *The Bahá'í Magazine (Star of the West)* in January 1930, vol. XX, pp. 301–5. His meeting with 'Abdu'l-Bahá in New York, July 22nd 1912, is mentioned on p. 230. (The transliteration of Persian and Egyptian names has been added by Mr Balyuzi.)

His delightful Highness the Prince shook hands with me and invited me to sit down in one of the comfortable rustic chairs at a little table under the Banyan tree. You will sit with us, O reader, for you, too, are in this enchanted garden to hear what a Prince, who is a savant and a philosopher, has to say about 'Abdu'l-Bahá. Only the Prince called Him, ' 'Abbás Bábá' which in Arabic means 'Abbás Father or Father 'Abbás.

'Yes, I knew 'Abbás Bábá,' commenced the Prince, 'He was a great friend of my brother, 'Abbás Hilmí II, the late Khedive. Also, Osman Murtadá, the Grand Master of Ceremonies of my brother had a great friendship with 'Abbás Bábá. I met your loved Teacher first early in 1912 on my way to Paris. Then when I was in New York in 1912, 'Abdu'l-Bahá was living in a house near Central Park, a home which His friends, (or do you call them His followers?), had prepared for Him. I was living in the Belmont Hotel in Fifth Avenue, and 'Abbás Bábá was kind enough to come and visit me there. I deeply appreciated this kind visit.'

Then His Royal Highness the Prince explained how proud he was to see a great Oriental moulding the spiritual thought of America. My host continued: 'Although we are sorry to see Orientals so backward in sciences, still we must not forget that some great generals, great leaders of thought and all religions have been born in the Orient. 'Abbás Bábá has proved to Europeans and to the entire West that great generals of the Spirit are still born in the East! As I love the Orient and am an Oriental, I was very proud of 'Abdu'l-Bahá's high station and prestige in the United States. Yours is a country of such stupendous wonder, such marked inventions, such marvelous strides in progress, and you saw the greatness of 'Abdu'l-Bahá.'

This earnest Prince spoke with such sincerity, his words were: 'I loved 'Abbás Bábá and admired Him, and I felt He loved me and was a good friend to me.'

'After this visit in New York,' the Prince recounted, 'I met 'Abbás Bábá again in Paris. He told me of His great conference in Oxford University. He told me, too, of His friends in Germany. Later on, we traveled together on the same ship coming back to Egypt. For four days we were always together. I was very sad when I heard of His passing, for I considered Him the most important man in our century. A man like 'Abbás Bábá cannot be replaced, that is my opinion. He had such a great spirit, such a powerful brain and such a grasp of realities!'

A GIFT FROM THE SHRINE OF BAHÁ'U'LLÁH

One of the pilgrims to the Holy Land, during the year 1920, was Ziaollah Asgarzadeh (Ḍíyá'u'lláh Aṣgharzádih) whom we have already met in these pages. He came from 'Iṣhqábád, and had a very valuable rug with him to present to 'Abdu'l-Bahá. The fascinating story of that rug will have to be told one day in greater detail. It had been intended for the Amír of Buḵhárá and was made of silk and gold thread. But the Russian Revolution of 1917 put an end to the Emirate. Asgarzadeh, while travelling in Central Asia, heard of the rug, hurried to purchase it, and managed to make his way to Afgḥánistán, thence to Bombay, where he took ship for Egypt.

On reaching Mount Carmel, Asgarzadeh gave the rug to Áqá Muḥammad-Ḥasan, who served in the Pilgrim House, and asked him to spread it in the doorway, in the path of 'Abdu'l-Bahá. When the Master came in and saw the rug on the floor He side-stepped it and asked whose rug it was. Asgarzadeh said that it was the Master's, his offering to Him. The only place for such a rug, said 'Abdu'l-Bahá, was the Shrine of Bahá'u'lláh; together they would place it in the Shrine.

Asgarzadeh then sought permission to give a feast for the occasion. When the day arrived the Master, mounted on His donkey, with the Bahá'ís following Him on foot, proceeded from the railway station outside 'Akká to Bahjí. On the way Asgarzadeh asked if they might sing, which

'Abdu'l-Bahá smilingly allowed. Asgarzadeh used to relate that they first sang poems by Bahá'í poets such as 'Andalíb and Varqá but, in the end, were so happy and elated that they sang any song which came to their minds. 'Abdu'l-Bahá rode on listening, silent and smiling, until they came within sight of the Shrine, when He turned round to say that it was time to stop singing.

That beautiful and precious rug remained in the inner Shrine of Bahá'u'lláh for more than a decade. Then the Guardian of the Faith sent it to the United States, with this message:

> Moved by an impulse that I could not resist, I have felt impelled to forego what may be regarded as the most valuable and sacred possession in the Holy Land for the furthering of that noble enterprise which you have set your hearts to achieve. With the hearty concurrence of our dear brother, Díyá'ulláh Asgharzádih, who years ago donated it to the Most Holy Shrine, this precious ornament of the Tomb of Bahá'u'lláh has been shipped to your shores.*

'The noble enterprise' mentioned by Shoghi Effendi was the construction of the Temple at Wilmette. Today that rug hangs in the Mashriqu'l-Adhkár, where it is highly prized.

* *The Bahá'í World*, 1930–1932, vol. iv, p. 210.

BIBLIOGRAPHY

Except for the lengthy extracts from *The Promulgation of Universal Peace*, quotations are reproduced in their original form, even though differing from the spelling and transliteration of Persian words adopted in this book. Persian texts not published in English have been translated by Mr Balyuzi.

'ABDU'L-BAHÁ. *'Abdu'l-Bahá in Canada*. Toronto: National Spiritual Assembly of the Bahá'ís of Canada, 1962.

—— *'Abdu'l-Bahá in Edinburgh*. London: National Spiritual Assembly of the Bahá'ís of the British Isles, 1963.

—— *Abdul-Baha in London*. Addresses, & Notes of Conversations. Chicago: Bahai Publishing Society, 1921.

—— *The Memorials of the Faithful*. Haifa: 1924.

—— *Paris Talks*. Addresses given by 'Abdu'l-Bahá in Paris in 1911–1912. First published 1912. 11th British ed. London: Bahá'í Publishing Trust, 1969. Published in the United States under the title *The Wisdom of 'Abdu'l-Bahá*. Wilmette, Illinois: Bahá'í Publishing Trust.

—— *The Promulgation of Universal Peace*. Discourses by Abdul Baha Abbas During His Visit to the United States in 1912. Vol. I, Chicago: Executive Board of Bahai Temple Unity, 1922. Vol. II, Chicago: Baha'i Publishing Committee, 1925.

—— *Some Answered Questions*. Collected and Translated from the Persian of 'Abdu'l-Bahá by Laura Clifford Barney. First published 1908. London: Bahá'í Publishing Trust, 1961.

—— *Tablets of 'Abdu'l-Bahá*. Cairo: Shaykh Faraju'lláh Dhakí al-Kurdí. Vol. II, 1330 A.H. (1911–12). Vol. III, 1340 A.H. (1921).

'ABDU'L-BAHÁ. *Tablets of the Divine Plan*. Revealed by 'Abdu'l-Bahá to the North American Bahá'ís during 1916–17. Wilmette, Illinois: Bahá'í Publishing Trust, 1962 (3rd ed.).

ABU'L-FAḌL, MÍRZÁ. *The Brilliant Proof. Burhäne Lämé*. Written December 28, 1911, in Syria, by the pen of Mirza Abul Fazl Gulpaygan. Chicago: Bahai News Service, 1912.

Bahá'í Revelation, The. A Selection from the Bahá'í Holy Writings. London: Bahá'í Publishing Trust, 1955.

Bahá'í World, The. An International Record. Vol. IV, 1930–1932. Vol. VII, 1936–1938. New York: Bahá'í Publishing Committee. Vol. XIII, 1954–1963. Haifa, Israel: The Universal House of Justice, 1970.

BAHÁ'U'LLÁH. *Gleanings from the Writings of Bahá'u'lláh*. Trans. by Shoghi Effendi. London: Bahá'í Publishing Trust, 1949.

—— *The Proclamation of Bahá'u'lláh* to the kings and leaders of the world. Haifa: Bahá'í World Centre, 1967.

BALYUZI, H. M. *Edward Granville Browne and the Bahá'í Faith*. London: George Ronald, 1970.

BLOMFIELD, LADY (Sitárih K͟hánum). *The Chosen Highway*. London: Bahá'í Publishing Trust, 1940. Reprinted Wilmette, Illinois: Bahá'í Publishing Trust.

BROWNE, E. G. (ed.) *Materials for the Study of the Bábí Religion*. Cambridge University Press, 1918.

—— (ed.) *A Traveller's Narrative* written to illustrate the Episode of the Báb. Vol. II, English Translation and Notes. Cambridge University Press, 1891.

CHAMBERLAIN, ISABEL FRASER. *Abdul Baha on Divine Philosophy*. Boston: The Tudor Press, 1918.

CHEYNE, T. K. *The Reconciliation of Races and Religions*. London: Adam & Charles Black, 1914.

Covenant of Bahá'u'lláh, The. A Compilation. London: Bahá'í Publishing Trust, 1963 (rev.).

DREYFUS, HIPPOLYTE. *Essai Sur Le Bahāisme*. Son histoire, sa portée sociale. First published 1909. 3rd ed. Paris: Presses Universitaires De France, 1962.

ESSLEMONT, J. E. *Bahá'u'lláh and the New Era*. First published 1923. Rev. 3rd ed. London: Bahá'í Publishing Trust, 1952.

FOREL, AUGUSTE. *Out of My Life and Work*. Trans. by Bernard Miall. London: George Allen & Unwin Ltd., 1937.

HALL, Mrs BASIL (Parvine). *The Drama of the Kingdom*. A Pageant Play the plan for which was given by Abdul Baha Abbas in London 17th January 1913. London: The Weardale Press Limited, 1933.

HAYDAR 'ALÍ, HÁJÍ MÍRZÁ. *Bihjatu's-Ṣudúr*. Bombay: 1913.

HOFMAN, DAVID. *A Commentary on the Will and Testament of 'Abdu'l-Bahá*. First published 1943. Rev. ed. Oxford: George Ronald, 1955.

HOLLEY, HORACE. *Bahaism: The Modern Social Religion*. London: Sidgwick & Jackson, Ltd., 1913.

—— *Religion for Mankind*. First published 1956. Rev. ed. London: George Ronald, 1966.

IVES, HOWARD COLBY. *Portals to Freedom*. First published 1937. 5th repr. London: George Ronald, 1969.

MAXWELL, MAY. *An Early Pilgrimage*. First published 1917. 3rd repr. London: George Ronald, 1970.

MU'AYYAD, Dr ḤABÍB. *Khátirát-i-Ḥabíb*. Memoirs of Ḥabíb. Ṭihrán: 1961.

NABÍL-I-A'ẒAM (Muḥammad-i-Zarandí). *The Dawn-Breakers*. Nabíl's Narrative of the Early Days of the Bahá'í Revelation. Wilmette, Illinois: Bahá'í Publishing Trust, 1932. Repr. 1953. London: Bahá'í Publishing Trust, 1953.

PHELPS, M. H. *Life and Teachings of Abbas Effendi*. With an introduction by Edward Granville Browne. First published 1903. 2nd ed. rev. New York: G. P. Putnam's Sons, 1912.

SHOGHI EFFENDI. *The Dispensation of Bahá'u'lláh*. London: Bahá'í Publishing Trust, 1947.

—— *The Goal of a New World Order*. London: National Spiritual Assembly of the Bahá'ís of the British Isles, 1931.

—— *God Passes By*. Wilmette, Illinois: Bahá'í Publishing Trust, 1944. 5th repr. 1965.

—— *The Promised Day Is Come*. First published 1941. Repr. Wilmette, Illinois: Bahá'í Publishing Trust, 1961.

—— *The World Order of Bahá'u'lláh*. First published 1938. Rev. 1955. 2nd impr. Wilmette, Illinois: Bahá'í Publishing Trust, 1965.

—— and SITARIH KHANUM (Lady Blomfield). *The Passing of 'Abdu'l-Baha*. Stuttgart: 1922.

STAR OF THE WEST. The Bahá'í Magazine. Vol. I (then titled *Bahai News*), Vols. III, IV, IX, X, XI, XII, XIV, XX, and XXIII. Published between 1910 and 1933 from Chicago and Washington, D.C., by official Bahá'í agencies variously titled.

THOMPSON, JULIET. *Abdul Baha's First Days in America*. From the Diary of Juliet Thompson. East Aurora, New York: The Roycrofters. (No date.)

—— *'Abdu'l-Bahá: The Center of the Covenant*. Wilmette, Illinois: Bahá'í Publishing Committee, 1948.

ZARQÁNÍ, MÍRZÁ MAḤMÚD-I-. *Kitáb-i-Badáyi'u'l-Áthár*. Diary of 'Abdu'l-Bahá's travels in Europe and America, written by His secretary. Bombay: Vol. I, 1914; Vol. II, 1921.

NOTES

The following abbreviations to titles in the bibliography are used in these notes:

Paris Talks	'Abdu'l-Bahá. *Paris Talks.*
Promulgation	'Abdu'l-Bahá. *The Promulgation of Universal Peace.*
Star	*Star of the West.*
Chosen Highway	Blomfield, Lady. *The Chosen Highway.*
God Passes By	Shoghi Effendi. *God Passes By.*
The Passing	Shoghi Effendi and Lady Blomfield. *The Passing of 'Abdu'l-Baha.*
'Abdu'l-Bahá in America	Thompson, Juliet. *Abdul Baha's First Days in America.*
Zarqání	Mírzá Maḥmúd-i-Zarqání. *Kitáb-i-Badáyi'u'l-Áthár.*

PART I

1. Browne (ed.), *A Traveller's Narrative*, vol. II, xxxvi.
2. Chase, Thornton, *What Went Ye Out For to See.*
3. Horace Holley was for over thirty years secretary of the chief administrative body of the Bahá'í community of North America, the National Spiritual Assembly of the Bahá'ís of the United States (and, until 1948, of Canada). In 1959 he was called to service at the World Centre of the Faith in Haifa, Israel, and died there in 1960.
4. Holley, *Bahaism: The Modern Social Religion*, pp. 211–13. Reprinted in *Religion for Mankind*, pp. 232–3.
5. Ives, *Portals to Freedom*, pp. 28–9.
6. *ibid.*, p. 253.
7. *Egyptian Gazette*, September 24th, 1913. Cited in *Bahá'í World*, vol. XIII, pp. 809–10.
8. Letter to Lady Blomfield, 1939, quoted in *Chosen Highway*, p. 221. The signet ring mentioned by Lord Lamington is now in the National Archives of the Bahá'ís of the British Isles, bequeathed by him in his will.

9. 'Abdu'l-Bahá told the Bahá'ís that this day was not, under any circumstances, to be celebrated as His day of birth. It was the day of the Declaration of the Báb, exclusively associated with Him. But as the Bahá'ís begged for a day to be celebrated as His, He gave them November 26th, to be observed as the day of the appointment of the Centre of the Covenant. It was known as Jashn-i-A'ẓam (The Greatest Festival), because He was Ghuṣn-i-A'ẓam—the Greatest Branch. In the West it is known as the Day of the Covenant.

10. Zarqání, vol. II, pp. 187 and 205–6.

11. Nabíl, *The Dawn-Breakers*, pp. 631–2. British ed., pp. 461–2.

12. Zarqání, vol. II, p. 206.

13. *Chosen Highway*, p. 46.

14. Zarqání, vol. II, p. 173.

15. The lunar Muslim month of fasting. It culminates in the festival known as 'Íd al-Fiṭr, which falls on the first day of the succeeding month. This Tablet is preserved in the International Archives at the Bahá'í World Centre, Haifa, Israel.

16. Generally referred to by the Bahá'ís as Áqáy-i-Kalím, or Jináb-i-Kalím. 'Kalím' means the 'Speaker'.

17. Cited *God Passes By*, p. 160.

18. *ibid.*, p. 161.

19. The 'Confectioner', a native of Shíráz.

20. Cited *God Passes By*, pp. 179–80.

21. Both quotations cited in Shoghi Effendi, *The Promised Day Is Come*, p. 62.

22. Cited *God Passes By*, p. 181.

23. Cited Shoghi Effendi, *The Dispensation of Bahá'u'lláh*, pp. 45–6. Also in *The World Order of Bahá'u'lláh*, p. 135.

24. Of the four Bahá'ís exiled to Cyprus, one was Mishkín-Qalam, an undisputed master of calligraphy, whose work is highly prized. Another was Mírzá 'Alíy-i-Sayyáḥ, the man who, in the years of the Báb's captivity in the mountain fortresses of north-western Írán, traversed vast distances on foot to keep a channel of communication between Him and His people. The other two were named Áqá 'Abdu'l-Ghaffár and Áqá Muḥammad-Báqir.

Mishkín-Qalam, Mírzá 'Alíy-i-Sayyáḥ, and another Bahá'í, Áqá Jamshíd-i-Gurjí (the Georgian), had earlier gone to Constantinople on the instructions of Bahá'u'lláh, to uncover the intrigues of partisans of Mírzá Yaḥyá. Four other Bahá'ís were also in Constantinople at that time, to sell some horses. They were: Áqá Muhammad-Báqir-i-Mahallátí, Áqá 'Abdu'l-Ghaffár, Darvísh Sidq-'Alí (a dervish), Ustád Muhammad-'Alíyi-Salmání (the barber). All were arrested. Ustád Muhammad-'Alí and Áqá Jamshíd were sent to Trebizond and on to Persia where they were handed over to Kurdish chieftains who, finding them innocent, set them free. Eventually they made their way to 'Akká.

Áqá 'Abdu'l-Ghaffár attempted to drown himself when the boat bearing the exiles dropped anchor in the bay of Haifa. But he was dragged out of the sea, and was sent with the other three to Cyprus, in the company of Mírzá Yahyá. He managed to escape, took the name of Mírzá 'Abdu'lláh, and found a house in 'Akká. Áqá Muhammad-Báqir and Mírzá 'Alíy-i-Sayyáh died in Cyprus. Mishkín-Qalam was allowed to leave Cyprus when the British Government took over the administration of the island in 1878. To 'Akká he went.

As to the supporters of Mírzá Yahyá, who were banished with Bahá'u'lláh to 'Akká, among them was a wife of Mírzá Yahyá, named Badrí-Ján; also her brother, Mírzá Ridá-Qulí; her nephew, Mírzá Fadlu'lláh (whose father, Mírzá Nasru'lláh, had died in Adrianople shortly before); and their attendant, Áqá 'Azím-i-Tafrishí. Badrí-Ján had, in fact, renounced her marriage to Mírzá Yahyá, leaving her two daughters with their father; her brother and nephew had followed suit and broken away from Mírzá Yahyá; and Áqá 'Azím had pledged his fealty to Bahá'u'lláh. Thus only two actively supported Mírzá Yahyá, in the party which landed at 'Akká with Bahá'u'lláh—Siyyid Muhammad-i-Isfahání, and Áqá-Ján Big-i-Khamsa'í. For further details see Balyuzi, *Edward Granville Browne and the Bahá'í Faith*, pp. 34-7.

25. Nabíl was a zealous adherent of Bahá'u'lláh, and had been constantly travelling the length and breadth of Persia, to spread the news of His Advent. At the instigation of the Persian Consul-General he was arrested and jailed in Egypt. When he was released and managed to enter 'Akká he was recognized by adversaries and had to flee the city and wander around the Holy Land.

26. Cited *God Passes By*, p. 185.

27. Citations from *God Passes By*, p. 184. See also Hosea ii. 15 and Ezekiel xliii.1-2. Hosea refers to it as 'the valley of Achor'.

28. Cited *God Passes By*, p. 187.

29. Hájí Mírzá Haydar-'Alí's autobiography is entitled *Bihjatu's-Sudúr* (Delight of Hearts). He, together with six of his fellow-believers, was arrested in Cairo at the prompting of the Persian

Consul-General, and was sent to Khartúm (Khartoum) in the Súdán. Banishment lasted for nine years, and was terminated by General Gordon in 1877. This arrest, transportation and exile entailed appalling sufferings. Later, Hájí Mírzá Haydar-'Alí travelled extensively throughout Persia and neighbouring countries, a teaching mission which lasted more than a quarter of a century. The evening of his heroic life was spent in the Holy Land where Western pilgrims knew him as the Angel of Mount Carmel. His story is an odyssey of the Bahá'í Faith. These quotations are taken from the Bombay edition, 1913, pp. 251–2 and 257.

30. 'Abdu'l-Bahá, *The Memorials of the Faithful*, pp. 55–6.

31. *ibid.*, pp. 31–2.

32. *God Passes By*, pp. 190–1.

33. Cited Shoghi Effendi, *The Dispensation of Bahá'u'lláh*, p. 47. Also in *The World Order of Bahá'u'lláh*, p. 136.

34. Esslemont, *Bahá'u'lláh and the New Era*, p. 39.

35. *ibid.*, pp. 40–1.

36. Zarqání, vol. II, p. 13.

37. Hájí Mírzá Haydar-'Alí, *Bihjatu's-Sudúr*, p. 253.

38. *God Passes By*, p. 222.

39. *Chosen Highway*, pp. 110–11, translated by Shoghi Effendi and sent for that book. For a longer version see *Star*, vol. XIV, pp. 356–7.

40. Citations from *God Passes By*, p. 238.

41. Shoghi Effendi, *The Dispensation of Bahá'u'lláh*, p. 47. Also *The World Order of Bahá'u'lláh*, p. 136.

42. Zarqání, vol. II, p. 192.

43. Paraphrase of Revised version; see Matt. xviii. 7 and Luke xvii. 1.

44. Hájí Abu'l-Hasan, the father of Mírzá Muhammad-Báqir Khán, had been a fellow-pilgrim of the Báb on the steamer which took them to Jiddah, the port of Mecca. On that boat Hájí Abu'l-Hasan witnessed such powers and extraordinary qualities in the young Siyyid, who was from his home town, that, in later months when he came to know Who the Báb was, he accepted Him.

45. Asgarzadeh was an outstanding Bahá'í who served the Faith with distinction for four decades in the British Isles, and who died in his field of pioneering in the Island of Jersey, April 1956. Because he went to Jersey at the beginning of the Ten Year Crusade (1953–63), he was designated by the Guardian of the Faith a Knight of Bahá'u'lláh. He was once a resident of

'Iṣhqábád (now Askabad, in the Soviet Republic of Turkmenistan).

46. Lady Sheil was the wife of Colonel Sir Justin Sheil, British
Minister in Ṭihrán (1849–53), who reported the martyrdom of the
Báb to Lord Palmerston, Secretary of State for Foreign Affairs.
His dispatch can be examined in the Public Records Office,
Chancery Lane, London.

47. Matthew Arnold, 'A Persian Passion Play', a lecture delivered before the Birmingham and Midland Institute, October
16th 1871. See *Essays in Criticism*. London: Macmillan & Co.,
1875. 3rd ed. Also later editions.

48. From *The World's Parliament of Religion*, vol. II, pp.
1125–6. London: 'Review of Reviews' Office, 1893. In a talk
entitled 'The Religious Mission of the English Speaking Nations',
by Rev. Henry H. Jessup, D.D., of Beirut, Syria. Also cited in
Bahá'í World, vol. XIII, pp. 814–15.

49. *Star*, vol. XXIII, no. 1, p. 28.

50. *Star*, vol. III, no. 13, pp. 14–15.

51. *Chosen Highway*, pp. 235–6.

52. *Bahá'í World*, vol. VII, p. 801.

53. *ibid.*, pp. 801–2.

54. May Maxwell, *An Early Pilgrimage*, pp. 12–13 and 15–16.

55. *ibid.*, pp. 41–2.

56. *Bahá'í World*, vol. VII, pp. 707–11. See her account, from
which the details in the following pages are drawn.

57. *ibid.*, pp. 710–11.

58. The third Bahá'í of the British Isles was Mrs Scaramucci.
It is not possible to ascertain, at this distance of time, when and
how she came into the circle of the Faith. She wrote a pamphlet
to introduce the Faith to the general public. But more widely
known was the pamphlet by Miss Ethel Rosenberg, under the
title of *A Brief Account of the Bahai Movement* (published by
the Priory Press, Hampstead, and J. M. Watkins, 21 Cecil
Court, St Martin's Lane, W.C., for the Bahai Society of London,
1911).

In the year 1906, Sarah Ann Ridgeway, 'a native of Pendleton,
a working-class district' close to Manchester, returned home from
the United States, where she had lived the years of her youth and
where she had embraced the Faith of Bahá'u'lláh. The honour of
pioneering in the north of England belongs to her. (See *The
Bahá'í Dawn*, Manchester, 1925, p. 3.)

Here, the present writer feels that he must call attention to a name totally forgotten, that of an Englishman who, in the opening decade of this century, gave his allegiance to Bahá'u'lláh. In 1910, Dr Susan I. Moody, an American Bahá'í, sent this report from Ṭihrán:

'Mr. William J. Patchin, aged 28 years, a native of London, England, died at Teheran, Persia, Dec. 31, 1910. He lived the Baha'i life and was constantly serving in the Cause. He had resigned his position with the Indo-European Telegraph Co. that he might go to Egypt to see Abdul-Baha, when he was suddenly summoned to the Supreme.' (*Bahai News*, vol. I, no. 18.)

59. *Star*, vol. XX, no. 1, p. 26.

60. As late as spring 1934, Mírzá Shu'áu'lláh inaugurated a publication which he named *Behai Quarterly*, from 7543 Twenty-sixth Ave., Kenosha, Wisconsin. It was short-lived and left no trace.

61. I. G. Kheiralla, Publisher, 4001 Grand Blvd., Chicago, 1900.

62. There is a letter in the possession of the present writer, written in December 1898 from 'Ishqábád by Ḥájí Siyyid Mírzá, the eldest son of Ḥájí Mírzá Siyyid Ḥasan (the Great Afnán), to his mother in Yazd. She was a daughter of Ḥájí Siyyid Muḥammad, that uncle of the Báb for whom Bahá'u'lláh revealed the *Kitáb-i-Íqán* (The Book of Certitude). Mírzá Ḍíyá'u'lláh had died on October 30th of that year, 1898. Ḥájí Siyyid Mírzá and two others of his brothers (one of them, Ḥájí Siyyid 'Alí, a son-in-law of Bahá'u'lláh) were at that time active partisans of Mírzá Muḥammad-'Alí. In that letter Ḥájí Siyyid Mírzá refers to Mírzá Ḍíyá'u'lláh as the Purest Branch, cavils at 'Abdu'l-Bahá for not visiting His half-brother while he lay ill in Haifa until the last day of Mírzá Ḍíyá'u'lláh's life, speaks of claims of divinity made for 'Abdu'l-Bahá, which, he says, the 'Branches' have rejected. When the writer of that letter returned to Yazd, his home town, his mother refused to meet him. Eventually he realized the enormity of the wrong he had done to 'Abdu'l-Bahá, and broke away from the violators.

63. Ḥájí 'Alí 'Askar, who had perforce abandoned home and taken the road to exile.

64. Dr Ali-Kuli Khan ('Alí-Qulí Khán), in the early days, used the *nom-de-plume*: Eshte'al al-Ebn Kalanter (Ishti'ál Ibn-i-Kalántar), in his writings and translations.

65. Browne, *Materials for the Study of the Bábí Religion*, p. 171.

66. Dr Moody (1851–1934), on whom 'Abdu'l-Bahá bestowed the title Amatu'l-A'lá—the Handmaid of the Most High—served the Faith and attended to the medical needs of the people of Ṭihrán, particularly the poor, from 1905 to 1924. Then she returned to the United States. But once again in December 1928 she set out for Ṭihrán. There she died and was buried, and many who were not Bahá'ís grieved over her death.

67. Phelps, *Life and Teachings of Abbas Effendi*, xxxvi and pp. 2–10.

68. Mírzá 'Alí-Aṣg̲h̲ar K̲h̲án, who also carried the title: Atábak-i-A'ẓam.

69. July 9th 1903, F.O. 60/666 (Public Record Office, Chancery Lane, London).

70. His father, S̲h̲ayk̲h̲ Muḥammad Báqir, responsible as he was for the death of the two brothers, Mírzá Ḥasan, Sulṭánu'sh-S̲h̲uhadá (the King of the Martyrs) and Mírzá Ḥusayn, Maḥbúbu'-sh-S̲h̲uhadá (the Beloved of the Martyrs), was stigmatized by Bahá'u'lláh as D̲h̲i'b (the Wolf). Thus it was that S̲h̲ayk̲h̲ Muḥammad-Taqí won the surname: Ibn-i-D̲h̲'ib (the Son of the Wolf). It was during the governorship of Prince Mas'úd Mírzá, the Zillu's-Sulṭán (eldest son of Náṣiri'd-Dín S̲h̲áh, but not his heir-apparent) that the above-mentioned brothers were martyred. In the year 1903, he was once again the governor of Iṣfahán. Jalálu'd-Dawlih, the governor of Yazd, was his son.

71. 'Abdu'l-Bahá, Tablets (Cairo), vol. III, p. 140.

72. Shoghi Effendi, *The World Order of Bahá'u'lláh*, p. 17.

73. See Balyuzi, *Edward Granville Browne and the Bahá'í Faith*, p. 107.

74. 'Andalíb means 'Nightingale'—the poet's soubriquet, conferred on him by Bahá'u'lláh. His name was Mírzá 'Alí-Aṣhraf; he was a native of Láhíján in the Caspian province of Gílán, but lived for many years in S̲h̲íráz, where he passed away. In 1888, Edward Browne met him in Yazd, and gave an account of their conversation in *A Year Amongst the Persians*. A letter in the handwriting of 'Andalíb exists, addressed to Edward Browne, but it is not known whether a copy of this letter ever reached him. Therein 'Andalíb encourages Browne to visit Bahá'u'lláh in 'Akká.

75. Cited in *The Covenant of Bahá'u'lláh*, p. 108.

76. *God Passes By*, p. 276.

77. The sarcophagus was the offering of the Bahá'ís of Rangoon, but, in particular, three Bahá'ís of that town helped

generously to provide it. They were Siyyid Muṣṭafáy-i-Rúmí, pioneer in Burma; Ḥájí Siyyid Mihdí, a native of Shíráz; and his son, Siyyid Ismá'íl. Siyyid Muṣṭafáy-i-Rúmí was martyred in Burma, at a very advanced age, during the Second World War, and was posthumously accorded the rank of a Hand of the Cause of God, by the Guardian of the Faith.

78. Zechariah vi. 12.

79. *God Passes By*, p. 276.

80. See a number of references in Balyuzi, *Edward Granville Browne and the Bahá'í Faith*.

81. *Chosen Highway*, p. 227.

82. *Abdul-Baha in London*, pp. 3–5.

83. *Chosen Highway*, pp. 149–50.

84. *ibid.*, p. 153.

85. *Abdul-Baha in London*, pp. 8–12.

86. *Chosen Highway*, p. 150.

87. Mírzá Abu'l-Faḍl, *The Brilliant Proof*, pp. 4–5.

88. *Chosen Highway*, pp. 182–3.

89. *Abdul-Baha in London*, p. 18.

90. *ibid.*, pp. 22–3.

91. *ibid.*, pp. 26–9.

92. *Chosen Highway*, pp. 173–4.

93. *Abdul-Baha in London*, pp. 84–5.

94. *ibid.*, p. 81.

95. *Chosen Highway*, p. 165.

96. *ibid.*, p. 166.

97. Holley, *Bahaism: the Modern Social Religion*, p. 175.

98. *Paris Talks*, pp. 15–16.

99. *Chosen Highway*, p. 186.

100. *Paris Talks*, pp. 28–30.

101. Bahá'u'lláh, *The Proclamation of Bahá'u'lláh*, p. 13.

102. *ibid.*, p. 63.

103. *Paris Talks*, pp. 114–16.

104. *ibid.*, p. 68.

105. *ibid.*, pp. 151–4.

106. *ibid.*, pp. 119–23.

107. *ibid.*, pp. 170–1.

108. *Chosen Highway*, p. 181.

109. *ibid.*, p. 185.

PART II

110. *'Abdu'l-Bahá in America*, p. 5.
111. *Promulgation*, pp. 1–2.
112. *ibid.*, pp. 9–10.
113. *ibid.*, pp. 7–8.
114. *'Abdu'l-Bahá in America*, p. 7.
115. *Promulgation*, p. 28.
116. *ibid.*, pp. 30–1.
117. *'Abdu'l-Bahá in America*, p. 11.
118. *Promulgation*, pp. 33–4.
119. *ibid.*, p. 39.
120. *ibid.*, p. 42.
121. *ibid.*, p. 43.
122. *ibid.*, p. 44.
123. *ibid.*, pp. 49–51.
124. *ibid.*, pp. 53–4.
125. *'Abdu'l-Bahá in America*, p. 16.
126. *ibid.*, p. 20.
127. *Promulgation*, pp. 67–8.
128. These nationalities are taken from Zarqání's account, but additional nationalities are mentioned in *Bahá'í World*, vol. VII, p. 219, in an account by Marzieh Gail (then Mrs Carpenter), entitled 'Commemoration of the Twenty-Fifth Anniversary of 'Abdu'l-Bahá's Visit to America'.
129. *Promulgation*, pp. 68–9.
130. *ibid.*, p. 89.
131. *'Abdu'l-Bahá in America*, p. 21.
132. *ibid.*, pp. 21–2.
133. *Promulgation*, pp. 107–8.
134. *'Abdu'l-Bahá in America*, p. 22.
135. *Promulgation*, pp. 119–21.
136. Thompson, *'Abdu'l-Bahá, The Center of the Covenant*, p. 22.
137. Ives, *Portals to Freedom*, pp. 82–8.
138. *Promulgation*, pp. 138–41.
139. *ibid.*, p. 137.
140. *ibid.*, pp. 142–3.
141. *ibid.*, pp. 145–6.
142. *ibid.*, pp. 148–9.
143. *ibid.*, pp. 155–7.

144. *ibid.*, pp. 157–65.
145. *'Abdu'l-Bahá in America*, p. 26.
146. *Promulgation*, pp. 171–7.
147. *ibid.*, pp. 178–9.
148. Zarqání, vol. I, p. 119.
149. *'Abdu'l-Bahá in America*, pp. 27–8.
150. *Promulgation*, pp. 186–8.
151. *ibid.*, pp. 189–91.
152. *ibid.*, pp. 192–7.
153. *ibid.*, p. 198.
154. Zarqání, vol. I, p. 128.
155. *Promulgation*, pp. 201–2.
156. 'Abdu'l-Bahá's citation of Scripture, as recorded by Zarqání, clearly referred to Christ's statement as recorded in Matt. xvi. 24; also see Mk. viii. 34 and Luke ix. 23.
157. *'Abdu'l-Bahá in America*, pp. 34–5.
158. *ibid.*, p. 35.
159. *Promulgation*, pp. 208–10.
160. *'Abdu'l-Bahá in America*, pp. 36–7.
161. *Promulgation*, p. 213.
162. *ibid.*, pp. 213–15.
163. *ibid.*, pp. 225–6.
164. The death of Grace Robarts Ober occurred on May 1st 1938, at the Annual Convention of the Bahá'ís of the United States and Canada, immediately after the conclusion of a rousing speech, calling for pioneers to gain the objectives of the first American Seven Year Plan. As soon as she sat down faintness overtook her. She was carried from the hall, and within moments she passed away. Her husband was the chairman of that convention. To him the Guardian of the Faith sent this cable: 'Heart overflowing grief sympathy dramatic ending noble life. Feel proud your dear wife's unforgettable services. Praying fervently for her departed soul. Love.' Harlan Ober himself died in July 1962, at his pioneering post in Pretoria, Union of South Africa.
165. See appendix IV.
166. *Promulgation*, pp. 233–4.
167. Ives, *Portals to Freedom*, pp. 115–16.
168. *ibid.*, pp. 120–28.
169. Alfred Lunt served the Faith of Bahá'u'lláh with such distinction that on his death in August 1937, the Guardian of the Faith sent this cable to the National Spiritual Assembly: 'Shocked

distressed premature passing esteemed well beloved Lunt. Future generations will appraise his manifold outstanding contributions to rise and establishment Faith Bahá'u'lláh American continent. Community his bereaved co-workers could ill afford lose such critical period so fearless champion their Cause. Request entire body their National representatives assemble his grave pay tribute my behalf to him who so long and since inception acted as pillar institution they represent. Convey Boston community assurance prayers, deepest brotherly sympathy their cruel irreparable loss.' (American *Bahá'í News* no. 110, p. 3.) And he wrote to an American Bahá'í: 'Words fail to express the sorrow and regret I feel at the untimely death of such a precious, ardent and capable champion of our beloved Faith. The loss is indeed irreparable, for he was the living embodiment of such a rare combination of qualities as few can display and none can surpass. I will continue to pray for his dear departed soul from the depths of my sorrowful yet grateful heart.'

170. *Promulgation*, pp. 247–55.

171. *ibid.*, pp. 257–8.

172. *Star*, vol. XIV, pp. 365–7.

173. *Promulgation*, pp. 278–83.

174. Apart from the three who had crossed the Atlantic with Him (see p. 171), Áqá Mírzá 'Alí-Akbar-i-Nakhjavání (father of Ali Nakhjavani, member of the Universal House of Justice) and Mírzá Valí'u'lláh Khán-i-Varqá (son of the martyr-poet Mírzá 'Alí-Muḥammad-i-Varqá, and appointed a Hand of the Cause by the Guardian of the Faith in 1951) had later come from the East to join His retinue. Aḥmad Sohráb, who became one of the two interpreters attending upon 'Abdu'l-Bahá, had been a resident of the United States. Dr Edward Getsinger had also accompanied 'Abdu'l-Bahá as far as Malden.

175. Cited '*Abdu'l-Bahá in Canada*, pp. 45–51.

176. Shoghi Effendi, *The Goal of a New World Order*, pp. 5–6, included in *The World Order of Bahá'u'lláh*, pp. 29–30.

177. *Promulgation*, pp. 291–6. Some words of the prayer translated from original text.

178. Cited '*Abdu'l-Bahá in Canada*, p. 48.

179. *Promulgation*, pp. 314–18.

180. Zarqání, vol. I, p. 252.

181. *Promulgation*, pp. 320–1.

182. *ibid.*, pp. 323–7.

183. William Jennings Bryan (1860–1925) was a prominent figure in the public life of America over several decades. He was an ardent advocate of the free-silver theory and bimetallism. Thrice defeated (1896, 1900, 1908) in the presidential elections as the Democratic candidate, he vigorously sponsored the candidacy of Woodrow Wilson in 1912, but resigned office under him in July 1915, as he believed that President Wilson's second note to Germany over the sinking of the *Lusitania* would lead to American entry into the war. He worked unceasingly for the cause of peace, but when the United States declared war on Germany in April 1917, he loyally supported the President, and even enrolled as a private in the army.

184. *Promulgation*, pp. 329, 331.

185. *ibid.*, pp. 332–6.

186. Zarqání, vol. I, p. 272.

187. *Promulgation*, pp. 337, 342.

188. *ibid.*, pp. 342–9.

189. *ibid.*, pp. 349–55.

190. *ibid.*, pp. 355–65. A few lines translated from the original text in Zarqání.

191. Zarqání, vol. I, pp. 310–11.

192. *ibid.*, vol. I, pp. 330–31.

193. *Promulgation*, pp. 371–2, 374.

194. *ibid.*, p. 376.

195. *ibid.*, pp. 388–9.

196. *ibid.*, pp. 393–4.

197. *ibid.*, p. 397.

198. *ibid.*, pp. 397, 399, 401–5.

199. *ibid.*, pp. 413–16.

200. Samuel Graham Wilson, D.D., who lived thirty-two years in Persia, published his *Bahaism and Its Claims* in 1915.

201. *Promulgation*, pp. 423–5.

202. *ibid.*, pp. 420–3.

203. *ibid.*, pp. 433–7.

204. *ibid.*, p. 443.

205. *ibid.*, pp. 444–7.

206. Zarqání, vol. I, pp. 396–9.

207. *Promulgation*, pp. 464–7.

PART III

208. *Chosen Highway*, pp. 162–3.

209. *ibid.*, pp. 159–60, for conversation.

210. See Balyuzi, *Edward Granville Browne and the Bahá'í Faith*, pp. 96–7.

211. *Chosen Highway*, p. 153.

212. See Balyuzi, *Edward Granville Browne and the Bahá'í Faith*, p. 102, n. 2.

213. Mushíru'l-Mulk was a brother of Husayn 'Alá, well known in recent years as the Prime Minister of Írán, and the Minister of Court. Their father 'Aláu's-Saltanih, who had the title of Prince as well, had himself been the Minister in London, and held the office of prime minister at a later date.

214. *Chosen Highway*, pp. 168–9.

215. Zarqání, vol. II, p. 52.

216. *Chosen Highway*, p. 172.

217. Many of the details and newspaper quotations in this account of 'Abdu'l-Bahá in Edinburgh have been drawn from *'Abdu'l-Bahá in Edinburgh* (see bibliography).

218. *Chosen Highway*, p. 168.

219. Zarqání, vol. II, pp. 85–6.

220. *ibid.*, vol. II, p. 148.

221. *Star*, vol. IV, pp. 67–8.

222. *ibid.*, vol. IV, p. 155.

223. Zarqání, vol. II, pp. 226–7.

224. *ibid.*, vol. II, p. 291.

225. *ibid.*, vol. II, p. 293.

226. *Star*, vol. IV, pp. 288, 290.

227. *ibid.*, vol. IX, p. 26.

228. *ibid.*, vol. IV, p. 316.

229. *The Passing*, pp. 30–1.

230. *Star*, vol. IX, p. 134.

231. Memoirs of Dr Mu'ayyad, p. 333.

232. *Chosen Highway*, pp. 202–5.

233. Sakínih Sultán was the widow of one of the martyrs of Yazd. She had a daughter named Fátimih, her only child, who died young, but left a baby, a solace for the stricken grandmother. Both because of her cruel bereavements and because of the services she had rendered (which included nursing both Mírzá Abu'l-Fadl and Shoghi Effendi, during his first year at the

university in Beirut), 'Abdu'l-Bahá always showed her a very generous measure of kindness. The tenderness of that kindness is shown in the many Tablets addressed to her. In a Tablet dated October 17th 1921, He tells her that although He is overburdened with work, with little time to write, He has written her that letter to ascertain her wishes regarding her grandson, Labíb. Whatever she chooses He will carry out; her wish is the same as His own, and He will never forget her services. The present writer knew this lady well during the years that he was a student in the American University of Beirut.

234. *God Passes By*, pp. 304–5.
235. 'Abdu'l-Bahá, *Tablets of the Divine Plan*.
236. *Chosen Highway*, pp. 219–20.
237. *ibid.*, pp. 222–5.
238. *Star*, vol. IX, pp. 187, 192–4.
239. *ibid.*, pp. 194–5. Letter dated November 19th 1918, from Acca, Palestine.
240. Star, vol. X, p. 156.
241. *ibid.*, vol. X, pp. 218–19.
242. *ibid.*, vol. X, p. 42. Translated by Shoghi Effendi, January 10th 1919, from the home of 'Abdu'l-Bahá, Haifa.
243. Cited *The Bahá'í Revelation*, pp. 208, 215–16.
244. *Star*, vol. XI, p. 288.
245. pp. 72–3.
246. *Chosen Highway*, pp. 214–15.
247. *Star*, vol. XII, pp. 136–7.
248. Forel, *Out of My Life and Work*, p. 342.
249. *God Passes By*, pp. 307–8.
250. *The Bahá'í Revelation*, pp. 220, 231.
251. *ibid.*, pp. 191, 195.
252. *The Passing*, pp. 9–10.
253. *ibid.*, pp. 3–9.
254. *Star*, vol. XII, pp. 277–8.
255. *The Passing*, p. 9.
256. *ibid.*, pp. 10–11.
257. *ibid.*, pp. 11–12.
258. *ibid.*, pp. 12–13.
259. *ibid.*, p. 13.
260. *Star*, vol. XII, pp. 263–4.
261. *ibid.*, pp. 264–5.
262. *The Passing*, pp. 14–15.
263. *Star*, vol. XII, pp. 266–7.

264. *ibid.*, p. 267.

265. *The Passing*, p. 15.

266. *ibid.*, pp. 15–17.

267. *ibid.*, pp. 19–21.

268. The words quoted, in the first two paragraphs of this chapter, are taken from the following writings of Shoghi Effendi: *America and the Most Great Peace* and *The Dispensation of Bahá'u'lláh*. Both essays are included in *The World Order of Bahá'u'lláh*; see pp. 89 and 143–4, for quotations.

269. Hofman, *A Commentary on the Will and Testament of 'Abdu'l-Bahá*, p. 20.

INDEX

Titles of books, periodicals, and Tablets are italicized. Footnotes are indicated by 'n.' after the page number; if the subject occurs both in the text and in a footnote, 'p. — and n.' is used. Back notes are shown as 'n. — '. Bold figures are used for principal themes, and for pages dealing with 'Abdu'l-Bahá's visits. His talks in the West, when quoted, are listed under 'Talks'. The subjects He dealt with are indexed. Page references to towns and countries are given, but as the events and persons associated with them are indexed, these references are not always analysed.